PRAISE FOR
The Rock, the Road, and the Rabbi

This is one of those unique "if" books that speaks deep into your soul with promise and possibility. Because *if* you've always wanted to visit the Holy Land, *if* you want a deeper understanding of the Bible, and *if* you enjoy great stories from a great storyteller—then this is a perfect book for you.

—Roma Downey, actor, producer, and president of LightWorkers Media

Kathie Lee Gifford has encouraged and inspired me for many years. This book will do the same for you. She escorts the reader to the land of the Savior, taking us on a heart-deepening journey of hope.

—Max Lucado, pastor and *New York Times* bestselling author

Living one's faith unashamedly and joyfully in the public square as my friend Kathie Lee Gifford has done is rare and beautiful, and has inspired me personally in my own faith. So it's no suprise that this rare and beautiful book should inspire me too. If it doesn't make you want to know God better—and make you want to visit Israel!—you obviously haven't read it yet. What are you waiting for?

—Eric Metaxas, *New York Times* bestselling author of *Bonhoeffer: Pastor, Martyr, Prophet, Spy* and host of the nationally syndicated *Eric Metaxas Show*

Kathie Lee Gifford's vibrant personality is revealed in her book *The Rock, the Road, and the Rabbi*. You can sense the thrill of her many treks through the Holy Land as she writes about its captivating beauty and its spiritually deep roots that have found a place in her heart, all because of the power of God's Word. Take time to read her innermost thoughts as she shares her experiences of walking where Jesus walked. "Seek [God] . . . and find him, though he is not far from any one of us" (Acts 17:27). Fix your heart on the Rock of salvation and walk the Road that leads to redemption with the Rabbi—the teacher who gives eternal life to those who seek Him.

—Franklin Graham, president and CEO, Billy Graham Evangelistic Association and Samaritan's Purse

The Bible is probably the single most significant written work in history, and yet it's so often misunderstood, distorted, or overlooked. In *The Rock, the Road, and the Rabbi*, Kathie Lee Gifford does the important work of studying and sharing this most foundational of books, hitting both the mind and the heart with the powerful impact of what she uncovers. I am grateful for what this book has done for my life, and you will be too.

—Allison Pataki, *New York Times* bestselling author of *The Accidental Empress*

The Rock, the Road, and the Rabbi will inspire and uplift readers everywhere. Whether you are a believer or not, a seeker or simply intrigued, this glorious walking tour of the Holy Land, with personal insights and stories by Kathie Lee Gifford, describes the sacred places of Israel and their meaning step by step. Rabbi Jason Sobel offers biblical and historical context with clarity and insight. From the stillness of the desert to the serenity of the Sea of Galilee, you will be swept into the beauty, wonder, and magnificence of these sacred places by two enthusiastic believers on a lifelong faith journey.

—Adriana Trigiani, *New York Times* bestselling author

A personal, inviting, and engaging encounter with both the Jesus of history, the man who walked the dusty landscape of first-century Judea and Galilee, and the Christ of faith, the one around whom the author's entire life revolves. Especially for Christians who know little about Jesus' Jewish background, this book is a fine place to begin your journey.

—James Martin, SJ, *New York Times* bestselling author of *Jesus: A Pilgrimage*

the ROCK, the ROAD, and the RABBI

My Journey *into the* Heart *of* Scriptural Faith
and the Land Where It All Began

KATHIE LEE GIFFORD

WITH RABBI JASON SOBEL

W PUBLISHING GROUP

AN IMPRINT OF THOMAS NELSON

Published in Nashville, Tennessee, by W Publishing, an imprint of Thomas Nelson.

Photos in the color insert were taken by Benjamin Wierda.

"He Saw Jesus"
Music by Brett James and Lyrics by Kathie Lee Gifford
© 2017, CassyCody Music Ltd (ASCAP) and Cornman Music (ASCAP)
All Rights Reserved. Used by Permission.

"Lead Me, Gentle Shepherd"
Music by David Pomeranz and Lyrics by Kathie Lee Gifford
© 2017, CassyCody Music Ltd (ASCAP) and Upward Spiral Music (ASCAP)
All Rights Reserved. Used by Permission.

Thomas Nelson titles may be purchased in bulk for educational, business, fund-raising, or sales promotional use. For information, please email SpecialMarkets@ThomasNelson.com.

Unless otherwise noted, Scripture quotations are taken from the Holy Bible, New International Version®, NIV®. Copyright © 1973, 1978, 1984, 2011 by Biblica, Inc.® Used by permission of Zondervan. All rights reserved worldwide. www.zondervan.com. The "NIV" and "New International Version" are trademarks registered in the United States Patent and Trademark Office by Biblica, Inc.®

Scripture quotations marked TLV are taken from the Tree of Life Translation of the Bible. Copyright © 2015 by the Messianic Jewish Family Bible Society.

Scripture quotations marked NKJV are from the New King James Version®. © 1982 by Thomas Nelson. Used by permission. All rights reserved.

Scripture quotations marked NLT are from the Holy Bible, New Living Translation. © 1996, 2004, 2007, 2013, 2015 by Tyndale House Foundation. Used by permission of Tyndale House Publishers, Inc., Carol Stream, Illinois 60188. All rights reserved.

Scripture quotations marked NASB are taken from New American Standard Bible®, Copyright © 1960, 1962, 1963, 1968, 1971, 1972, 1973, 1975, 1977, 1995 by The Lockman Foundation. Used by permission. (www.Lockman.org)

Scripture quotations marked ESV are taken from the ESV® Bible (The Holy Bible, English Standard Version®), copyright © 2001 by Crossway, a publishing ministry of Good News Publishers. Used by permission. All rights reserved.

Italics used in Scripture passages are the author's own emphasis, save for material quoted from the TLV translation.

Any Internet addresses, phone numbers, or company or product information printed in this book are offered as a resource and are not intended in any way to be or to imply an endorsement by Thomas Nelson, nor does Thomas Nelson vouch for the existence, content, or services of these sites, phone numbers, companies, or products beyond the life of this book.

ISBN 978-0-7852-1600-1 (eBook)
ISBN 978-0-7852-2268-2 (special edition)
ISBN 978-0-7852-2287-3 (special edition)

Library of Congress Control Number: 2017956361

ISBN 978-0-7852-1596-7

Printed in the United States of America

18 19 20 21 22 LSC 10 9 8 7 6 5 4 3 2 1

The most important fact I want to emphasize at the beginning of this book is this: *I am not a biblical scholar or an expert in biblical studies.* I am simply a lifetime student of the Word of God and a seeker of truth.

But in my search for a deeper understanding of the Bible, I have met extraordinary people such as my friends Emilie and Craig Wierda, to whom I am most grateful for first inviting me along this amazing journey.

And finally I thank God for Ray Vander Laan, Rod Van Solkema, and Rabbi Jason Sobel, three men who have taken me up steep slopes, led me deep into the desert, explained ancient mysteries, and revealed what Scripture means in its original form. Most importantly, they have relit a passion in my innermost being for the Bible and rekindled my desire for the Lover of my soul: Jesus, the Messiah.

For that I am eternally grateful, and to them I dedicate *The Rock, the Road, and the Rabbi.*

—KATHIE LEE GIFFORD

CONTENTS

CONTENTS

INTRODUCTION

Lord, You Want Me to What?

*The steadfast love of the LORD never ceases; his mercies never come
to an end; they are new every morning; great is your faithfulness.*
—LAMENTATIONS 3:22–23 ESV

Before I began my new job as cohost of the fourth hour of *The
Today Show* in 2008, I felt the Lord tugging at my spirit with
the words of Matthew 6:33: *Kathie, seek first My kingdom and My righteousness, and all these things will be given to you as well.*

I remember responding, "Lord, You know that's what I am trying to do—put You and Your kingdom first in my life."

Then I felt Him gently rebuke me: *You're not listening. I said to seek
Me first!*

"Lord, do You mean first thing in the morning before anything
else?" I questioned.

In my heart, I sensed His clear answer: *Yes.*

Wow. I already got up earlier than most—usually right before
dawn. But with my new duties at *Today*, I would be leaving my home

in Connecticut shortly after 6:00 a.m. for the hour-long commute into New York City.

"Really, Lord? Before I go into work?"

Yes. I felt Him tenderly remind me, *As you begin your day, so goes your day.*

So I began to awaken before 4:00 a.m. and pray for an hour for my family members, friends and colleagues, world situations, and personal concerns. Then I would open the Scriptures and study God's Word for an hour more, with my puppies and the birds outside my window as my only company.

This new discipline soon became the best part—and my favorite part—of the day. I began to understand and cherish the Scriptures that talk about the joy of seeking God in the morning:

- "Let the *morning* bring me word of your unfailing love, for I have put my trust in you. Show me the way I should go, for to you I entrust my life" (Psalm 143:8).
- "It is good to praise the LORD and make music to your name, O Most High, proclaiming your love in the *morning* and your faithfulness at night" (Psalm 92:1–2).
- "In the *morning*, LORD, you hear my voice; in the *morning* I lay my requests before you and wait expectantly" (Psalm 5:3).
- "O God, You are my God; *early* will I seek You; my soul thirsts for You; my flesh longs for You in a dry and thirsty land where there is no water" (Psalm 63:1 NKJV).
- "He will make your righteous reward shine like the *dawn,* your vindication like the noonday sun" (Psalm 37:6).
- "The path of the righteous is like the *morning* sun, shining ever brighter till the full light of day" (Proverbs 4:18).

Through this process of getting up early every morning to study God's Word, I have experienced the truth of my favorite Bible verse: "I can do all things through Christ who strengthens me" (Philippians 4:13 NKJV).

Where do we get everything we need in life? From the Lord our God.

How does He strengthen us? With His Word.

Changing my morning routine has changed my life. I began not only to study the Word, but also to memorize as much as I could so that Scripture would become a living, breathing part of me. No textbook needed, no study guide necessary—just the pure, life-giving, sustaining Word of God settled deep in my soul.

Ever since then, I have been passionate about knowing and understanding the Bible. It breaks my heart to watch so many people desperate to find meaning, cures, and answers from a world that only wants to promote products, gain profit, and exploit human need.

Every answer to every question and every single desire and need anyone will ever have is already available for us in God's Word. The problem is that too few people are willing to do the work of searching for it! "Ask and it will be given to you," Jesus tells us. "Seek and you will find; knock and the door will be opened to you" (Matthew 7:7). In other words, make an effort!

Many of us have become so complacent, spoiled, and comfortable that we don't realize we are miserable. Isaiah 55:2 says: "Why spend money on what is not bread, and your labor on what does not satisfy? Listen, listen to me, and eat what is good, and you will delight in the richest of fare." I believe this is how our faith grows stale, our joy diminishes, and our passion for God runs dry.

We know that eventually we will die if we don't eat food. But we will all die spiritually if we stop feeding on His Word! "*Taste* and see that the LORD is good," Psalm 34:8 says. When we fill our lives with everything but the very thing we need most to thrive in our faith—His Word—we become lukewarm. We become bored and indifferent. We fall out of love with God.

One of my favorite verses is Psalm 18:30: "As for God, his way is perfect: The LORD's word is flawless." Friends, this is either a fact or a lie. There is no middle ground.

This is why I have grown so passionate about learning what the Bible really says. If I am going to base my life on something, it has to be the truth, the whole truth, and nothing but the truth, so help me, God! But how can we live the truth if we don't even know it?

Granted, there are mysteries in Scripture that will remain mysterious because God wills them to. But Jesus said in John 8:32, "You will know the truth, and the truth will set you free." Even Pontius Pilate asked Jesus, "What is truth?" (John 18:38).

Everyone wants to know what truth is, but too often in our world the truth is manipulated by individuals, organizations, or the media to accomplish certain agendas. It seems impossible to wade through all the informational garbage.

The word *truth* occurs in the Bible more than two hundred times. Obviously, God places immeasurable value in the truth, and He longs for each of us to seek it, find it, and apply it to our lives. The Bible is our treasure map. We can use its parables, psalms, numbers, prophecies, and personal stories of faith to guide our understanding. But this process requires great effort on our part. All too often we are so overwhelmed by technology, our personal dramas, and our endless ambition that we neglect to study God's Word. Imagine how it breaks the heart of our heavenly Father—who loves His children and longs to lead us into all joy, peace, and hope—when He sees us putting all our energy into everything but the one thing that can bring us life.

One of the saddest things I've encountered through the years when I try to share the gospel of salvation through Jesus, the Messiah, as taught in the Bible, is that many people dismiss the message immediately because of what they have already heard and therefore believe about what the Bible says.

They say they can't put their faith in a book that maintains the earth was created in seven days. They say they can't put their faith in a vengeful God who wants mankind to fear His judgment or they'll be sent to hell. They hate the apostle Paul's admonition for wives to be submissive to their husbands. They refuse to even pick up a Bible, read it, or study it in any way, even though most reasonable people agree it is the single most influential piece of literature ever written in all of history.

When people share their concerns with me, I always respond in the same way: "You have to understand what the Bible actually says, not what you've been told by others who are usually misinformed."

For instance, the word in Genesis 1:1–5 translated "day" is the Hebrew word *yom*, which refers to a period of time with a beginning and an end. It is unlikely it was a twenty-four-hour solar day, because the sun, moon, and stars do not appear until the fourth "day."

As to the issue of fearing God, I thought it would be fascinating to look up what the word *fear* actually means in ancient Hebrew.

I discovered that the word *yirah*, translated "fear," has a range of meanings.

In Jewish thought, there are three levels of fear. First, there is the fear of punishment or pain (*yirat ha'onesh*).[1] This is the sense in which we usually think of the word *fear*. Second, there is the fear of breaking God's law (*yirat ha'malkhut*).[2] This is the fear of being punished by God for sin. The third type of fear is a deep reverence for and awareness of the presence of God (*yirat ha'rommemnut*): "The fear of the LORD leads to life; then one rests content, untouched by trouble" (Proverbs 19:23).[3] This is the healthy type of fear that draws us near to God. "There is no fear in love. But perfect love drives out fear, because fear has to do with punishment. The one who fears is not made perfect in love" (1 John 4:18). If we "fear" God in this way, then we will be aware of God's presence all around us. I love this thought!

On the subject of submission, I thought it would be interesting to test what I had been learning from my rabbinic study and go to the original text. I searched for what "submit" means in the original text of Ephesians 5:22, where Paul exhorts, "Wives, submit yourselves to your own husbands as you do to the Lord." I found the Greek word *hupotasso*. Basically, it means "to identify with" or "to be in support of." This is different from the English translation, which is taken from the Greek word *hupeiko*, meaning "submit to."

The biblical meaning of submission has nothing to do with being a doormat or a second-class citizen, or even a slave of any kind. Instead, it seems to point to what most of Jesus' teaching points to: be kind to one another, love one another, be of service to one another, and treat others the way you want to be treated.

The truth is that some people aren't aware of the facts about

God's Word, and others choose to ignore them. The Bible is not an ancient, dead book. Hebrews 4:12 tells us, "The word of God is alive and active."

God is a covenant-keeping, faithful, unchanging Father to us all in a world where everything else changes from one moment to the next.

In this book you will have the exciting opportunity to discover the *truth* of the Bible and learn what many passages in the Scriptures really mean. You will experience the Rock (Jesus), the Road (the Holy Land), and the Rabbi (the Word of God) as you have never experienced them before!

Come deeper as we explore the land of Israel and mine the treasures of God's Word together. There is so much more!

PREFACE

My Love Affair with Israel

Pray for the peace of Jerusalem:
"May they prosper who love you."
—PSALM 122:6 NASB

My love affair with the land of Israel began the moment I took my very first step onto the Promised Land in June of 1971. I was seventeen years old, and my father's high school graduation gift was a trip for me and my mother to attend the first Jerusalem Conference on Biblical Prophecy. I missed my graduation ceremony, but I couldn't have cared less. I was where it all happened! All the stories I had heard, all the Scriptures I had studied since I was a young girl—*everything* I believed from the Word of God had taken place thousands of years before in this land I was experiencing for the very first time! That thought took my breath away all those years ago. It still does today.

I have returned to Israel many times during the last forty-five years, and each time I have come back a totally transformed person.

Why? you might ask. *What is so magical about a small piece of rocky terrain roughly the size of New Hampshire that gives it the power to completely redirect, redefine, and ultimately redeem a human heart?*

That question is the essence of this book. I want to take you to the Holy Land. I want you to experience the thrill of discovering the Word of God in its original languages of Hebrew and Greek, because I believe with all my soul that the answer to every question any person will ever ask is hidden in that land and in the Word of God in its purest form.

Come! Let's go to the land, let's hear the Word, and let's be transformed by the wonder of it all.

Meet the Good
Rabbi: Jason Sobel

I first met Rabbi Jason Sobel in December 2016 during the Christmas rush at Rockefeller Center. I had heard about him for several years from friends I respect very much, and to a person, their regard for him and the depth of his teaching was extraordinary. "You *have* to meet him!" my friends told me. "His teaching will change your life."

So Jason and I sat across from each other at my favorite New York City restaurant, Neary's Pub, and ordered the famous lamb chops. I instantly warmed to him. Rabbi Jason is the kind of person who gives you a big smile and a bear hug that leaves you breathless.

I expressed to Rabbi Jason my exasperation with what Christmas has deteriorated into: a massive, crass, commercial circus that has nothing to do with the birth of Jesus Christ. I challenge anyone to find a baby in a manger anywhere! (Okay, they still have one at the end of the Christmas Spectacular at Radio City Music Hall. But that's it.)

I remember throwing up my hands and declaring to Rabbi Jason that I basically hated the whole furious frenzy.

He gave me a wry smile and said quietly, "I can give you a good reason to love December 25."

I couldn't imagine such a reason. "Please!" I pleaded.

For the next three hours, I listened as the good rabbi unpacked the secret of this biblical story in a way that left me in awe. (He will share it later in this book.)

Throughout these chapters, I have asked Rabbi Jason to take us deeper into the Scriptures—the same ones we have read over and over through our lives without ever mining the treasures that lie beneath. This is Jason's extraordinary gift. Every time you think he's finished with his point, he flashes a smile and says, "But wait! There's more!" And there always is. So much more!

Rabbi Jason Sobel is a colorful, funny, delightful, brilliant, given-to-rapping Messianic Jew. That term *Messianic Jew* simply means he is a Jewish individual who believes that the Messiah, who was prophesied 353 times in the Old Testament, has already come into the world in the person of Jesus Christ. Simply put, Messianic Jews believe that Jesus was and is the Messiah (or "Anointed One").

By that definition, I, too, am a Messianic Jew. My father was a Jew, so I am Jewish by birth. And I believe the Messiah has not only already come, but He is going to come again, this time to reign in His kingdom in a new heaven and a new earth.

Jewish friends of mine have often teased me about my *chutzpah*, a Yiddish term I always took negatively to mean "a little pushy." So imagine my surprise when Rabbi Jason explained to me that it actually means "holy boldness." Much better!

I want to be bold in my witness for Jesus, but I also want to be sensitive to the Holy Spirit. It's so easy to completely turn off people whose hearts are not ready to hear the Word.

Rabbi Jason taught me that Jesus came to undo all that we lost in the garden of Eden. He came to undo the ten plagues Moses brought down in the first exodus from Egypt, because Jesus is the final exodus—becoming the one and only Doorway into heaven, the restored Garden that awaits believers.

Another thing Rabbi Jason taught me is that from the first letter to the last, the Bible points to Jesus. On the third day after the crucifixion, two of Jesus' disciples were discussing everything that had happened in Jerusalem during the Passover. Jesus appeared to them on the road to Emmaus and said: "'Did not the Messiah have to suffer these things and then enter his glory?' And beginning with Moses and all the Prophets, he explained to them what was said in all the Scriptures concerning himself" (Luke 24:26–27). Jesus' statement on the road to Emmaus is very similar to one made by the rabbis who state in the Talmud, "The prophets prophesied only of the days of the Messiah."[1]

All of Scripture is meant to point to the Messiah in some way. For example, as Rabbi Jason explained to me, the first letter of Genesis is the Hebrew letter *bet*, and the last word of the book of Revelation is the Hebrew word *amen*, which ends in the letter *nun*. The first and last letters of the Bible spell the Hebrew word *Ben*, which means "Son." From the very first to the very last letter, everything in the Bible points to the Son!

When the old and the new are connected in this way, we experience what the two disciples experienced on the road to Emmaus when they exclaimed, "Were not our hearts burning within us while he talked with us on the road and opened the Scriptures to us?" (Luke 24:32). This type of Emmaus experience can happen repeatedly as you discover the Jewish roots and foundations of the Scriptures.

Throughout *The Rock, the Road, and the Rabbi,* Jason will provide his own unique thoughts and insights into many of the places we visit, the Bible passages we examine, and the truths we discover. You'll see his contributions in a different font throughout the book.

So join us, won't you? Come to the land, to the Word, and to the wonder of Israel—and to the Scriptures through which they all come together.

Meet the Tour Guide:
Ray Vander Laan

In April 2012, my husband, Frank, and I went to Israel together for the first time. To say he didn't want to go would be an understatement. He was dreading it, and this from a man who had traveled all over the world as an athlete and sportscaster! But our dear friends Emilie and Craig Wierda had told me about a man named Ray Vander Laan, who was considered one of the greatest Bible teachers in the world, and about a tour he was leading in Israel.

My heart was hungry for more truth, but Frank felt he already had all the truth he needed. He had become a Christian decades earlier as a young boy growing up in poverty during the Depression. His parents were Christians, and his father worked as an itinerant oilman in California and Texas. According to Frank's mother's Bible, they moved twenty-nine times before Frank went to high school in Bakersfield, California. Frank remembered eating dog food—and being grateful for it—when life was particularly harsh. But his family always found a church each time they came to a new town, and many times that church was all they had other than one another.

What Frank didn't realize until our trip to Israel is that he had a *religion* all his life, but he never had a *relationship* with the living God. Begrudgingly, he agreed to go to Israel with me because he knew how much it meant to me. This trip became the prototype for what we now call the Rock and Road Experience.

Frank and I arrived at Ben Gurion Airport in Tel Aviv at noon after a ten-hour flight from New York City. I think most of the people in our tour group thought we would head to our hotel in Jerusalem, relax for the rest of the day, and then begin our study of the Holy Land rested and refreshed the next morning. But that's because we did not yet know our leader, Ray Vander Laan. Oh, we'd read his bio. We knew he was a teacher of biblical studies from Holland, Michigan, and the founder of That the World May Know Ministries. We knew he had a master's degree from Westminster Theological Seminary and had completed graduate studies that were the equivalent of an Orthodox rabbinical degree from Yeshiva University in New York City. But what we didn't know was *why* he had gone to such extensive lengths to study the Bible.

We soon discovered that Ray was an extremely memorable individual. Do you remember Indiana Jones from *Raiders of the Lost Ark*? Well, I immediately dubbed our teacher "Michigan Ray"! He not only looked like Harrison Ford, he even dressed like him and wore an Indiana Jones–style hat straight out of the Paramount Studios wardrobe! But Ray's message was completely his own.

"The problem with the Bible," he explained on the first day of our study tour, "is that the Bible was written *by* Middle Easterners *for* Middle Easterners. But we try to understand it with a Western mind-set. We try to apply our own principles and our Western understanding to a culture that is completely foreign to us."

That made sense to me. Our foreign policy has tried to do the same thing with nation building in the Middle East, with disastrous results. The difference between the Eastern and Western mind-sets is apples and oranges. Or more accurately, hummus and hot dogs. Culturally and historically, the East and the West are worlds apart. So how do we bridge that chasm when it comes to learning Scripture?

"By understanding what the Word of God—the Bible—*really* says," Ray explained.

After our flight landed, we were instructed to gather our luggage, put on our hiking boots, and grab our Bibles. There would be no lounging by the pool that day!

Then came one of my favorite memories on the entire Israel tour. We climbed straight up a mountain for about an hour to reach Gezer, a once-thriving biblical city that is now in ruins. I remember eighty-two-year-old Frank looking at me without an ounce of humor and declaring, "I am on the first flight out of here tomorrow."

"I'm right behind you," I said, wondering why we had agreed to such a trip.

When all of us jet-lagged pilgrims finally made it to the top of the mountain, I noticed Michigan Ray wasn't even out of breath.

The view was stunning. "Look down there," Ray pointed, "down to where we started out. See that tiny white ribbon following alongside the Mediterranean Sea? That's the Via Maris, or 'The Road of the Sea.' It's an ancient trade route dating back thousands of years." It was a beautiful sight, and it set the stage perfectly for Ray's first teaching session.

"People always ask, *Why the Jews?* Out of all the nations, why did God choose this stubborn, brilliant, but rebellious people to bring His message of salvation to the world?"

Ray clasped his worn leather Bible for emphasis and pointed below.

"Whoever controlled *that* road controlled the world at that time," he explained to our group. "It would be like God choosing Wall Street or Hollywood today. But in Jesus' time, that road was the center of commerce in the Middle East. To the north were Syria, Lebanon, and Turkey; to the east was Mesopotamia; to the south were Egypt, Libya, and Ethiopia. And to the west? To the west was Caesar."

MORE FROM RABBI JASON

We often refer to Jews as the "chosen people" because God made the nation out of a chosen couple, Abraham and Sarah. Part of God's covenant with Abraham and his children was giving them the land of Israel. This begs the question: why did God choose that land?

As Kathie mentioned, Israel's geographic position is key, since it functions as a land bridge between Asia and Africa. But from a spiritual perspective, there is even more. I believe the land God promised Abraham has the same geographic boundaries as the garden of Eden. When they ate of the forbidden fruit, Adam and Eve compromised Paradise and brought sin into the world. But through Abraham, Sarah, and their seed (the Messiah), God will restore heaven to earth, unifying Abraham's biological children with those in the nations who place their faith in Jesus.

CHAPTER 1

THE BROOK OF ELAH

David and Goliath

*[May] God . . . give you the Spirit of wisdom and of revelation in
the knowledge of him, having the eyes of your hearts enlightened,
that you may know what is the hope to which he has called you.*

—EPHESIANS 1:17—18 ESV

The next day of our Israel tour, we traveled by bus and then foot
(uphill again!) to the Valley of Elah—the place where David
famously defeated Goliath. Nobody was grumbling anymore. Not
even Frank. We had learned a great truth the day before: the harder
the climb, the greater the blessing on the mountaintop.

When we finally reached the ridge where the Israelites had looked
out with terror across the valley to where the Philistines waited to
attack, the first thing that struck me was how completely unchanged

it is. There is nothing there but the imagination you bring with you. And as you recall the familiar story of David and Goliath recorded in 1 Samuel 17, you can truly envision the drama that took place there some three thousand years ago.

Ray has the extraordinary gift of enabling people to see a familiar story with new eyes.

He explained, "Many people think the miracle in the story is how David, a young shepherd boy, was able to defeat the giant, Goliath—the champion of the Philistines, Israel's enemy. But the truth is that any shepherd worth his salt already knew how to defeat his foes. Shepherds were trained from their earliest days to protect their flocks from any enemy, including lions and bears. The Scriptures tell us that David had already done this. In 1 Samuel 17:36, David tells King Saul that he 'has killed both the lion and the bear.'

"So while King Saul and the entire Israelite army cowered in fear for forty days, this young shepherd, who was probably between twelve and fourteen years old, spurned the king's offer of his own armor and instead reached into the Brook of Elah, picked up five smooth stones, placed them in his shepherd's pouch, and approached the giant without fear. David said to Goliath in 1 Samuel 17:45, 'You come against me with sword and spear and javelin, but I come against you in the name of the Lord Almighty, the God of the armies of Israel, whom you have defied.'"

Ray paused to let all of this sink in.

"The miracle of David and Goliath is that David had an intimate *relationship* with the living God!" he bellowed. "That's what makes a miracle!"

Then Ray instructed all of us to go down to the brook and pick up a stone. By now we had learned to do what he said without questioning him. I will never forget the look in Frank's eyes as this man who was in six Halls of Fame obediently reached down to pick up his stone, just as a young shepherd boy had done three thousand years ago.

Ray also picked up a stone from the brook. As he held the stone in his hand, he looked at each of us, as if to the core of our souls, and asked: "What is *your* stone? Where are you going to throw it?"

He literally "rocked" our world. Frank and I and everyone in the group were never the same again.

This experience lit a fire in my belly, and it satisfied a deep longing in Frank's soul. Though the rest of the trip was profoundly moving and illuminating, it was this truth he learned in the Valley of Elah—that religion is nothing without relationship—that gave Frank a strong sense of peace and purpose until the day he died. Finally, at the age of eighty-two, he had found his stone.

As I stood on the mountaintop of Elah, I was filled with a sense of overwhelming awe. I was thrilled to be hearing for the first time what the ancient text truly meant. Centuries ago, Jesus said, "You will know the truth, and the truth will set you free" (John 8:32).

And I was starting to feel free, indeed.

As Ray concluded the day's teaching, he called each of our names, one by one, and challenged us to throw our stone wherever the Lord has placed us. "That's why every one of us who are created in the image of the Creator is on this planet," Ray said. "We are supposed to partner with God to bring His *shalom* to the chaos of this world. Genesis 1:1–2 says, 'In the beginning God created the heavens and the earth, . . . and the Spirit of God was hovering over the waters.' Think of Genesis 1:2 like this: '*Shalom* hovered over the chaos.'"

Ray explained that the word *shalom* has been diluted through the centuries from its original meaning to now mean "peace." But according to Ray, *shalom* really means God's *perfection*. *Shalom* encompasses all the characteristics of God—His righteousness, His justice, His unfailing love, His forgiveness, His holiness, and yes, His peace as well. *Shalom* is everything that is inherent in the one God and everything He planned for those He created. The garden of Eden was perfect, and all of creation, including human beings, was perfect—because God was, and is, and shall forever be *perfect*.

"So," Ray repeated, "we are to bring God's *shalom* to the chaos of this world."

There it was: our purpose! This is what gives meaning to our lives—what drives our passion, what fuels our very soul, and what ultimately fulfills our personal destiny.

But as we would soon discover, Ray had only begun to shake our foundations.

Come . . . to the Brook of Elah!

MORE FROM RABBI JASON

WHY DID DAVID CHOOSE FIVE SMOOTH STONES?

Over a forty-day period, the Philistine giant Goliath mocked and demoralized the army of Israel. Even worse, he ridiculed the Lord. Goliath's actions exposed the fear and lack of faith in the hearts of King Saul and his soldiers. But then David came along, and he couldn't tolerate the way the Lord's name was being insulted. He couldn't stand idly by as the people cowered in fear before this pagan blasphemer, even if he was a giant skilled in war. David was provoked to act.

So David went to Saul and said he wanted to fight Goliath on behalf of the king and his people. Saul, for good reason, was hesitant to allow young David to fight, but he conceded. He offered David his armor, but David decided not to wear it because it was too big. Instead, he would use a slingshot and five smooth stones from the river. Sounds crazy, right?

What is the significance of David using five stones? To answer this question, we need to dig deeper to understand this story from a Jewish perspective.

The name Goliath comes from the Hebrew root *gimmel, lamed, hei*, which means "to expose, reveal, or exile." He revealed the fear and exposed the weakness in the Israelites and their army. If Goliath had been a professional wrestler, he could have been called the Banisher or the Exiler.

I believe the five stones are key to understanding the story of David and Goliath. The Hebrew language is alphanumeric. This means that numbers can be written with letters. For example, the number five in Hebrew is written with the letter *hei* (ה), which is the fifth letter of the Hebrew alphabet. According to some Jewish mystics, the letter *hei* is connected to the divine breath of God that releases His creative power and potential. This is alluded to in the Hebrew text of Genesis 2:4, which says, "These are the genealogical records of the heavens and the earth when they were created, at the time when ADONAI *Elohim* made land and sky" (TLV). The Hebrew word translated "created" is *bara*, which means "created out of nothing." In this verse, *bara* has the letter *hei* inserted into it, which is grammatically incorrect.

There is no good grammatical reason for this word to include the letter *hei* unless the text is trying to allude to some deeper truth. But what? Remember, the letter *hei* is often seen as the letter of the divine breath of God, which, along with the Word of God, is the means by which creation came to be: "By ADONAI's word were the heavens made, and all their host by the breath of His mouth" (Psalm 33:6 TLV). So the letter *hei* in the word translated "created" in Genesis 2:4 alludes to the divine breath releasing God's creative power.

This truth can also be seen in the life of Abraham and Sarah. God promised Abraham and Sarah that they would conceive a child, but years went by without their having a son. As a sign that they would bear children even in their old age, that the promise would be fulfilled, the Lord changed their names:

> For My part, because My covenant is with you, you will be the father of a multitude of nations. No longer will your name be Abram, but your name will be Abraham, because I make you the father of a multitude of nations. . . . As for Sarai your wife, you shall not call her by the name Sarai. Rather, Sarah is her name. And I will bless her, and moreover, I will give you a son from her. I will bless her and she will give rise to nations. Kings of the peoples will come from her. (Genesis 17:4–5, 15–16 TLV)

The Lord changed Abram's name to AbraHam, and Sarai's to SaraH. There is a one-letter difference between their new names and their old ones—the addition of the letter *hei*, or H in English. The Lord added this letter to their names because it represented His creative power to accomplish the impossible!

Now it should make more sense why David picked up five stones. David needed the supernatural power that comes with the divine breath in order to punish Goliath, the wicked blasphemer, to restore honor to the divine name, and to bring *shalom* to the chaos. This is what the letter *hei*—the fifth letter of the Hebrew alphabet and the number five—represents in Hebraic thought.

In other words, David needed the *hei*, the divine empowerment of God's Spirit, to obtain victory and overcome the impossible!

The way to overcome the impossible has always been the same. Don't fear the giants. The Lord is with you always. Just believe and fight! You already have the victory.

CHAPTER 2

En Gedi

David's Waterfall

*Let the one who hears say, "Come!" Let the one
who is thirsty come; and let the one who wishes
take the free gift of the water of life.*

—REVELATION 22:17

One of my favorite places in Israel is En Gedi. This oasis in the
desert, directly west of the Dead Sea, is a steep climb dotted
with ancient caves where young David hid from his enemy, King
Saul, for years and cried out to God in dozens of profound psalms.
All David's poetry about strongholds, hiding places, refuge, rocks,
and living waters come alive here. We can only wonder what was
going through David's mind during his time in the wilderness.

Perhaps David thought of Abraham, who was promised that he

would have a child, only to have to wait and trust for decades for that promise to come true when he was one hundred years old. David had been anointed king of Israel by the prophet Samuel when he was a young boy, only to wait until he was thirty to finally sit on the throne of the kingdom of Israel.

Haven't we all experienced excruciating times of waiting for God to answer our prayers? But the wait isn't idle time; the waiting period is our opportunity to be active and alive and growing, which is why it is so important that we persevere. As Isaiah 40:31 reminds us: "Those who hope in the LORD will renew their strength. They will soar on wings like eagles; they will run and not grow weary, they will walk and not be faint."

God's promise about the waiting time is as big a part of His plan as the actual moment when God's promise comes true. I doubt we are ever the same person when the promise is fulfilled that we were when the promise was made.

Although the landscape is bleak and the land is parched and dry, an amazing thing happens the higher you climb in En Gedi. Life begins to bloom all around you, wildlife bounds effortlessly on the heights, and suddenly, unexpectedly, streams and waterfalls of living water appear as if from nowhere.

The most famous of these waterfalls is the extraordinary David's Waterfall.

You catch your breath when you come upon it, and you can easily imagine how David and his men were overjoyed and praised God when their parched tongues tasted the water flowing from it and their weary, sun-scorched bodies stood beneath its blessed refreshment. You will never read the Psalms the same way after experiencing En

Gedi. The realization of God's unfailing love and faithfulness overwhelms you, and you weep tears of gratitude and praise.

Ray explained that the Judean mountains are made of limestone, so they are porous in nature, not rock-solid like granite or marble. "There—directly north, some seventeen miles from here—lies the town of Bethlehem. It's conceivable that the rain that fell in Bethlehem two thousand years ago in the time of Jesus is the very water falling over us here in En Gedi right now."

Imagine waiting two thousand years for living water! There have been times in my life, I confess, when I felt as if I was waiting that long for God's promises to be filled. Yet His timing is always perfect.

Come . . . to En Gedi!

LEAD ME, GENTLE SHEPHERD
(Inspired by En Gedi)

Lead me to the rock that is higher than I.
Hide me 'neath Your wings as You lift me through the sky.
Give me living water that I may thirst no more,
And when I go through storms, my Lord, lead me safely to the
    shore.

Chorus:
O lead me, Gentle Shepherd,
Let me hear Your tender voice.
And when we reach the crossroads,

Guide me toward the better choice.
Spirit, give me wisdom, show me Your sweet shalom.
Then lead me on to glory, Lord,
Lead me on to home.

Let me know Your truth, that I may understand
That nothing is created except by Your command.
In You I have my being, You give me every breath.
And You, and You alone, my Lord, have conquered even death.

Repeat Chorus

Tag:
One day the clouds will open
And all will see Your face,
And bow before Your lordship,
And praise You for Your grace.
And we will raise our voices in glorious harmony
And reign with You forever for all eternity.

—LYRICS BY KATHIE LEE GIFFORD

CHAPTER 3

THE JUDEAN WILDERNESS

Psalm 23

Surely your goodness and love will follow me
all the days of my life,
and I will dwell in the house of the LORD
forever.

—PSALM 23:6

While our tour group was in the wilderness of En Gedi, Ray Vander Laan reminded us of another well-known Bible passage that was likely written while David was in the wilderness: Psalm 23.

Most of us are familiar with this psalm, perhaps the most famous of all the psalms. On the surface, Psalm 23 seems almost like poetry, setting a beautiful, bucolic scene of the peaceful relationship between a shepherd and his flock. But as Ray explained, it is so much deeper than that.

The first line, "The LORD is my shepherd," is obvious. There is only one leader of a flock of sheep. And in Jesus, we have a benevolent, tender, and protective Shepherd who knows His sheep—and His sheep know Him.

Jesus said, "My sheep listen to my voice; I know them, and they follow me" (John 10:27). They follow Him because they *trust* Him. He has never let them down. Sheep can't see very well, but they have a heightened sense of hearing. They follow the shepherd's voice.

The next line in Psalm 23 is interesting: "I shall not want" (v. 1 NKJV). Perhaps a better translation is, "I have everything that I need because of Him."

The shepherd provides everything the sheep needs, even leaving the flock to go looking for the one lost member who might be in danger.

The next line is, "He makes me to lie down in green pastures" (v. 2 NKJV).

The truth is, there were no green pastures in Israel at that time—not in the way we think of rolling, grassy, lush fields. There were only small patches of grass in the Judean wilderness, barely visible except late in the day when the setting sun caused them to reflect light.

Ray explained that the shepherd's job was to lead his sheep to these life-giving spots so that they would be given exactly what they needed for that day. No more. This kept them in a constant state of trusting.

"He leads me in the paths of righteousness" (v. 3 NKJV).

"Paths of righteousness" are what the Hebrews called the ancient, well-worn paths that are still clearly visible winding through the hillsides today. Shepherds have used these same routes for centuries.

The Twenty-Third Psalm is a beautiful example of God's provision for each of us. He promises He will take care of us. He expects us to trust Him, and He gives us just what we need when we need it. In other words, "we live by faith, not by sight" (2 Corinthians 5:7). This is what leads to the eventual restoration of our souls.

Thinking about that restoration reminds me of a vivid memory from my precious father's last days. He was home under hospice care, and day after day my mom, my sister Michie, my brother Dave, and I sang hymns and prayed over him, holding him and whispering our love. One day we recited Psalm 23 over him. Finally, as my mother spoke the words, "Your rod and Your staff, they comfort me" (v. 4 NKJV), Daddy suddenly sat up, took a deep breath, and passed into eternity.

I believe with all my heart that Daddy went directly into the waiting, loving arms of his Shepherd, and it gives me great peace to know the truth of 2 Corinthians 5:8: "To be absent from the body [is] to be at home with the Lord" (NASB).

The rest of Psalm 23 is about the abundant, victorious life God promises to all His "sheep" if we continue to listen to His voice and follow in His footsteps.

Come . . . to the Judean wilderness!

CHAPTER 4

MOUNT CARMEL

Elijah and the Prophets of Baal

*"How long will you waver between two opinions? If the LORD
is God, follow him; but if Baal is God, follow him."*

—1 KINGS 18:21

The Old Testament book of 1 Kings records a dramatic showdown between the God of Israel and the false god Baal. At this
time, Israel had experienced a civil war and was divided into two
kingdoms. The Northern Kingdom maintained the name Israel,
and the Southern Kingdom was called Judah. The people of Israel
had largely abandoned the God of Abraham, Isaac, and Jacob. They
had been seduced by the false god Baal, who was worshiped by the
people who were not driven out of the Promised Land as God had
commanded.

The ultimate test of "Which is the greater God?" took place at the summit of Mount Carmel during the reign of the evil king Ahab and his even more evil queen, Jezebel. The prophet Elijah suggested that the followers of Israel's God (known as Yahweh) and the followers of Baal meet and "test" which was the one, true God.

In 1 Kings 18, we learn that King Ahab and Queen Jezebel had led Israel into unprecedented evil by worshiping pagan gods. Jezebel was from Phoenicia, and she was a priestess in the Baal cult. When she came to Israel, she set up a whole cult center to Baal that included 450 priests and 400 priestesses to Baal and Baal's consort, Asherah.

Baal is the pagan word for "Lord," and there were many different kinds of Baals in the pagan world, such as the "wisdom" Baal, the "military" Baal, the "health and wealth" Baal, etc.

But the supreme Baal was the "rain" Baal. This Baal was the god of fertility, who controlled the weather and provided rain. He was considered the god of the thunderstorm, and he was depicted as having lightning in his hands.

It was believed that this Baal would go into hibernation in the underworld during the summer season, causing the rain to stop. When fall came, Baal returned to earth to have sex with his consort, Asherah, thus bringing forth the rain again.

Today we understand they were in essence saying the rain symbolized Baal's sperm and the earth symbolized Asherah's womb. So, in order to get the gods to fertilize the land, the pagan believers mimicked these gods with their so-called worship. They would come to one of the Baal worship centers, marked by Asherah poles, and have sex with one of the priests or priestesses in hopes of enticing Baal and Asherah to mate. These centers were essentially houses of prostitution. Obviously, these pagan religious practices were completely contrary to the laws passed down to the Hebrews by Moses.

In times of severe drought or crisis, as they became more desperate, the Baal followers even sacrificed their children, either their own or the firstborn of a clan or family, in an attempt to win Baal's favor. In recent excavations near the capital city of Samaria, ruins have been found of a Baal temple built by King Ahab. Among the temple ruins were jars that contained the remains of infants and children who had been sacrificed in that evil place.

We can imagine what was happening during the years of drought described in 1 Kings 17. The people were starving, which caused them to become desperate, leading to sexual immorality and infanticide. This sets the stage for the great showdown between King Ahab and his false god, Baal, and the prophet Elijah and his God, Yahweh. Which of them would be the true "storm" God and send the saving rain? It was one of the most dramatic confrontations in the entire Bible.

The showdown took place at Mount Carmel, which means "the vineyard of God"—a reminder of what Israel was called to be for the world. But the people had forgotten the one, true God, and they had forgotten why the Lord had given them the land in the first place—so they would be a light to the nations, a kingdom of priests, declaring Yahweh to a seeking, hurting, and lost world.

The mountaintop was packed with people who still worshiped Yahweh, still said their prayers, and still sang their songs. But they had added the worship of Baal alongside their worship of Yahweh, making the pagan Baal equal to the Lord of all creation! This was the blasphemy that enraged the sovereign God. During the showdown on Mount Carmel, God sent down fire from heaven and proved to all who were present that He alone is God.

I believe it is this same kind of blasphemy today that breaks God's heart when we add false gods to our own worship. What have we allowed in our own lives to be equally or even more important to us than God?

The day our tour group visited this site—April 26, 2012—happened to be Israel's Independence Day (*Yom Ha'atzmaut*), commemorating the Israeli declaration of independence in 1948. Ray had just finished recounting the extraordinary victory of the God of Israel over Baal, when, just at that moment, sirens wailed below in the Valley of Jezreel. Then Israeli fighter planes emerged from the hidden silos beneath the ground and screeched through the skies directly above us. It was exhilarating beyond description. Even now as I write these words, my soul leaps at the memory of it.

God is still winning the victory. He is still fulfilling His promises. He is still sovereign over all things and all nations. There is a God in Israel! And He still loves His people and the land they were called to.

Come . . . to Mount Carmel!

CHAPTER 5

CAESAREA AND HERODIUM

Herod the Great

When King Herod heard this he was disturbed,
and all Jerusalem with him.

—MATTHEW 2:3

Other than Jesus, there is perhaps no biblical character more fascinating than Herod the Great. If Jesus is the greatest story ever told, then I believe Herod is the greatest story *never* told.

While there are a number of people named Herod in the Scriptures, we read about Herod the Great only in a couple of places—first as the king the wise men visited when they were seeking the place where the Messiah was to be born (Matthew 2:1–12), and then later when an enraged Herod sent his soldiers to Bethlehem to kill every male child under the age of two years old in the hopes of destroying any future threat to his throne and kingdom (Matthew 2:16).

But according to the historian Josephus and other chroniclers of the era, Herod the Great, who was born around 73 BC, lived a life of extraordinarily ruthless ambition, unbounded intellect, viciousness, and architectural genius.

Herod murdered the father of his favorite wife, Mariamne. He also drowned her brother and then murdered her as well, claiming she had committed adultery. He executed his most trusted friend, his barber, and three hundred military leaders in one day. He also killed three of his sons, suspecting them of treason. Finally, at the end of his life, he locked up three thousand of the leading citizens of Israel with orders that they be executed at the hour he died, to assure there would be sorrow and mourning on that day. Josephus wrote that Herod "put such abuses upon [the Jews] as a wild beast would not have put on them, if he had power given him to rule."[1]

Looming just a short distance away from Bethlehem is one of Herod's eleven palaces, Herodium, which Herod selected as the place where he would be entombed.

Herod was the governor of Galilee (appointed by Marc Anthony) when in 40 BC the Parthian Empire conquered Judea and named a new king. Herod was more shrewd than loyal. He declared allegiance to Rome and fled Jerusalem with as many as five thousand people, including his family, under cover of night. Josephus wrote that, while fleeing, his mother's chariot overturned and trapped her underneath. When she miraculously emerged unscathed, Herod declared his gratitude to the gods and decided to one day be buried at that very site.[2]

For two thousand years, experts insisted that Herod's tomb was not in Herodium. But then in 2007, Herod's burial place was finally discovered by Ehud Netzer of Hebrew University, just where Josephus had written it was.

It is fascinating to climb down the cistern at Herodium and see where the earth has been packed and pushed forward to raise the height of the mountain. (One can only imagine how many slaves died to accomplish this.) Why would Herod go to so much trouble to raise the mountain? Because there was another mountain the same size next to it, and Herod, being the narcissist he was, demanded that his palace or burial site be higher than the one next door.

All of Herod's magnificent palaces were one day's journey from each other—from the north to the farthest south, to Masada, in the Dead Sea region. These palaces were, in essence, his escape route should things go wrong with the Jews or, even more dangerously, with Caesar.

Herod the Great needed Caesar because he needed Caesar's army, but Caesar needed Herod for a reason that has been lost to history. This is perhaps the most fascinating aspect of Herod's story.

Caesarea Maritima (also called Caesarea by the Sea) is an extraordinarily beautiful city on the coast of the Mediterranean, best known in the Bible as the place where Herod Antipas, the son of Herod the Great, imprisoned the apostle Paul. When you visit this city, you will see a plaque that mentions Pontius Pilate. We can assume Pilate was one of the thousands of soldiers who sailed to Israel on Caesar's ships to this man-made harbor at Caesarea. Only recently have experts finally discovered how King Herod was capable of going 120 feet into the Mediterranean Sea to pour concrete more than two thousand years ago. Why did he go to such trouble? If Caesar's ships arrived carrying soldiers, then what did they return with? The answer is surprising: King Herod and his family had a product that Caesar desperately wanted and desperately needed—the ancient version of Viagra.

It's important to understand the historical context. The Jews were the first monotheistic culture in history. They believed in one God and one God only. The Greco-Roman world of Herod's day was polytheistic. They believed in many gods, and much of their worship was sexual in nature. To facilitate this "worship," Herod had a product made from a substance extracted from the balsam tree, among other ingredients, that functioned as an aphrodisiac! Whether it actually worked, no one knows; but we do know from Josephus's historical writings that Caesar had a voracious appetite for this product, and he kept his ships coming and going between Capri, where he spent most of his time, and Caesarea Maritima on Israel's west coast, where Herod and his family made sure Caesar's ships were filled to capacity with their valued product.[3]

One of my favorite memories of Caesarea was when our group toured the ancient hippodrome, or athletic arena. Frank jumped up on a huge rock and immediately went into "sportscaster mode," holding an imaginary microphone to his mouth and saying, "Good evening, ladies and gentlemen, and welcome! This arena is rocking!" I don't recall his exact words, but I remember so well the joy in Frank's voice as he stood there in the arena. On our first trip to Israel with Ray Vander Laan in 2012, we visited the palace of Herodium, and I have a vivid memory of Ray teaching us the story of the Jewish Zealots' revolt against Rome in AD 70. The Zealots fled to the high spots in Israel in order to hold off the Roman assault. The most famous of these mountaintop fortresses is Masada next to the Dead Sea (see "Masada" on page 166). But they also went to Herodium.

Ray told us that when the Zealots broke into Herod's tomb, they discovered the sarcophagus, or box, that held Herod's remains. Archaeologists believe the Zealots smashed the box into six thousand pieces and blew Herod's ashes into the wind. This is symbolic of how despised Herod still was to the Jews seven decades after his death.

We were sitting in the area of the ancient synagogue on top of the palace when Ray recounted the story. Suddenly he threw his hat onto the ground and yelled, "Herod!" His voice echoed. *Herod! Herod!*

"Was it worth it?" *Worth it? Worth it?*

"Would you do it all again?" *Again? Again?*

The words of Mark 8:36 came to my mind: "For what will it profit a man if he gains the whole world, and loses his own soul?" (NKJV).

Herod had everything—a kingdom, a family, a thriving business, and a brilliant, creative mind. Yet he used all these things selfishly, narcissistically, and cruelly to build a monument to himself at the expense of everything and everyone else. He eventually died at his palace in Jericho, roaming the palace and murmuring, "Mariamne, Mariamne." He had lost his brilliant mind and his body wasted away. Josephus tells us that he stank so badly, even his servants hated to come near him.[4]

Every day as I read the newspapers, I see evidence that nothing has changed throughout the centuries.

Only what we build for God's kingdom will last. Nothing else is worth it.

Come . . . to Caesarea and Herodium!

CHAPTER 6

BETHLEHEM

Church of the Nativity

But you, Bethlehem Ephrathah,
though you are small among the clans of Judah,
out of you will come for me
one who will be ruler over Israel,
whose origins are from of old,
from ancient times.

— MICAH 5:2

I was deeply disturbed when our tour group visited modern-day Bethlehem. Scripture tells us Bethlehem was the birthplace of Jesus, the Messiah, prophesied in Micah 5:2 sometime between 750 BC and 686 BC (seven hundred years before Jesus' birth): "But you, Bethlehem Ephrathah, though you are small among the clans of Judah, out of you will come for me one who will be ruler over Israel, whose origins are from of old, from ancient times."

Today, the city of Bethlehem is controlled by the Palestinian Authority, and it feels—as my daughter, Cassidy, described it—"darkly oppressive." There are military checkpoints as you enter and exit. It hardly feels joyful or anything like the way the shepherds would have experienced it two millennia ago, as a place of great rejoicing at the Savior's birth.

Come . . . to Bethlehem!

More from Rabbi Jason

The Significance of Bethlehem

Shortly after the birth of Jesus in Bethlehem, an angel of the Lord appeared to shepherds guarding their sheep at night and announced to them, "Today in the town of David a Savior has been born to you; he is the Messiah, the Lord" (Luke 2:11). And the sign given to them was that they would find "a baby wrapped in cloths and lying in a manger" (v. 12). Of all the possible signs that could have been given to these shepherds, why did the Lord choose a baby lying in a manger and wrapped in swaddling clothes? Why was this so significant?

To answer this question, we need to dig deeper and explore the Jewish context in which the New Testament was written. Good students of the Bible are like detectives who ask lots of questions of the text. The first question we need to ask is: *Who are these shepherds? Is there anything unique about them?*

I believe these were no ordinary shepherds. They were Levitical shepherds, trained and tasked with the responsibility of tending and guarding the flocks used for sacrifices in the temple in Jerusalem.

Next, we must ask, *What is so significant about the location in which they found Jesus?* When it was time for one of their flock to give birth, the shepherds would bring the sheep into one of the caves surrounding Bethlehem that were used for this purpose. These birthing caves were kept in a state of ritual purity since these lambs were destined to be used as sacrifices in the temple. In fact, many of the male lambs born around Bethlehem would be used for the Passover.[1]

Since there was no room in the local inn, Mary and Joseph used one of these caves around Bethlehem. Messiah was not born in a stable behind some Econo Lodge or Motel Six. He was born in one of the many caves used for birthing these sacrificial lambs, because He Himself would be the ultimate sacrificial Lamb.

Not only would the location of Jesus' birth be significant to these shepherds, but so would the fact that Jesus was swaddled in cloths.

These shepherds were responsible for making sure that the newborn lambs did not contract defects, for only animals without spot or blemish could be used as a sacrifice in the temple. Baby lambs are very clumsy when they are born, so many scholars believe that these shepherds would swaddle their newborn lambs in order to prevent these future sacrificial lambs from becoming blemished by injuring themselves on jagged parts of the cave.

Another key aspect of swaddling in ancient Israel was "salting" a newborn. After Jesus was born, Joseph would have washed and scrubbed Him with salt water. Practically, the salt killed any bacteria found on an infant's body. But there is a lot of spiritual symbolism in this act as well.

Salt was symbolic of friendship and loyalty in the ancient world; it was a sign of covenant, as in the phrase "a covenant of salt" (2 Chronicles 13:5; Leviticus 2:13; Numbers 18:19). A common expression to denote friendship in Middle Eastern culture is, "There is salt between us." A salt covenant is used to denote the eternal covenant of friendship and kingship that God made with David and his heirs: "Don't you know that the LORD, the God of Israel, has given the kingship of Israel to David and his descendants forever by a covenant of salt?" (2 Chronicles 13:5). Jesus was not only born in Bethlehem, which is the city of David, but He was also the promised Son of David, the Messiah and King who came to fulfill the Davidic covenant—God's promise that one of David's descendants would live on the throne forever—and to establish the new covenant spoken of in Jeremiah: "'The days are coming,' declares the LORD, 'when I will make a new covenant with the people of Israel and with the people of Judah'" (31:31).

Salt was also an indispensable part of every sacrifice offered in the temple, as we read in Leviticus: "You are to season with salt every sacrifice of your grain offering. You are never to allow the salt of the covenant of your God to be lacking from your grain offering. With all your sacrifices you must offer salt" (2:13 TLV).

Not only was Messiah born in the same location as the temple offering, but He was also washed in salt as part of the swaddling process, which points to His future sacrifice as the Passover Lamb of God who would take away the sins of the world and inaugurate the new covenant (Jeremiah 31:31).

Messiah came to make a covenant with us, and He was so committed to us that He chose to die in order establish it, demonstrating how seriously He takes His friendship with us! This is what John 15:13 alludes to: "Greater love has no one than this: to lay down one's life for one's friends." Messiah was "the Lamb who was slain from the creation of the world" (Revelation 13:8), so He needed to be salted as our true sacrifice to erase our sin and bring us into a covenant friendship with the Lord. Now, that's a true friend. Isn't it amazing? We must make sure we are valuing His friendship and taking full advantage of it.

Not only was the process of swaddling significant to the shepherds, but I believe the actual garments in which the baby Jesus was swaddled were meant to be a sign to them as well. Let's explore their deeper meaning.

One of the oldest symbols of the Jewish faith is the menorah, a seven-branched candelabrum used in the temple. The Kohanim, the Levitical priests, lit the menorah in the sanctuary every evening and then cleaned it out every morning, replacing the old wicks with new ones.

What were the wicks of the menorah made from? The priests' tunics. Any priestly garment that became so dirty to the point that its stains could not be washed out was no longer acceptable to be worn during priestly service. These unusable garments were not destroyed; instead, they were cut up, and the fabric was used for another holy purpose. The tunics of the ordinary priests were used to make wicks for the menorah that was to burn continually in the Holy Place in the temple.

This is speculation, but I believe Jesus' swaddling clothes could have been made from the torn priestly garments that would have been used to make the wicks of the menorah. But where would Joseph and Mary have gotten them? My guess is that Mary got these cloths from her cousin Elizabeth, who was married to the priest Zechariah. As soon as Mary entered the home of Elizabeth, who had miraculously conceived in her later years, the unborn baby in her womb leaped, filled with the Holy Spirit. Elizabeth cried out, "You are blessed among women, and blessed is the fruit of your womb. Who am I, that the mother of my Master should come to me? For even when I just heard the sound of your greeting in my ear, the unborn child leaped with joy in my womb. Blessed is she who trusted that there would be a fulfillment of those things spoken to her by ADONAI" (Luke 1:42–45 TLV).

So the shepherd priests, who encountered angels, went to a place where the lambs used for the sacrifices were born and swaddled. There, they saw the baby Jesus swaddled like a sacrificial Passover lamb in priestly garments that were used for the lighting of the menorah in the temple, which symbolized the eternal presence and promise of God! Now it should make more sense as to why a baby wrapped in swaddling clothes and lying in a manger would be such a significant sign to these shepherds, for it pointed to Jesus being both the Lamb of God and the Light of the World.

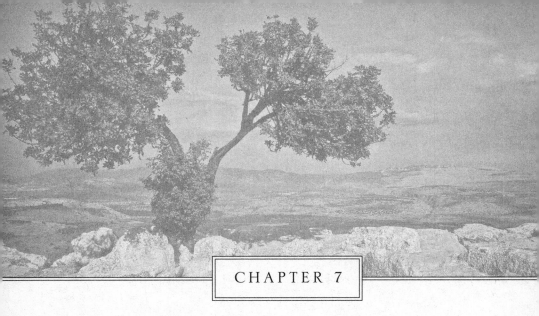

CHAPTER 7

NAZARETH

Jesus Was a What?

*"Isn't this the carpenter? Isn't this Mary's son and the
brother of James, Joseph, Judas and Simon?"*

—MARK 6:3

Our tour group was gathered, as usual, on top of a mountain
when Ray asked us a question: "How many of you know
what Jesus and Joseph, his earthly father, did for a living before He
began His ministry as a rabbi when He turned thirty?"

Every one of us answered, "He was a carpenter." Smug bunch
we were, indeed.

Then Ray again rocked our world by replying, "Actually, no.
Jesus wasn't a carpenter, although there is no doubt that he did work
with wood at times, along with other items."

Now, at this point, I was wondering what I was doing on a mountaintop 5,710 miles away from home with a guy who obviously didn't even know the basics of the Bible—with ten days of the tour to go!

This was the moment my life changed.

Ray explained, "The word translated 'carpenter' in Matthew 13:55 and Mark 6:3 for how Joseph and Jesus made a living is the Greek word *tektōn*. It means 'builder.' You see, when the writers of the King James Version were translating the Greek into the English, they assumed, 'Oh, these guys were carpenters. Just like us.'

"The problem with that is that there were no trees that could be used for building in Israel at that time like there were in England. All the wood in Israel came from the cedars of Lebanon, which were cut down, made into rafts, and floated along the Via Maris—'The Road of the Sea'—adjacent to the Mediterranean. There, they were broken apart and taken to the various construction sites."

Ray paused for his point.

"You see, there were only rocks in Israel. This is an example of one of the many poor translations in the Bible."

And then Ray gave us a stunning insight.

"Jesus was not a carpenter. Jesus was a stone mason."

I was shaken to the depths of my soul. Suddenly everything made sense! I remembered several Bible verses that referred to stones and building with stones:

- "Let any one of you who is without sin be the first to throw a *stone* at her" (John 8:7).
- "On this *rock* I will build my church" (Matthew 16:18).

- "The *stone* the builders rejected has become the cornerstone" (Psalm 118:22).

Then I asked the most profound question I have ever asked a man of God. "Ray, if we are wrong about something as simple as this in the Bible, what else are we wrong about?"

Ray looked at me with a mischievous grin and a piercing light in his eyes. "Everything," he answered.

And that's when I fell in love all over again with the journey, especially after Rabbi Jason explained Ray's revelation about Jesus' profession.

Come . . . to Nazareth!

MORE FROM RABBI JASON

JESUS THE PROMISED MASTER CRAFTSMAN

The Greek word *tektōn* can be translated as "stone mason" or "architect." All these concepts are significant in reference to Jesus, since they connect back to Him as the architect of creation.

The first word of Genesis in Hebrew is *bereshit* (pronounced "ber-ee-sheet"), which is commonly translated as "in the beginning." But *bereshit* can also be translated as "through the firstborn," since the Hebrew letter *bet* is also the preposition "through," and *reshit* (pronounced "re-sheet") can mean "firstborn." So Genesis 1:1 can be translated, "Through the firstborn, God created the heavens and the earth." And who is God's Firstborn? It is Jesus. The New Testament tells us He was the "firstborn over all creation" (Colossians 1:15) and "the firstborn from the dead" (Revelation 1:5).

Jesus is the *Tektōn*, the Architect of all creation. This reading aligns perfectly with the apostle John's understanding of creation. In John 1:3, he states, "Through him all things were made; without him nothing was made that has been made."

But there is more. The word *tektōn* can also be translated as "craftsman." The fact that the New Testament calls Jesus a *tektōn* is amazing, since Israel's Messiah is seen as a "craftsman," based upon the rabbinic understanding of Zechariah 2:1–4, which says:

> Then I lifted up my eyes and behold, I saw four horns! I said to the angel speaking with me, "What are these?"
>
> He said to me, "These are the horns that have scattered Judah, Israel and Jerusalem."
>
> Then ADONAI showed me four craftsmen. I asked, "What are these coming to do?"
>
> He answered, "These are the horns that scattered Judah, so that no one could raise his head, but the craftsmen have come to frighten them, to cast down the horns of the nations that have lifted up their horn against the land of Judah to scatter it." (TLV)

Commenting upon the four craftsmen mentioned in Zechariah 2, the rabbis in Jewish tradition state: "Who are the four craftsmen? Messiah son of David, Messiah son of Joseph, Elijah, and the righteous [High] Priest, [who will serve in the messianic era]."[1]

Jesus is the messianic craftsman whom Zechariah spoke about. The mention of two Messiahs in this passage might seem confusing. But in Jewish thought, "Messiah son of Joseph" is the one who will suffer to redeem God's people, and "Messiah son of David" is the one who will defeat God's enemies to establish the messianic kingdom. So, while many Jews see these two roles being fulfilled by two separate individuals, the New Testament teaches that Jesus at His first coming came as Messiah son of Joseph, who suffered as the "Lamb of God, who takes away the sin of the world" (John 1:29), and at the Second Coming will reveal Himself as Messiah son of David, who will establish God's kingdom as the Lion of Judah. When these two aspects of Messiah—"lamb" and "lion"—have been fully realized in the world, then the promise of Isaiah 65:25 will be fulfilled:

> "The wolf and the lamb will feed together.
> The lion will eat straw like the ox,
> but dust will be the serpent's food.
> They will not hurt or destroy
> in all My holy mountain," says ADONAI. (TLV)

Jesus is the promised master craftsman and architect of creation who brings order out of chaos and *shalom* to our lives in this world and in the world to come! You don't have to wait to begin to experience His peace until His kingdom comes—you can have it right now as He promised: "*Shalom* I leave you, My *shalom* I give to you; but not as the world gives! Do not let your heart be troubled or afraid" (John 14:27 TLV).

What sets humankind apart from all other creatures? Only we are made in the image of God (in Hebrew, *b'tzelem Elohim*). The word for "image" in Hebrew is *tzelem*. It is derived from the Hebrew word *tzel*, which means "shadow."[2] A shadow does not act independently but is a reflected image. Thus, to be made in God's image means to reflect the image of our Creator. How is this to be accomplished? In Jewish thought, it means that we are to imitate God in all His ways, or as Paul wrote in the New Testament, "Be imitators of me, just as I also am of Messiah" (1 Corinthians 11:1 TLV).

Bringing light out of darkness and order out of chaos was one of God's first actions as Creator. We are called to do the same—to bring order and *shalom* to the chaos of the world around us. When we imitate our Creator, we allow God's light to shine in the midst of the darkness, thereby displaying our good works to others so they might glorify our Father in heaven (Matthew 5:16). Living as image-bearers brings order and *shalom* to a broken world, infuses our lives with meaning, and reflects God's image to those around us.

God longs to show the world His goodness through the way we live. But unfortunately, His goodness and peace can't flourish in the midst of chaos. The Lord always brings order before He fully manifests His blessing of peace. For this reason, when we care for His creation by working with Him to bring order out of chaos, we show His goodness to the world. As Jesus taught, "Let your light shine before men so they may see your good works and glorify your Father in heaven" (Matthew 5:16 TLV).

CHAPTER 8

THE JUDEAN DESERT

The Temptation of Christ

*Jesus, full of the Holy Spirit, left the Jordan and
was led by the Spirit into the wilderness, where
for forty days he was tempted by the devil.*

—LUKE 4:1—2

S cripture tells us that after His baptism by John the Baptist, Jesus
left the Jordan River and went straight into the Judean desert,
where He was tempted by Satan for forty days.

Jesus, full of the Holy Spirit, left the Jordan and was led by the
Spirit into the wilderness, where for forty days he was tempted
by the devil. He ate nothing during those days, and at the end
of them he was hungry.

The devil said to him, "If you are the Son of God, tell this stone to become bread."

Jesus answered, "It is written: 'Man shall not live on bread alone.'"

The devil led him up to a high place and showed him in an instant all the kingdoms of the world. And he said to him, "I will give you all their authority and splendor; it has been given to me, and I can give it to anyone I want to. If you worship me, it will all be yours."

Jesus answered, "It is written: 'Worship the Lord your God and serve him only.'"

The devil led him to Jerusalem and had him stand on the highest point of the temple. "If you are the Son of God," he said, "throw yourself down from here. For it is written: 'He will command his angels concerning you to guard you carefully; they will lift you up in their hands, so that you will not strike your foot against a stone.'"

Jesus answered, "It is said: 'Do not put the Lord your God to the test.'"

When the devil had finished all this tempting, he left him until an opportune time. (Luke 4:1–13)

Even though I have been to the desert region before and I know what to expect, I am always stunned by the bleakness and harshness of this part of Israel. I can't imagine lasting one day in the unrelenting and suffocating heat and brutal terrain. It is the most unwelcoming landscape one can experience, yet this is where Jesus was determined to go to strengthen Himself before beginning His earthly ministry.

The desert is a metaphor for our darkest experiences in life. The desert either destroys you or prepares you to emerge stronger and more powerful than ever before. I think too often we try to escape the hard tests in our lives as quickly as possible because, let's be honest, no one loves to suffer.

But if we can at least be aware that there is a deep and abiding purpose for our trials, it can give us hope that our suffering is never in vain. James 1:2–4 says: "Consider it pure joy, my brothers and sisters, whenever you face trials of many kinds, because you know that the testing of your faith produces perseverance. Let perseverance finish its work so that you may be mature and complete, not lacking anything."

God can and does use *everything* for His great purpose. As Romans 8:28 tells us, "We know that in all things God works for the good of those who love him, who have been called according to his purpose."

In the Judean desert, Satan offered up his kingdoms and his riches and his power to Jesus—if He would only bow down to him. Jesus responded to each of Satan's temptations in the same way: by quoting Scripture. Over and over, Jesus responded to Satan's temptations by declaring, "It is written . . ."—and this is the way we, Jesus' followers, should respond as well.

Because of Jesus, we can respond to the temptations of Satan by saying:

- "Get behind me, Satan!" (Matthew 16:23).
- "I am more than a conqueror because of Jesus Christ who loves me" (paraphrase of Romans 8:37).
- "I am a child of God, I am the offspring of the King, and therefore I am an heir to His kingdom! And just like Jesus, I still have work to do."

Come . . . to the Judean desert!

CHAPTER 9

THE SEVEN STREAMS

Jesus Calls His Disciples

As Jesus walked beside the Sea of Galilee, he saw
Simon and his brother Andrew casting a net into the
lake, for they were fishermen. "Come, follow me," Jesus
said, "and I will send you out to fish for people."

—MARK 1:16—17

Much has been made of the story of Jesus calling His first
disciples to follow Him. It's an extraordinary picture of a
young, inexperienced rabbi, fresh from His testing in the Judean
wilderness and eager to start sharing His *good news* (the Greek word
translated as "gospel") with a hurting world.

The whole area of the Sea of Galilee is breathtakingly beautiful. When you visit today, you feel as though the entire landscape is

strangely unchanged. The town of Tiberius on the west coast of the sea is the only developed spot, with charming hotels, restaurants, and a boardwalk allowing tourists to buy a ticket for a boat ride out onto the famous lake where Jesus calmed the storm and walked on the water.

There are no high-rise office buildings or residential developments in this area, and you find yourself grateful that it is still unspoiled. It makes it so much easier to imagine this place two thousand years ago, where Scripture tells us many of the stories involving Jesus took place.

Near the newly discovered ancient synagogue in Magdala, sitting directly on the Sea of Galilee, is a small, beautiful Catholic chapel called the Church of Peter's Primacy. I love it because it is simple and not ornate in decoration. The chapel, built in 1933, includes the ruins of a fourth-century church that commemorates the traditional spot where it is believed that Jesus called His disciples.

Scripture records the event like this:

One day as Jesus was standing by the Lake of Gennesaret [Sea of Galilee], the people were crowding around him and listening to the word of God. He saw at the water's edge two boats, left there by the fishermen, who were washing their nets. He got into one of the boats, the one belonging to Simon, and asked him to put out a little from shore. Then he sat down and taught the people from the boat.

When he had finished speaking, he said to Simon, "Put out into deep water, and let down the nets for a catch."

Simon answered, "Master, we've worked hard all night and haven't caught anything. But because you say so, I will let down the nets."

When they had done so, they caught such a large number of fish that their nets began to break. So they signaled their partners in the other boat to come and help them, and they came and filled both boats so full that they began to sink.

When Simon Peter saw this, he fell at Jesus' knees and said, "Go away from me, Lord; I am a sinful man!" For he and all his companions were astonished at the catch of fish they had taken, and so were James and John, the sons of Zebedee, Simon's partners.

Then Jesus said to Simon, "Don't be afraid; from now on you will fish for people." So they pulled their boats up on shore, left everything and followed him. (Luke 5:1–11)

The reason scholars believe this to be the actual location where this account happened is strictly scientific. It is the only place around the entire lake that seven separate streams of fresh water flow into it. According to Rabbi Jason, the number seven in Hebrew symbolizes completeness and perfection. It is used 735 times in the Bible—54 times in the book of Revelation alone. The number derives much of its meaning from being tied directly to the creation of the world (seven days) and to the seven annual Holy Days in the Hebrew calendar (see "An Overview of God's Appointed Feasts" on page 142). And Jesus performed seven miracles on God's Sabbath (Matthew 12:9–14; Mark 1:21–26, 29–31; Luke 13:10–13; 14:1–4; John 5:1–9; 9:13–16).

It is believed that because of these seven strong streams, fish were attracted to this area of the lake; therefore, the fishermen were too. While it looks like a calm beach you might find anywhere, because it receives seven streams of living water beneath the surface, it was the optimal place for teacher to meet student, for rabbi to meet disciple, and for God Himself to meet mankind.

Come . . . to the Seven Streams!

MORE FROM RABBI JASON

PETER'S CATCH OF 153 FISH AND SECOND CHANCES

In John 21, after the death and resurrection of Jesus, the disciples went fishing in the same area—or as some believe, the very same spot— where Peter and several other disciples were first commissioned by the Lord to become fishers of men (Matthew 4). This means Peter's recommissioning and the disciples' new season of ministry to the Lord commenced in the very same spot where it all began at Tagbah, on the shores of the Sea of Galilee.

After fishing all night, Peter and several of the disciples had caught nothing. How could these experienced fishermen catch absolutely nothing? I believe there is a clue found in the Hebrew word for "fish." In Hebrew, the word for "fish" shares the same root constants (*dalet, aleph, gimmel*) as the Hebrew term that denotes anxiety, worry, and fear. The disciples, especially Peter, were fishing from a place of worry, fear, and anxiety. Not only were they scared the authorities might do to them what they had done to Jesus, but they were probably concerned about their future. Though they had been Jesus' inner circle of disciples, they had fled and hidden in His greatest hour of need; only John had not left Him. Surely they felt they had failed the Lord and had questions about their roles as leaders. When we fish from a place of worry and fear, our nets will remain empty like the disciples' nets. We must follow and serve the Lord not by fear but by faith!

At dawn, Jesus, whose identity remained hidden from the disciples temporarily, asked if they had caught any fish. After the disciples said no, Jesus, still unrecognizable to them, told them, "Throw your net on the right side of the boat and you will find some" (John 21:6). There were so many fish in the net this second time that they were barely able to pull it in.

Describing this great catch, John tells us, "There were 153 fish, many of them big; but the net was not broken" (v. 11 TLV). The large catch of fish was meant to remind the disciples that they had nothing to fear. Jesus had and would always provide for them if they remained faithful in following His instructions.

But of course, there is more! Every detail in the Bible is there for a reason. God does not waste words. Often, deeper truth is found in the details. One of the interesting details in this passage is that the catch of fish totaled 153. What is this detail meant to communicate to us?

First, I think it connects us back to Peter himself—his restoration after having denied the Lord three times the night Jesus was arrested and brought to the high priest Caiaphas's house (Matthew 26:69–74). But it also connects us to Peter's recommissioning, which happens later in this chapter.

In Matthew 16:15, Jesus asked the disciples, "But who do you say I am?" Peter responded by saying, "You are the Messiah, the Son of the living God" (v. 16 TLV). Jesus said to Peter:

> "Blessed are you, Simon son of Jonah, because flesh and blood did not reveal this to you, but My Father who is in heaven! And I also tell you that you are Peter, and upon this rock I will build My community; and the gates of *Sheol* will not overpower it. I will give you the keys of the kingdom of heaven. Whatever you forbid on earth will have been forbidden in heaven and

what you permit on earth will have been permitted in heaven."
(vv. 17–19 TLV)

I believe that Peter's confession can at least loosely be connected to the number 153 on several levels. First, 153 is the numerical value of the phrase, "I am the LORD your God" (Isaiah 43:3), as in "For I am ADONAI [the Lord] your God, the Holy One of Israel, your Savior" (TLV). Thus, the number 153 in John 21 hearkens back to Peter's confession that Jesus is Lord, which was the foundational confession upon which the church was built.

The number 153 is also the value of *HaPesach*, which is the Passover lamb described in Exodus 12:21: "Go, select lambs for your families and slaughter the Passover lamb" (TLV). Thus, the number 153 connects Peter's confession with Jesus' subsequent prediction of His death and resurrection, which links His divine nature and death as the suffering servant Messiah who is "led like a lamb to the slaughter" (Isaiah 53:7).

There is another textual link that connects John 21 and Peter's confession in Matthew 16. There are only two places in the New Testament where Jesus called Peter "Simon son of Jonah": Matthew 16:17 and John 21:15 ("Son of Jonah" is found in some ancient Greek manuscripts, while others say "Son of John"; but I believe Jonah is the better reading based upon the context and connection with Matthew 16). This is no coincidence but is meant to connect these two passages. Peter acted like Jonah by denying the Lord and running away.

Even though Peter had acted like Jonah, the Lord wanted to communicate to Peter that he was forgiven. He wanted to let Peter know that he was still "the rock" whom the Lord would use to be the first to publicly proclaim the good news to Israel, as well as be the first to bring the gospel to the Gentiles, which would occur in Acts 10 when

Peter preached to the Roman centurion Cornelius and his family. On account of the Lord's graciousness, "the keys of the kingdom" would still be entrusted to Peter to open the gates of salvation to the Jews first and to the Gentiles as well (Romans 1:14).

One final meaning of the number 153: as I mentioned above, John 21 happens in the same location or right near the place that Jesus first called Peter and Andrew, his brother, to be His disciples by saying, "Follow Me, and I will make you fishers of men" (Matthew 4:19 TLV). According to Jerome, an early church father, there were 153 species of fish in the Sea of Galilee, which ties back to the disciples being fishers of men.[1] Like Peter and the disciples, every follower of Jesus is called to cast their nets by faith for the purpose of drawing people into the kingdom of God.

CHAPTER 10

CANA

Turning Water into Wine

*What Jesus did here in Cana of Galilee was the
first of the signs through which he revealed his
glory; and his disciples believed in him.*

—JOHN 2:11

Much has been made of the fact that Jesus performed His first miracle at a wedding in the Galilean village of Cana by turning six large stone pots of water into wine. And He didn't turn the water into just average wine—it was the best wine possible!

Wine is mentioned 235 times in the Bible, according to *Young's Analytical Concordance to the Bible*. Some instances are variations of the word, as in *winepress*, but it is impossible to ignore the consistent presence and significance of wine in the biblical world. Interestingly, compared to the hundreds of uses of *wine*, the words *drunk* or *drunk-enness* or *drunken* appear only eighty-one times in the Bible.

In Genesis 14:18, we read that Melchizedek, the priest of the Most High God at Salem (the ancient name for Jerusalem), "brought out bread and wine" for Abram and his companions. Many scholars believe Melchizedek was a preincarnate manifestation of Jesus—meaning that Jesus Himself came to earth earlier than when He was physically born to the Virgin Mary. Others disagree, but what is not disputed is that a blessing of "an abundance of . . . wine" was prophesied as a heritage to the chosen people—the Jews—in Genesis 27:28.

In that passage, Isaac said to Jacob, "May God give you heaven's dew and earth's richness—an abundance of grain and new wine." The Hebrew word translated "wine" in this verse (*tirosh*) does not mean unfermented grape juice, as some have suggested, because *tirosh* is an intoxicant if used in excess. Israel has a very hot, desert-like climate and there was no refrigeration in biblical times, so it was impossible to maintain freshness for any length of time or to keep grape juice from fermenting.

Wine is the most common alcoholic beverage mentioned in the Scriptures. In some places, it is used in sacrificial or medicinal ways, such as when Paul suggested that Timothy "stop drinking only water, and use a little wine because of your stomach and your frequent illnesses" (1 Timothy 5:23).

The Bible says clearly in Psalm 104:14–15 that God gave wine to make men *glad*. Referring to the Lord's provision for His people, the psalmist said, "He makes . . . wine that gladdens human hearts."

Of course, the Bible does mention drunkenness, as in the story of Noah in Genesis 9:20–22 and Lot in Genesis 19:30–38. Jesus, in

Luke 21:34, told His followers not to get drunk. The apostle Paul exhorted in Ephesians 5:18, "Do not get drunk on wine." You cannot get drunk on grape juice, no matter how much you imbibe!

Finally, we must remember how Jesus used the cups of wine at the Last Supper (see "An Overview of God's Appointed Feasts" on page 142), and how we continue to remember His sacrifice on the cross each time we take communion (1 Corinthians 11:24).

When Jesus turned the water into wine in Cana, the six stone pots that contained the wine held twenty to thirty gallons each. This was no small miracle!

In the Bible, God had directed His people to make wine a part of their festivals throughout the year, celebrating God's bounty with gratitude and joy. This wedding in Cana was a celebration—and Jesus enhanced the celebration with His first public miracle.

Come . . . to Cana!

MORE FROM RABBI JASON

JESUS' FIRST MIRACLE AND THE SIX STONE POTS

As Kathie indicated, Jesus' first miracle involved six stone pots of water that He turned into wine. Every word in the Bible is there for a reason, so what is significant about the number six?

The first thing we need to understand is that in numerology, six is the number of creation. The Bible tells us the Lord created the world in six days. Genesis 1:1, the first verse of the Bible, contains six words in Hebrew. The sixth day of creation is the day God made the first man and woman, the crowning culmination of all creation. And not only was man created on the sixth day, but in Jewish thought, Adam and Eve sinned on the sixth day, which is Friday on the biblical calendar.

But there is something even deeper about the number six that we need to understand. As I mentioned previously, the Hebrew language is alphanumeric, which means numbers are represented by letters. The number six in Hebrew is represented by the sixth letter in the Hebrew alphabet, *vav*. This is so important because *vav* is the letter used in Genesis as the conjunction that connects heaven and earth: "God created the heavens and [*vav*] earth."

In other words, the fall broke the *vav*, the connection between heaven and earth. So God in His goodness sent Jesus as the second Adam to reverse the curse in order to restore the connection between heaven and earth. Jesus died on the sixth day, a Friday, to make atonement for the sin of the first man and woman so the blessings we lost in Eden could be restored! Isn't it mind-blowing the way the Lord connects all of this?

Now it should make sense why the first miracle of turning the water into wine involved six stone pots that were filled to the brim. Jesus came to restore the Lord's original blessing for creation.

Jesus' first miracle is symbolic of what the Lord wants to do in you. Like the water into wine, God wants to transform you from ordinary to extraordinary. In Messiah you are a new creation: "the old has gone, the new is here!" (2 Corinthians 5:17). Ask God today to transform any emptiness in your life into fullness.

Jesus performed His miracle at a wedding in Cana of Galilee. But of all the miracles Jesus could have performed, why was His first recorded miracle turning water into wine? To answer this question, we must understand the apostle John's purpose for writing his gospel, which was to demonstrate that "Jesus is the Messiah, the Son of God" (John 20:31). The Messiah, according to the Torah and Jewish tradition, was going to be greater than Moses, as the Lord states in Deuteronomy 18:18: "I will raise up for them a prophet like you [Moses] from among their fellow Israelites, and I will put my words in his mouth. He will tell them everything I command him."

What was the first miracle Moses performed to demonstrate to Israel and Pharaoh that he was the redeemer sent by God to deliver them? He turned water into blood. But Jesus, the greater Moses, turned water into wine because He did not come to bring death, but so that we might have life and have it more abundantly (John 10:10).

Wine is one of the primary signs of the abundant blessings of the coming messianic kingdom. The messianic prophecy in Amos 9:13 states, "The mountains will drip sweet wine and all the hills will melt over" (TLV); the one in Isaiah 25:6 says, "On this mountain, ADONAI-Tzva'ot will prepare a lavish banquet for all peoples—a banquet of aged wine—of rich food, of choice marrow, of aged wine well refined" (TLV). By turning the water into wine, Jesus demonstrated that He was the promised prophet, the greater Moses, who came that we might begin to experience the abundant life of the messianic kingdom here and now through faith in Messiah Jesus.

It is also significant that Jesus performed the miracle of turning water into wine "on the third day" of the week (John 2:1). If there is a number or detail in the Scripture, it is there for a reason. The third day is one on which many traditional Jews get married, because it is the only day God blessed twice (Genesis 1:10, 12).

The third day is also connected to revelation. It was on the third day that the Lord descended on Mount Sinai and Moses led the people out of the camp to encounter the Lord (Exodus 19:16–17). Just as Moses and the Israelites experienced the revelation of God's glory on the third day, so Jesus revealed His glory on the third day.

The third day prophetically is one of redemption, restoration, and resurrection. Abraham offered his son Isaac on the third day (Genesis 22:4). And concerning the third day, the prophet Hosea declared: "Come, let us return to the LORD. He has torn us to pieces but he will heal us; he has injured us but he will bind up our wounds" (Hosea 6:1). Moses' first miracle on the third day was meant to point to Messiah's death and resurrection from the dead, which is the primary way Messiah makes known His glory to Israel and to the nations. By faith in Messiah, you can experience a third-day miracle by which you become a new creation, transformed from water into wine by the Lord's touch!

CHAPTER 11

CAPERNAUM

Headquarters of Jesus' Ministry

Leaving Nazareth, [Jesus] went and lived in Capernaum,
which was by the lake in the area of Zebulun and Naphtali.

—MATTHEW 4:13

Although Jesus grew up in the town of Nazareth, Scripture tells us He moved to Capernaum to establish a sort of headquarters for His earthly ministry (Matthew 4:13). This was strategic. Capernaum sits on the northwest coast of the Sea of Galilee. It was an important commercial stop along an ancient trade route.

This location of Capernaum was the first time our tour guide, "Michigan Ray," explained to us the use of parables in first-century Jewish life. Apparently Jewish men were not allowed to become rabbis, or teachers, until they were thirty years old. At that time, they would gather disciples and travel through the countryside speaking to the local people along the way and in the various synagogues on the Sabbath.

For centuries experts have debated the New Testament's claim in Matthew 4:23 that Jesus spoke in synagogues throughout Galilee, because they claimed there were no synagogues in Galilee at that time. They argued that the people simply went to Jerusalem and the temple for all the festivals and sacrificial offerings demanded by the law of Moses (see "An Overview of God's Appointed Feasts" on page 142).

But archaeologists have discovered the remains of ancient synagogues in Migdal, Capernaum, Herodium, Qumran, Masada, and most recently Magdala, where a synagogue was found eighteen inches below the ground. And in August 2016, *Kehila News Israel* announced the recent discovery of another synagogue at Tel Rechesh in lower Galilee, just four inches underground.[1]

I believe it is only a matter of time before even more sites are discovered, because historically the synagogue was central to the Jewish people and the Jewish faith. In fact, synagogues are still central to the Jewish faith—just as churches, temples, and mosques are equally important in modern society to the faiths they represent. They are the places where people of similar beliefs assemble to worship, celebrate, and pass on their traditions and faith to future generations.

The role of the rabbi in the Jewish faith is central to understanding the Jewish people. Rabbis were trained to be "good shepherds" to the common people who, like sheep, were simple-minded and in desperate need of leadership. The word *rabbi* means "teacher," and because most people in first-century Israel were uneducated in a formal sense, it was left to the rabbis to explain the fundamentals of the faith to the needy, seeking, often confused individuals who followed them on their travels through the countryside.

The rabbi would often begin by simply commanding, "Come!" and the people would follow and begin their journey with him. It was understood that the people were never to ask, "Where are we going?" or "What are you going to teach us when we get there?" If that sounds condescending, I assure you it was not. I am certain it was thrilling, not unlike taking a ride in an amusement park that promises thrills and chills, but you never know when they will come!

During our tour of Israel, Ray would begin each day with us all circled around him. Then we would recite the ancient Hebrew *Shema*, recorded in Deuteronomy 6:4: "Hear, O Israel, the LORD our God, the LORD is one." Jewish people have been reciting this verse every morning and evening since before the birth of Jesus. The Shema is the foundational Jewish prayer and their central declaration of faith. The purpose of reciting the Shema (which means "to hear") is to declare love and allegiance to the Lord, the God of Abraham, Isaac, and Jacob. It is also meant to testify to the world that God is One, that there are no other gods, and therefore we must serve and worship Him alone, even if this means laying down our lives. You can't imagine the beauty and power these words convey when you hear them in the land where they were first spoken.

After we recited the Shema, Ray—in an action meant to mimic these first-century rabbis—would thunder the command, "Come!" He would go up the mountain, and we would follow this mountain goat of a man at breakneck speed.

Rabbis in the first century were aware that the people who listened to them were uneducated, peasant folk for the most part. So the rabbi typically spoke of things the average person could under-stand through their senses—what they could see or smell or hear or touch or taste. Teaching in parables was an art form of communi-cation at the most primal level, and nobody did it better than Jesus.

Out in a field, you could picture Jesus pointing and saying, "Consider the lilies of the field, how they grow" (Matthew 6:28 NKJV). There are flowers everywhere in Israel. But instead of lilies as we envision them, they are more like huge red poppies dominating the landscape. They are just gorgeous!

At the time of Jesus, Capernaum was the "Millstone Capital of the World." Even when you visit today, you will notice many centuries-old millstones casually strewn about.

It's important to understand how crucial millstones were to the economy and to the everyday life of Middle Easterners. Simply put, a millstone is a pair of large, round stones used together in grist-mills for grinding wheat or other grains. Think of it as an ancient Cuisinart! The people's food supply depended largely on them.

Jesus said, "If anyone causes one of these little ones—those who believe in me—to stumble, it would be better for them to have a large millstone hung around their neck and to be drowned in the depths of the sea" (Matthew 18:6).

I have no doubt that Jesus spoke these very words right there in the heart of Capernaum, where the Sea of Galilee sits only yards away. The people could not have missed His meaning. I'm sure they loved the beauty and simplicity of Jesus' teachings just as we do today, and they appreciated that He never spoke down to them or belittled them as the Pharisees and Sadducees routinely did.

Jesus knew the longing in the people's hearts to understand the truths He was teaching them. And He loved the purity of their desire to know their Father more intimately. They needed hope, and Jesus delivered hope to them on a daily basis for the next three years.

Right next to the synagogue in Capernaum is an excavated site most archaeologists agree is the home of Peter's mother-in-law, not one hundred yards away from the synagogue. Scripture records that Jesus visited this home during His stay in Capernaum:

- "When Jesus came into Peter's house, he saw Peter's mother-in-law lying in bed with a fever" (Matthew 8:14).
- "As soon as they left the synagogue, they went with James and John to the home of Simon [Peter] and Andrew. Simon's mother-in-law was in bed with a fever, and they immediately told Jesus about her. So he went to her, took her hand and helped her up. The fever left her and she began to wait on them" (Mark 1:29–31).
- "Jesus left the synagogue and went to the home of Simon [Peter]. Now Simon's mother-in-law was suffering from a high fever, and they asked Jesus to help her. So he bent over her and rebuked the fever, and it left her. She got up at once and began to wait on them" (Luke 4:38–39).

I think it's fascinating that at this point in Scripture, only angels and women have served Jesus—the angels after His temptations in the wilderness (Matthew 4:11) and Peter's mother-in-law after He healed her. Later, we will hear of Mary (the sister of Lazarus and Martha) anointing Jesus with expensive perfume: "Mary took about a pint of pure nard, an expensive perfume; she poured it on Jesus' feet and wiped his feet with her hair. And the house was filled with the fragrance of the perfume" (John 12:3).

This was a demonstration of profound worship, and "life" always takes place just steps from where "worship" has been offered. Scripture says that God inhabits the praises of His people (Psalm 22:3). When we pray and we praise, we release the power of heaven to respond to our faith. Abraham was called a friend of God because of his faith, not because of his wealth or intelligence or strength or his standing in society. James 2:23 says, "The scripture was fulfilled that says, 'Abraham believed God, and it was credited to him as righteousness,' and he was called God's friend."

Millennia later, we continue to be called "God's friends" when we believe His promises to be true.

Come . . . to Capernaum!

MORE FROM RABBI JASON

JESUS, FORGIVENESS, AND 70 X 70

As Kathie explained above, Capernaum was the center of Jesus' ministry after He was run out of Nazareth (Luke 4:14–33). Capernaum is also the location where Jesus taught His disciples the true meaning of forgiveness. Peter asked Jesus: "'Lord, how often shall my brother sin against me, and I forgive him? Up to seven times?' Jesus said to him, 'I do not say to you, up to seven times, but up to seventy times seven'" (Matthew 18:21–22, NKJV).

Peter thought he was being very spiritual by being willing to forgive someone up to seven times. So Jesus' response—commanding him to forgive someone up to 490 times—must have been quite a shock! Everything Jesus did and said was very purposeful. He never wasted a word. So the number of times He instructs us to forgive must have some deeper significance. But what is it?

As we have already discussed, every word in Hebrew has a numerical value, and these values frequently communicate deeper spiritual insights. That is certainly the case here.

The number 490 is the numerical value of the biblical Hebrew word *tamim*, which means "complete," "perfect," or "finished." A person who can't forgive will always live an imperfect and incomplete life that lacks a true understanding of the "finished," gracious work of the cross. The number 490 is also the value of the Hebrew phrase "Let your heart be perfect" (1 Kings 8:61, my translation). Forgiving helps make us complete, and it is key to perfecting our hearts before the Lord.

But there are some even deeper connections. In Hebrew, the word for "my nativity" (*moladati*) and Bethlehem (*Beit Lechem*)—the city where Messiah was born, which means "House of Bread"—each individually adds up to 490. This makes perfect sense, since Jesus was born so that we might be forgiven. And forgiveness is associated with bread in the Lord's Prayer, which says: "Give us this day our daily bread. And forgive us our debts as we also have forgiven our debtors" (Matthew 6:11–12 TLV). Just like a person can't live without their daily bread, an individual can't survive without forgiveness.

The psalmist wrote, "If you, LORD, kept a record of sins, Lord, who could stand?" (Psalm 130:3). We need to learn to forgive and to be forgiven. How do we celebrate the forgiveness Messiah has brought us? By partaking of the broken bread of the Lord's Supper, concerning which Jesus said, "This is my body given for you; do this in remembrance of me" (Luke 22:19). Jesus, who is the Bread of Life, was born in Bethlehem, the House of Bread, so that we might both experience forgiveness and extend the bread of forgiveness to others. When we fail to forgive, it's like we are spiritually withholding food from a starving person!

Forgiveness is not an elective; it is a requirement for followers of

Jesus. We must forgive because we have been forgiven by the Lord. Extending forgiveness should not even be dependent on receiving an apology, as Paul wrote: "Bear with each other and forgive one another if any of you has a grievance against someone. Forgive as the Lord forgave you" (Colossians 3:13). For this reason, forgiveness is one of the greatest acts of faith and a true sign of faithfulness to the Lord. We must forgive because we have been forgiven. The practical benefit of forgiveness is that it frees us as well as the other person. Unforgiveness keeps you imprisoned and chained to your past, but forgiving is a key that sets you free.

Don't delay! Ask yourself as well as the Lord, "Whom do I need to forgive today?" Do you need to forgive yourself, a friend, or a family member? May the Lord give you the faith and grace right now to forgive in Jesus' name.

CHAPTER 12

THE SEA OF GALILEE

The Other Side

That day when evening came, he said to his
disciples, "Let us go over to the other side."

—MARK 4:35

One of the things that struck me the first time I visited the Sea of Galilee was how few boats were out on the water and how few buildings were along the magnificent coastline.

I asked Ray about this, and he laughed. "Well, historically, Jews hate the water."

"What?" I exclaimed. "But it's gorgeous! And it's prime real estate."

"Not to Jews. Think about it. All kinds of bad things happened on water: Jonah was in the belly of a fish for three days. Noah and the flood. Storms always came upon the Sea of Galilee. Jews are afraid of what the water represents—the chaos! The list is endless."

That is likely the reason that even the fishermen I observed around the Sea of Galilee stayed so close to shore when they fished.

I asked a friend who is involved in Israeli politics about the lack of development, and he explained that all the land surrounding the Sea of Galilee is owned by the government, so it's not available for purchase. But even if it were, it would probably be bought by non-Jews, who don't have negative views of the water.

Personally, I'm grateful that this pristine, magnificent landscape will likely never be developed. I imagine that today the Sea of Galilee looks very similar to what it must have been when Jesus walked along the shores.

Imagine how the disciples must have felt when Jesus told them to "go over to the other side of the lake" (Luke 8:22). Most of the disciples had spent their entire lives in the Galilee region. They had fished in the Sea of Galilee, even making their living as fishermen. They knew better than anyone the perils of this body of water. They knew that severe squalls could develop within minutes, with swells of waves up to twenty feet high. In other words, they knew a person could die out on that lake and never be found in the depths of the water (which is eighty-five feet at its deepest).

They also knew that on "the other side" were the pagan cities of the Decapolis—thriving, modern, vulgar, and forbidden by their Jewish law.

Yet here was Jesus, a righteous Jew, telling them to get in the boat and purposefully set out for the very place they had spent their entire lives avoiding. The disciples must have freaked out when

Jesus suggested this. This was unheard of! This was strictly forbidden! This was dangerous! And this was crazy!

They got in the boat anyway, and then look what happened:

> So they got into a boat and set out. As they sailed, he fell asleep. A squall came down on the lake, so that the boat was being swamped, and they were in great danger.
>
> The disciples went and woke him, saying, "Master, Master, we're going to drown!"
>
> He got up and rebuked the wind and the raging waters; the storm subsided, and all was calm. "Where is your faith?" he asked his disciples.
>
> In fear and amazement they asked one another, "Who is this? He commands even the winds and the water, and they obey him." (Luke 8:22–25)

Immediately they encountered a storm. I'm sure the disciples all thought, *See? I told you so.*

Jesus calmed the storm, but the worst was yet to come!

When they arrived at the shore, immediately a demon-possessed, naked, violent, bloody-from-cutting-himself man came screaming at them from the tombs! This man was the picture of death, except he wasn't dead. It had to be terrifying to the disciples.

But not to Jesus. Jesus was the only one who got out of the boat.

What I love about this story is the reason that Jesus got in the boat in the first place—to go over to the other side and save this one, pathetic, seemingly hopeless man!

Jesus came to bring His *shalom* to the chaos, to dress this man in a robe of righteousness, and ultimately to set him free! Free to go home to his family and his neighbors as a living testimony to God's mercy and forgiveness and redemption.

What boat does Jesus want us to get into?

Where does He want us to sail?

Whom does He want us to greet in love and mercy when they run screaming at us in their chaos?

Ray concluded his teaching of this story by reminding us that at the end of the gospel of Mark, we see Jesus exchanging places with this man on the cross. Now Jesus was the one who was naked, crying out, bloodied, and driven into the tomb. This is how we are made whole—Jesus exchanges His life for ours, His cleanness for our uncleanness.

He defeats evil by absorbing evil into Himself.

He brings His *shalom* to the chaos by taking on all the world's chaos so He can offer us true peace.

Come . . . to the Sea of Galilee!

CHAPTER 13

MAGDALA

Mary Magdalene and the Women Jesus Loved

*When Jesus rose early on the first day of the week, he appeared first
to Mary Magdalene, out of whom he had driven seven demons.*

—MARK 16:9

Mary Magdalene holds a very special place among the followers of Jesus. She was not like any typical disciple—in fact,
she lacked any relevance at all to the people of her day. She was
not a man, not a fisherman, not a tax collector. She was obviously
a woman—but no ordinary woman. Mary of Magdala, a village
recently discovered along the southern shores of the Sea of Galilee,
is mentioned twelve times in the Gospels, more than most of the
apostles.

Both the gospel of Mark and the gospel of Luke record that Jesus had cast seven demons out of Mary Magdalene at some point in His earthly ministry (Mark 16:9; Luke 8:2). The Bible tells us she was present at Jesus' crucifixion and was the first on the scene at His grave after the resurrection:

> Early on the first day of the week, while it was still dark, Mary Magdalene went to the tomb and saw that the stone had been removed from the entrance. So she came running to Simon Peter and the other disciple, the one Jesus loved, and said, "They have taken the Lord out of the tomb, and we don't know where they have put him!" (John 20:1–2)

I believe Jesus was the first and greatest feminist in history because of the value He placed on the women He met during His lifetime. Jesus overruled centuries of customs and traditions in the ancient world that often resulted in women being treated as second-class citizens. Just as importantly, Jesus actively elevated women above their normal status and role in both the secular culture of His day and in first-century Judaism.

For example, Jesus talked to the Samaritan woman, who was considered to be doubly unclean because she was not only female but also a foreigner. Yet look at Jesus' interaction with her: "When a Samaritan woman came to draw water, Jesus said to her, 'Will you give me a drink?'" (John 4:7).

I love the way Jesus saw into her heart. Instead of drawing water with the other women during the coolest hours of the morning or late afternoon, she was alone at the well at noon—a sure sign she was avoiding the other townspeople due to her terrible reputation.

Jesus told this Samaritan woman the truth about herself, but not in a condemning way. Instead, He treated her with respect and valued her in a way no man ever had, certainly none of her five previous husbands. Scripture says that after her encounter with Jesus, the Samaritan woman went back to her village and told the people all about Jesus—and they, in turn, went out to meet Him. Jesus made this downtrodden, much used, and tainted woman a star in her own community! Jesus never left anyone the same after an encounter with Him.

Jesus also called a woman who had been crippled a "daughter of Abraham," implying equal status with a man, or "son of Abraham." In Luke 13:16, He said, "Should not this woman, a daughter of Abraham, whom Satan has kept bound for eighteen long years, be set free on the Sabbath day from what bound her?" Calling a woman "a daughter of Abraham" was unparalleled in Scripture, and in fact, it occurs nowhere else in the Bible!

There is perhaps no greater evidence of the value Jesus placed on women than the fact that He welcomed them into His inner circle of devoted followers, with perhaps as many as half of His followers being female (including Mary Magdalene, Joanna, Susanna, and Mary and Martha, among others). Throughout the Bible, women had an important role in the leadership of God's people and their redemption.

In John 19:25–27, we see that Jesus loved and honored His mother, Mary, so much that even in His last hours, before His death on the cross, He was concerned for her welfare:

Near the cross of Jesus stood his mother, his mother's sister, Mary the wife of Clopas, and Mary Magdalene. When Jesus saw his mother there, and the disciple whom he loved standing nearby, he said to her, "Woman, here is your son," and to the disciple,

"Here is your mother." From that time on, this disciple took her into his home.

As the firstborn son in a Jewish family, Jesus was held responsible for every member. But we read in John 7:5 that before His resurrection, "Even his own brothers did not believe in him," which meant that He couldn't leave His beloved mother in their care. So He chose to entrust the care of His mother instead to the apostle John.

After His resurrection, Jesus showed compassion to Mary Magdalene. In Mark 16:9, we read, "When Jesus rose early on the first day of the week, he appeared first to Mary Magdalene, out of whom he had driven seven demons." I love that in her grief and fear, Mary Magdalene didn't recognize Jesus until He tenderly said her name: "Jesus said to her, 'Mary.' She turned to him and cried out in Aramaic, 'Rabboni!' (which means 'Teacher')" (John 20:16). This reduces me to tears every time I think of it because I, too, experience grief, confusion, and fear. And the thought that Jesus might lovingly whisper my name—seeing me, knowing me, loving me—is as profound an experience as I can imagine. How tender! How revolutionary! Jesus is the radical lover of women!

It is difficult for us in our modern, Western culture to fathom a world where women were worth less than a camel, required to remove themselves from society during each menstrual cycle, forbidden to talk to any men outside of their family, or even to count change from their hands into the hands of a male. During that time, a husband could divorce his wife, but a wife had no legal option to leave her husband, no matter how abusive he might be. There are many more examples of the lower status women received in ancient Israel—and pretty much everywhere else in the civilized world.

But, for me, there is one story in Scripture that showcases Jesus' love and respect for women: the woman caught in adultery.

Come . . . to Magdala!

MORE FROM RABBI JASON

THE WOMAN CAUGHT IN ADULTERY AND WHY JESUS WROTE IN THE SAND

Yeshua went to the Mount of Olives. At dawn, He came again into the Temple. All the people were coming to Him, and He sat down and began to teach them.

The *Torah* scholars and Pharisees bring in a woman who had been caught in adultery. After putting her in the middle, they say to *Yeshua*, "Teacher, this woman has been caught in the act of committing adultery. In the *Torah*, Moses commanded us to stone such women. So what do You say?" Now they were saying this to trap Him, so that they would have grounds to accuse Him.

But *Yeshua* knelt down and started writing in the dirt with His finger. When they kept asking Him, He stood up and said, "The sinless one among you, let him be the first to throw a stone at her." Then He knelt down again and continued writing on the ground.

Now when they heard, they began to leave, one by one, the oldest ones first, until *Yeshua* was left alone with the woman in the middle. Straightening up, *Yeshua* said to her, "Woman, where are they? Did no one condemn you?"

"No one, Sir," she said.

"Then neither do I condemn you," *Yeshua* said. "Go, and sin no more." (John 8:1–11 TLV)

Some Torah scholars and Pharisees brought a woman who was caught in adultery to Jesus. They wanted to know Jesus' opinion as to the punishment this woman should face. They thought this question would trap Jesus, for if He said that they should stone her, then He would be viewed as cruel. But if He said that the adulterous woman should be forgiven and the law not followed, then He could be accused of violating the Torah and being too liberal. Jesus, who operated in the Spirit of wisdom, responded in a way that prevented them from entrapping Him but also demonstrated the heart of the Father. He turned the tables on these leaders when, after writing in the dirt, He said, "The sinless one among you, let him be the first to throw a stone at her" (John 8:7 TLV). That statement had a powerful effect on those who heard it. The accusers of the woman caught in adultery left one by one.

It seems from the text that Jesus' act of kneeling down and writing in the dirt also played a key part in causing the Torah scholars and Pharisees to leave without saying a word.

Why did Jesus do this, and what could He have written that would have had such a profound effect? There is no way to be certain, but there seem to be a few clues in the text. There are four key components to what Jesus did:

- Jesus used His finger to write.
- Jesus wrote with His finger twice.
- Jesus wrote specifically in the dirt, and
- Jesus knelt to write.

First, let's explore the first and second clues, Jesus' use of His finger and writing in the dirt twice.

After bringing the Israelites out of Egypt, the Lord brought them to Mount Sinai and gave them the Ten Commandments on two stone tablets that were "written by the finger of God" (Exodus 31:18 TLV). But as Moses was coming down Mount Sinai to give the people the two tablets, he saw them worshiping a golden calf. What did Moses do? He smashed the tablets that were "written by the finger of God" because he saw the people committing idolatry, which is a spiritual form of adultery in the Lord's eyes: "backsliding Israel committed adultery" (Jeremiah 3:8 TLV). It was fitting that Moses smashed the two tablets of testimony, because they symbolized in rabbinic thought the traditional Jewish wedding contract known as a *ketubah*, given to every bride on her wedding day.

God in His grace did not divorce Israel because of her spiritual adultery, but forgave her after Moses pled for forgiveness. After going up Sinai again, Moses came down with another set of tablets. This second set of tablets was a key sign that the Lord had forgiven Israel and was giving her a second chance. Moses descended with the second pair of tablets on the Day of Atonement, the holiest day of the year. On this day, Israel's high priest was commanded to enter into the Holy of Holies to sprinkle the blood of the special animal sacrifices on the mercy seat of the ark, in hopes that the Lord would accept his offering and forgive their sins (see "An Overview of God's Appointed Feasts" on page 142), which points to the Lord's grace and forgiveness.

When Jesus wrote in the dirt, it was just a few days after the Day of Atonement. Jesus' action of writing in the dirt reminded these leaders that they, too, were guilty of breaking the Ten Commandments and needed atonement, which they had just fasted and prayed for less than a week prior. And it was during this season of the Day of Atonement that the Lord had forgiven Israel, who had acted as an unfaithful wife by committing spiritual adultery through idolatrous actions.

If the Lord had forgiven Israel during this same season for a similar sin, then what right did the religious leaders have to condemn this woman? In summary, Jesus' writing in the dirt reminded the Pharisees and Sadducees of the Ten Commandments given by the finger of God, and His writing in the dirt twice reminded them that God had given Israel a second chance by giving them a second set of tablets. In light of this, who among them was worthy to cast the first stone?

The third aspect of this story that needs to be examined is why Jesus wrote in the dirt. I believe it was to remind these leaders where they came from. Man was created from the dirt (Genesis 2:7), and as such we are all weak and vulnerable to temptation. Jewish tradition says there was once a rabbi named Simcha Bunem who carried two slips of paper, one in each pocket. On one piece it was written, "For my sake the world was created" and on the other piece, "I am but dust and ashes." Every person has such worth that the world was created for them, but on the other hand, we need to be humble, for we come from the dirt and are all sinners who fall short of God's glory (Romans 3:23).

And finally, I love the fact that Jesus knelt to write. Think about it for a moment. Several influential men were standing around this woman, pointing accusatory fingers at her as she probably knelt down in fear and shame. What did Jesus do? He knelt as well, in part to get down on her level. He did not stand over her but got down in the dirt with her. This is such a beautiful picture of the love of Jesus! He meets us where we are and never looks down on us.

Jesus was clear that this woman should sin in this way no more. Yet even though she was guilty, Jesus didn't condemn her, but showed her grace and told her she was forgiven and free to go.

CHAPTER 14

GALILEE

The Woman Who Was Healed by a Touch

*[Jesus] said to her, "Daughter, your faith has healed
you. Go in peace and be freed from your suffering."*

—MARK 5:34

It's difficult in our modern culture to imagine what life was like in Israel during the time of Jesus. The Jews experienced terrible suffering under Roman rule—physically, emotionally, and spiritually.

The Romans were brutal, violent oppressors who took every opportunity to whip their subjects into submission. They despised the Jewish faith and saw it as inferior to their polytheistic worldview. The Jews, in return, despised the Romans because of their oppressive taxes and their "unclean" culture and pagan religion. And more than anything, the Jews resented the Romans' absolute power over their daily life and worship.

Daily living for every Jew was an act of faith. They spent each waking moment trying to keep not only the Torah—the Mosaic law—but also the extra six-hundred-plus man-made laws imposed on them by the Pharisees and the Sadducees. We can't imagine the weight of such a legalistic burden on everyday life. No one could be pure enough, or holy enough, or without blemish before God under such self-righteous leaders.

The Pharisees and the Sadducees, however, took great pains to parade their intellectual and spiritual superiority before the people. Jesus saved His sternest words for these individuals. In Matthew 23:27, Jesus said: "Woe to you, teachers of the law and Pharisees, you hypocrites! You are like whitewashed tombs, which look beautiful on the outside but on the inside are full of the bones of the dead and everything unclean."

Jesus came to ease the burdens on the Jewish people. In Matthew 11:28–30, He said: "Come to me, all you who are weary and burdened, and I will give you rest. Take my yoke upon you and learn from me, for I am gentle and humble in heart, and you will find rest for your souls. For my yoke is easy and my burden is light."

No wonder the people's hearts soared when they heard Him teach! No one in their world ever spoke such words of life or hope or compassion to them. Such love! Jesus' words still have the same effect today on those whose hearts are open to His tender message of grace.

Perhaps no one in the ancient world longed for Jesus' message of grace more than the women in first-century Israel. As we mentioned in the previous chapter, it is important to understand the status of women in ancient times. Their freedoms were severely limited by the Jewish law and traditions. They were basically confined to their father's or their husband's home and had no authority of their own.

During this time women were considered inferior to men and weren't even allowed to testify in court trials, as they were not deemed to be credible witnesses. They were considered second-class citizens, excluded from worship among the men, with little more status than slaves.

But Jesus consistently demonstrated that He had a high respect and value for women.

One of my favorite stories of Jesus' love for women is in Mark 5, when He healed a woman whose menstrual cycle had caused her to suffer for twelve years. She touched the hem of His garment (a major violation of the law as a woman), and He broke the law as well by talking to her in public:

> And a woman was there who had been subject to bleeding for twelve years. She had suffered a great deal under the care of many doctors and had spent all she had, yet instead of getting better she grew worse. When she heard about Jesus, she came up behind him in the crowd and touched his cloak, because she thought, "If I just touch his clothes, I will be healed." Immediately her bleeding stopped and she felt in her body that she was freed from her suffering.
>
> At once Jesus realized that power had gone out from him. He turned around in the crowd and asked, "Who touched my clothes?"
>
> "You see the people crowding against you," his disciples answered, "and yet you can ask, 'Who touched me?'"

But Jesus kept looking around to see who had done it. Then the woman, knowing what had happened to her, came and fell at his feet and, trembling with fear, told him the whole truth. He said to her, "Daughter, your faith has healed you. Go in peace and be freed from your suffering" (Mark 5:25–34).

Rabbi Jason has some beautiful insights about this story of Jesus' love for the woman with the issue of blood.

Come . . . to Galilee!

MORE FROM RABBI JASON

JESUS AND THE WOMAN WITH THE ISSUE OF BLOOD

Yeshua got up and began to follow him, with His disciples.

Just then a woman, losing blood for twelve years, came from behind and touched the *tzitzit* of His garment. For she kept saying to herself, "If only I touch His garment, I will be healed."

But then *Yeshua* turned and saw her. "Take heart, daughter," He said, "your faith has made you well." That very hour the woman was healed. (Matthew 9:19–22 TLV)

A woman who had been suffering with bleeding for twelve years reached out and grabbed the hem of Jesus' garment. Jesus responded by saying, "Someone touched me; I know that power has gone out from me" (Luke 8:46). The woman, realizing that she could not hide, "came trembling and fell at his feet," telling Jesus why she had touched Him and how she had been healed instantly.

The bleeding woman had every reason to be fearful. Among religious

Jews, it was—and still is—considered immodest and inappropriate to touch a man, even one's husband, in public. But even worse, this woman was ritually unclean and could spread her impurity to any person she touched (Leviticus 15:25–27). She could have faced serious consequences for such a bold action.

But this woman was desperate. Imagine not being touched by family or friends for twelve years. She had lived for over a decade in a perpetual state of shame as an outcast who was excluded from the social and spiritual life of her community. She felt she had nothing to lose, so she took a big risk. When she touched the hem of Jesus' garment, she was instantly healed! Though Jesus became ritually unclean by her touch, she became clean, and more importantly, whole again.

Notice this woman's fear: "The woman, knowing what had happened to her, came and fell at his feet and, trembling with fear, told him the whole truth" (Mark 5:33). Notice also Jesus' gentle response: "Daughter, your faith has healed you. Go in peace" (v. 34). This underscores how radically differently Jesus dealt with women than did other men of His day. Rather than being upset with her, which would have been the normal reaction from a rabbi or Levitical priest, He commended the woman's faith.

But of course, there is something more! A key detail often overlooked in this passage is that the woman touched "the edge of his cloak" (Matthew 9:20). She did not just touch the fringe, but rather His *tzitzit*, the ritual tassels placed on each corner (*kanaf*, in Hebrew) of every four-corner garment. These *tzitzit* are described in the book of Numbers:

> Adonai spoke to Moses saying, "Speak to *Bnei-Yisrael*. Say to them that they are to make for themselves *tzitzit* on the corners

of their garments throughout their generations, and they are to put a blue cord on each *tzitzit*. It will be your own *tzitzit*—so whenever you look at them, you will remember all the *mitzvot* of ADONAI and do them and not go spying out after your own hearts and your own eyes, prostituting yourselves. This way you will remember and obey all My *mitzvot* and you will be holy to your God. I am ADONAI your God. I brought you out of the land of Egypt to be your God. I am ADONAI your God." (Numbers 15:37–41 TLV)

These *tzitzit* were meant to remind Israel to faithfully follow the Lord by obeying His commandments. It is no coincidence that they were to be placed on all four corners of the garment.

The root of all sin goes back to the garden of Eden. The result of Adam and Eve's disobedience was exile for them and all their descendants after them. Living in exile means living in a perpetual state of disconnection and separation that ultimately leads to death if not remedied. There are four aspects to exile: spiritual, emotional, relational, and physical.

The promise of redemption from exile is also connected to the number four. At the Passover Seder, there are four cups of wine that correspond to the four aspects of redemption mentioned in Exodus 6:6–7 (TLV): "I will bring you out," "I will deliver you," "I will redeem you," "I will take you to Myself" (see "An Overview of God's Appointed Feasts" on page 142). At the final redemption, the Lord will "lift up a banner for the nations, and assemble the dispersed of Israel, and gather the scattered of Judah from the four corners of the earth" (Isaiah 11:12 TLV).

Also, there is a messianic promise that states, "For you who revere

My Name, the sun of righteousness will rise, with healing in its wings" (Malachi 3:20 TLV). The word for "wings" in this verse literally means "corner" and is the same word used for the tassels on the four corners, known in Hebrew as the *arba kanfot*. This woman reached out and grabbed one of the four "wings" of Jesus' tunic.

This bleeding woman had been living in exile on all four levels. She had no physical contact with family and friends, could not publicly worship in the temple, was isolated and alone, and lived in a perpetual state of physical pain. But she found a fourfold healing by touching one of the four corners of Jesus' garment, and thus she became an example of the messianic redemption that we can begin to experience right now when we reach out and touch Him! Like her, we must have the faith to boldly reach out and seize the Lord so that we might find help and healing in our time of need.

Just like the woman with the issue of blood was viewed as unclean, many religious leaders in Jesus' day viewed the Gentile nations as unclean and unworthy. This perspective was due to the fact that the nations of the world were pagan at this time, and their cultures were dominated by idolatry, bloodshed, and sexual immorality. Despite this, Jesus had a very different view of Gentiles. He did not focus on their sin but on God's promise of redemption for all people.

Just like the woman who grabbed hold of Him and found personal redemption, one day all the nations of the world will do the same. As the prophet Zechariah wrote:

"Many peoples and powerful nations will come to seek ADONAI-Tzva'ot in Jerusalem, and to entreat the favor of ADONAI." Thus says ADONAI-Tzva'ot, "In those days it will come to pass that ten men from every language of the nations will grasp the corner of the garment of a Jew saying, 'Let us go with you, for we have heard that God is with you.'" (Zechariah 8:22–23 TLV)

One day all peoples will grab hold of the Lord by attaching themselves to God's people. When this happens, exile will end and the world will be healed!

On a more personal and practical level, women were not seen as equal to Jewish men. But Jesus and the New Testament make it clear that "there is neither Jew nor Greek, there is neither slave nor free, there is neither male nor female—for you are all one in Messiah *Yeshua*" (Galatians 3:28 TLV). This does not mean there are no longer any differences or distinctions between men and women or Gentiles and Jews; rather, it implies a spiritual equality. There are no second-class citizens in God's kingdom.

CHAPTER 15

CAESAREA PHILIPPI

The Gates of Hades

I tell you that you are Peter, and on this rock I will build
my church, and the gates of Hades will not overcome it.

— MATTHEW 16:18

Caesarea Philippi was an especially pagan city known for its worship of Greek gods and its temples devoted to the ancient god Pan. It was located north of Bethsaida along the Syrian border.

While Jesus and His disciples were in Caesarea Philippi, He asked them an important question:

> When Jesus came to the region of Caesarea Philippi, he asked his disciples, "Who do people say the Son of Man is?"
>
> They replied, "Some say John the Baptist; others say Elijah; and still others, Jeremiah or one of the prophets."

"But what about you?" he asked. "Who do you say I am?"

Simon Peter answered, "You are the Messiah, the Son of the living God."

Jesus replied, "Blessed are you, Simon son of Jonah, for this was not revealed to you by flesh and blood, but by my Father in heaven. And I tell you that you are Peter, and on this rock I will build my church, and the gates of Hades will not overcome it." (Matthew 16:13–18)

This Scripture passage has been misunderstood for centuries. Jesus asked His disciples, "Who do you say that I am?" And He is asking the same of us today. Many will respond, "Jesus was a good man." Or "Jesus was a prophet." But Peter answered, "You are the Messiah, the Son of the living God" (v. 16).

The Hebrew word for Messiah means "the Anointed One." Peter meant that Jesus was the long-awaited Savior, spoken of throughout the Old Testament by the prophets, who would come and redeem Israel and save it from its sins.

This was a profound understanding and statement of faith for a simple, uneducated fisherman! The truth of it was stunning, especially in that completely pagan setting. In response, Jesus gave Simon, son of Jonah, a new name: Peter (*petros* in Greek). Here is where many biblical scholars agree that a major misunderstanding occurred centuries ago. The word *petros* describes a shifting, moving rock. The word *petra*, which is used in the next phrase ("and on this rock [*petra*] I will build my church"), is defined as solid rock.

Then Jesus continued, "And the gates of Hades will not overcome it" (v. 18).

Understanding the setting of this biblical scene is essential to understanding the Scriptures. When Jesus posed this question to His disciples, they were likely standing in front of a large pagan temple in Caesarea Philippi called the Gates of Hades. This temple was believed by the Greeks at the time to be the entrance to hell and to the precipitous cavern beneath it, so deep it couldn't be measured.

I don't believe, based on this understanding of the actual words used by Jesus, that Jesus intended to base His church on a man, an imperfect human being, as awesome as Peter was. Because we know very soon from Scripture that this same Peter would deny three times that he even knew Jesus!

Instead, Jesus was saying that He would base His church on the *truth* of what Peter answered: "You are the Messiah, the Son of the living God" (v. 16). This is the *petra*, the solid rock, the cornerstone of the church.

Peter agreed, later saying to the Jewish leaders, "Jesus is 'the stone you builders rejected, which has become the cornerstone'" (Acts 4:11).

In biblical times, a cornerstone was used as the foundation and standard upon which a building was constructed. It was the most important stone in the building process. In fact, the cornerstone was so important that if it were removed, the entire structure could collapse.

Jesus saw deeply into Peter's heart. He saw his love, He saw his faith, and He saw his courage to speak the truth about Jesus, the "Anointed One," the prophesied Messiah. But Jesus also knew that in the near future, on the night before Jesus would be crucified, that same Peter would deny Him three times and later weep bitterly because of his betrayal. Matthew 26:75 tells us, "Then Peter remembered the word Jesus had spoken: 'Before the rooster crows, you will disown me three times.' And he went outside and wept bitterly."

The church, meaning the entire body of Christ—the building of believers—was not built on the frailty of one human being but on the eternal power of the divine Savior of the world, who stood at the very "gates of Hades" in Caesarea Philippi and proclaimed the truth.

Come . . . to Caesarea Philippi!

More from Rabbi Jason

Who Do You Say That I Am?

After leaving the area of Bethesda, Jesus and His disciples went on a thirty-two-mile journey to Caesarea Philippi. To fully understand why Jesus took His disciples on such a long journey to this site, we must understand a bit about the history of this city.

Caesarea Philippi is located on the southern slopes of Mount Hermon in northern Israel. In the time of Joshua, Caesarea was known as Baal Gad (Joshua 11:16–17), named for the fertility god Baal, who was the primary deity worshiped by its inhabitants. The Greek conquest under Alexander the Great led to the hellenization (Greek influence) of Caesarea Philippi and its eventual renaming to Paneas, after the Greek god Pan. Pan was worshiped as the god of the shepherds, flocks, hunters, and mountain wilds, and he was associated with "Pan-ic sex," which was sex for the sake of personal pleasure and lust.

After being conquered by Rome, the city was put under the authority of Herod the Great. In honor of Caesar, Herod built a marble temple that he dedicated to the Roman emperor in 20 BC. Herod's son Philip expanded the city and renamed it Caesarea, to honor Caesar. To distinguish it from Caesarea Maritima, the port city built by Herod, it was referred to as Caesarea Philippi.

Caesarea Philippi is mentioned twice in the New Testament

(Matthew 16:13; Mark 8:27; both accounts of the same event). After arriving in Caesarea Philippi, Jesus asked His disciples, "Who do people say the Son of Man is?" (Matthew 16:13). Then He asked them possibly the most important question found in the Scriptures: "Who do you say I am?" (v. 15).

It seems strange that of all the places that the Lord could have asked this question, He chose Caesarea Philippi. Caesarea Philippi was the "Sin City" of Israel, where the people worshiped Caesar, Baal, and Pan through sexual immorality and wild partying. Yet if you think about it, this was a great location for Jesus to ask His disciples about who they thought He was. These disciples would have been surrounded by temptation as well as the sounds of people proclaiming their allegiance to some of the most popular gods of their day.

It was in this setting that Jesus chose to test not only His disciples' understanding of His identity but also their commitment to Him. Peter responded to His Master's questions by saying, "You are the Messiah, the Son of the living God" (v. 16). Peter's answer was meant to communicate that Jesus was the promised divine, messianic, Davidic king, who alone was to be served.

In response to Peter's great confession, Jesus declared:

"Blessed are you, Simon son of Jonah, for this was not revealed to you by flesh and blood, but by my Father in heaven. And I tell you that you are Peter, and on this rock I will build my church, and the gates of Hades will not overcome it. I will give you the keys of the kingdom of heaven; whatever you bind on earth will be bound in heaven, and whatever you loose on earth will be loosed in heaven." Then he ordered his disciples not to tell anyone that he was the Messiah. (Matthew 16:17–20)

Let's unpack Jesus' response. First, He made it clear that Peter's confession had heavenly origins and was revealed to him by divine inspiration. Peter's statement was not a guess but a God-thought that had been granted to him from above.

Second, as Kathie mentioned above, Jesus made a play on words by using two Greek words, *petros* and *petra*. *Petros* is Peter's Greek name and is best translated as "small stone." *Petra*, on the other hand, means a boulder or foundation stone of a building. Peter, who was a small stone, made a confession of faith that was going to be the huge rock and foundation stone upon which the church would be built. The meaning of the Greek word for "church" used here is *ekklesia* (or *ecclesia*), and its Hebrew equivalent is *edah*, which means "congregation." But what is important here is that the Hebrew word *edah* comes from the Hebrew word *eid*, which means to "bear witness" or "give testimony."

In Jewish thought, there is one key place that the idea of confession and bearing witness are connected. The central Jewish confession of faith is the Shema: "Hear, O Israel: The LORD our God, the LORD is one. Love the LORD your God with all your heart and with all your soul and with all your strength" (Deuteronomy 6:4–5). This declaration is meant to remind us morning and evening that the Lord is the one and only true God. He alone is to be worshiped. By reciting the Shema, Jews declare their loyalty to the King of kings and bear witness to His kingship.

To underscore this bearing-witness component, in Deuteronomy 6:4 there are two letters that are written larger than all others. The first enlarged Hebrew letter is found in the first word, *Shema* (שמע, "hear"); the second larger letter is found in the very last letter of the last word in this verse, which is *echad* (אחד). The enlarged *ayin* of *Shema* and the enlarged *dalet* of *echad* spell *eid*, which is the Hebrew word for "witness"—the same word we looked at above.

What is the point? Peter's confession functioned as a sort of New Testament version of the Shema, which would become a foundational confession of all followers of Messiah. Many of the early Christian martyrs died proclaiming, "Jesus is Lord!"

Jesus then went on to say, concerning the church, that "the gates of Hades will not overcome it" (Matthew 16:18). What exactly was He trying to communicate? A city is only as strong as its gates. In ancient times, cities were protected by walls that usually had one central gate. An invading army attacked the gates of the city since they were the most vulnerable point.

Hades (sometimes called Sheol) is the place where the dead descend after this life. A common belief in antiquity was that there were gates that stood at the entrance to the underworld, which was the realm of the deceased. Once these gates closed, the individual was prevented from experiencing the life of God's kingdom.

The church has been given the mission and the power to break down the gates of death (Hades/Sheol) and open the gates of the kingdom, so that people are delivered from death by declaring, like Peter, that Jesus is the messianic King and Son of God. In Acts 2, during Pentecost, we see that Peter began to use what might be described as "keys of the kingdom" to exercise spiritual authority and unlock the door of salvation by sharing the gospel with Cornelius and his family. Acts 10 tells us that they became the first Gentiles to believe the gospel and be filled with the Holy Spirit.

But there is something more! One day while I was meditating on this verse, I felt the Lord ask me in a still, small voice, *Jason, who do you say I am?* For a moment I was confused. I said, "Lord, You are my Messiah, my Redeemer, and King." But then I realized that this was not actually the question being posed to me. Jesus wanted me to ask Him the opposite: "Lord, who do You say I [Jason] am?" There are so many people who want to define us. And whatever defines us has power over us.

Identity is destiny. If you allow your life to be defined by lies or by people who do not truly know who God created you to be, then you will be robbed of both your true identity and your full destiny. Our identity must come from and be found in the Lord. Like Peter, each one of us must answer Jesus' question, "Who do you say I am?" How we answer this question will shape our eternal destiny for better or worse.

But we also must ask Jesus, "Who am I in Your sight?" In other words, "Who do You say I am based on Your infinite and eternal perspective?" Understanding the answer to these questions on a deep level is a key to experiencing the abundant life Jesus promised us (John 10:10).

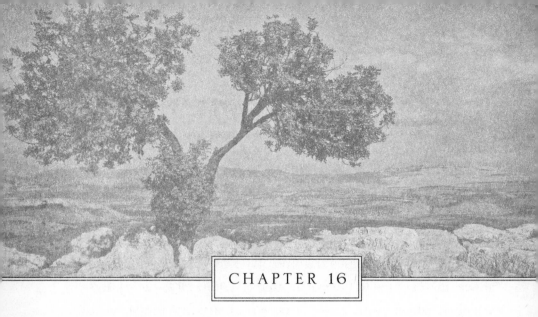

CHAPTER 16

THE POOL OF SILOAM

Healing a Blind Man

"Go," he told him, "wash in the Pool of Siloam" (this word means
"Sent"). So the man went and washed, and came home seeing.

—JOHN 9:7

The gospel of John tells us that Jesus healed a blind man at the
Pool of Siloam (John 9:1–11). The exact location of this pool
was debated for centuries until June 2004, when, during construction work to repair a large water pipe south of Jerusalem's Temple
Mount at the southern end of a ridge known as the City of David,
archaeologists Ronny Reich and Eli Shukron discovered two ancient
stone steps. As the work progressed, the excavation revealed that
these steps were part of the ancient Pool of Siloam from the Second
Temple period, which was during the time of Jesus.

This was no wading pool they had discovered; it measured 225 feet in length. The pool was fed by waters from the Gihon Spring, located in the Kidron Valley. Because these were naturally flowing spring waters, they qualified under Jewish law to be used as a *mikvah*, or ritual bath—something required for all Jews entering the temple to worship.[1]

Adjacent to this extraordinary archaeological find is something equally astounding: Hezekiah's Tunnel, mentioned in 2 Kings 20:20, an amazing underground tunnel that is fascinating to explore. It was used to funnel floodwaters from the temple, but it is widely believed to have also been used as an escape route for the Zealots—the ancient Jewish sect that sought to overthrow the occupying Roman government—when Titus destroyed Jerusalem in AD 70. Evidence suggests that a group of Zealots hid from the Romans deep within adjacent rooms in the tunnel. Carbon-dated bones have been discovered that give credence to this theory.[2]

Rabbi Jason's explanation of the Pool of Siloam once again helps my faith grow ever deeper in a loving God.

Come . . . to the Pool of Siloam!

More from Rabbi Jason

The Man Born Blind and Divine DNA

Immediately after Jesus left the temple in Jerusalem, He came across a man born blind from birth. Upon seeing this blind man, His disciples asked Him, "Rabbi, who sinned, this man or his parents, that he was born blind?" (John 9:2). Jesus responded that this man's blindness was not the result of any transgression committed by him or his parents. It occurred so that God's power might be brought to light in him.

Jesus then spat in the dirt, made mud with His saliva, placed it on the eyes of the blind man, and told him to go wash in the Pool of Siloam. After washing, the man was miraculously healed and could see for the first time in his life!

We must understand how the Lord performed this miracle to comprehend the full magnitude of this miracle and its deeper message. The most important part of this miracle was the use of saliva to make the mud. This was a man born blind from birth, which means he was born with a genetic defect. He therefore needed to experience healing on both a spiritual and genetic level to be fully cured. If you have ever taken a DNA test or watched an episode of CSI, then you know that one way to get DNA is through saliva. Through His saliva, Jesus was transferring His perfect DNA to this blind man to supernaturally heal him of his genetic defect. In the same way that the Lord created Adam out of the dirt of the ground, Jesus performed a new creation miracle that brought new life to this man.

But there is something more! Jesus' use of spittle was also meant to communicate an important message about His origin and position as God's firstborn Son and legitimate heir to His Father's kingdom. In that culture, the firstborn son was entitled to a double portion of his father's estate. The right of receiving the blessing of the firstborn could be contested if it were proved that the one in question was the firstborn of his mother but not his father, or if he was deemed to be illegitimate because he was born out of wedlock.

There was a belief among some first-century rabbis that the saliva of the firstborn son had healing properties and could be used to prove that the son in question had the right to receive the blessing of the firstborn. There is an example in the Talmud in which a son was proved to be the firstborn because his saliva was used to heal a man's ailing eyes, which was supported by the following statement: "The spittle of the firstborn of a father is healing, but that of the firstborn of a mother is not healing."[3] But this example is minor in comparison to the miracle Jesus performed in John 9. Jesus did not restore the sight to an individual like in the example above, but He actually gave sight to a man who never had it at all. This type of miracle was unheard of and unprecedented; it was a prophetic fulfillment of Isaiah 35:4–5: "Behold, your God! . . . He will save you. Then the eyes of the blind will be opened" (TLV).

There were individuals who questioned the parentage of Jesus and accused Him of being an illegitimate son. Many had doubts about who was His true father. Jesus Himself implied in His teaching that He did not have a human father but a heavenly One. Jesus said He was the One who came from and was sent by the Father. The miraculous healing of the man born blind should have proved Jesus' claim of being God's Son because only the saliva of the Father's firstborn could supernaturally heal in this way. Unfortunately, many of the Judean leaders rejected this sign. The irony is that the one born blind could see, but those who claimed to have a deep knowledge of the Scriptures remained spiritually blind.

Healing this man's eyes demonstrated that Jesus was the promised Messiah, the only begotten Firstborn of our Father in heaven. It also revealed the Lord's overwhelming mercy, kindness, and power! Nothing is impossible with God, even congenital diseases. He truly is the Great Physician! And apart from having our eyes opened by His grace, we remain blind.

CHAPTER 17

THE DECAPOLIS

The Prodigal Son

Not long after that, the younger son got together all he had, set off for a distant country and there squandered his wealth in wild living.

—LUKE 15:13

Many people are familiar with Jesus' parable of the prodigal son, recorded in Luke 15:11–32:

There was a man who had two sons. The younger one said to his father, "Father, give me my share of the estate." So he divided his property between them.

Not long after that, the younger son got together all he had, set off for a distant country and there squandered his wealth in wild living. After he had spent everything, there was a severe famine in that whole country, and he began to be in need. So he went and hired himself out to a citizen of that country, who sent him to his fields to feed pigs. He longed to fill his stomach with the pods that the pigs were eating, but no one gave him anything.

When he came to his senses, he said, "How many of my father's hired servants have food to spare, and here I am starving to death! I will set out and go back to my father and say to him: Father, I have sinned against heaven and against you. I am no longer worthy to be called your son; make me like one of your hired servants." So he got up and went to his father.

But while he was still a long way off, his father saw him and was filled with compassion for him; he ran to his son, threw his arms around him and kissed him.

The son said to him, "Father, I have sinned against heaven and against you. I am no longer worthy to be called your son."

But the father said to his servants, "Quick! Bring the best robe and put it on him. Put a ring on his finger and sandals on his feet. Bring the fattened calf and kill it. Let's have a feast and celebrate. For this son of mine was dead and is alive again; he was lost and is found." So they began to celebrate.

Meanwhile, the older son was in the field. When he came near the house, he heard music and dancing. So he called one of the servants and asked him what was going on. "Your brother has come," he replied, "and your father has killed the fattened calf because he has him back safe and sound."

The older brother became angry and refused to go in. So his father went out and pleaded with him. But he answered his father, "Look! All these years I've been slaving for you and never disobeyed your orders. Yet you never gave me even a young goat so I could celebrate with my friends. But when this son of yours who has squandered your property with prostitutes comes home, you kill the fattened calf for him!"

"My son," the father said, "you are always with me, and everything I have is yours. But we had to celebrate and be glad, because this brother of yours was dead and is alive again; he was lost and is found."

Many scholars believe Jesus shared this parable while in Capernaum, just a few miles from the Decapolis, across the Sea of Galilee. The Decapolis (literally "ten cities") is believed to be the place where the seven Canaanite nations who inhabited the land before the Hebrews arrived to conquer it fled to survive Joshua and his army:

- "This is how you will know that the living God is among you and that he will certainly drive out before you the Canaanites, Hittites, Hivites, Perizzites, Girgashites, Amorites and Jebusites" (Joshua 3:10).
- "He overthrew seven nations in Canaan, giving their land to his people as their inheritance" (Acts 13:19).

In Jesus' day, the Decapolis was a Hellenistic (Greek-influenced) area, deeply entrenched in pagan worship and therefore forbidden to any Jew who wished to remain ritually clean, pure, or holy before God. In our vernacular, the setting of this parable would be as if one of our sons left his Christian home for Las Vegas—Sin City, baby! And the prodigal son succumbed to all the depravity that infamous mecca had to offer.

There is an ancient road that follows the coast of the Sea of Galilee from Capernaum to the Decapolis. In this parable, it is noteworthy that the father saw his son returning home from "a long way off" (Luke 15:20) and picked up his robe and ran for joy toward his precious "sin-soaked" son. In Jesus' day, the father's action would have shocked his audience. No decent Jewish man would be so immodest as to lift his robe, nor would he embarrass himself by running toward a son who had brought him and the family so much shame. By all rights, the prodigal son should have been dead to him. But the beauty of it is the exact opposite! His son was alive! He was coming home, and he was sorry! The father simply could not contain his glorious joy.

Of course, the father in this parable is a metaphor for God, our heavenly Father, and how He acts whenever one of us, His children, repents and returns to the Father's House (see "Bet Av" on page 122). In Luke 15:7, Jesus said, "I tell you that in the same way there will be more rejoicing in heaven over one sinner who repents than over ninety-nine righteous persons who do not need to repent."

The father in the story embraced his son with total abandon, oblivious to the stench of the sweat and the pigs and the debauchery. He called for the fattened calf to be butchered for a homecoming feast; he threw his best robe over his son's filth, and he put his signet ring on the son's grimy finger, signifying the son's place of importance in the family. The father put shoes on his son's feet. He treated him as royalty instead of what he actually was: an ingrate, a degenerate, and a profound disappointment to everyone, mostly his father.

This story is one of the most moving examples of a father's mercy in all of literature. As you are standing in Capernaum, it is easy to imagine the extraordinary scene that Jesus described just up the ancient road.

But lost in many sermons on this parable is the story of the older son—the "good" son—who came home from working hard in his father's field to the sound of music and merriment and rejoicing.

When told the news of his brother's unexpected return, the older son became belligerent, hurt, and combative. He refused to go into the party to welcome his brother home. Some would say he had good reason. After all, the older son didn't cause his father pain, embarrassment, disappointment, or sorrow.

I believe this son represents those of us who are "Pharisees" in our hearts. We keep all the rules, we do everything required of us, and we are faithful and loyal believers. But we lack what our Father cares about most: love, compassion, mercy, grace, and forgiveness. These are the things the prodigal son's father expressed to his beloved son—who was once lost but now is found.

This is a perfect picture of redemption. We can only imagine the reaction of the Pharisees in Jesus' audience that day. Did they recognize themselves in the person of the unloving but faithful son?

Do we?

Come . . . to the Decapolis!

CHAPTER 18

THE MOUNT OF OLIVES

The Triumphal Entry

When he came near the place where the road goes down the
Mount of Olives, the whole crowd of disciples began joyfully
to praise God in loud voices for all the miracles they had seen:
"Blessed is the king who comes in the name of the Lord!"

—LUKE 19:37—38

The Mount of Olives, or Mount Olivet, is part of a mountain ridge east of and adjacent to the Old City of Jerusalem. Olive groves once covered its slopes, and a small grove—the Garden of Gethsemane—remains there to this day. What surprises some first-time visitors is that this place has been used as a Jewish cemetery for more than three thousand years. Many Jews believe the Messiah will someday arrive in Jerusalem through the Mount of Olives—and when He does, the dead will rise from their graves and walk to the Temple Mount. Therefore, many Jewish believers wish to be buried at this site, only a few meters away from the Old City, with their feet facing the Temple Mount.[1] Headstones are arranged row after row, representing approximately 150,000 graves, creating an almost surreal tableau as you face the city of Jerusalem while standing on the Mount of Olives.

The Mount of Olives is one of my favorite places in all of Israel, for it features prominently in the Scriptures in the life of Jesus. Yet according to the Bible, the Mount of Olives will also play an important role in the second coming of Jesus during the end times.

There are a few areas on the Mount of Olives that are nothing short of thrilling for me.

One of them is the ancient road that descends from the top of the mountain to the bottom at the foot of the Kidron Valley. This is the road on which Jesus rode on the foal of a donkey on Palm Sunday, the last week of His life. To the left, you can see many ancient graves, which brings to mind the time when Jesus was criticized because the people were waving palm leaves and crying, "Blessed is the king who comes in the name of the Lord!" (Luke 19:38). Some of the Pharisees in the crowd became angry and told Jesus, "Teacher, rebuke your disciples!" (v. 39). Jesus answered, "I tell you, if they [the people] keep quiet, the stones will cry out" (v. 40).

It's deeply moving to walk this ancient road, knowing that these very graves were the stones Jesus was referring to. Along the short way down, Scripture tells us in Matthew 23:37 that Jesus saw the magnificent city before Him and exclaimed, "Jerusalem, Jerusalem, you who kill the prophets and stone those sent to you, how often I have longed to gather your children together, as a hen gathers her chicks under her wings, and you were not willing."

Jesus knew exactly what was to befall Him in the week ahead. Yet His every spoken word was about His concern for others, not for Himself. That would come later, on His last night on earth during the agony of the Garden of Gethsemane.

One of the most profound teachings I've ever received happened during our tour of Israel at a specific place on the Mount of Olives.

It was unusual for Ray to care much where we sat, as long as we were comfortable and within earshot. But on this day, he had all eighteen of us sit on a stone wall with our backs to a very bushy area, looking out facing south. It couldn't have been more than thirty feet from one end of us to the other. Because Ray had never arranged us this way, we were already intrigued.

"I want you to look directly behind you," Ray began. "See all that overgrown bush there against that wall?"

We could all see it perfectly. The wall that the foliage was growing on was barely visible it was so pervasive.

Ray directed our attention back to him as he pulled out his wallet and took out a small laminated card, the size of a driver's license.

"Look here." He pointed at the tiny black speck in the middle of the card. "See this?"

We could all barely make it out.

"That," he explained, "is a mustard seed, among the smallest seeds in all of the botanical world. It's smaller than a speck of pepper."

He let that settle in, and it truly was extraordinary to wrap our minds around it.

"Now," he said, "look back at all that growth behind you again."

Naturally, we obeyed, wondering where all this was going.

"That is the most feared plant in all of Israel, the mustard plant. It's feared because once it takes root it can't be destroyed. You can try to burn it out, stomp it out, tear it out, but eventually it takes over everything in its way."

Ray paused, lifted up his Bible, and said: "The mustard seed is the kingdom of God! Once it gets planted, nothing can stop it! I wonder if the disciples made the connection to Jesus' other teaching—that if we have faith even as small as this, we can say to that mountain. . . ." He pointed to something we hadn't noticed before: Herodium in the distance!

". . . Be gone! And it will be thrown into that sea!"

Now we looked where he was pointing at a stunning image: the Dead Sea!

Ray reminded us that the rabbis always taught what the simple people could see and hear and smell and taste and touch. The weight of what he was teaching was overwhelming: this is the only spot on the Mount of Olives where these three things—the mustard plant, Herodium, and the Dead Sea—are visible.

Thus, Jesus had to have been standing *right there* when He shared this parable!

We all just sat there, stunned.

I could easily picture Jesus standing exactly where Ray was standing. I moved my eyes behind me there, then to my right, then before me again—and I began to weep.

Ray continued: "The kingdom of God is us! It is all of us as believers. If we just believe, we can say to that mountain—the world's way, Herod's way, Satan's way—be gone, into that sea, the Dead Sea, which is already dead!"

Come . . . to the Mount of Olives!

MORE FROM RABBI JASON

THE TRIUMPHAL ENTRY AT THE MOUNT OF OLIVES

Jesus rode down the Mount of Olives into Jerusalem on a donkey during what has become known as the Triumphal Entry. But did you ever wonder why He chose to ride on a donkey? Every one of Jesus' actions was intentional. He came to fulfill everything that was prophesied by Moses and the prophets concerning the Messiah so that the world might know that He was the promised Redeemer.

Speaking of the coming Messiah, the Old Testament prophet Zechariah wrote:

> Rejoice greatly, daughter of *Zion*!
> Shout, daughter of Jerusalem!
> Behold, your king is coming to you,
> a righteous one bringing salvation.
> He is lowly, riding on a donkey—
> on a colt, the foal of a donkey. (Zechariah 9:9 TLV)

So Jesus the Messiah came riding on a donkey in fulfillment of this prophecy. But there is much more meaning as to why a donkey was chosen. Horses are a symbol of military might, wealth, and strength. Donkeys, on the other hand, are symbolic of humility and peace. At His first coming, Messiah came as the humble lamb of God riding on a donkey. But at His second coming, He will descend from the heavens riding a white warhorse ready to vanquish all evil from the world (Revelation 19:11–16).

Still deeper, the donkey plays a key role in the history of the redemption of God's people. We see this in the life of Abraham, the father of the Christian faith. Abraham in Hebraic thought went through ten tests. The final test was the offering of Isaac upon the altar as a sacrifice to the Lord, which demonstrated his great faith (Hebrews 11). But it was also meant to paint a portrait of God the Father's willingness to offer His only Son on our behalf. In Genesis 22, Abraham put his supplies on a donkey when he went on the three-day journey to offer Isaac, who was a type (or symbolic figure) of Messiah, as a burnt offering on Mount Moriah (Genesis 22:3).

Moses also made use of a donkey when he was sent by God to redeem the children of Israel from Egypt. In Exodus 4:20, Moses put his wife and children on a donkey.

Abraham's and Moses' use of a donkey was ultimately meant to point to the Messiah who would also use a donkey when He came to usher in the start of the messianic kingdom that would come through His sufferings.

Jesus' riding on a donkey not only underscored His humility, but also pointed to the fact that He was the greater Abraham. As Jesus said, "Abraham rejoiced to see My day; he saw it and was thrilled" (John 8:56 TLV). Jesus was also the greater prophet like Moses, who came to bring about an even greater redemption (Acts 3:22). Thus the work of redemption that began with Abraham and was taken to the next level by Moses was advanced further by Jesus, who at His Second Coming will bring complete transformation to all of creation.

When you truly welcome Jesus into your life as King and Savior, like the crowd seemed to do during His Triumphal Entry—crying out, "Blessed is the king who comes in the name of the Lord!" (Luke 19:38)— you begin to experience not only personal salvation, but also real new-creation transformation.

Gezer, next to the Via Maris—the ancient trade route known as the "Road of the Sea."

Gezer is really our first stop right off the plane in Tel Aviv. It's a lot steeper of a climb than it appears.

En Gedi. The glorious oasis in the desert next to the Dead Sea. David hid near here from King Saul and wrote many of his psalms in the caves deep within the Rock.

En Gedi. The sheer beauty of it is astounding and totally worth the steep, hot climb.

En Gedi. David's waterfall.

The Judean Desert in the afternoon.

Caesarea Maritima.
Herod's brilliant
man-made harbor,
ready to receive
Caesar's ships.

Caesarea Maritima. The amphitheater and
sports complex known as the Hippodrome.

Mount Carmel. Where Elijah challenged
the prophets of Baal.

The Sea of Galilee.
Beyond beautiful!

Mount Carmel. This is what the mustard plant looks like at its peak in the spring.

Mount Arbel. One of the ancient paths.

Mount Arbel. This is at the top, with the Sea of Galilee in the distance.

Mount of Olives. See the Kidron Valley at the base of the mountain.

Mount of Olives. With my three favorite people in the world: Cody Gifford, Cassidy Gifford, and Christine Gardner.

Mount of Olives. Some of the ancient graves in the Kidron Valley.

Mount of Olives. The ancient road Jesus rode down on Palm Sunday.

The Garden of Gethsemane. Virtually unchanged since Jesus prayed here to be delivered from the suffering ahead—"yet not my will, but yours be done."

Herodium. Herod's palace near Bethlehem. Breathtaking.

The Jericho Road. Jesus and His disciples traveled it when they "went up to Jerusalem."

Arad in the Negev Desert. Where God made His covenant with Abraham.

The Church of the Holy Sepulchre. Where most scholars believe Jesus was crucified and resurrected.

The Via Dolorosa. Marking the stations of the cross.

Jerusalem. An ancient road in the Arab
section of the city.

The Dead Sea. An evening view.

The Temple Mount. The most sacred site in
Israel for Jews and Muslims.

Jerusalem. Near the Western Wall.

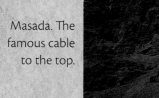

Masada. The
famous cable
to the top.

Masada (seen in the top-right corner). It was Herod's favorite palace.

Masada. For those who choose the hard way to the summit. Most take the cable car.

Masada. One of several water cisterns. Another example of Herod's architectural genius.

Qumran. Next to the Dead Sea, where the ancient Essenes wrote and hid the famous Dead Sea Scrolls.

Qumran. The actual caves—site of one of the greatest archaeological discoveries of our time.

Modern-day Bethlehem. Seen from Herod's palace at Herodium.

Bet Shean, in the Decapolis. A place forbidden to the ancient Jews, yet Jesus came here to save a demon-possessed man because He loved him.

Chorazin. One of the sites where an ancient synagogue has been discovered.

The Jordan River. In all its glory.

My daughter Cassidy's baptism in the Jordan River. Our precious brothers Remi Adeleke and Rod Van Solkema holding her against the strong current.

My son Cody's baptism in the Jordan River. He is forever bonded with these two amazing men of God.

During His Triumphal Entry into Jerusalem from the Mount of Olives, Jesus wept over the city. He saw that it would be destroyed because the people did not recognize or receive Him as the promised Messiah, the one spoken of by Moses and the prophets (Luke 19:39–44). The Mount of Olives is the location of the Olivet Discourse, in which Jesus described the prophetic future of Jerusalem and some of the key signs of the end times (Matthew 24–25; Mark 13; Luke 21:5–36).

Perhaps most importantly, it was from the Mount of Olives that Jesus ascended into heaven forty days after His resurrection (Acts 1:9–12). Of all the locations Jesus could have chosen to ascend from, why did He choose this place and not a more prominent one, such as the Temple Mount?

The prophetic significance of the Mount of Olives is likely the primary reason the Lord chose this site as the place of His ascension. The prophet Ezekiel saw God's glory depart from the Temple of Solomon and Jerusalem by way of the Mount of Olives (Ezekiel 11:22–23). Ezekiel also prophetically saw the Lord's glorious presence returning from the east, coming over the Mount of Olives, and entering into the future messianic temple of God (Ezekiel 43:1–5).

Finally, Zechariah prophesied that at the coming of Messiah, "His feet will stand on the Mount of Olives which lies to the east of Jerusalem, and the Mount of Olives will be split in two from east to west" (Zechariah 14:4 TLV). Messiah's ascent to heaven was meant as a precursor and sneak preview of His ultimate return, as described in Zechariah. This was confirmed by the angels in Acts 1:11, who said to the disciples, "Men of Galilee, . . . why do you stand here looking into the sky? This same Jesus, who has been taken from you into heaven, will come back in the same way you have seen him go into heaven.'

We must actively look for, long for, and pray for the Messiah's coming, like the apostles who watched Him ascend into heaven. Think how your life would be changed if you passionately longed for and lived every day as if this would be the moment Jesus would return!

CHAPTER 19

THE UPPER ROOM

The Passover Seder

"Say to the master of the house, 'The Teacher says, "Where is the guest room in which I may eat the Passover with My disciples?"' Then he will show you a large upper room, furnished and prepared; there make ready for us."

—MARK 14:14–15 NKJV

I have visited the Armenian section of Jerusalem, where the traditional sites of the Tomb of David and the Upper Room are believed to be, though there is little there now to confirm it. However, we know clearly from Scripture what took place in the Upper Room.

I'm going to let Rabbi Jason lead us through this section about the room that would change history forever.

Come . . . to the Upper Room!

MORE FROM RABBI JASON

THE LAST SUPPER, PASSOVER, AND THE UPPER ROOM

The Upper Room is the site of many important events in the lives of Jesus and the apostles. As Passover approached, the disciples asked Jesus, "Where do You want us to go and prepare for You to eat the Passover?" (Mark 14:12 TLV). Jesus responded by saying that they would see a man carrying a jar of water and that this man "will show you a large upper room, furnished and ready" (v. 15 TLV). This final meal that Jesus ate with His disciples, commonly referred to as the Last Supper, was really a Passover Seder (ceremonial meal) that Jesus and His disciples celebrated. Not only did Jesus eat the Passover with His disciples, but He also taught them how the key elements of the Passover Seder pointed to and found their ultimate fulfillment in Him.

The Passover Seder is a special meal eaten on Passover, centered around drinking four cups of wine (or grape juice). Each of the four cups has deep spiritual significance and symbolizes the four distinct promises God made to the Jewish people in Exodus 6:6–7.

The first cup is known as the cup of sanctification. Jesus began His Seder by reciting the blessing over this first cup. We read about this in Luke 22:17–18: "And when He had taken a cup and offered the *bracha* [blessing], He said, 'Take this and share it among yourselves'" (TLV). During a Passover Seder, we respond to the cup of sanctification by crying out, "God, make us holy. Set us apart for Your plans and holy purposes for our lives."

The second cup is commonly referred to as the cup of plagues. During this part of the Passover meal, we remember that God redeemed us with great signs and great wonders. We remember that

God, through Moses, turned water into blood, and that Messiah's first miracle turned water into wine because He is greater than Moses.

The third cup is known as the cup of redemption. When we drink this cup, we are reminded of the blood of the Passover lamb that was put upon the doorposts of the house. At the Passover Seder, when Jesus blessed the cup and gave it to His disciples, He did that with this third cup, the cup of redemption. He said to His disciples, "Drink from it, all of you; for this is My blood of the covenant, which is poured out for many for the removal of sins" (Matthew 26:27–28 TLV).

Blood played a central role in Israel's deliverance from bondage in Egypt. God told the children of Israel that in order to be spared from the final and worst plague, the death of the firstborn, they would have to slaughter a lamb and place its blood on the doorposts of their home. Any family that failed to do so would lose their firstborn in this plague. Just as the blood on the doorposts of the house in Egypt saved Israel from the plague of the death of the firstborn, those who belong to Jesus have been bought by the blood of the Lamb of God. We do not have to experience the wrath of God and His judgment because Jesus died for us as the ultimate Passover lamb! Whenever we partake of the Lord's Supper, we are symbolically drinking and spiritually partaking of the third cup, the cup of redemption.

The fourth cup is the cup of acceptance or thanksgiving. This cup looks to the future, to the coming of the kingdom. It was over the fourth cup that Jesus said, "I will never drink of this fruit of the vine from now on, until that day when I drink it anew with you in My Father's kingdom" (v. 29 TLV). When we drink the fourth cup in the Passover Seder, we acknowledge and give thanks for our acceptance as children of the King, knowing our position, power, and authority in Messiah.

A second key element of the Passover is the *matzah*, the unleavened bread (plural, *matzot*). *Matzah* is to be eaten for seven days during Passover and serves as a reminder that God brought Israel "out from the land of Egypt in haste" (Deuteronomy 16:3 TLV). *Matzah* bread has almost a corrugated look, with holes like dotted lines running vertically alongside rows of browned pockets of dough. *Matzah* is symbolic of both redemption and affliction. The affliction that the bread represents is the centuries of slavery in Egypt endured by the children of Israel. The brown stripes running the length of the bread recall the lashings of Israel's taskmasters in Egypt. It is also known as the bread of freedom and healing, when God redeemed His people from Egypt with an "outstretched arm" (Exodus 6:6 TLV).

We can also see Jesus represented in the *matzah*. See Isaiah 53:4–5:

> Surely he took up our pain
> and bore our suffering,
> yet we considered him punished by God,
> stricken by him, and afflicted.
> But he was pierced for our transgressions, . . .
> the punishment that brought us peace was on him,
> and by his wounds [stripes, NKJV] we are healed.

Jesus' "bread of affliction" was the weight of our sins. The *matzah's* holes stand for His piercings, and the brown stripes represent His stripes by which we are healed and set free from bondage to sin and our own "Egypts." These are personal prisons that confine and limit us from being who God wants us to be and doing what He has destined for us.

The *matzah* is broken during the fourth step in the Seder called *yachatz*, which means "to break." During the Last Supper, *matzah* was the bread Jesus lifted, broke, and "gave it to his disciples, saying, 'Take and eat; this is my body'" (Matthew 26:26). In fact, communion can be seen as a mini-Passover each time we partake. Did you realize there was such deep meaning in so thin a cracker?

A third key traditional element of the Passover Seder that was also part of the Last Supper was the bitter herbs (*maror*, in Hebrew). God commanded Israel to commemorate the Passover with *matzah* and bitter herbs (Exodus 12:8; Numbers 9:11). The bitter herbs are meant to remind us of how the Egyptians embittered the lives of our ancestors with hard labor (Exodus 1:14). The most commonly used bitters include romaine lettuce, horseradish, and endives.

Whether you eat a fresh slice of horseradish or a leaf of romaine lettuce, you should be thinking of the bitterness of slavery during *maror*. Traditionally, we dip the *maror* in the *charoset* (the apple-nut-wine-cinnamon mixture that represents the mortar used for the bricks) to taste a small amount of sweetness along with the bitter flavor. One reason for this is that even during the most bitter years of slavery, the promise of redemption that God made to Abraham added sweetness to Israel's suffering.

On the night Jesus was betrayed, John 13:25–27 shows how He revealed His betrayer:

Then he who leaned on *Yeshua's* chest says to Him, "Master, who is it?"

Yeshua answers, "It's the one I will give this bit of *matzah* to, after I dip it." After dipping the *matzah*, He takes it and gives it to Judah from Kriot, the son of Simon. And with that bit, satan entered into him. Then *Yeshua* tells him, "What you're about to do, do quickly!" (TLV)

So in addition to the bitterness of slavery, this step during the Passover Seder represents the bitterness of separation from Jesus as exemplified by Judas.

A fourth element, and the most central element of the Seder in the first century, was the Passover lamb. The command to eat the Passover lamb is first found in Exodus 12:8, which states: "They are to eat the meat that night, roasted over a fire. With *matzot* and bitter herbs they are to eat it" (TLV). The offering of the Passover lamb was meant to be a reminder of blood placed on the doorposts of the Israelites' homes in Egypt.

But not just any lamb would be acceptable to be eaten in fulfillment of the commandment of Passover. The Passover lamb had to be slaughtered as a sacrifice to the Lord (*korban*, in Hebrew), in the designated location that had been chosen for offerings. Deuteronomy 16:5–6 states: "You may not sacrifice the Passover offering within any of your gates that ADONAI your God is giving you. Rather, at the place ADONAI your God chooses to make His Name dwell, there you will sacrifice the Passover offering in the evening at sunset—the time of your coming out from Egypt" (TLV).

Since the destruction of the second Jerusalem temple by the Romans in AD 70, there has been no Passover sacrifice offered in the fulfillment of this prophecy. For this reason, Jews of European descent don't eat lamb today and will not do so until the temple in Jerusalem is restored.

Jesus taught that He was the true Passover lamb and the promised Messiah who came to bring about a greater Exodus. Moses came to redeem Israel from slavery in Egypt, but Messiah Jesus came to bring deliverance from sin and death. From the perspective of the New Testament, true freedom is found in God's Son, Jesus, of whom it is written, "If the Son sets you free, you will be free indeed!" (John 8:36 TLV).

God the Father sent His Son, Jesus, so that everyone who receives and believes in Him might find freedom and everlasting life in the world to come! Just like Israel had to apply the blood of the Passover lamb to the doorposts of their homes so that death would pass over their first-born sons, so every one of us must apply the blood of Jesus, the greater Passover Lamb of God, so that death and judgment will pass over us!

CHAPTER 20

BET AV

The Father's House

*My Father's house has many rooms; if that were not so, would I
have told you that I am going there to prepare a place for you?*

—JOHN 14:2

I wish everyone could go on a Rock and Road Experience trip to
Israel with Rod Van Solkema and his beautiful wife, Libby. They
are an amazing team. Rod is a pastor in Grand Rapids, Michigan,
but he thinks of himself more as a coach. It's obvious on a trip with
him that he is both. He is also a compassionate, passionate lover of
Jesus and the Word of God.

Libby is not only a great support system for Rod, but she is also
an excellent, gifted teacher as well. I always looked forward to the
times when Rod would ask Libby to share one of her parables with

In John 14:2, Jesus was teaching about the Bet Av. He told His disciples, "In My Father's house are many mansions" (NKJV). However, this is an example of a poor translation of Scripture. The word *mansions* in some translations of John 14:2 implies a life of lavish privilege, living in heaven on streets of gold. But it is the exact opposite. It is a picture of the church becoming the bride of Christ.

The Bible talks about how Jesus is the lover of our soul in Song of Solomon 1–2, using the concept of marriage as a picture and an expression of the unity and intimacy that completes a human being. Jeremiah 3:14 describes us as being married to the Lord. In heaven, our concept of earthly marriage will be replaced by a heavenly, perfect marriage to the One who gave Himself in love for us. What a concept!

A better Greek translation of John 14:2 is "rooms," not mansions: "My Father's house has many rooms." In this passage, Jesus is referring to Bet Av as it related to Jewish wedding customs. In ancient times, the father's house was designed to be able to add a room for a newly married son. After an engagement, the prospective groom would return to his father's house and begin to build a new room for himself and his bride. That's why Jesus told His disciples, "I go to prepare a place for you" (John 14:2 NKJV).

After the marriage, the groom and his bride would be given this new room as their own—a place where they could privately explore their new life together in an intimate setting. In this fashion, the Bet Av, or father's house, would continue to grow as the family did.

Come . . . to the Father's house!

CHAPTER 21

GARDEN OF GETHSEMANE

"Not My Will, but Yours"

He withdrew about a stone's throw beyond them, knelt down and prayed, "Father, if you are willing, take this cup from me; yet not my will, but yours be done."

—LUKE 22:41–42

*G*ethsemane means "oil press." The Garden of Gethsemane is mentioned in Matthew 26:36: "Then Jesus went with his disciples to a place called Gethsemane, and he said to them, 'Sit here while I go over there and pray.'"

Mark 14:32 says it like this: "They went to a place called Gethsemane, and Jesus said to his disciples, 'Sit here while I pray.'"

In Aramaic, Gethsemane is a place or enclosed piece of ground to which Jesus and His disciples retired. In John 18:1, this place is described as a garden (*kepos,* in Greek): "When he had finished praying, Jesus left with his disciples and crossed the Kidron Valley. On the other side there was a garden, and he and his disciples went into it."

Scholars dispute the exact location of the Garden of Gethsemane, but that didn't spoil our tour group's experience. We know it could be anywhere in a general area, so it didn't really matter to me where it was exactly. It was there, somewhere close, and no academic argument can mar the experience for me or millions of others who seek Him.

On the Mount of Olives, right next to the Church of Mary Magdalene, there is an ancient grotto where an equally ancient geth-semane, or oil press, still exists. It is here that many scholars believe Jesus and His disciples spent the last week before Jesus' crucifixion.

Once deep inside this beautiful grotto, it is not difficult to accept that this could, indeed, be the actual place where Jesus and His disciples slept before Jesus was betrayed by Judas, arrested, and led to His suffering at the hands of the Sanhedrin and Pontius Pilate.

Come . . . to the Garden of Gethsemane!

More from Rabbi Jason

Gethsemane, Eden, and the Anointed One

After celebrating Passover, Jesus and His disciples walked to the Mount of Olives, to the Garden of Gethsemane (Matthew 26:36). The fact that Jesus spent the final hours before His arrest in a garden is significant. First, the fall of man occurred in a garden—so Jesus, who is the second Adam, also entered into a garden as He prepared to give His life to atone for the sin of the first man and woman.

Second, one of the primary titles ascribed to Jesus is "Christ." Growing up, I thought this was His last name. Instead, Christ is the Greek equivalent of the Hebrew word *Mashiach* (Messiah), which means "the Anointed One." Why is this so significant? In ancient Israel, kings were anointed with olive oil as a sign of being chosen and empowered by God to rule. Thus, the term *Messiah* in Judaism came to refer to the promised messianic King and Redeemer who would be anointed with olive oil and, more importantly, by the Spirit of the Lord to establish the kingdom of God.

According to Isaiah, it is out of an olive stump that "a shoot will come forth out of the stem of Jesse, and a branch will bear fruit out of His roots," and "the *Ruach* of ADONAI [Spirit of the Lord] will rest upon Him" as the anointed Messiah from the line of David (Isaiah 11:1–2 TLV). It's amazing to think that Jesus spent one of the most important moments of His life in an olive garden, which is the very type of tree that was most symbolic of His role as Messiah (Jeremiah 33:15; Zechariah 3:8; 6:12).

As Kathie explained, Gethsemane comes from the Aramaic word meaning "olive press." Olives went through three pressings to remove every ounce of oil. The three pressings of the olives are connected to the three times Jesus asked His heavenly Father to "let this cup pass from Me" (Matthew 26:39, 42, 44 TLV). Like an olive in a press, Jesus was being crushed by the weight of humanity's sin, so that by His pressing of the oil, the light of salvation might be released into our lives. The crushing that Jesus experienced for you and me was so severe that He sweated blood (Luke 22:44).

But there is something more! Jesus asked His three closest disciples—Peter, James, and John—to watch and pray with Him (Matthew 26:38). At the start of Messiah's ministry, He was led into the desert, where while fasting and praying He was tested three times by Satan. At the end of His ministry, Jesus seemed to be undergoing a final and similar test. While it was important for Him to pass the test, He wanted His disciples, especially Peter, to gain the spiritual strength needed to pass the test as well.

Three times the disciples fell asleep, even though the Lord asked them to tarry with Him in prayer. Jesus knew Satan wanted to sift Peter and the disciples like wheat but, would not be able to due to His intercession for them (Luke 22:32). Jesus wanted the disciples to pray with Him so that they might be able to resist temptation. This is only speculation, but perhaps Jesus hoped that if Peter had tarried with Him in prayer for those last few hours and had not fallen asleep three times, he would have had the strength to not deny Him three times.

All of us must be vigilant to watch and pray so that we don't succumb to the temptation to deny the Lord when we go through the olive presses of life and feel like we are being crushed by our situation and circumstances. We must remember that it is the crushing that brings out the true inner value and worth of the olive, which is the oil.

CHAPTER 22

GOLGOTHA

The Triumph of the Cross

Carrying his own cross, he went out to the place of the Skull (which
in Aramaic is called Golgotha). There they crucified him, and
with him two others—one on each side and Jesus in the middle.

—JOHN 19:17–18

When we were screening Mel Gibson's movie *The Passion of the Christ* at our home, I began to sob uncontrollably during the scene where Jesus falls and, in spite of His agony, says to His mother: "Behold, Mother. I make all things new." My daughter, Cassidy, who was eleven years old at the time, said: "Don't cry, Mommy. It has a happy ending, remember?"

Don't you just love the innocence and truth of children? But what she didn't understand was that I wasn't crying tears of pain, but tears of joy. She was right, of course. It *does* have a happy ending because of Jesus' sacrifice. He made eternal life possible for every human being.

I have read the biblical account of Jesus' arrest, "trial," scourging, and crucifixion hundreds of times. I take comfort in knowing that account is based on eyewitness testimonies by the Gospel writers. Many scholars believe the gospel of Mark to be one of the earliest writings in the New Testament, most probably written to Christian believers in Rome before the destruction of Jerusalem in AD 70. Mark begins his gospel by declaring that Jesus was the Messiah long prophesied in the Old Testament; thus, He is the Son of the living God, the Anointed One, the long-awaited deliverer of Israel.

Interestingly, I learned that the biblical narrative of Jesus' last day on earth parallels almost exactly what was known as the Roman Triumph. What originally was seen as a tragic defeat for Jesus and His kingdom was eventually found to be the exact opposite: the greatest triumph in history.

The Bible tells us that Jesus was born during the reign of the Roman emperor Caesar Augustus, who was the son of the assassinated Julius Caesar. Caesar Augustus vowed to build a temple to honor his murdered father and to hold a dedication ceremony to proclaim his father as divine. During that ceremony, a comet streaked through the sky—a sign that Caesar Augustus declared as confirmation that he himself must be "the Son of God," if his father, Julius Caesar, was God. From that period on, the Roman people believed Caesar Augustus to be the divine "Son of God."

What began as a way to honor conquering generals soon became limited to the emperors, proclaiming their sovereignty and divinity. The ceremony began with the Roman soldiers who assembled at the Praetorium, where the guards were stationed. Then a purple robe (the color of royalty) would be placed on the emperor and a wreath would be placed on his head. "Hail Caesar!" they would shout, and the people would chant, "Triomphe!" as the emperor and the guards wound their way along the Via Sacra in Rome to arrive at the Capitoline, or "head hill." There, a bull would be sacrificed by someone who had been carrying an instrument of death.

The emperor would then be offered a bowl of wine, which he would refuse or sometimes pour out on the head of the sacrificial bull.

Finally, the emperor would ascend the steps of the Capitoline, accompanied by someone on his left and someone on his right.

The entire population would declare him as their "savior"— their divine Caesar, proclaiming, "Hail Caesar, Lord and God!" Then they would all look for signs in the heavens to confirm their leader's coronation.

Ray brilliantly described how the description of Jesus' last days in Mark's gospel, including Jesus' suffering, perfectly paralleled the Roman procession known as a triumph.

After Jesus had been sentenced to death by Pontius Pilate, He was taken to the Praetorium in Jerusalem by the Roman guards. There, they stripped Him, threw a purple robe over Him, and placed a crown of thorns on His head. Then they mockingly worshiped Him, shouting, "Hail, the King of the Jews" and bowed down to Him, striking Him and spitting on Him.

After they had tired of this sport, they led Him away along the Via Dolorosa to be crucified. Jesus carried His own cross (instrument of death) until He collapsed beneath it. A passerby, Simon of Cyrene, was forced to carry Jesus' cross for Him to Golgotha ("the Place of the Skull").

There, the soldiers laid Jesus on the cross and crucified Him along with two revolutionaries, one on His left and one on His right. They offered Him sour wine, which He refused.

Pontius Pilate had insisted that a sign (a *titulus*—a placard that identified His so-called crime) reading "THE KING OF JEWS" be nailed to Jesus' cross. As He suffered, the crowd around Him taunted Him, "Hail, the King of the Jews." They hurled blasphemies and insults on Him.

Once Jesus gave up His spirit, there was an earthquake and the curtain at the entrance to the Holy of Holies in the temple was split in two from the top to the bottom.

Signs, indeed.

But perhaps the greatest irony was what was said by the Roman centurion who had watched the entire event: "Surely this man was the Son of God!" (Mark 15:39).

Much debate continues to exist regarding the definitive spot where Jesus was crucified—known as Golgotha—and the location of the actual tomb where Jesus was buried and resurrected on the third day. Most biblical scholars believe that the Tomb of the Holy Sepulcher is where Jesus was crucified and that He was buried close by. Others, a much smaller group, believe that the Garden Tomb was the true burial site of Jesus.

I personally have no way of knowing the truth, but I must say that when I am at the Garden Tomb, I feel deeper in my spirit His very presence.

It doesn't ultimately matter where it happened. It matters that it *did* happen!

If you visit Rome today, you will no doubt want to explore the Coliseum, built during AD 70–80. This is the largest amphitheater in the Roman world and was constructed in large part with the spoils of war after the destruction of Jerusalem and the Jewish revolt in AD 70. Even now you can still see the Titus Arch (named after the general who conquered the land), a menorah, and the trumpets and the table representing the conquered Jewish state.

The Coliseum in Rome was built to honor Caesar and the Roman kingdom, which appeared to be the most powerful "god" at the time. But the true Kingdom, and the true King, are alive and well all over the world today. The True Triumph.

Come . . . to Golgotha!

MY BROTHER: THE JEWISH BAPTIST PREACHER

Far from the land of Israel, on an island called Manhattan, stands a beautiful, historic church on 57th Street, across from Carnegie Hall. Many visitors to New York City who pass by this church are surprised to see this plaque next to its doors:

CALVARY BAPTIST CHURCH, 1847
Reverend David Epstein, Senior Pastor

Many think, "Am I seeing things? A Reverend *Epstein* of a *Baptist* church?"

Yes. My brother, Dave, is indeed the pastor of this wonderful church and has been for the last twenty years. When I told him about this book, he was quick to understand my desire to get people to truly dig deep into the greater meaning of the Scriptures.

I was delighted when he agreed to make this contribution to our efforts with insights on two of the most important Scripture readings related to our Lord's sacrifice and what it really means for us.

FATHER FORGIVE THEM . . . (LUKE 23:32—43)
By David Epstein

In Luke 23 we have the graphic story of three dead men walking: Jesus and two robbers, all condemned to death and executed together. What's so interesting is that, according to the accounts in Matthew and Mark, everyone was mocking and cursing Jesus, including the two criminals—and then Luke gives us the rest of the story.

Suddenly, around noon, three hours into the crucifixions, one robber had a change of heart. He rebuked his partner in crime, acknowledging his own guilt and the innocence of Jesus. More, he asked Jesus to "remember me when you come into your kingdom" (v. 42).

What happened? What led to this man's transformation? Jesus made seven statements while on the cross for six hours—but the only thing He said for the first three hours between 9:00 a.m. and noon was, "Father, forgive them, for they do not know what they are doing" (v. 34). The grammar indicates that Jesus offered this prayer for forgiveness more than once. The imperfect active indicative translated in most versions as "Jesus said" actually indicates more continuous or repeated action, not a onetime statement. The biblical Greek word ἔλεγεν literally means "He was saying"; therefore, this prayer for forgiveness was the recurring theme for three hours.

The only way to understand one man's transformation is by the amazing power of forgiveness—God's love. The result was: "Remember me." And the response of Jesus was: "Truly I tell you, today you will be with me in paradise" (v. 43).

So why did one man embrace forgiveness and the other refuse it? Only God knows. The real question is: *Which of the two are you?*

THEY SHALL NEVER PERISH . . .
(JOHN 10:27–30)
By David Epstein

Everything we love the most in life can be lost. Does that include salvation itself? Can we lose God's love? In John 10:28, Jesus, while describing Himself as the Good Shepherd who loves and sacrifices His life for His sheep, declared: "I give them eternal life, and they shall never perish." How strong is this promise?

In biblical Greek, the strongest negative that exists is called emphatic negation. It occurs when the negative particle of the indicative mood, ου, in concert with the negative particle of the non-indicative mood, μη, is joined to the verb—in this case, απολωνται, which means "to perish" or "to be destroyed."

What Jesus means is this: Those who genuinely believe in Him will never lose His love—they are saved and secure forever. No one who follows Him will ever, under any circumstances, for any reason, perish. Jesus isn't a liar. His death was not in vain ("the Good Shepherd gives His life for the sheep"), His promise is not in doubt ("they shall never perish"), and His power is not in question ("no one will snatch them out of my hand" or "my Father's hand"—a two-fisted salvation).

Therefore, salvation is not just a gift that God gives to us, which is wonderful enough, but we are a gift exchanged between the Father and the Son. Salvation is not just something that belongs to us; more importantly, we belong to Him. When will the Father take back the gift He gave to His Son? When will the Son take back the gift He gave to His Father? *Never!*[1]

When Jesus went to the cross, He didn't say, "Father, I hope this works." He said, "It is finished." That phrase, τετελεσται, is a biblical Greek word signifying a completed action in the past, on the cross, with continuing life-changing consequences in the present. It means paid in full. Mission accomplished. You can go to the bank on it!

Jesus didn't die on Good Friday so the whole world *might* get saved, only to get lost again. Jesus died on Good Friday so the whole church *would* get saved—and stay saved forever. There is no "maybe," or "hope so," or "might be" in the death of Jesus. There is only "yes" and "know so" and "shall be."[2]

MORE FROM RABBI JASON

GOLGOTHA, THE CRUCIFIXION, AND ADAM

Have you ever wondered why Jesus had to die on a cross? The answer given by most people is that this was a common means of execution by the Romans. But surely something as important as the death of God's Son was not based solely upon Rome's proclivity for brutal means of execution like crucifixion. There must be something more.

How did sin enter the world? The first man and woman took from the tree of the knowledge of good and evil, and they ate the one thing in the garden of Eden that the Lord had prohibited (Genesis 3:6). Their disobedience led to the fall and their exile from Eden.

Redemption required a repair (*tikkun*, in Hebrew) for their sin. The first man and woman could not correct what they had done. What did God do? Since sin entered by means of a tree, God put His Son on a tree, in the form of a cross, to redeem us from the sin of the first man and woman. The Lord put Jesus, the second Adam, back on the tree for you and me to restore and make restitution for what had been stolen from the tree in the garden.

The first Adam brought death by means of a tree, but the second Adam brought life by means of His death on one! Concerning this, the apostle Paul wrote: "For since death came through a man, the resurrection of the dead also has come through a Man. For as in Adam all die, so also in Messiah will all be made alive. But each in its own order: Messiah the firstfruits; then, at His coming, those who belong to Messiah" (1 Corinthians 15:21–23 TLV).

Thank God for the tree, for it is the means by which the Lord sets us free and makes eternal life possible.

As always, there is even more. As Jesus hung on the cross, He had a crown of thorns on His head. Have you ever wondered why? The Roman soldiers put a crown of thorns on His head to mock His claim to be King Messiah. But the deeper spiritual reason for the crown of thorns also ties back to the garden of Eden. The sign of the curse of creation was that the ground would "produce thorns and thistles" (Genesis 3:18). By wearing a crown of thorns at His crucifixion, Jesus, the second Adam, took upon Himself the curse of creation, to undo it for the purpose of restoring the blessing!

Not only was Jesus' head pierced, but His hands, feet, and side were pierced as well. His hands were pierced, for it was with human hands that Adam and Eve stole from the tree. His side was pierced, because it was Eve, the one taken from Adam's side, who led Adam into temptation—I believe that by having His side pierced, Jesus was making atonement for the woman's role in the fall. Finally, Jesus' feet were pierced, because the first messianic prophecy states that the seed of the woman, meaning the messianic seed, would come and crush the head of the serpent, as stated in Genesis 3:14–15:

> ADONAI *Elohim* said to the serpent, "Because you did this,
> Cursed are you above all the livestock
> and above every animal of the field.
> On your belly will you go,
> and dust will you eat
> all the days of your life.
> I will put animosity
> between you and the woman—
> between your seed and her seed.
> He will crush your head,
> and you will crush his heel." (TLV)

Messiah's hands and feet were pierced so that He might overcome sin, Satan, and death for our sake. And Jesus wearing the crown of thorns demonstrates that He loved us so much that He was willing to identify with our pain and suffering and taste death so that we might experience life!

CHAPTER 23

JERUSALEM

The Jewish Festivals

*The LORD said to Moses, "Speak to the Israelites and say to
them: 'These are my appointed festivals, the appointed festivals
of the LORD, which you are to proclaim as sacred assemblies.'"*

—LEVITICUS 23:1—2

I think if you ask most believers if they have ever heard that
everything important in Jesus' life took place during one of
the traditional Jewish festivals, they would probably say no. Most
wouldn't even be able to list the Jewish festivals, much less describe
the importance of them in Jewish life. This is typical of the problem
we are up against as we try to educate Christians regarding the
foundations of our faith. Perhaps if we could learn how important
Jesus felt these festivals were, we might grow to understand how
important they should be to us as believers.

The city of Jerusalem is an integral part of these Jewish festivals. The Lord declared, "I have chosen Jerusalem for my Name to be there" (2 Chronicles 6:6). Thus, Jerusalem became the spiritual center of Israel, the place where God would place His name, causing His presence to dwell in the temple. Jerusalem was the place of pilgrimage, for everyone in Israel was commanded by God to appear before Him three times a year—during the three pilgrimage festivals of Passover, Pentecost, and Tabernacles—to offer sacrifices and firstfruit offerings in the temple.

Understanding the setting and celebration of these Jewish festivals brings new light to familiar stories of Jesus' life. For example, Jason explained to me during our first meeting in December 2016 that on the night that Jesus was born, the shepherds in the fields and the sheep they were tending were not ordinary sheep or shepherds. (He mentioned these truths earlier in this book, but they are worth repeating.)

The Bible is clear that the land directly surrounding Jerusalem was controlled by the Levitical priests, and everything either grown, raised, or born in that area was for one purpose: to be sacrificed on the altar of God in the temple of God for the people of God. Bethlehem is only three miles away from Jerusalem.

When we understand the Jewish feast of Passover, we realize the sheep that the shepherds were tending were born for the same reason that Jesus was born: to die for the forgiveness of sins! And just as Jesus was perfect, these lambs raised to be Passover sacrifices had to be perfect, too, without any defect or blemish. Do you know what shepherds in Bethlehem used to do to assure a sheep's perfection when it was first born? They wrapped the newborn lamb in swaddling cloths and laid it in a manger!

When the angel explained this sign to the Levitical shepherds, they would have understood the significance of finding the newborn baby wrapped in swaddling cloths and lying in a manger, because they knew that this baby was holy—set apart for sacred use—and in fact, this baby would be "the Lamb of God, who takes away the sin of the world!" (John 1:29), as John the Baptist later described Him.

Do you see how understanding the Jewish feasts can shed new light on the Scripture? If you don't have goose bumps right now, I haven't done a very good job of explaining this!

As Rabbi Jason explains next, every major event in Jesus' life happened on a Jewish holiday.

Come . . . to Jerusalem!

MORE FROM RABBI JASON

AN OVERVIEW OF GOD'S APPOINTED FEASTS

Every follower of Jesus should be interested in the biblical holidays because Jesus Himself celebrated the Jewish festivals! More importantly, every major event in Jesus' life occurred on one of these Jewish holidays. For instance, Jesus is said to have been born around the time of Sukkot, the festival that focuses on God's presence, provision, and protection. Jesus' death was on Passover, the holiday that promises redemption. As we saw in chapter 19, the Last Supper of our Lord was a Passover Seder.

The biblical holidays are part of the inheritance of all followers of Messiah. Understanding the holidays gives us a deeper understanding and greater insight into the person and work of Jesus. Since much of Jesus' life and ministry revolved around the Jewish festivals, a fuller revelation of Jesus can be ours when we grasp the significance of these appointed times.

On the lighter side, as you study the Jewish feasts, you will find that our God is not merely about fasting; He is also very fond of feasting. He is a God of celebration. He wants you to come and join His party. Now let's take a moment to briefly explore the spiritual meaning and transformative nature of these biblical holidays.

Leviticus 23 describes the calendar of yearly feasts for God's people, breaking them into three cycles. The weekly celebration of the Sabbath (*Shabbat*, in Hebrew) is the first holiday mentioned. This Hebrew word means "rest." God rested on the seventh day and commanded Israel to do the same in the Ten Commandments (Exodus 20:8). From the days of Moses to the present, the Jewish people have celebrated the *Shabbat* starting at sundown on Friday and ending at sundown on Saturday. God rested on the seventh day, so we do as He did.

The spring holidays are Passover, Firstfruits, and Pentecost. These are holidays that reflect God's work of the past and were fulfilled in the first coming of Messiah. If you're scratching your head, let me explain briefly.

PASSOVER AND REDEMPTION

The focus of Passover (*Pesach*, in Hebrew) is redemption, which leads to freedom. The Lord redeemed the Israelites from Egypt, freeing them from the bondage of slavery. Centuries later, Jesus (*Yeshua*, in Hebrew) died as the Passover Lamb to redeem us from death and break the bondage of sin. Redemption in the days of Moses was meant to mirror the future redemption through the death of Messiah. Jesus is the ultimate fulfillment of the promise of redemption.

THE FEAST OF FIRSTFRUITS AND THE RESURRECTION

During the celebration of Firstfruits (*Yom HaBikkurim*, in Hebrew), the focus is resurrection. This was an agricultural holiday that celebrated the firstfruits of the harvest, which were brought from the fields to the temple on the second day of Passover. Fittingly, thousands of years later, Jesus was brought back from the dead during this festival. In 1 Corinthians 15:20, Paul tells us, "But now Messiah has been raised from the dead, the firstfruits of those who have fallen asleep" (TLV). Though Jesus fulfilled the promise of this holiday in His resurrection, there is also a prophetic fulfillment of this feast in which the firstfruits of the harvest symbolize the future resurrection of believers at the end of the age.

PENTECOST, SINAI, AND THE GIFT OF THE HOLY SPIRIT

The Feast of Pentecost (*Shavuot*, in Hebrew) focuses on revelation. This holiday commemorates the giving of the Torah to Moses on Mount Sinai. During Jesus' time on earth, He gave the Holy Spirit to the disciples in Jerusalem on Pentecost. There is something significant about the fact that God chose the same day, both in the Old Testament and New Testament, to give the gift of Word and Spirit. In Genesis 1, the Spirit hovered over the formless surface of the watery earth, then God spoke the words, "Let there be light," and there was light (Genesis 1:3). Word and Spirit combined to bring about new creation and greater revelation.

During His lifetime, Jesus fulfilled the focus and promise of all three spring holidays—redemption, resurrection, and revelation.

THE FEAST OF TRUMPETS AND THE RETURN OF MESSIAH

The fall holidays are *Rosh Hashanah* (Feast of Trumpets), *Yom Kippur* (Day of Atonement), and *Sukkot* (Feast of Tabernacles). These holidays are awaiting their prophetic future fulfillment.

Rosh Hashanah (Feast of Trumpets) is the Jewish New Year and is "trumpeted in" with the blowing of the *shofar* (a ram's horn). This holiday points to repentance (changing one's way of thinking and being), resolving to make a better life, and ideally returning or regathering to God. At the sound of the *shofar* in a day yet to come, God will gather all His people from the four corners of the earth to Himself at the return of Messiah (Isaiah 27:13; 1 Corinthians 15:52; 1 Thessalonians 4:16).

THE DAY OF ATONEMENT AND THE REDEMPTION OF ISRAEL

Yom Kippur means "atonement," or to repair a wrong so that we can be one with the Holy One. (Notice the word *atonement* can be broken down as at-one-ment.) This feast also focuses on repentance and redemption and forgiveness from the sins of the previous year. In the future fulfillment of this holiday, all Israel, as well as all the nations, will look upon the One they pierced and recognize Him as the Messiah (Zechariah 12:10). This will result in the fullness of redemption being realized. In Jewish thought, this is the final redemption.

THE FEAST OF TABERNACLES AND THE MESSIANIC KINGDOM

Sukkot (Feast of Tabernacles) is a time for rejoicing. This holiday commemorates the wandering of the Israelites in the desert. The shelters (*sukkot*, in Hebrew) relate to the temporary structures in which they lived as they wandered. This holiday commemorates how God provided manna from heaven to feed them, water from the stones to quench them, and a pillar of cloud by day and fire by night to guide them. Ultimately, it reflects God's presence, provision, and protection. Many Messianic Jews believe that Jesus was born during this holiday. When the future promise of Sukkot is fulfilled, the kingdom of God will be established, and we will all rejoice. According to the prophet Zechariah, all the nations of the world will join the Jewish people in

Jerusalem to celebrate the Feast of Tabernacles. "Then all the survivors from all the nations that attacked Jerusalem will go up from year to year to worship the King, ADONAI-Tzva'ot, and to celebrate *Sukkot*" (Zechariah 14:16 TLV).

In addition to the fall and spring holidays, which are known as the major holidays and are found in Leviticus 23, there are two other minor but key Jewish holidays mentioned in Scripture: Purim and Hanukkah.

THE FEAST OF PURIM, ESTHER, AND THE PROVIDENCE OF GOD

Purim is found in the book of Esther. Intrigue, sabotage, fear, courage, romance, and rising to one's destiny may sound like a soap opera, but the story of Esther is a chronicled struggle between good and evil, where the hidden hand of God isn't seen but is at work on behalf of His people. The story of Esther and the celebration of Purim is ultimately about God working all things together for the good (Romans 8:28). At Purim, we realize that when we cannot see the providential hand of God, we must trust the heart of God. Realizing the goodness of the Father stirs us to rejoice!

THE FEAST OF DEDICATION AND THE LIGHT OF THE WORLD

Hanukkah is the Feast of Dedication found in both the book of Daniel and the gospel of John. It commemorates the miraculous rededication of the temple in Jerusalem after it was defiled by the Greeks. It honors and celebrates the miracles God did, such as one night's *cruse* (jug) of oil for the menorah providing eight nights' worth of light and the victory of the outnumbered Israelites over the Greeks. God delivered the many into the hands of the few, proving Zechariah 4:6, which declares, "'Not by might nor by power, but by my Spirit,' says the LORD Almighty." Some believe that Jesus called Himself "the light of the world" in John

8:12 during Hanukkah, while others believe He made this statement during Sukkot. In John 10, Jesus went up to Jerusalem with His disciples to celebrate the Feast of Dedication. This holiday's prophetic fulfillment will occur when the light of the Messiah shines forth to all the ends of the world and we become the light that God calls us to be.

Why is learning about these Jewish festivals so important? It is in looking back at what God has done that we can see forward to His future plans for us. "'For I know the plans I have for you,' declares the LORD, 'plans to prosper you and not to harm you, plans to give you hope and a future'" (Jeremiah 29:11).

CHAPTER 24

THE UPPER ROOM AND TEMPLE COURTS

Pentecost Sunday

When the day of Pentecost came, they were all together in one place. Suddenly a sound like the blowing of a violent wind came from heaven and filled the whole house where they were sitting. They saw what seemed to be tongues of fire that separated and came to rest on each of them.

—ACTS 2:1–3

During our first Rock and Road Experience tour with Ray, he explained to us that two important events occurred in Acts 2:1–3. The first thing that happened is the Holy Spirit entered the room and rested on all the believers there. The second is that the disciples traveled a short way to the steps leading up to the temple.

Come . . . to the Upper Room!

More from Rabbi Jason

The Upper Room, Pentecost, and Sinai Revisited

The Upper Room was not only the place of the Last Supper, but it was also where the disciples prepared themselves to receive the gift of the Holy Spirit on Pentecost (Acts 2).

It is impossible to fully grasp the outpouring of God's Spirit (and what is commonly understood as the birth of the church) without first understanding the biblical roots of Pentecost. *Pentecost*, which means "Fifty Days," is the Greek term for the biblical Jewish holiday known as *Shavuot*, the Feast of Weeks (Exodus 34:22; Leviticus 23:9–22; Deuteronomy 16:10).

God commanded Israel upon entering the Promised Land to count seven complete weeks, starting on the second day of Passover, and on the fiftieth day to celebrate *Shavuot/Pentecost*. *Shavuot* in part was an agricultural holiday that began on the second day of Passover with the offering of the firstfruits of the barley harvest and culminated fifty days later with the offering of the firstfruits of the wheat harvest.

Jesus died on Passover. He also rose from the dead on the holiday called Firstfruits (*Yom HaBikkurim*), which was an agricultural holiday that took place on the second day of Passover. In ancient times, an offering of the firstfruits of the barley harvest was given to the Lord. It would be waved before the Lord as a sign of thanksgiving and in eager expectation of greater blessing to come. If you had a good early harvest, it was a guarantee that you would also have an abundant later harvest. Not only were the firstfruits a sign of the greater harvest to come, but the feast started the forty-nine-day countdown to Shavuot/Pentecost.

149

Nothing is random with God. Therefore, it is appropriate that Jesus, who died on Passover, would arise from the dead as "the firstfruits of those who have fallen asleep" (1 Corinthians 15:20). After He rose, He instructed the disciples to "not leave Jerusalem, but wait for the gift my Father promised. . . . For John baptized with water, but in a few days you will be baptized with the Holy Spirit" (Acts 1:4–5). Jesus' resurrection on the Feast of Firstfruits started the countdown to Pentecost, which was His Father's gift—the biggest biblical God party on record, where God literally rocked the house, and there were three thousand salvations in one day! Jesus not only died as the Passover Lamb but was raised from the dead on the day the firstfruits of the barley were offered in the temple!

Why did Jesus choose Pentecost Sunday as the day to pour out the Holy Spirit? To understand this question, one must know the key historical event that happened on this day. It was on the fiftieth day of Israel's coming out of Egypt that the Lord descended upon Mount Sinai and spoke the Ten Commandments to Israel. Thus, Shavuot is also known as *Zeman Mattan Torateinu*, or "the Time of the Giving of the Torah."

It is critical to understand that the Torah and the Spirit were given on the same day, the fiftieth day. But why is this so important? At the start of creation, "The earth was chaos and waste, darkness was on the surface of the deep, and the *Ruach Elohim* [Spirit of God] was hovering upon the surface of the water. Then God said, 'Let there be light!' and there was light" (Genesis 1:2–3 TLV). How does the Lord bring life out of the chaos and the darkness? By His Word and Spirit! In the same way that the original creation was birthed through Word and Spirit, the work of the new creation begins by God giving His Word and climaxes in the giving of His Spirit on the exact same calendar day so that we might experience the life and light of God's transforming power!

But there is still more! On the Day of Pentecost in the New

Testament, "a sound like the blowing of a violent wind came from heaven and filled the whole house where they were sitting. They saw what seemed to be tongues of fire that separated and came to rest on each of them. All of them were filled with the Holy Spirit and began to speak in other tongues as the Spirit enabled them" (Acts 2:2–4).

From a Jewish perspective, Acts 2 is considered to be a reenactment of Mount Sinai or, better yet, a second Sinai experience. The booming of the wind was like the thunderings at Sinai, and the tongues of fire over the disciples' heads were akin to the cleft tongue that came out of the mouth of God when He uttered the Ten Commandments. *Targum Neofiti*, an ancient Aramaic paraphrase of the Hebrew Bible, describes the giving of the Ten Commandments by the mouth of God, "like torches of fire, a torch of fire to the right and a torch of flame to the left. It flew and winged swiftly in the air of the heavens and turned around and became visible in all the camps of Israel and . . . became engraved on the two tablets of the covenant."[1]

In Acts 2, God again imprinted His Word as He did on Sinai. This time the stone of Sinai was replaced as God wrote His new covenant: "I will make a new covenant with the people of Israel. . . . I will put my law in their minds and write it on their hearts" (Jeremiah 31:31, 33). God does not want His Word to remain written on stone tablets; He wants His words to be written on our hearts by the power of the Spirit!

As God redeemed Israel, He has redeemed us through Messiah, and by His power He is transforming all who believe into new creations with new identities and purpose. Israel was called a royal priesthood, a holy nation, on Mount Sinai. Peter declares the same for us:

> But you are a chosen people, a royal priesthood, a holy nation, God's special possession, that you may declare the praises of

him who called you out of darkness into his wonderful light. Once you were not a people, but now you are the people of God; once you had not received mercy, but now you have received mercy. (1 Peter 2:9–10)

Peter himself became a new creation during Pentecost. Instead of the cowering coward who denied Jesus three times, he became *Petra* (Peter), living up to the name Jesus gave him, which means "rock." Peter, filled with the power of the Holy Spirit, preached his first sermon and birthed the early church during this Pentecost. Just as in Genesis, as the Spirit hovered over the deep, God spoke the Word, and creation occurred. As it was in the beginning, so it was on that Shavuot (Pentecost) in Jerusalem—the union of Word and Spirit swelled the ranks of the followers of Yeshua by three thousand new creations that day. Word and Spirit resulted in newness of life!

Remember, what God has done in the past, He wants to do again in the present and the future. The past is more than events that have already happened. Those events reflect the heart of God and what He desires to do in and through you. Seek the Lord for your own personal Pentecost as individuals and as a church, and watch the amazing work of transformation that comes through His Word and Spirit.

CHAPTER 25

THE TEMPLE MOUNT

The Spiritual Center of the World

I have chosen Jerusalem that My Name would abide there.
—2 CHRONICLES 6:6 TLV

The Temple Mount in Jerusalem is a deeply moving, almost otherworldly place to visit. I always have dual emotions when I enter the courtyard that leads to the Western Wall. I can't help but cry for all that was lost due to Israel's disobedience to God and His law, resulting in the numerous times that it was destroyed. And yet there were also those thrilling times when the people of Israel repented of their sins and asked for God's forgiveness. And God faithfully answered their prayers.

It's almost a metaphor for our own spiritual ups and downs. No doubt the Temple Mount is steeped in history and future end times significance.

Come . . . to the Temple Mount!

MORE FROM RABBI JASON

JERUSALEM, THE SPIRITUAL CENTER OF CREATION AND OUR FUTURE HOME

New York is known as the "city that never sleeps." There is a palpable energy to New York City that makes it unique. On a spiritual level, Jerusalem is similar. Jerusalem abounds with the palpable presence of God that makes the city spiritually electric. Just walking the streets of the Old City can be a spiritual experience. But what makes the city of Jerusalem so special and unique?

The uniqueness of Jerusalem can be attributed to the fact that it is the city chosen by God to be the spiritual center of Israel and ultimately the whole world. Concerning Jerusalem, the Lord declared, "I have chosen Jerusalem that My Name would abide there and I have chosen David to be over My people Israel" (2 Chronicles 6:6 TLV). Israel was chosen to be the political center but more importantly the spiritual center, the place where God would place His Name and cause His presence to dwell in the temple.

One of the primary reasons Jerusalem is the spiritual center of the world is the Temple Mount.

To better understand this, we must go back to the first book of the Bible. The father of faith and the first Hebrew patriarch was Abraham. Abraham went through ten trials of faith that demonstrated both his faithfulness and complete, loving devotion to the Creator of all. At his first trial, Abraham heard the divine command, "Get going out from your land, and from your relatives, and from your father's house, to the land that I will show you" (Genesis 12:1 TLV). At the tenth and final trial, Abraham heard similar words: "Take your son, your only son whom you love—Isaac—and go to the land of Moriah, and offer him there as a burnt offering on one of the mountains about which I will tell you" (Genesis 22:2 TLV).

To which mountain did the Lord lead Abraham? It was Mount Moriah in Jerusalem, the same mountain that the Lord chose for the site of the temple, His abode in this world. God is love (1 John 4:8), and Mount Moriah is the place where one of the first and greatest demonstrations of love for the Lord occurred through Abraham. Can there be any greater act of love than offering your beloved child who was born supernaturally in old age in fulfillment of the Lord's promise? Abraham was not just offering the one he most loved, but he was putting his entire future on that altar. What an act of radical love!

It was on this mountain that God's covenant was confirmed for the final time to Abraham, which caused the Lord to choose the summit of Mount Moriah as the site of the temple's Holy of Holies, the ultimate embodiment of the relationship between God and His people, Israel. Mount Moriah is the location where Abraham demonstrated his great love for God and the place where the first commandment was most tangibly demonstrated for the first time! This is also the place where Abraham met and paid tithes to Melchizedek, the king of the city of Salem.

The site of Mount Moriah was also significant for King David. In 2 Samuel 24, Satan incited King David to take a census of the people. When David realized that his decision to number the people was sinful in the sight of God, he turned to the Lord and prayed to be forgiven. In response, the Lord sent the prophet Gad to King David. Gad told David that he must choose one of the following punishments: either seven years of famine, three months of running from his adversaries who would seek his life, or three days of pestilence from the Angel of the Lord (2 Samuel 24:11–13).

David chose the third of these three options, declaring that he would rather "fall into the hands of the LORD, for his mercy is very great" (1 Chronicles 21:13). As a result, God sent an angel to bring a plague throughout the land. Upon reaching Jerusalem, the Lord commanded the angel to desist. As the angel of the Lord stood by the threshing floor of Ornan the Jebusite on Mount Moriah, David's eyes perceived this angel "standing between heaven and earth, with a drawn sword in his hand extended over Jerusalem" (v. 16). The angel then commanded David through the prophet Gad to build an altar to the Lord on this site. This is believed to be the very same site at which Abraham offered Isaac and encountered the Lord! This was the site of Solomon's temple, the very place where the presence of God dwelled among His people.

Even in Babylonian exile, after the temple was destroyed, Daniel prayed three times a day toward the Temple Mount in Jerusalem at the time the daily sacrifices should have been offered.

In 538 BC, Zerubbabel, the leader of the tribe of Judah, returned as part of the first wave of exiles who came back to Jerusalem (Ezra 1:1–2). By command of the Persian king Cyrus, Zerubbabel, who was appointed as the governor of Judah, began to rebuild the temple with the assistance of the high priest Joshua (Ezra 3:2–3, 8). It took several years to rebuild the temple's foundation, and construction was delayed due to hostility from the Samaritans (Ezra 4:1–5). Because of this political opposition, the work of the temple was stopped for seventeen years (Ezra 4:21). Through the support of Ezra and the prophetic encouragement of Zechariah and Haggai, Zerubbabel resumed the work on the temple. After several years of construction, in 516 BC the temple was finally finished and dedicated with great joy (Ezra 6:16). The temple built by Zerubbabel is often referred to as the Second Temple.

Upon seeing the Second Temple, some of the Jewish returnees from Babylonian exile felt a tremendous sense of disappointment. In their eyes, it fell far short of the beauty and glory of Solomon's temple. It was much smaller, less ornate, did not house the ark of the covenant, and its dedication was not accompanied by any miracles such as the presence of God consuming the sacrifices on the altar.

Even though all the above was true, the Lord spoke through the prophet Haggai, saying, "'The glory of this latter House will be greater than the former,' says ADONAI-Tzva'ot. 'In this place, I will grant *sha-lom*'—it is a declaration of ADONAI-Tzva'ot" (Haggai 2:9 TLV). How was this fulfilled? God used Herod the Great to bring this prophecy to pass. Herod began a large-scale renovation of the temple and expansion of the Temple Mount. The work on the Second Temple was one of the largest construction projects of the first century BC. Because of the immense resources Herod invested, the Second Temple became one of the wonders of the ancient world. Herod's motivation, according to the historian Josephus, was to make a name and legacy for himself— but God used this ambition to fulfill His promise made through Haggai about the glory of the latter House (Haggai 2:3–9). This is a great reminder that God can use anyone, even if they are not aware of it, to fulfill His plans and purposes. The Second Temple stood on the Temple Mount from 516 BC until AD 70, when it was destroyed by the Romans.

Like Daniel did when he was in exile, traditional Jews still pray toward the Temple Mount in Jerusalem. It was and always will be the holiest site and the place of the Lord's abode. Jews pray at the Western Wall (*kotel*, in Hebrew) for this reason. The Western Wall is the only remaining wall of the Temple Mount, so the Western Wall remains are holy ground due to their proximity to the Holy of Holies.

But of course there is more! Song of Solomon 2:9 states: "Look! He is standing behind our wall—gazing through the windows, peering through the lattice" (TLV). Many Jewish rabbis interpret "our wall" in this verse as referring to the Western Wall. The reason is that the Hebrew word for "wall" in this passage is *kotel*, the Hebrew name for the Western Wall.

Song of Solomon 2:9 is also seen as connected to another promise that the Lord made to King Solomon in 1 Kings 9:3: "The LORD said to him: 'I have heard the prayer and plea you have made before me; I have consecrated this temple, which you have built, by putting my Name there forever. My eyes and my heart will always be there.'" These verses are a promise that the Western Wall will never be destroyed because the Lord keeps watch over it in perpetuity.

The Zohar, a mystical commentary on the Torah, takes it a step further, explaining that the Hebrew word *kotel* can be broken into two parts, *ko* and *tel*. The letter *ko* has the numerical value of twenty-six, which is the same as the tetragrammaton (הוהי), the four letters in Hebrew that are often translated into English as YHVH or Yahweh. *Tel* is Hebrew for "hill." Thus, the name *kotel* is meant to allude to the fact that God's presence will always dwell on the Mount of God at the Western Wall.

For two thousand years, the Jewish people have mourned the destruction of the Second Temple. Each year, on the ninth day of the Hebrew month of Av (the day the temple was destroyed in AD 70), observant Jews fast, mourn, and pray for the rebuilding of the temple in Jerusalem. But why would the Lord allow the temple to be destroyed? The choice of the location for the temple was connected to—and symbolic of—its spiritual foundation, which was love. The First Temple was destroyed because of idolatry, and the Second Temple was destroyed due to a senseless hatred that Jewish people had toward one another.

Thus, the First Temple was destroyed when Israel broke the first and greatest commandment, which is, "Love the LORD your God with all your heart and with all your soul and with all your strength" (Deuteronomy 6:5). The Second Temple was destroyed when Israel broke the second greatest commandment, which is, "Love your neighbor as yourself" (Leviticus 19:18).

When love was lost, God's house crumbled because its foundation was destroyed! Jesus came proclaiming and embodying the love of God. He offered the cure that could have prevented the temple's destruction as well as the painful tragedy of exile that resulted and continues to this day.

Love builds; hate destroys. The questions we must ask ourselves as we reflect on the reason for the destruction of the temple are: "Have I learned lessons of love?" and "Whom am I harboring hate and offense in my heart toward?" Hatred and offense build fences that block us from having a real, meaningful connection to God and others. If we harbor offense and bitterness in our hearts, then we are also guilty of contributing to the destruction of God's house, the temple. But if we come in the opposite spirit, one of gratuitous radical love, then we are helping to pave the way for the return of Jesus and the restoration of God's temple in Jerusalem, a place of worship for Israel and the nations!

Clearly, the Temple Mount is important to the Jewish people. But how important should it be for Christians? I believe this is an important question to answer.

On at least three occasions, Jesus lamented over Jerusalem. Jesus even wept over the impending destruction of Jerusalem because of their senseless hostility and rejection of Him as their Messiah:

As He drew near and saw Jerusalem, He wept over her, saying, "If only you had recognized this day the things that lead to *shalom*! But now they are hidden from your eyes. For the days will come upon you when your enemies will surround you with barricades and hem you in on all sides. And they will smash you to the ground—you and your children within you. And they won't leave within you one stone upon another, because you did not recognize the time of your visitation." (Luke 19:41–44 TLV)

If Jesus was saddened over Jerusalem's fate, should we not be as well? Should not those who call themselves His disciples also care for Jerusalem and the Jewish people? As the psalmist exhorted, "Pray for the peace of Jerusalem: 'May they prosper who love you'" (Psalm 122:6 NASB). This promise of prosperity is rooted in the promise that God made to Abraham concerning his descendants: "I will bless those who bless you, and the one who curses you I will curse. And in you all the families of the earth will be blessed" (Genesis 12:3 NASB). Praying for Jerusalem and the Jewish people is one way to bless Israel and experience the promise that is attached to it.

By praying for Jerusalem and the Jewish people, we are not just demonstrating concern for the city that the Lord loves, but also our desire to see His kingdom come on earth as it is in heaven. The final redemption of the world is dependent upon Israel's acceptance of Jesus as King Messiah:

O Jerusalem, Jerusalem who kills the prophets and stones those sent to her! How often I longed to gather your children together, as a hen gathers her chicks under her wings, but you

were not willing. Look, your house is left to you desolate! For
I tell you, you will never see Me until you say, "*Baruch ha-ba
b'shem* ADONAI. Blessed is He who comes in the name of the
LORD!" (Luke 13:34–35 TLV)

The phrase Jesus uses, "*Baruch ha-ba*," is a common Hebrew expression of welcome used to greet the groom as he walks down the aisle,
and it is used on doormats of Jewish homes in Israel. Until the Jews, as
a whole, welcome Jesus as Redeemer and Son of David, the messianic
kingdom will not be established on earth.

And what is the name of this home? The apostle John answered
this for us: "I also saw the holy city—the New Jerusalem—coming down
out of heaven from God, prepared as a bride adorned for her husband"
(Revelation 21:2 TLV). It is to this New Jerusalem that all believers will
regularly make the pilgrimage:

Then all the survivors from all the nations that attacked
Jerusalem will go up from year to year to worship the King,
ADONAI-*Tzva'ot*, and to celebrate *Sukkot*. Furthermore, if any
of the nations on earth do not go up to Jerusalem to worship
the King, ADONAI-*Tzva'ot*, they will have no rain. (Zechariah
14:16–17 TLV)

"Then they will bring all your kinsmen from all the nations,
as an offering to ADONAI, on horses and in chariots, and on
litters, mules and camels, to My holy mountain Jerusalem," says
ADONAI, "just as *Bnei-Yisrael* bring their grain offering in a clean
vessel to the House of ADONAI. I will also take some of them as
priests and for Levites," says ADONAI.

"For just as the new heavens and the new earth, which

I will make, will endure before Me"—it is a declaration of
ADONAI—"so your descendants and your name will endure."
(Isaiah 66:20–22 TLV)

In other words, Jerusalem was not just the home of David, the
prophets, and the Jewish people, but is destined to become your home
as well. In that day, Jerusalem will be a "house of prayer for all nations"
and will fulfill its ultimate destiny to be the spiritual center of God's
kingdom! It was the place of His Father's house! His Father is our Father,
so we will all one day go up to Jerusalem to worship and rejoice with
the Lord in the New Jerusalem! As we say at the end of every Passover
Seder, "Next Year in Jerusalem" or, better yet, "the New Jerusalem!" May
we all have the same heart for this amazing city and the Promised Land
as David and the Son of David, Jesus!

Should we not take seriously the command to pray for the peace
of Jerusalem and seek its well-being? All who pray for the peace of
Jerusalem will prosper.

CHAPTER 26

THE DEAD SEA

"The Waters Shall Be Healed"

*Moreover, in that day living waters will flow from
Jerusalem, half toward the eastern sea and half toward the
western sea, both in the summer and in the winter.*

—ZECHARIAH 14:8 TLV

The Dead Sea is one of the most extraordinary places in the
world. It is more than four hundred meters below sea level and
is considered the lowest point on dry land on planet Earth.

The water in the Dead Sea is almost ten times saltier than the
ocean, making it completely inhospitable to any life form. Tourists
flock to this site to enjoy the phenomenon of buoyantly floating
on the surface, completely incapable of sinking in the hypersaline
water. The beauty treatments made from the various rich minerals

in the region are legendary, and it's not uncommon to watch a sea full of people floating and laughing with their faces covered in Dead Sea mud masques.

We are told by the experts that the water level of the Dead Sea has been receding at the alarming rate of one meter a year because of water being diverted from the Jordan River for agricultural purposes and the natural evaporation caused by the sea's own mineral works.

Gazing on the area now, it's almost impossible to believe that it was once a rich, fertile landscape—so inviting, in fact, that Abraham's nephew Lot chose it from all the land as far as his eye could see. Scripture tells us, "Lot looked around and saw that the whole plain of the Jordan toward Zoar was well watered, like the garden of the LORD, like the land of Egypt" (Genesis 13:10).

What? This devastated wilderness, this wasteland, was once a garden? How is that even possible? Well, the Scriptures give us a clue: "Then said he unto me: 'These waters issue forth toward the eastern region, and shall go down into the Arabah; and when they shall enter into the sea, into the sea of the putrid waters, the waters shall be healed. And it shall come to pass, that every living creature . . . shall live; and there shall be a very great multitude of fish . . . that all things be healed. . . .'" (Ezekiel 47:8–9 JPS Tanakh).[1]

A miracle is happening this very moment in the Dead Sea. Perhaps prophetic Scripture is even being fulfilled as recently as these past five years. A young tourist named Samantha Siegel discovered something extraordinary in the waters: freshwater ponds with actual fish and green plants along the shores! She took video of the fish swimming in the water,[2] and soon scientific experts and the naturally curious were on the scene to discover the truth.

A team of researchers from Ben Gurion University in the Negev Desert sent researchers to the floor of the Dead Sea. This had never been done before, because this super-saline environment renders regular scuba gear completely inoperable.

How they did it is not as important as what they found in 2011. The divers discovered huge craters on the seafloor, fifteen meters across and twenty meters deep, full of fresh fish and covered with mats full of microorganisms, with freshwater flowing from the craters![3]

While this discovery baffles the scientific world, it causes people of faith to rejoice. Much further research shall no doubt continue, but in the meantime, we believers can find encouragement in our walk with the Rabbi and gain strength from the Word of God, which never changes.

Come . . . to the Dead Sea!

CHAPTER 27

MASADA

The Jews' Last Stand against Rome

Live as free people.
—1 PETER 2:16

Masada is one of the most extraordinary sites in all of Israel. One of Herod's most architecturally astounding palaces, it sits directly next to the Dead Sea, just twelve miles east of Arad in the Negev Desert. The fortress of Masada was built between 37 and 31 BC, but it gained notoriety when it was besieged by the Roman Empire at the end of the first Jewish-Roman War. Approximately 960 Jewish rebels famously committed mass suicide rather than be overrun by the Roman legion.

In AD 73, the Roman governor Lucius Flavius Silva began building a siege ramp against the western face of the mountain to attack the Israelites. The ramp was completed in the spring, allowing the Romans to finally breach the wall of the fortress with a battering ram on April 16.

Originally, the Jewish rebels at the top of Masada threw stones at those building the ramp to fend off their enemies. To counter this tactic, the Romans made previously captured Jewish prisoners work at the forefront of the ramp. The Jewish rebels chose not to kill their fellow Jews, knowing full well it might mean their own demise.

When the Romans finally entered the fortress, they discovered that the Jewish defenders had set everything but the food store-room on fire and had chosen to kill themselves rather than become Roman slaves. Apparently ten lots were drawn, and ten men were chosen as executioners; the rest lay down side by side and bared their necks. Finally, the last Jewish Zealot killed the remaining nine and then took his own life. The food was left untouched so the Romans would know without a doubt that the Jewish men, women, and children of Masada had not starved to death but had chosen freedom.[1]

By the way, the final day of the siege was the first day of Passover, the holiday on which the Jews celebrate their freedom from the bondage of slavery.

The lots have been discovered and can be seen today in the Israel Museum in Jerusalem. Eleven pottery shards have been excavated from the mountain. Each bears a name, including the name of the Zealot leader, Ben Yair.

We know most of these facts through the historical writings of Josephus, who had access to the Roman commanders at the time. Further testimony came from the only survivors of the Roman siege of Masada: two women and five children who had hidden during the final hours.[2]

Interestingly, coins have been found on the mountain that date all the way back to the Maccabean kings. And today, this is the site where the newest members of the Jewish army take their vows of allegiance to the state of Israel. Masada has become an eternal symbol of the Jewish fight for freedom.

Come . . . to Masada!

CHAPTER 28

THE QUMRAN CAVES

The Dead Sea Scrolls

*The grass withers and the flowers fall, but
the word of the Lord endures forever.*

—1 PETER 1:24–25

The Dead Sea Scrolls, one of history's greatest archaeological finds, were discovered between 1946 and 1947, just as the nation of Israel was being reestablished after ceasing to exist since the fall of Jerusalem to the Roman Empire in AD 70.

Talk about timing!

Some 981 ancient parchment scrolls were found in eleven caves along the northwest shore of the Dead Sea. This area is only thirteen miles east of Jerusalem, and as noted in chapter 26, it is 1,300 feet below sea level, making it the lowest point in the world.

Scholars have identified the remains of between 825 and 870 separate scrolls, and they can be divided into two categories: biblical and nonbiblical. Fragments of every book of the Old Testament except the book of Esther have been discovered, including nineteen copies of the book of Isaiah, twenty-five copies of Deuteronomy, and thirty copies of Psalms.

Interestingly, prophecies by Ezekiel, Jeremiah, and Daniel that are not included in the Bible were also written in the scrolls. And miraculously, the Isaiah scroll, found fundamentally intact, is one thousand years older than any previously known copy of the book of Isaiah.

Together, the Dead Sea Scrolls are the oldest group of Old Testament manuscripts ever found. And the way they were discovered was nothing short of miraculous.

Apparently a local Bedouin shepherd left his flock to look for a stray. As he searched, he came across a cave in the crevice on the mountainside. No one knows exactly why, but he threw a stone deep into the dark interior of the cave, only to be startled by the sound of shattered pots. When he entered the cave, he found a collection of large clay jars, most of them empty. But a few were intact and their lids were still tightly in place. When the shepherd looked further, he was disappointed at first to discover nothing in them but some old scrolls.

The truth is, this shepherd had stumbled upon one of the greatest archaeological discoveries of all time!

It is believed that the scrolls were originally written by a Jewish sect known as the Essenes sometime between 200 BC and AD 68. Though they are not mentioned by name in the New Testament, the Essenes were well documented by Josephus. They were a strict, Torah-believing, apocalyptic Jewish sect who felt that the religious leaders at the temple in Jerusalem were corrupt and had fallen away from the sacred text of Moses. They were led by a priest they called "The Teacher of Righteousness," who was opposed by the established religious leaders of the Pharisees and the Sadducees.[1]

The Essenes called themselves the "Sons of the Light," and they referred to their enemies as the "Sons of Darkness." Interestingly, they also called themselves "the poor" and members of "the Way" (the earliest name given to believers in Jesus). The Essenes believed the Holy Spirit dwelled within them, therefore they lived in "the house of holiness." Some experts believe that John the Baptist had at one time been a member of the Essene sect.

In addition to the Scripture scrolls, the Qumran caves housed many writings that were not Scripture. It's fascinating that certain biblical figures such as Abraham, Enoch, and Noah are mentioned in these additional scrolls, containing previously unknown stories about them. One scroll gives additional stories about Abraham and provides an alternate explanation of why God asked Abraham to sacrifice Isaac, his son! This Qumran text introduces a satanic figure called "Mastemah," who basically goads God into testing Abraham's faith, eerily reminiscent of Satan convincing God to test Job.[2] Numerous theories abound and are sure to be argued among scholars and lay-people alike for decades to come.

Of course, these additional sources are separate from Scripture. I just think it is interesting that they exist! These scrolls—though not Scripture—can shed extra light on the Scriptures themselves.

One of the most unusual of the Dead Sea Scrolls is the Copper Scroll, which records a list of sixty-four underground hiding places throughout Israel that are believed to be the locations of treasures from the temple in Jerusalem, hidden away for safekeeping.

Most curious is that, although the Qumran community existed during the time of Jesus' ministry, none of the scrolls mention Jesus or any of His followers by name. Regardless, the Dead Sea Scrolls reveal a community with many incredible parallels to the Jesus movement at the time. They prove that Christianity is rooted in Judaism, and the scrolls have been called "the evolutionary link" between Judaism and Christianity.

Come . . . to the Qumran Caves!

CHAPTER 29

TEL AVIV

The Mediterranean Capital of Cool

"Your prayers and gifts to the poor have come up as a memorial offering before God. Now send men to Joppa to bring back a man named Simon who is called Peter. He is staying with Simon the tanner, whose house is by the sea."

—ACTS 10:4–6

When you visit the modern, sophisticated city of Tel Aviv, it's almost impossible to picture what it once was during biblical times. Today, Tel Aviv bustles with chic hotels, five-star restaurants, and boutiques and galleries selling the latest, hottest styles—all along the natural beauty of the Mediterranean Sea. The *New York Times* called Tel Aviv "the capital of Mediterranean cool."[1]

At times when I am in Tel Aviv, I almost feel as if I am in Santa Monica, California, because the resemblance is so extraordinary.

There's a common saying in Israel today: "Jerusalem prays; Tel Aviv plays." The contrast in the two very different cities is striking.

The small ancient village of Joppa, now known as Jaffa, still survives in Tel Aviv today. Though it is now a thriving, cultural oasis of restaurants and art galleries, it was once home to the oldest seaport in the world. It was also the home of Simon the tanner, where the apostle Peter received a crucial vision from God that completely transformed his faith (Acts 10:9–16). From this extraordinary experience, Peter set out to visit the home of Cornelius the centurion, just a short journey north in Caesarea Maritima, an event we looked at previously in chapter 9. There, Cornelius and his entire household heard Peter's testimony regarding Jesus the Messiah, and the Bible tells us every member was saved. This little, picturesque seaside port in Tel Aviv is the place where a miracle occurred in one Jewish man's heart, which, in turn, set off miracles in the hearts of millions of Gentiles worldwide.

Ironically, ancient Joppa is the same port that the prophet Jonah set out from centuries before in an attempt to flee from the Lord, who had told him to go to Nineveh, also to save the lives of non-Jewish sinners in desperate need of salvation. Jonah didn't want to go. Peter didn't want to go. You know what? Sometimes I don't want to go. But we are all called to get out of our biases and our preconceived ideas of what a ministry looks like and "Go into all the world and preach the Good News to everyone" (Mark 16:15 NLT).

Come . . . to Tel Aviv!

CONCLUSION

What Is Your Stone?

*[David] took his staff in his hand, chose five smooth stones
from the stream, put them in the pouch of his shepherd's bag
and, with his sling in his hand, approached the Philistine.*

—1 SAMUEL 17:40

I returned to the *Today Show* eight days after Frank passed into glory. My children, Cody and Cassidy, came to support me, standing in the wings. On that day, I felt the Lord leading me to share something deeper about Frank than most people knew. I had no idea what I was going to say, but I had a lifetime of experience of God's faithfulness to give me the words that He would want me to share.

I told the audience that, as a child, Frank had asked Jesus into his heart as Lord and Savior. He had considered himself a Christian his whole life. But he came to realize in the Holy Land that he actually had a religion all his life, but the joy resides in the *relationship* one has with our loving God, regardless of where or how often you go to church. This was profound for him—and life-changing.

At this writing, the video of that show, which went viral imme-diately, has reached over seventy million views.[1]

So even while we grieve losing our precious husband, father, and friend, we know that Frank Newton Gifford threw his last stone, bringing God's *shalom* to the chaos of the world.

What is your stone? What is your gift? How will you know it?

What is the one thing that you can do that no one else can do but you?

What is your stone?

Going Home

August 9, 2015

Precious in the sight of the LORD is the death of his faithful servants.

—PSALM 116:15

August 9, 2015, dawned as a glorious, perfect summer Sunday. I was up early to help Cassidy get ready to leave for a flight to Santa Fe where she would begin a new film. I headed downstairs while it was still dark to let the dogs out, start the coffee, and begin my daily ritual of Scripture, prayer, and devotions while my husband, Frank, slept in upstairs. Two hours later, around 7:00 a.m., I heard the scale in Frank's bathroom declare: "Your weight is 178 pounds."

Perfect, I thought to myself. *It's going to be a good day. That's his favorite weight.*

Then Frank went about his typical morning routine: he showered, dressed in what he knew to be my favorite outfit of black jeans and a crisp white shirt, and came downstairs to pour his Dunkin

Donuts coffee and help himself to a big piece of cornbread while he opened his Bible on the big Restoration Hardware table and sat in his favorite chair, in his favorite room, in his favorite place in the world—our home in Connecticut on the Long Island Sound.

At 7:45 I saw him sitting there contentedly. As I climbed the steps to our bedroom, I told him, "I'm going to get ready for church, Frank Gifford." (I have always called him that since the day I met him.)

"Okay," he responded.

I took my time getting ready, finally heading down the staircase at 8:30, noticing the time and thinking, *Oh good, we've got an hour to have another cup of coffee before we need to leave for church.*

It's funny the things you remember.

As I descended, I looked into the sunroom, where I'd last seen him less than an hour before, but he wasn't seated at the table.

"Lamb?" I asked, thinking he might have stepped outside to watch the boats go by in the harbor.

I continued toward the sunroom and suddenly stopped in my tracks. There, on the floor just inside the sunroom, was my precious husband, lying on his back. The coffee cup had fallen, though not broken, and the coffee had spilled onto the floor.

I began to scream for help, knowing Cody was asleep on the second floor and our beloved friend Elvia Medina was in the kitchen.

Not knowing what else to do, I began to give Frank mouth-to-mouth resuscitation, praying all the while that Frank would come to, not knowing if he'd had a stroke or maybe choked on the cornbread.

Cody appeared and immediately began to give his father chest compressions, and Elvia ran to call 911. All I can remember clearly of these moments was the extraordinary, supernatural peace I was experiencing. I was able to rejoice at the same time I was trying to save Frank's life, just as Cody was. This is what the Bible calls the peace that passes all understanding (Philippians 4:7). I now know without a doubt that it is a real thing.

Finally, the EMTs arrived and confirmed to us what we already knew to be true: Frank was gone. One of them said to me after examining Frank: "Mrs. Gifford, I hope this comforts you. Your husband never knew he hit the ground." In other words, Frank never suffered.

I cried for joy hearing these words. They did comfort me, because it was an answer to prayer.

You see, my husband wasn't afraid of anything after the extraordinary life he had lived, except for one thing: he never wanted to be a burden on his family. He never wanted to be hooked up to machines or lose his dignity because of an illness.

"Please tell me if it ever gets to that, you'll pull the plug," he used to tell me.

"Honey," I'd answer each time, "I love you, but I'm not going to prison for you."

"Then trip over it!" he used to say, laughing.

But I knew his heart and I knew his wishes, and I prayed every day that when the Lord took him home, it would be instantaneously— right into Jesus' loving arms.

That's exactly what happened. When I first saw Frank lying on the floor, his eyes were wide open in astonishment as if he'd suddenly seen something amazing. Because he had.

I believe Frank saw Jesus, and Jesus took his breath away.

Isaiah 61:1–3 says:

He has sent me to bind up the brokenhearted . . .
and provide for those who grieve in Zion—
to bestow on them a crown of beauty
instead of ashes,
the oil of joy
instead of mourning,
and a garment of praise
instead of a spirit of despair.
They will be called oaks of righteousness,
a planting of the LORD
for the display of his splendor.

All of us who loved Frank beyond words experienced this same joy and peace and comfort on that day and in the days that came after.

People would say, "I'm so sorry you lost your husband." And I would always reply: "Oh, he isn't lost. I know exactly where he is."

How could we all have this otherworldly, supernatural, doesn't-make-any-human-sense joy? Because we all know Jesus personally, and His promises to us are real and His Word is true.

We know we will all see Frank again someday. And I will see my father and mother and everyone else who has passed on to glory through their faith in Jesus, the Messiah.

This is only the beginning, and there will be no end.

So I encourage you to find your stone and throw it at the chaos of this world. Serve the living God and find your purpose in Him. Rejoice in hope and overflow with joy. Lift up your hands and worship Him in spirit and truth with awe and wonder. Sing praises to His name and cast your crowns at His feet. And thank Him that you are like "an olive tree flourishing in the house of God; I trust in God's unfailing love for ever and ever" (Psalm 52:8).

Amen.

On June 16, 2017, I had the great joy of meeting Brett James in Nashville. Brett is one of the most successful songwriters in country music, and together we wrote this song about Frank's passing.

HE SAW JESUS

A little kiss, a little coffee, a little moment to pray.
Our Sunday mornings always started that way.
Makeup in the mirror, hummin' a gospel song.
When I came down the stairs I knew something was wrong.
He was lyin' on the floor. He was in a better place,
And I could tell for sure by that sweet look on his face . . .

[Chorus]
He saw Jesus. He saw Jesus.
And He took his breath away.
He was a man who never wanted to leave his house,
But he went home that day.
He saw the heavens open,
Saw the Father's open arms.
When you see that kind of love, how could you stay?
He saw Jesus. He saw Jesus,
And He took his breath away.

No, I didn't lose him. I know right where he is.
See, he was never really mine. He was always His.
And tho I miss his kisses, and I can't fill the empty space,
It helps when I remember that sweet look on his face when . . .

[Repeat chorus]

Now I know every Sunday morning when I kneel down to pray,
He'd want me to live, he'd want me to love, each and every day,
'Til I see Jesus, I see Jesus and He takes my breath away.
I'm in no hurry to leave this world behind,
But I know I'll go to a better place.
I'll see the heavens open, see the Father's open arms,
And when I feel that kind of love what can I say
But thank You, Jesus, thank You, Jesus, as You take my breath
    away.
So I'll keep breathing, I'll keep breathing,
'Til He takes my breath away.

AFTERWORD

It is the last day before this manuscript is due to the publisher. I am filled with a sense of wonderful relief that we have made the deadline, and yet a tangible anxiety nips at the edges of my mind: Did I get everything right? Did I acknowledge every source properly? Did I leave anything out that could truly bless or persuade or explain better what I long to share of my love of the Rock, the Road, and the Rabbi?

The answers to these questions are: no, hopefully, and probably!

As much as I long to understand what the words in Scripture mean, I don't agonize over the things I don't understand. There is much you just can't Google to get an answer for or you get so many divergent answers that you're more confused than when you initially asked the question.

So I embrace the miracles, the majesty, and the mystery of the Bible. I love the Scripture that says: "Now we see things imperfectly, like puzzling reflections in a mirror, but then we will see everything with perfect clarity. All that I know now is partial and incomplete, but then I will know everything completely, just as God now knows me completely" (1 Corinthians 13:12 NLT).

What a relief! And what a glorious "hope and future" awaits us (Jeremiah 29:11)!

And my favorite: "Eye has not seen, nor ear heard, nor have entered into the heart of man the things which God has prepared for those who love Him" (1 Corinthians 2:9 NKJV).

As I close this book, I rest in the assurance of Romans 8:28: "All things work together for good to those who love God, to those who are the called according to His purpose" (NKJV).

God, who knows me and loves me anyway, will forgive my shortcomings, my mistakes, and my misguided good intentions. He has done so every day of my life.

He knows my heart, and He forgets all my iniquities. Therefore, I will hit the Send button and trust that He will use this flawed effort to help bring His *shalom* to the chaos of this world. This world He created. This world full of people and creatures He loves. This world He died for, and this world He is yet coming to redeem.

Shalom Shalom
—Kathie Lee
Greenwich, Connecticut
June 30, 2017

Next year in Jerusalem!

APPENDIX

The Rock and Road Experience

What joy for those whose strength comes from the LORD,
who have set their minds on a pilgrimage to Jerusalem.
—PSALM 84:5 NLT

In October 2016, a group of fifty seminarians, messianic students, and pastors from The King's University in Dallas, Texas, traveled to Israel for a Rock and Road Experience—a Bible study tour of Israel led by Rod and Libby Van Solkema. They were the first of what I hope will result in similar groups setting out every week from every state in America to study the rabbinic way in the Holy Land.

My prayer is that evangelical Christians and Jews will agree to sponsor and fund these trips in order to bless them, and to bless Israel as well, filling planes and buses and hotels and mountaintops with seekers of deeper truth in their spiritual journeys.

Many of my Israeli friends tell me the only true friends Israel has are American evangelical Christians, because we love the Rock

(Jesus), the Road (the Holy Land), and the Rabbi (the Word of God). And we love the Jewish people. And, by the way, because of the teachings of Jesus, we also love everyone else who lives in the land.

How glorious would it be to go and then sponsor someone on such a trip? This is how we can impact the kingdom exponentially.

The first fifty will return and bring fifty others, who will return with others until one day, Lord willing, a Rock and Road Experience group will be on the Mount of Olives when the Lord Jesus Himself returns to the very spot!

Zechariah 14:4 tells us, "On that day his feet will stand on the Mount of Olives, east of Jerusalem, and the Mount of Olives will be split in two from east to west, forming a great valley, with half of the mountain moving north and half moving south."

ROCK AND ROAD EXPERIENCE TESTIMONIALS

There were so many lessons that impacted my faith during our trip to the Holy Land, but my biggest takeaway was the importance of relying on the body of Christ. During the second day of our trip I took a fall that resulted in a ligament tear in my left ankle. Being a former Special Forces medic, I knew the injury was serious. I had to make a decision to stay and push through, or head home. I decided, "This is a once-in-a-lifetime opportunity; therefore I'll endure the discomfort to continue the journey!" For the remainder of the trip my team/family encouraged and helped me along the way. Some helped me up mountains, Vicki gave me one of her walking sticks,

Rod and Kathie and many others prayed for me, Cody checked on me constantly, and Joe (who is also a former Navy SEAL) lifted my spirits by making lighthearted fun of me. By the end of the trip, I knew that there was no way I could have made it through on my own. As I was taught in the SEAL teams, I needed to rely on teamwork to accomplish the goal, and during the trip that lesson was further reinforced.

The Rock and Road Experience strengthened me as a teammate and reminded me of the importance of relying on my community, the body of Christ, and because of that I am greatly appreciative of Kathie and the Rock and Road Experience.

— REMI ADELEKE

We had the very good fortune of having Ray, Rod, and Jason as spiritual leaders during our multiple times in Israel. We learned a lot from each of them, even though individually they had a slightly different perspective.

Being in Israel brings the Bible to life. We truly feel like we walked in the footsteps of Abraham, David, John the Baptist, and most importantly Jesus. We felt the emotions Abraham must have experienced ending up in the Zin desert while obeying God's directive to walk almost 1,400 miles to arrive there. While in En Gedi, we could almost hear David expressing his beautiful thoughts, which he later wrote in the book of Psalms. Words cannot begin to express the emotions both of us felt at being baptized again in the Jordan River near where we believe John baptized Jesus. As we walked through the poppies and olive trees in the Garden of Gethsemane, we could almost feel the weight of the world and the pain upon Jesus' shoulders as He prayed on the night of His betrayal.

We are indebted that our visits to Israel have aided our continuous journey to grow closer to Christ and God!

We wish you God's blessing!

— KAREN AND WAYLAND

Unbeknownst to me when I asked to join the tour to Israel, it would change my life forever.

I walked the path of Jesus and became closer to God. I understand the Bible more from walking the path of Jesus' life. It brought it all to life for me. I could visualize all the stories in the Bible. I will forever feel connected to each person on the trip. I have many fond memories: riding the elevator with Blakely on the first night of the trip, walking the snake trail (Masada) with Rocky, the day we spent in Caesarea Maritima and Rod's moving story about his friend, and walking through the Hasmonean Aqueduct made me believe I can do anything! I will always be thankful to have met the group of strong women on this trip and shared this experience together. I will remember Rod on the edge of every rock formation, sharing all his knowledge of the Bible, thinking he was going to fall over the edge (though he was protected). Libby telling me we were going to be friends. Without a doubt meeting my roommate Stephanie, and my bus partners, Susan and Lisa.

I do not think life is an accident. God has a plan for all His sheep. Kathie Lee was the shepherd who brought us all together.

I'm forever grateful to you, Kathie.

— MARY CASALINO

The images that you may have in your mind of the Bible are brought to life by the Road that is Israel. My pilgrimage to Israel strengthened my convictions, solidified the cracks that I had created in my own faith, and ultimately brought me closer to the Rock that is Jesus Christ.

Jesus saved my soul years ago; however, in Israel, He took a broken believer and pieced that believer back together. He showed me all the answers I had been looking for and knocked down walls that I had spent years building. Aside from the growth in my personal relationship with the Rock, Jesus restored my faith in humanity. I now see God and Jesus more completely and more fully. I see His plan for mankind. I am forever grateful for my opportunity to explore this land with some of the people I love most.

My hope, in this little testimony, is that anyone on the fence about going to Israel or on the fence about their own personal faith might take the next step and reach out to our Rock. He is waiting patiently.

— CHRISTIANA GIFFORD

Picture in your mind an entire country the size of New Jersey. That's Israel—263 miles from north to south and 71 miles from east to west. Jesus' footprints covered an incredibly small square footage when you think about the impact He made across the world and for so many generations.

The landscape of Israel was unlike anything I had expected. Israel is a beautiful country, stretching from mountains to desert to rivers and seas. On our second day, we made our way into the Israeli Zin desert, where the Israelites spent most of their forty years of wandering; the two days spent there were enlightening to my spirit. It's easy to view the desert as barren, arid land where very little could grow, much less thrive, but I learned that the desert shaped the story of God's people. When He leads you into a spiritual desert, it's to draw you away from the distractions and noise of a fruitful land, and into a space that requires dependence and focus on Him alone.

The Bible refers to the desert more than any other physical place. Most of us are familiar with the Israelites' forty years of wandering through the dusty, mountainous, sandy terrain—their conversations full of grumbling, complaining, and doubting the God who had led them out of slavery in a miraculous show of protection and provision. They felt lost and stranded as they wandered deeper and deeper into the deserted unknown. What they (and we!) failed to realize, is that God didn't just deliver them from their captors and take His hands off, but He led them into the desert and continued to be their guide for those forty years, ultimately leading them directly into the Promised Land flowing with milk and honey. As we feel the temperatures and heat rise around us, when we're in the middle of fiery trials, it is imperative that we press into a God who provides and protects us, and who is leading us through the deserts and into His promised land of riches and glory.

As we trekked through the Zin desert and worked our way across the rocky landscape, we saw movement above us on the mountain. We realized that the movement was the agile balancing of small deer (they looked like goats in our eyes) nimbly traversing their environment. We watched them in amazement as we read the Scripture in Habakkuk about God equipping His people with the feet of the deer.

My time in the desert (literally) will forever change the way I prepare my heart for my times in the desert (figuratively). Rather than plead with God to deliver me out of the deserts He leads me into, I will recognize that when He draws me away from my place of comfort, it is to speak to me intimately and in silence . . . in His Holiest of Holies. Second, my prayers will receive a transformative renovation.

Rather than praying that God would take the desert away from me, I will pray like Habakkuk that instead, God would give me the feet of the deer to equip me to traverse the desert well.

—ANNE NEILSON

Our journey to the Holy Land began with an inauspicious initial destination: Hadassah Hospital. Considering Mom is the Energizer Bunny incarnate, it comes as no real surprise that she occasionally overexerts herself; and the first morning of our trip to Israel proved to be no different.

A powerful combination of jet lag, hitting the ground running, and shooting for *Today* at the Western Wall had led to some understandable fatigue (she'd kill me if I said "age-related" fatigue—so I'll hope this escapes her finely tuned editorial eye). Not one to miss the party, however, Mom marched forward bravely, leading our group full steam ahead into the beautifully vibrant Israeli countryside. She performed her leadership function admirably, until I realized that she was nowhere to be found—and attendance is something of a leadership prerequisite.

Unbeknownst to me, our human Energizer Bunny had suffered a mild case—she'd refute this diagnosis, but no one ever questioned her flare for the dramatic!—of heat exhaustion, and was resting comfortably at the bottom of a lush hillside as our group took in the stunning vista of the ancient Via Maris defining the Mediterranean coastline to the West.

As mere precaution, we escorted her to Hadassah Hospital to confirm everything was in working order. One of my most memorable experiences occurred shortly thereafter, and that was bearing witness to the incredible professionalism and unity displayed by a diverse multicultural staff at Israel's busiest healing center. From beginning to end, Christians, Jews, and Muslims worked together around the clock to ensure that my mother received world-class care.

In a region of the world often criticized for its cultural, ethnic, and religious divisions, what I witnessed was nothing short of God's mercy working through His children—irrespective of where they hailed from or what beliefs they subscribed to.

James 1:17 tells us, "Every good and perfect gift is from above, coming down from the Father of the heavenly lights, who does not change like shifting shadows." My first impression of Israel, therefore, was an unexpected yet mighty display of these perfect gifts. The kind words of a stranger. The quiet patience of a doctor. And the love for one's neighbor—especially for those seemingly different than ourselves.

— CODY GIFFORD

Walking the Bible, step by step from Old Testament to New Testament, made my religious education come to life! To stand on a spot and realize there are twenty-seven layers of history underfoot and that a stone bearing the engraving, "Entry to Solomon's Kingdom" had just been unearthed at bottom; to sail across the Sea of Galilee and walk the streets of Capernaum where Jesus ministered; and to take bread and wine in the Garden of Gethsemane while looking across at the Temple Mount, all while reading the Scripture and touching these places intimately as Thomas touched the wounds of Jesus . . . I cried tears of relief and revelation on a level that it is hard to find words to explain. I wish this gift, this grace to every being on earth.

— KELLY YAEGERMANN

There aren't enough words to describe the life-changing impact of my trip to Israel. It was refreshing. It was enlightening. It was powerful. I studied in the Holy Land during a time of my life where I was seeking direction from God. Immediately, He began to speak to me through our dynamic leaders, Rod and Libby, the land we explored, and our team members. Every day was like drinking the most refreshing cup of water. I always wanted more because it was something I had never experienced before.

Your life will be transformed after studying in the Holy Land. The Gospel stories will come alive in new and unusual ways. Your relationship with Jesus will never be the same.

— KYLE MICHAEL MILLER

I was honored to be a part of Kathie Lee's Rock and Road Experience in Israel last year. Aside from our having a chance to sing the songs we had written in various biblical settings (surreal and thrilling, to say the least), having been raised in the Jewish faith, I got a much more profound understanding of how the Old and New Testaments worked together.

As a result of climbing Israel's extraordinary mountains, bathing in its rivers, and traversing its ancient deserts, I experienced a renewed and quietly personal connection with God and my own spiritual nature. In terms of Jesus Himself, I was blown away to learn of His unflinching bravery and willingness to speak His powerful truths directly into the faces of the Roman and religious hierarchy of the day. Where most spiritual teachers through the centuries would clois-ter themselves away in some holy place and have their students come to them to "sit at the hem of their garment," not Jesus. He brought His message of love for one's fellows and of being living messengers of God's love to everyone everywhere and risked life and limb to do so.

My gratitude, respect, and love for Him is boundless, and I thank

Kathie Lee, Rod, Libby, and the others for this indescribable and unforgettable experience.

— DAVID POMERANZ
Award-winning recording artist and songwriter

On our last night in Israel, I was quite simply overwhelmed with the goodwill and beautiful spirit of my new family, the wonderful group I had been privileged to travel the Holy Land with. When I saw Kathie Lee at dinner I just had to say, "I think you brought me here to learn about Christ and what it means to be a Christian. But now that I have been here, I really think I want to be Jewish." Of course, she had the best answer anyone could give. She said, "The good news is that you can be both!"

I had arrived in Israel with, what I learned, one might call a "mustard seed" of faith. I knew that I had also brought a mountain of doubt in my carry-on. Learning about Judeo-Christian history and culture helped me see that "faith" is exactly as improbable as it sounds. To me, faith is an openness of the heart to allow the wonders in. Of course, being me, I still question everything, but that little seed is planted deeply. I believe that God loves every one of us, even the reluctant.

— VICTORIA KENNEDY

On October 28, 2016, I arrived in the land of Israel with approximately fifty other individuals. The group was comprised of pastors, faculty, and students from The King's University. Over an eleven-day span, we ate, rode the tour bus, and hiked a total of eighty-five miles together. It was a beautiful experience to observe God's people coming together to learn more about the Bible, the land, the people, and ourselves.

One of my most memorable events occurred on the third day, when the group climbed the mountain fortress of Masada. It was here where God spoke to me through Psalm 119:105, which declares, "Your word is a lamp for my feet, a light on my path." As I ascended Masada with the others, I began to better comprehend that this spiritual journey can only be accomplished one step at a time. It requires patience, perseverance, and a strong walk with God if I am to finish this race. However, I cannot become so concerned about my own spiritual well-being that I forget to acknowledge the wounded standing on the side of the mountain. Helping my fellow brothers reach the summit of Masada gave me the greatest joy because no one was left behind.

This trip and specifically this event changed my life because I began to realize it doesn't matter how fast I run, the most important goal is ensuring all of God's children finish the race.

— TERRY JACKSON

Walking the ancient paths in Israel was an experience like none other in my life. The atmosphere as well as the terrain exudes God's story wrought and etched in the fabric of the land. Walking in the footsteps of our predecessors in the faith was not only a journey in time but also a journey within.

Having served in ministry over four decades, I came to the Holy Land at the end of my own wilderness. Unbeknownst to me, God was both escorting me and awaiting my presence in specific places: the Jericho road, the caves of Adullam, and ultimately the desert. Upon the same fierce landscapes that Abraham's, Moses', and David's scorched souls encountered the living God, He was faithful to meet me in my own raw vulnerability.

What was said of Him is true: "A bruised reed he will not break, and a smoldering wick he will not snuff out" (Isaiah 42:3).

— ANONYMOUS

Being in Israel was a life-changing experience. Seeing the Scripture come to life, experiencing the land Jesus walked, and touching the promises of God is indescribable. I am more in love with the Lord and His Word than I could ever imagine, a love that grows in revelation of Him daily, through His Word and through His land.

Experiencing Israel gave me new eyes to "see" His Scripture through God's lens—His perspective—and removed the cultural blindness of my Western world lens.

— SARAH SANDERS

Visiting the land of Israel is stepping into a pivotal place in history, the present, and the days to come. Israel holds utmost importance for understanding the God of the Bible. It is also a fundamental location of world history and modern technology. It stands in the center of global politics.

Israel has something to offer everyone. Whether the feel of the ancient stones, the aroma of spices in the markets, the breathtaking sunsets over the sea of Galilee, or the feeling of arriving at an ancient homeland, Israel is a place that once experienced will never be forgotten.

— SHAWN MOIR

I was not supposed to be on this, my first, trip to Israel, but God . . .

Israel changed me in more ways than a brief story can tell. It has had a way of flowing to the plethora of deep places in my life and overflowing every valley.

Two important events occurred. First, praying at the Kotel connected me to Jewish people in an unusually significant way, where our prayers and the presence of God blended in a beautiful cacophony. Second, I told God that because a Christian in a high place blessed me, I wanted to be a blessing to another and He could use me. On the way home during the layover in San Francisco, Sarah and I met Chuck Norris and his wife, and I asked if I could pray for them. Coincidentally, they were on their way to Israel.

— KIM BEARD

On the fourth day of our trip that Kathie Lee had so graciously donated, our guide affectionately known as Rabbi Coach Rod (Rod Van Solkema) led us up a rocky road to a mountain, which many believe was the mountain where Moses received the Ten Commandments. At its crest, there was a wide, open area where our team of weary sojourners could spread out (at the encouragement of Rod) to pray and seek the God of Israel. I positioned myself behind a large rock and cried out to the Lord for the salvation of His people and His land that His Word so often attributes as key to the restoration of the world.

God never abandons those with whom He starts. Behind the rock, I had a unique sense of proximity to the divine presence as I cried out to God for all Israel "to hear" and "love the LORD" as Deuteronomy 6 states, and as the Rabbi *Yeshua* (Jesus) taught and emulated (Matthew 22:37; Luke 13:34). Hearing God's voice was distinctive for Moses on the mount then, as His voice is distinctive for all who have an intimate relationship with Him today (Hebrews 3:13–15; Psalm 95:7–8).

I will never be the same.

— J. AXTELL

Life is not a straight line! From October 27 to November 8, 2016, an unexpected change occurred in my life that caused the linear path I was on to take a turn, shall we say? There's the saying, "Life events happen"—i.e., death of a loved one, birth of a child, et al. However, toward the winding down of year 2016, a Tuesday night, before retiring to bed, while checking email, I discovered an unusual subject line: "You have been invited." I was a student—one of a group of fifty—chosen to travel to the Holy Land in an all-expenses-paid trip to Israel gifted by a philanthropist! We would go on the Rock and Road Experience, hiking the mountains of Israel.

Although there were many sacred and holy occurrences that happened there, I'd rather share a page out of my journal that I wrote upon returning home to Detroit, Michigan, that sums it up better.

November 9, 2016

To My Bet-Av Fam! I think I'm the last to get back home: Deee-troit!!

> We climbed Masada! *(hard)*
> We climbed Mt. Sinai! *(strenuous/arduous)*
> We climbed Mt. Arbel! *(rocky)*
> We climbed Mt. Olivet! *(very vertical)*
> We climbed Jericho! *(steep/steep)*
> We climbed foothills! (felt like mountains . . . LOL!)
> We crouched down w/ flashlights into caves!
> We partook of communion together!
> We hiked the "hot desert" together!
> We cooled off in En Gedi together!
> We swam together in the Dead Sea at night, floating, gazing at the stars! *(so fun)*

We had conversations about a lady who interrupted our lives—
Kathie Lee Gifford!

We cried together!

We encouraged together!

We prophesied to one another and together!

We prayed for one another!

We prayed for each other's families!

We prayed for each other's fears!

We even disagreed w/ one another!

We walked through Jaffa Gate together!

We experienced countless, beautiful hotels together! *(7 to be exact!)* Wow!

We spent 12 days together!

We spent 2 days of travel together!

We've walked Israel together! *(beautiful land)* *(God's land!)*

We were from every race and ethnic group: African American, Aussies, Chinese, Jewish, Caucasians, Scottish, et al. . . . but we became Bet-Av—family.

— JODI A. MATTHEWS
The King's University student, Jewish Messianic Studies Program

Israel rocked my soul.

Aside from frequently feeling inspired by Kathie's stories about her own time in the Holy Land, prior to arriving there myself I didn't know exactly what to expect.

Despite the various conflicts surrounding Israel, the land has remained one of the most beautiful and often undisturbed places—consisting of some of the warmest people I've ever met.

I will never forget the immense sense of peace I felt while traveling through the different cities and regions in Israel, and even more significantly, how much His presence seemed to permeate the entire land. The very last day of our journey, after having heard about all of the recent archaeological discoveries such as the Seal of Hezekiah uncovered in the ancient City of David, we met an Israeli tour guide who concluded the trip with a profound message. This enchanting young woman shared with us how "She"—meaning Israel—is getting ready for our Savior's return. "She is getting ready." I am too.

— ERIKA BROWN

This walk through Israel took me from chaos, which we spoke of often, to peace. When standing on the ground where David probably stood as he slew Goliath, where Jesus wept the night He was arrested, where the tablets were found, I saw with my own eyes how real this history is.

I had my birthday with my new friends in a boat on the Sea of Galilee, where Jesus appeared walking on water to His friends He loved. I saw how close we were traveling into the real history of the beginnings of our Christ. We got up each day with a group that started as strangers, who through morning prayer became our cohesive insula, and together we took the same journey as Christ's forebears. All this made the holy days of Easter much more as I returned home to Washington.

— BOBBI SMITH

Stop me if you've heard this one: A Hindu, a Sikh, and a group of Catholics and Christians head to Israel. . . .

Sure, it sounds like the start of a weird joke. But for me, Israel was a longtime dream. Growing up in Israel West—also known as northern New Jersey—I always imagined going to the Promised Land. I had always felt there was an energy in the land that was connected to my own, and the two times my husband and I tried to make the trip, Middle Eastern travel restrictions prevented us from going.

Fast-forward a few years, and Kathie Lee Gifford invited my husband and me on a trip she was putting together with her friends and family. I immediately said yes. My husband, Agan, had a previous work commitment he couldn't bail on, so I decided to go alone. But as she does, Kathie said she'd pray on it. And if you don't know—when Kathie Lee prays, things start to happen. Within weeks, Agan's longstanding work trip was canceled, and the two of us were heading to Israel together; our baby daughter would stay with my parents.

The first time I read the story of David and Goliath, we were sitting on rocks in the Valley of Elah. And the first time I read David's Psalms about living water, his thirst for God, and his confidence in being guided by his Shepherd despite being aggressively hunted by Saul, we were in En Gedi, the cool water falling freely in the middle of the dry, cracked desert. I had never read the Bible before, and the stories were literally coming to life, right in front of our eyes. And it was clear—like so many things in Israel—this wasn't an accident. It was divine order.

As we lay in bed at night, Agan and I talked about the day, the walk, the stones. We had conversations we'd never even considered before, thoughts and prayers fueled by the teachings or readings of the day. The truth is, we had cleared some rocky terrain in our marriage already—our infant daughter was diagnosed with and beat cancer before her first birthday. And it was impossible not to see the parallels—the signs that were placed all over the land, seemingly just for us, to remind us that we were going the right way, in life, with each other, always guided by a guide. The Guide.

We left Israel different than when we arrived—still Sikh, still Hindu—but with Shema on our lips and in our hearts, with a deep gratitude for Israel and all her lessons. And our marriage was stronger because of it.

For us, the Promised Land had kept its promise, and then some.

— RAAKHEE MIRCHANDANI

NOTES

INTRODUCTION

1. John J. Parsons, "The Awe of the Lord," hebrew4christians.com/Scripture/Parashah/Summaries/Eikev/Yirah/yirah.html.
2. Ibid.
3. Ibid.

MEET THE GOOD RABBI: JASON SOBEL

1. Babylonian Talmud, Sanhedrin 99a.

CHAPTER 5: CAESAREA AND HERODIUM

1. Flavius Josephus, *Antiquities of the Jews*, Book XVII, translation available at sacred-texts.com/jud/josephus/ant-17.htm.
2. Dean Smith, "Tomb of Herod the Great Discovered," OpenTheWord.org, April 24, 2017, opentheword.org/2017/04/24/tomb-of-herod-the-great-discovered/.
3. Flavius Josephus, *Antiquities of the Jews*, Book XV, translation available at penelope.uchicago.edu/josephus/ant-15.html.
4. Flavius Josephus, *The Wars of the Jews*, Book I, translation available at sacred-texts.com/jud/josephus/war-1.htm.

CHAPTER 6: BETHLEHEM

1. Mishnah Shekalim 7:4.

CHAPTER 7: NAZARETH

1. Talmud, Babylonian Sukkah 52.

2. "Inflection of *tzel*," pealim.com, pealim.com/dict/4242-tzel/.

CHAPTER 9: THE SEVEN STREAMS
1. Oppians, *Halieutica or Fishing*, translation available at penelope.uchicago.
edu/Thayer/E/Roman/Texts/Oppian/Halieutica/1.html.

CHAPTER 11: CAPERNAUM
1. Amir Tsarfati, "Ancient Synagogue Where Jesus
Taught Discovered in Galilee," *Kehila News Israel*,
August 16, 2016, kehilanews.com/2016/08/16/
ancient-synagogue-where-jesus-taught-discovered-in-galilee/.

CHAPTER 16: THE POOL OF SILOAM
1. Bible Archaeology Society Staff, "The Siloam Pool: Where Jesus Healed
the Blind Man," *Bible History Daily*, July 2, 2017, biblicalarchaeology.
org/daily/biblical-sites-places/biblical-archaeology-sites/
the-siloam-pool-where-jesus-healed-the-blind-man/.
2. Ibid.
3. Babylonian Talmud, Bava Batra 126b.

CHAPTER 18: THE MOUNT OF OLIVES
1. Rick Westhead, "Jerusalem's Mount of Olives Cemetery Running
Out of Room," *Toronto Star*, December 16, 2012, thestar.com/news/
world/2012/12/16/jerusalems_mount_of_olives_cemetery_running_
out_of_room.html.

CHAPTER 22: GOLGOTHA
1. Dave Epstein, "Found and Lost?" in *Nelson's Annual Preacher's
Sourcebook*, O. S. Hawkins, ed., vol. 3 (Nashville, TN: Thomas Nelson,
2013), 161.
2. Ibid.

CHAPTER 24: THE UPPER ROOM AND TEMPLE COURTS
1. Moshe Weinfeld, *Normative and Sectarian Judaism in the Second Temple
Period* (London: T & T Clark, 2005), p. 274.

CHAPTER 26: THE DEAD SEA

1. Ezekiel 47:8–9, JPS Tanakh, Bible Hub, biblehub.com/jps/ezekiel/47. htm.
2. Samantha Siegel, "Fish Living by the Dead Sea—Prophecy of Ezekiel Unfolding," July 21, 2016, youtube.com/watch?v=x5A3GkuRaMI.
3. Adam Eliyahu Berkowitz, "Fulfillment of the Dead Sea Prophecy Has Begun," Breaking Israel News, July 27, 2016, breakingisraelnews. com/72711/fulfillment-dead-sea-prophecy-begun/#/.

CHAPTER 27: MASADA

1. Aviva and Shmuel Bar-Am, "Masada, Tragic Fortress in the Sky," *Times of Israel*, April 13, 2013, timesofisrael.com/ masada-tragic-fortress-in-the-sky/.
2. Flavius Josephus, *The Wars of the Jews*, Book VII, chapter 9, translation available at sacred-texts.com/jud/josephus/war-7.htm.

CHAPTER 28: THE QUMRAN CAVES

1. Jewish Virtual Library, jewishvirtuallibrary.org/ teacher-of-righteousness.
2. Jeffrey L. Sheler, "The Reason God Tested Abraham," *U.S. News and World Report*, June 29, 1997, money.usnews.com/money/ personal-finance/articles/1997/06/29/the-reason-god-tested-abraham.

CHAPTER 29: TEL AVIV

1. Henry Alford, "Seizing the Day in Tel Aviv," *New York Times*, July 20, 2008, www.nytimes.com/2008/07/20/travel/20telaviv.html.

CONCLUSION

1. "Watch Kathie Lee's Touching Tribute to Husband Frank Gifford," Today.com, August 17, 2015, www.today.com/video/watch-kathie-lees-touching-tribute-to-husband-frank-gifford-506707523589.

About the Authors

KATHIE LEE GIFFORD is the three-time Emmy-winning cohost of the fourth hour of *TODAY*, alongside Hoda Kotb. The Gifford-Kotb hour has been hailed as "appointment television" by *Entertainment Weekly*, and "*TODAY*'s happy hour" by *USA Today*.

Prior to NBC News, Gifford served as cohost of *Live with Regis and Kathie Lee* for fifteen years, where she received eleven Emmy nominations. She was also a correspondent for *Good Morning America* for three years. In 2015, she was inducted into the Broadcast & Cable Hall of Fame. Her Broadway musical, *Scandalous*, for which she wrote the book and the lyrics, received a Tony nomination for its lead actress. Also a songwriter, Kathie recently wrote "He Saw Jesus" and "Jesus Is His Name," as well as the score and script for the movie *A Reel Life*.

Gifford has authored three *New York Times* bestselling books, including *Just When I Thought I'd Dropped My Last Egg*, *I Can't Believe I Said That*, and the popular children's book *Party Animals*. Her book *Good Gifts: One Year In the Heart of a Home* raised over $1 million for the Salvation Army.

Gifford lends support to numerous children's organizations, including Childhelp, the Association to Benefit Children, the Salvation Army, and the International Justice Mission. A devoted humanitarian, she received an honorary degree from Marymount University for her humanitarian work in labor relations.

Gifford has two children, Cody and Cassidy, and resides in Connecticut.

About the Authors
(continued)

RABBI JASON SOBEL is a thought leader, spiritual guide, and Jewish follower of Yeshua (Jesus). He is cofounder of Fusion with Rabbi Jason, an organization dedicated to sharing teachings and resources that reveal deeper insights into the Jewish roots of the Scriptures. Learn more at www.rabbisobel.com.

Join Rabbi Jason on a Rock, Road, and Rabbi Tour of Israel!

Visit www.rockroadrabbitours.com to learn more about this unique experience designed around the rabbinic approach to learning and living the biblical text. A Rock, Road, and Rabbi Tour is a "Road to Emmaus" encounter—your eyes will be opened as the Old and New Testament connect in high definition.

You will never see Jesus and the Bible the same way again!

*Career Management
and Survival
in the Workplace*

❧ ❧ ❧ ❧ ❧ ❧ ❧ ❧ ❧ ❧ ❧ ❧ ❧ ❧ ❧ ❧

Manuel London

Edward M. Mone

Career Management and Survival in the Workplace

Helping Employees Make
Tough Career Decisions,
Stay Motivated, and
Reduce Career Stress

 Jossey-Bass Publishers

San Francisco • London • 1987

CAREER MANAGEMENT AND SURVIVAL IN THE WORKPLACE
Helping Employees Make Tough Career Decisions, Stay Motivated, and Reduce Career Stress
by Manuel London and Edward M. Mone

Copyright © 1987 by: Jossey-Bass Inc., Publishers
433 California Street
San Francisco, California 94104
&
Jossey-Bass Limited
28 Banner Street
London EC1Y 8QE

Library of Congress Cataloging-in-Publication Data

London, Manuel,
    Career management and survival in the workplace.

    (The Jossey-Bass management series)   (The Jossey-Bass
social and behavioral science series)
    Bibliography: p. 213
    Includes index.
    1. Career development.   2. Employee motivation.
3. Job stress.   I. Mone, Edward M.   II. Title.
III. Series.   IV. Series: Jossey-Bass social and
behavioral science series.
HF5549.5.C35L65   1987   658.3'14   86–46334
ISBN 1–55542–043–5 (alk. paper)

Manufactured in the United States of America

The paper in this book meets the guidelines for
permanence and durability of the Committee on
Production Guidelines for Book Longevity of the
Council on Library Resources.

JACKET DESIGN BY WILLI BAUM

FIRST EDITION

Code 8719

A joint publication in
The Jossey–Bass Management Series
and
The Jossey–Bass
Social and Behavioral Science Series

For Marilyn and Ceil

Contents

Preface

In a world filled with change and uncertainty, career survival is uppermost in many people's minds. Indeed, many people may find themselves making tough career decisions throughout their lives. Staying motivated to make these decisions requires being resilient, understanding oneself and the environment, and having a clear sense of career direction along with the flexibility to modify that direction as conditions change. How people react to stressful work events will depend on, and be affected by, their career motivation.

Career Management and Survival in the Workplace is about career survival. It addresses the problems involved in helping employees face tough career decisions throughout their careers, not just when they start them, of keeping employees motivated in our increasingly volatile work world, and of helping employees to cope with and prevent career stress.

This book is for human resource professionals, corporate career counselors, and managers who develop programs and policies affecting employees' careers. Human resource professionals play a key role in how people view their careers and whether they realize the opportunities that are available to them. The human resource professional's role is to help keep employees motivated, committed to the company, and satisfied with their jobs. The difficulty is how to do this in a changing, often turbulent work environment.

Economic, Social, and Organizational Trends

The work world is more complex and challenging today than it was a generation ago. There are changes in how and

where work is done. Advances in computers and telecommunications have made working at home viable for some people. In addition, people's values are changing. Today, "doing your own thing" is increasingly accepted. Thus, many people are striving for a well-balanced life, placing equal value on work, family, and leisure, rather than emphasizing one to the exclusion of the others. Men's and women's roles are changing with the increase in the number of dual-career couples. Men and women are more often sharing childcare and household responsibilities.

For companies, too, today's competitive environment demands flexibility, quality products, high standards of service, and attentive responses to customers' needs and problems. Most companies are under increasing pressure to improve productivity and reduce costs while remaining innovative. Moves to improve productivity and reduce costs often involve staff reductions, particularly among middle managers. And flatter organizational structures mean fewer promotional opportunities. Thus, corporations are developing people for jobs with more autonomy, responsibility, and higher pay, not necessarily for promotion to a higher level. The meaning of career success is changing to include alternatives to promotion, such as signs of competence, power, and status. The increased variety of career alternatives emphasizes the importance of flexible career planning with room for specialists and for generalist managers.

Within organizations, management styles are changing from authoritarian to participatory. Employees are more often involved in decision making, rewarded for innovations, and encouraged to interact across and within departments. Companies are also experimenting with more flexible organizational structures, such as matrix structures, and with systems that are less bureaucratic and more responsive to individual and corporate needs. These systems include group incentive programs that reward team performance, as well as systems that give managers the discretion to reward good performers with substantial financial incentives.

In the face of these changing conditions on the part of organizations and changing expectations on the part of employees, people need the motivation to respond with flexibility to new conditions and opportunities that offer greater responsibility, and autonomy and the self-confidence to create their

own opportunities when necessary. And, in either case, they need a clear sense of career identity and a definite career direction.

Overview of the Contents

Chapters One through Four focus on career decisions. Chapter One describes the types of difficult career decisions employees face. We discuss decisions employees make because they want to (for instance, because they want to change jobs, change careers, retire, or start working after raising a family) as well as decisions that occur because opportunities arise or a negative event occurs, such as being fired. The human resource professional's task is to help people deal with all these decisions.

Chapter Two explores how well employees know what they want from their careers and how this sense of direction influences their approach to career decision making. We illustrate the value of helping employees analyze their needs, ambitions, and skills and explore the environment for opportunities that fit what they want. In both Chapters One and Two, we discuss the value of encouraging people to explore alternatives and try out different career directions.

Chapters Three and Four provide a guide for human resource professionals in counseling employees as they make career decisions. Chapter Three describes how people make career decisions. We cover decision stages from identifying the problem to committing oneself to a choice. Chapter Four outlines strategies that can be used to help people make career decisions. After describing different approaches, we show how the way a person makes a decision depends on the needs of the situation and on one's decision-making style.

Keeping employees motivated is a major goal of human resource programs. This is the topic of Chapters Five through Nine. Chapter Five defines and gives examples of the three components of career motivation: *career resilience* (believing in oneself and being willing to take risks), *career insight* (understanding one's strengths and weaknesses and being aware of opportunities in the environment), and *career identity* (having a sense of career direction). This chapter also offers a self-reflection guide to help employees assess their own career motivation.

Chapter Six shows how the career motivation components combine to form patterns that influence career development and change. This chapter offers a way to help employees analyze their career assets and liabilities and establish a career strategy that is meaningful for them.

Chapter Seven reveals how the boss, company, and job can support employees' career motivation. For instance, positive reinforcement and opportunities for achievement enhance career resilience. Feedback on job performance and information about career opportunities increase career insight. Opportunities for leadership and encouragement for involvement in professional activities contribute to career identity.

Chapter Eight continues our discussion of the role of the organization in employee development and career management. This chapter proposes ways to evaluate sources of support for career motivation and provides more information about company policies and a description of twenty-one company programs that affect career motivation. A corporate strategy for meeting the needs of different departments is described, and an example is given of how one department developed a training and evaluation process to ensure employee competence and growth. The chapter also offers a method for evaluating career programs.

Chapter Nine describes how employees can gain and lose support for career motivation. We offer guidelines for increasing employees' motivation by changing the environment and helping employees understand the role they play in developing their own careers.

The tough career decisions discussed earlier in the book constitute a specific type of career stress. Having a solid foundation of career resilience, insight, and identity paves the way for smooth career transitions. The last five chapters of the book help the human resource professional understand career stress and how employees cope with it. Chapter Ten reviews sources of career stress, including various forms of role conflict and ambiguity. Special attention is given to the career stress faced by women and minorities. This chapter also presents questions that can be used to evaluate the sources of stress in a company.

Chapter Eleven describes the stress of making career decisions and undergoing career transitions. Examples are given

of people who have experienced major transitions. Chapter Twelve begins our discussion of ways to prevent career stress, and Chapter Thirteen discusses how organizations can help reduce their employees' career stress through their personnel programs and policies. For instance, redesigning jobs, changing reporting relationships, and training supervisors to recognize and cope with symptoms of stress in their subordinates are ways of making work more satisfying for the employee. Employee counseling and health fitness programs are ways to reduce the symptoms of stress and to prevent future stress.

Chapter Fourteen examines how employees' reactions to stress are affected by their career resilience, and how their resilience is affected by the stress they experience. The chapter suggests what can be done to help employees handle stress more constructively and how both employee and organizational factors affect career survival. Individuals' characteristics, such as career resilience, influence their efforts to find supportive work settings and their control over their environments. Simultaneously, organizational factors, such as available rewards and opportunities, influence career survival and motivation.

Throughout the book, we describe people facing a variety of career situations. We include men and women in early, middle, and late career, some making tough career decisions, some demonstrating different levels of career motivation, and others coping with various stressful environments. These examples demonstrate our points and, we hope, enhance the reader's understanding by demonstrating development and change. To this end, many of the cases described early in the book are referred to again in subsequent chapters, and when we mention a person who was introduced earlier, we refer to the chapter where that individual was first described.

Career Management and Survival in the Workplace also includes a number of exercises designed to encourage self-reflection. These are not extensive writing exercises. Rather, they are meant simply to help employees think about their career decisions, their career motivation, and their sources of, and reactions to, career stress. These exercises may be integrated into career programs or they may be used separately in career counseling.

We believe that individual, environmental, and organizational factors interact to affect how people make career decisions and transitions. The environment, in the form of the company, boss, job, and larger socioeconomic conditions, affects the decisions and transitions people are likely to face, as well as strengthens or weakens their career motivation. Nevertheless, people need to be proactive in first understanding themselves and the environment and then in acting to make decisions in line with their needs, abilities, and ambitions—and to cope effectively with and even prevent career stress. In this context, career development takes on new meaning—one aimed not at helping people advance but rather at helping them survive in the corporate world. Toward that end, we describe several career programs that provide the resources to promote better career decisions, enhance motivation, and cope with stress. These include a workshop for managers on their role as developers (Chapter Seven); a method for developing career paths and parallel opportunities for training and increased compensation to enhance skill development and motivation (Chapter Eight); and a workshop on coping with organizational change (Chapter Thirteen).

Acknowledgments

This book grew out of our discussions about how people react to changing work environments. These discussions were a source of mutual support and the start of a friendship. We are grateful to our families, Marilyn, David, and Jared London, and Ceil Mone, for their reactions to our ideas and for their patience during the many evenings, weekends, and vacation days of writing and revising. We are also grateful to G. Robert Dobbs for providing a supportive work climate where new ideas in career and management development can be discussed and evaluated. It is also an environment of considerable change, and this has given us direct experience in career survival.

Somerset, New Jersey   Manuel London
March 1987   Edward M. Mone

The Authors

Manuel London is a district manager in charge of employee development and organization effectiveness at AT&T. London has been involved in organizational research and program development for AT&T since 1977. From 1974 to 1977 he taught in the business school at the University of Illinois in Urbana. He received his B.A. degree (1971) from Case Western Reserve University in philosophy and psychology and his M.A. (1972) and Ph.D. (1974) degrees from Ohio State University in industrial and organizational psychology.

London's main research activities have been in manager development and career decisions. He has also conducted research on the relationship between work and nonwork behavior and has written on ethical issues in personnel decisions. He is a consulting editor for the *Academy of Management Journal* and a member of the editorial boards of *Personnel Psychology* and the *Journal of Management Development*. He has written more than thirty papers and is the author of the books *Managing Careers* (1982, with S. A. Stumpf) and *Developing Managers* (1985).

Edward Mone is a staff manager in charge of career and management development at AT&T. He received his A.B. degree (1973) in economics and his M.A. degree (1977) in college counseling and student development, both from Hunter College, City University of New York. He is currently studying for his Ph.D. degree in organizational psychology at Teachers College, Columbia University.

Mone's main research activities have been in leadership behavior, management development, and career planning in large organizations. Mone has been involved in the design and implementation of management and organization development programs at AT&T since 1982. From 1977 to 1982 he maintained a private practice as a career and job search consultant in New York City.

Career Management
and Survival
in the Workplace

One

The Tough Career Decisions
Facing Employees

Most people face major career decisions several times in their lives, for instance, when they graduate from college and when they retire from work. Career decisions also rise when people are unhappy at work, when their employers are unhappy with them, and when new opportunities emerge. This chapter concerns the reluctance and anxiety many people feel about making career decisions and their lack of understanding about the control they have over their choices.

Let's begin with some definitions. A *decision* is a commitment to act. A *decision process* begins with identifying a problem and ends with action being taken. Decisions are important when they change a person's life. Important decisions arise because of problems people must solve or transitions they must make. Decisions are difficult when people must choose between two or more alternatives that seem to have equally desirable or undesirable features.

A *career decision* is a commitment to make a change in one's work: to change employers, change jobs within the same organization, change occupations, retire. A career decision may also be a commitment to take on a new assignment or even to adopt a new attitude toward an old job. Sometimes people make a career decision when they make a decision about another part of their lives. For example, deciding to have children may influence whether one spouse quits work for a while or cuts down on work-related travel to be home with the family. For the most

1

part, this book is about career decisions that involve major transitions: selecting one's first job, deciding to change companies, making a mid-career change, taking early retirement.

When Career Decisions Are Necessary

Half the battle in making a career decision is realizing that there is a decision to be made. The spark that creates that realization may be negative feedback on job performance or perhaps new information that a desired promotion will not materialize. Perhaps a person reads a recruitment ad in the employment section of the newspaper. A friend might be getting a better job, or a relative may encourage him or her to look for a job that pays more. The employee might see a revival of *Death of a Salesman* at the community theater and begin to think about values and priorities. Most likely, a combination of events over time causes people to look for alternatives.

The passage of time and rising expectations account for many career decisions. Some occur simply because people get older. For example, a young person graduates from high school or college and looks for a job. Career decisions also occur because people want them to. For instance, a person may be unhappy with work and search for a job offering more money, better chances for promotion, or more exciting tasks.

Career decisions arise also in response to an opportunity. For instance, a friend offers a person a new job. Here, a quick decision may be necessary to decide initially whether to treat the opportunity seriously. If the person decides to consider the offer, then a careful decision process ensues.

Still other times people are forced to make a career decision. Examples are being fired and being forced to retire. Consider Jim Marsh. Jim was a thirty-five-year-old assistant professor at a well-known private university. At the end of his sixth year at the school, his department chair refused to recommend him for tenure. He could stay for only another year. This decision came as a shock to Jim, as he had been told by the department chair and others over the years that he had been doing reasonably well. He was the author of two books, the recipient of a large grant, and was liked by his students. However, al-

though Jim enjoyed academic life, he began to feel that the lack of financial rewards and the difficulty of securing a tenured position were not worth the effort. A social scientist by training, he thought his research skills and knowledge of organizational behavior would be valuable to a company.

Jim decided to find another job as soon as he could—if possible, before the next school year began. He applied for a few teaching jobs because this was familiar territory, but he also embarked on a major search for alternatives. He contacted friends in the business world, some of whom were his former students. He asked their advice: What opportunities were available? How could he find out about them? What would be the best way to market himself? What should he put on his resume? One contact led to another. People promised to circulate his resume. Jim also considered enrolling in a six-week retraining program at a major university; the program was designed to acquaint people holding doctorates in the humanities and social sciences with business issues. A friend who had been through the program said it was a valuable way to get job interviews and build a network of contacts. Jim felt that he would try the program if nothing came along before it began.

Deciding to Consider a Career Change

At times when making a career decision is necessary, some people react by not making a decision, some have to be pushed into making a decision, and some take the initiative for making the decision themselves. How people react to making a career decision and the type of decision process that results often depend on personality characteristics.

Not Making a Decision. Sometimes people know they need to consider changing a job or career. They feel they deserve better. They grow tired of putting up with a demanding boss or with routine work. But they do nothing. They resign themselves to their lot, or they tell themselves that the right job will come along eventually—that they will wind up with the promotion they want or with the income and life-style they dream about. But they fail to do anything to attain these goals.

Being Pushed into a Decision. To some extent, all people are dreamers, not acting as forcefully as they should. It is as though they believe in the "job fairy," who will one day come and make things right. Sometimes the "job fairy" comes in the form of a push. For example, people who were fired may say that it was the best thing that could have happened to them. They say this in retrospect, of course, not while they are experiencing the pain of rejection and the uncertainty of finding another job. But they eventually find their way and often for the better. This was true in Jim Marsh's case. He found a position in a market-research department of a large corporation. If he had received tenure, he probably would never have known what he missed.

Pushing Oneself into a Decision. Decisions individuals seek for themselves result from a perceived imbalance between the way things are and the way they should be. For instance, a person may be dissatisfied with his or her boss, the job, or other aspects of the work. Opportunities for career growth may not be as great as hoped. Or job performance may not reach the person's expectations.

These people believe in their ability to bring about positive change. Psychologists call them *internally controlled*. They tend to attribute positive events and outcomes to themselves, and they are also willing to accept blame. They do not wait around for something to happen.

This set of questions can be used to assess how much control people believe they have over their lives (answer true or false).

1. If I work hard, I'll be rewarded.
2. What happens to me in this organization is my doing.
3. I determine what happens to my career.
4. People are as successful as they make themselves.
5. My future in this organization will be determined by factors beyond my control.
6. No matter how hard I try, I can't affect what happens to me.
7. I have little control over my work (what I do, how I do it).
8. I am at the mercy of others.

"True" answers to statements 1 through 4 reflect internal control, while "true" answers to 5 through 8 do not. People with internal control push themselves into finding a situation that will provide the rewards they know they deserve.

This same characteristic is seen in those who view themselves in a positive light and have self-confidence. People can answer true or false to these statements to assess their self-confidence.

1. I am confident about my abilities. ⊤
2. I am an effective person. ⊤
3. I am good at what I do. ⊤
4. I have a lot to be proud of.
5. I feel incompetent.
6. I wish I had more ability.
7. I feel inferior to others.
8. People don't respect my opinion.

"True" responses to statements 1 through 4 and "false" responses to statements 5 through 8 suggest high self-confidence; reverse responses indicate low self-confidence. To give people increased understanding of their self-confidence, you can ask them to think of other statements that describe how strongly they believe in themselves.

For all these scales, we have included only a sample of items that reflect the personality characteristic. You can probably think of other items that indicate internal control and self-confidence (or standardized scales can be used for this purpose; see Robinson and Shaver, 1974). The goal is to get people to think about their belief in themselves and in their ability to control their environment and achieve their goals.

Tom Fenton provides an example of an internally controlled, self-confident person. He had been with a large consumer-product company for twenty years when he decided to leave. Starting as a middle-level manager in one of the operating units, Tom had transferred to the headquarters marketing department ten years ago at a time when there was an increased emphasis on market strategy and sales.

In recent years, Tom felt that the company had been moving backward. He felt that the company's new creed, "customer satisfaction," was more lip service than anything else. It seemed clear to him that his boss and his boss's boss had little idea of the direction their departments should be taking and the direction the company as a whole should be taking. This lack of direction led to anxiety and confusion. Tom also thought that the company was going back on its implicit "psychological contract" with its employees. He felt that there had been more job security and far more concern for people in the past than he could see today. These observations sparked the idea in Tom's mind that it might be better for him to leave at this time than to stay. It took him six weeks of considerable thought and deliberation to make the decision.

To help make the decision, Tom turned to a friend outside the company who was a marketing consultant. His friend's advice was that Tom should establish a marketing plan for himself that would entail a careful examination of career alternatives within the company as well as outside. Tom's strategy would be to speak to a number of people about career opportunities. The approach he would take in talking to these key individuals would be to seek their advice, not ask for a job. Within the company, Tom spoke to the president, two vice-presidents, and at least ten directors in many different units. They were as uncertain as he was about the direction the firm was taking. They all talked about the transition the company was undergoing and would continue to undergo, probably for the next three to five years. Increasingly, Tom realized that if he stayed, he would not be better off three years from now than he was today. Also, the company would probably be laying off or retiring many of its managers because of a surplus of middle managers as well as of managers at higher levels. Advancement opportunities were not likely to come Tom's way. In addition to people within the company, Tom talked to people who had recently left the company. Tom realized that leaving the company was risky, but he got nothing but positive reactions from these people. They had done well and found many opportunities to grow. Overwhelmingly, they wondered why he was still with the company.

Given this encouragement to leave, Tom decided to approach his supervisor to ask about the financial package the company might offer him if he were willing to quit. Tom felt that if he acted now, the company would negotiate a package that would be lucrative for him as well as fair for the firm. If Tom waited and got caught in large-scale layoffs, the economic incentives might not be so good. As it turned out, Tom was able to negotiate a favorable agreement.

Tom was extremely self-confident about his skills and marketability. The more he talked with people outside the company, the more he realized they were impressed with his abilities and background. Tom's ambition was to become the president of a small firm. He knew that if he stayed with his current company, he would not get the type of experience he needed to be attractive to a small business as its chief executive officer. Company presidents are generally hired from the ranks of vice-presidents, and he was unlikely to attain this position within the company. Tom's desire was to become vice-president of a small firm and, after perhaps a series of such positions, to become the president of a company—perhaps one he would found himself.

Once Tom made the decision to leave, the rest was fun. He rationalized that he was leaving a different company from the one he joined twenty years ago. Further, he felt that because the company had violated the psychological contract, he was under no obligation to stay. Although the decision to leave was difficult, he felt he had made the right choice based not on emotion but on a careful consideration of his career and what he could find in the company versus what was available outside. Given that he clearly could not meet his goals internally, he saw no reason to stay. A financial settlement that would allow him to live for as long as a year without working provided enough security for him to leave. In addition, he felt this was the best time to leave. It would put him ahead of the many marketing people who would be searching for jobs in several months, and leaving in February, as he expected to, would be an advantage, according to Tom's consultant friend, because many companies are then in the process of implementing new budgets and looking for people to direct new projects.

Evaluating the Alternatives

Janis and Mann (1977) present a model of how people make career decisions. The process begins, as we have discussed, with some input—new information or perhaps an event that they did not expect. The next step is to ask themselves a series of questions about the risks involved.

Risk entails giving up something of known value for something of potentially higher value. Some people take risks with their careers. Their propensity is to take the more exciting, higher-value career choice even though it has a lower probability of success than the alternative with a lower value. Other people are security oriented. They would rather be sure about what is going to happen even if it means giving up an opportunity for improving their position.

Take the example of Tom Fenton, described earlier. For a while, Tom had been gathering information about his company. This information bothered him, but there was little risk in doing nothing. As he became increasingly uncomfortable with his situation, the risks of doing nothing seemed to increase. However, Tom did not at first see any available alternatives. Changing companies would be a big step, especially after twenty years. Tom had to investigate the alternatives open to him. Talking to acquaintances inside and outside the company highlighted the negatives of staying and revealed a few positive alternatives. There was risk in leaving, but a financial incentive lowered that risk.

Stress Resulting from a Lack of Alternatives

Suppose Tom did not have viable alternatives. If the labor market or economic conditions had not been so good, he might have decided to stay. He might have told himself that things were not so bad. This is called *defensive avoidance*. However, it probably would not have been easy for Tom to rationalize away his discontent. His feelings that his skills were underutilized and undervalued by the company would not have been consistent with his self-concept as an effective, productive person. Fortunately for Tom, he had the time to search his environment

and find several desirable alternatives. Jim Marsh, described earlier, also had time to thoroughly explore alternatives.

Many people do not have or do not allow themselves the luxury of a thorough search for alternatives. When there are no alternatives (or when one perceives there are none) and the present state is more negative than positive, the person is likely to be defensive or avoid the situation. Eventually, stress builds up and panic ensues. A person in this state is unlikely to take advantage of whatever time is available to search for new alternatives. Errors in judgment are likely to occur, as the person simply copies others' behavior. The person is likely to be irritable, impossible to reason with, and unproductive. The individual feels trapped. This sudden realization that the job fairy will never come and it is too late to do anything about it is the stuff mid-career crises are made of.

People differ in how much stress they can take before they make a major career decision. When things get bad at work—for example, when people are under pressure to produce or when they are not getting along with their co-workers—they may react by being late for work, leaving early, being absent, or reducing their job performance in other ways. They may slowly withdraw from work without actually leaving their jobs. A small increase in job tension may even be enough to make them quit suddenly.

Fortunately, situations often change before people quit. Negative aspects disappear or do not seem so bad over time. The positive aspects of a situation may increase or become more obvious than they were. Whether these changes actually occur or are in a person's mind does not matter. People run into trouble when reality becomes so negative that it cannot be ignored or when they distort reality to such an extent that they cannot function any longer. Basically, it is a matter of degree. There is nothing wrong with seeing the glass half full rather than half empty. But there is something wrong with saying the glass is full when indeed there is not a drop to drink.

Summary

This chapter explored when people make career decisions—sometimes because they want to and other times

because they have to. Some people face negative situations and would be better off looking for alternatives. But an implicit belief in the job fairy makes them wait and hope that things will turn out well without their taking action. People's self-confidence and sense that they control what happens to them are an important foundation for taking positive action.

People are sparked into such action when they perceive that the value of possible career alternatives exceeds the value of staying where they are. They evaluate the risks of staying versus the risks of alternative courses. If they do not see viable alternatives, they are likely to be defensive, to avoid the issue, or to rationalize away the current negative situation. If they realize that the risks of staying are great but feel there is no time to search for alternatives, they are likely to be "hypervigilant," perhaps changing to a job that is far worse than their present one. The ideal case is recognizing the need to make a change, having the time to make a decision, and then making it. This presumes that people know what they want in a job—the topic of the next chapter.

Two

What People Want
from Their Careers:
Establishing a Sense
of Direction

Once people realize that they must make a career decision, the next problem they face is knowing what they want. This knowledge is crucial in searching for alternatives and then evaluating them. People who do not have a good idea of what they want from their careers are not likely to make a satisfying decision, and they will probably find themselves making career decisions over and over again. Although many people are never completely sure of what they want, some sense of career direction is important for guiding their decision process. Otherwise they flounder.

Assessing Abilities and Job Preferences

Case Histories. We begin this chapter by returning to Tom Fenton, introduced in the previous chapter. Tom's case is an example of a deliberate, detailed decision to find the best job. We then consider cases of other people who were not so definite about their career ambitions. In them we will see the stress resulting from uncertainty and ambivalence.

Once Tom left the organization, his marketing strategy was to speak to ten to fifteen people he knew well. He had breakfast with one close friend who recommended a number

of other people to talk to. Each meeting led to new contacts. His strategy was to seek advice, not a job. Many of the people he talked to knew of opportunities within their own companies, or they suggested other fruitful ideas. In the end, Tom had the names of many more people than he could possibly contact.

Several issues were salient for Tom in making a decision: whether to work for a large or small company, whether to stay in the same industry, and whether to relocate. In discussing his alternatives with his wife, Tom mentioned the status of working for a large, established company. Tom had several opportunities with large organizations such as the one he had just left, and he had several opportunities with small companies. In addition, some of his job offers were in totally different industries. Staying with the same industry seemed less important to Tom than having a job that used a broad spectrum of his skills. Fortunately, he had had a sequence of jobs that gave him fairly broad marketing experience at responsible levels of management. Clearly he did not have to limit himself to one industry. Another consideration was relocation. With a daughter still in high school, Tom felt that this was not the best time for a move. However, he considered opportunities in other parts of the country.

At the time of our interview with him, Tom had three solid job offers and had decided to accept one. The evening we spoke, he had to call the other two to tell them that he would not be available for further discussions. In fact, he had to cancel several interviews for the next day because he would be starting his new position.

The job Tom chose carried the title of executive vice-president. He would be working for a small, local, but highly profitable land-development organization. He would be managing a group of about 100 people, many of whom were in real estate sales. Tom was able to write his own employment contract. Because the company had considerable cash to invest, it often bought businesses, refurbished the properties, and then sold them quickly. Tom convinced the company to hold on to the businesses for a year or so, build them up, and then sell them at an increased profit. Tom was responsible for these ventures. He had substantial control over the whole process of seek-

ing out new businesses, establishing the case for purchasing them, negotiating the purchase, overseeing the operation, and ultimately making a profit. When a business opportunity arose, Tom felt that he could find someone within the organization or hire someone from outside to build the business and make it attractive for profitable resale.

Although Tom was moving into a new industry, the skills he had learned over the years would serve him well. He would still be in marketing and sales. He would still be responsible for developing business plans, establishing strategy and tactics, and carrying them out.

He felt that if the job did not work out, he would still be developing his career. He could say that he had been an executive vice-president. He planned to maintain the network that he initiated in his career search because even if he succeeded, his intention was to move on to new executive-level jobs until he was the chief of his own organization.

One of the offers Tom had was in a different city. He admitted that this opportunity was probably better than the one he took. It would have involved establishing new marketing areas for a consulting firm that developed and implemented data systems for other organizations. This firm was highly profitable, and it was certainly in a growing area of the high-tech industry. But leaving his employer of twenty years and embarking on a risky career path were transitions enough for Tom at this time. It did not seem worthwhile to uproot his family. He felt there would be other opportunities in the future if the present one did not work out. Meanwhile, he would be getting the experience he felt he needed.

In making this career decision, Tom was driven by high self-confidence and an unwillingness to accept the status quo. He made a careful decision, taking into account responsibility, title, economic conditions, and location. But despite the careful consideration, it seemed to us that he was unsure about the new position he was taking. He regretted not having the prestige of working for a large, recognizable firm. Perhaps he was enamored of the job title. He could see better opportunities elsewhere, and he was already preparing for the possibility of failure.

He reasoned that if he did not perform as well as the new company hoped or he hoped he would, he would have the contacts and strategy to find a comparable, if not better, position. Even if the job went sour, he would be able to paint the experience in a positive light.

A dynamic, aggressive person, Tom felt he knew himself well. He was also a thoughtful individual who was concerned about others and believed he could implement this concern at the same time he enhanced the productivity of the people working for him. Overall, Tom felt he knew where he was going and what he wanted. He had a vision for himself, and he had considered what he would do depending on how well the new opportunity worked out. He was excited about his prospects, and he clearly differentiated between what he wanted in the short term and how that would contribute to what he wanted in the long term.

We next consider someone who also had a vision for himself but did not have the courage to act on it—at least not at the time. As a result he faced a tough career decision.

Harvey Monroe was a twenty-seven-year-old manager who had been in his job for about a year when we interviewed him. He was raised in an inner city in the Northeast. After one semester at a state teacher's college, he left school. An F in calculus did him in. He then enrolled in a course at a major university in his home town and was admitted as a freshman the next year. He played football during his freshman year and was on the dean's list both semesters. He paid for school by working in the admissions office and giving tours to prospective students.

Harvey started at a well-known law school with a small scholarship and $200 in his pocket. Finding working and studying impossible, he transferred to a lesser-known law school at a branch of the state university. He lived with friends, held a succession of part-time jobs, and borrowed as much money as he could to make ends meet. He was tempted to quit school when he had only a few courses left. However, he persevered. Living on charge cards for a few months, Harvey finally received his law degree.

When Harvey interviewed for his job with a large service company, he wanted to be a corporate attorney. He was told that the company did not hire neophyte attorneys; they hired only lawyers with corporate experience. When the company asked him whether he would be interested in a management-development program, he could not refuse; he needed the money badly. He also thought the job would develop his business interests and give him good experience and a challenge. He liked the fact that there was a degree of risk; he would be fired after the first year if he did not demonstrate potential for advancement.

Other jobs he considered after graduating from law school involved little more than routine work. As a law clerk in a large firm, he would be in the back office with twenty other associates. He did have an offer from a small law firm to work as an associate for two years and then ideally become a partner. But the practice involved general family litigation, which he did not like. Another job with a government regulatory commission as a clerk writing opinions did not offer much in the way of law experience. He was enticed by a job as a corporate attorney for a paper company, but this position did not materialize.

Harvey's first management job with the service company was in the customer-relations department at headquarters. This department acted as a liaison between the company and its customers. Harvey's task was to ensure that customer orders were delivered according to company guidelines. Harvey enjoyed it. His law background gave him a broader view than many of the managers in the department had.

After five months, his boss was transferred to another department, and Harvey went along. His new position was tracking repair records in the management office for special services. His assignment was to get the repair time down, which he managed to do, although not to the extent he had hoped. The job required educating himself about the nature of the work, meeting with higher-level managers to outline a plan, developing a training program for repair people, and running the program.

Harvey was transferred again after six months, once again following his boss. Harvey had been on this job for only two weeks when we talked to him. The position required keeping

equipment records. He had two people reporting to him, the first time he had had responsibility for subordinates. By this time, Harvey thought of his boss as a mentor. His boss was a "golden-boy hot shot" who was "bright as a whip and respected in high places," according to Harvey. Harvey saw him as a "down-to-earth person"—someone he could talk to.

Harvey mentioned that he was uncomfortable working for the company because his peer group from law school felt that his job was beneath him, even though he was earning more than most of them. His friends' attitude could have been the result of jealousy, although Harvey did not see it that way. Harvey said that he would prefer to be in the company's legal department, and he claimed that the coordinator of the management-development program at first led him to believe that if he had a good first year he might be able to get into the legal department. (A conversation we had with the coordinator indicated otherwise, however.) Harvey felt that he did have a successful first year, but he now realized the company had no intention of moving him into the legal department.

The month before our interview with Harvey, he had taken three weeks off to study for the bar exam. He had not yet received the results, but he said that the exam was easier than he expected it would be. Harvey's heart seemed to be in practicing law. He said that he could practice part-time as long as it did not interfere with his job. However, he could not get into extensive cases because most people would want a lawyer who worked full-time. His friends told him that he could be a great politician, and they called him "the Senator." They said he should serve the community. But it was impossible for Harvey to quit the company now because of the debts he incurred in school.

We have already seen that self-confidence makes a difference in career ambitions and the career outcomes people are willing to accept. Harvey Monroe and Tom Fenton were similar in that they both believed in themselves. However, unlike Tom Fenton, who had a record of prior accomplishments, Harvey Monroe overstated his abilities. Remember that he barely finished his law degree. Both Tom and Harvey were frustrated

because their career prospects did not seem to be in line with their ambitions and abilities. Tom made a crucial mid-career switch. Harvey, still trying to establish himself, had yet to redirect his career. He was increasingly dependent on what seemed to him to be a high income and a secure job. He said that he felt bored and underutilized. Tom had taken accurate stock of his abilities, while Harvey saw himself as more competent than he probably was. Having insight into one's own abilities and motivation can be crucial for career success. Misunderstanding one's goals or overstating one's abilities is likely to lead to poor career choices.

For Patricia Stewart, an administrative assistant in an accounting office in New York City, a new job offer made her assess her goals and motivation. Living in a New Jersey suburb, she was thrilled when a neighbor suggested that she apply for a vacant position in the personnel department of a local company. At first, the offer was enticing, and she accepted it. However, when her current employer heard about the opportunity, he gave her an attractive counteroffer. Patricia also learned that the new job involved lower benefits, slower increases in pay, and less vacation time; and she would have to buy a car. Patricia felt committed to the new job because she said she would take it; she felt committed to her neighbor, who was looking forward to working with her. But Patricia also felt as though she were deserting her current employer.

The weekend during which she made the final decision was agony for her. She went over it a dozen times. She was not sure what she wanted, and she found herself pulled in different directions. Some of the issues had nothing to do with the job. For instance, Patricia did not want the embarrassment of telling her neighbor that she did not want the new job. In the end, Patricia decided to accept her current employer's counteroffer. She realized that better opportunities could be found in New Jersey than the job she had been offered. Meanwhile, she could stay where she was appreciated and doing well. Her final decision seemed so simple and obvious to her once she had made it.

Sometimes, making a decision is like climbing a hill. People find out how little they know about themselves and their

goals. They do not see the whole picture until they get to the top. Ultimately, certain criteria become more salient than others, and the decision is evident. That is not to say that self-insight helps one avoid the agony of making a decision. Career decisions lead to change, and most people resist change.

Studies of Job Preference and Career Interests. Everyone differs in career needs, job preferences, and the type of organization he or she wants to work for. Nevertheless, some research specifies the factors most people believe make a job desirable and how career stage influences people's preferences.

One study, conducted over a thirty-year period, asked 57,000 job applicants at a public utility to rank the importance of ten factors that make a job good or bad (Jurgensen, 1978). Men and women differed somewhat in their preferences. The order for men (from high to low preference) was security, advancement, type of work, company, pay, co-workers, supervisor, benefits, hours, and working conditions. Women considered type of work more important than any other factor, followed by company, security, co-workers, advancement, supervisor, pay, working conditions, hours, and benefits. People believed that others value pay most, even though they did not say that about themselves. The changes over the thirty-year period were inconsequential except that there was a decrease in the importance of advancement and security. Type of work eventually replaced security as the most important factor for men.

A study of M.B.A.s selecting a first job after graduation found that most were concerned with pay and fringe benefits followed by opportunities to use skills, exercise responsibility and leadership, and act autonomously (Feldman and Arnold, 1978).

Career stage may affect what people want from a job and career (Veiga, 1983). During the early part of their career, when people are trying to establish themselves, they want jobs where they can learn and develop, thereby improving their advancement potential and marketability inside or outside the organization. As their careers mature, they often become impatient about

advancement (as did Tom Fenton). However, whether they change jobs or not is likely to be affected by community and family ties (for example, children in school and a working spouse) as well as by career opportunities. As they approach retirement, they become concerned with company benefits. They also worry about stagnating. People are likely to retire when they feel their job skills are obsolete, they have poor health, they have attained their career goals, their jobs are stressful or boring, they have attractive leisure pursuits, or they have lost the desire to compete and work at a fast pace (Beehr, 1986).

Employees' career preferences are guided by their interests, and they tend to make career decisions on the basis of these interests—that is, they choose occupations that match their interest patterns. Career interests are fairly well crystallized by the end of adolescence. One career-counseling model measures people on a set of six interests and then tries to match them to occupations that allow them to follow those interests (Holland, 1973). For instance, people with artistic interests are matched to jobs that require creativity, such as those in advertising, design, and journalism; people with social interests are matched with jobs that serve or help people, such as nursing and teaching.

Understandably, a person's preferences and interests may help in career decisions. However, we believe that no one set of interests or preferences determines career success. Rather, a combination of needs, values, and interests constitutes a person's career motivation. Some of these are fairly stable characteristics; they set the foundation for establishing a meaningful career direction. Other characteristics, especially one's interests and preferences and expectations for pursuing them, can change because of the opportunities and information available. Chapters Five and Six identify these stable and varying characteristics and suggest ways employees can assess them in themselves and use this information in making satisfying career decisions.

Assessing the Environment

Understanding the context in which one works is also important in making successful career decisions. Tom Fenton inves-

tigated his environment thoroughly before making a decision. Harvey Monroe, however, accepted his job as a manager hoping that he would be allowed to transfer to the company's legal department. He later discovered that the legal department's policy was to hire people who had legal background, not to transfer current managers who had studied law. Nevertheless, he harbored the fruitless hope that the policy could be altered in his case. But Harvey also assessed the environment well enough to know that he was making a better living than he would as a private attorney, at least initially. Also, he knew that it would be a struggle to start a law practice.

Others' opinions are also part of the environment. Harvey Monroe was influenced by his friends, who flattered him into thinking that he would be a successful politician, a dream he had not given up. Patricia Stewart was concerned about her neighbor's opinion of her decision. In this case, her neighbor clouded the real issue—what she wanted from a career. For Tom Fenton, acquaintances were helpful in clarifying opportunities. But he was also swayed by the arguments of friends who had already left the company. To some extent, his friends may have been justifying their own decisions by describing how happy they were and by persuading Tom to follow their lead. Fortunately, Tom also talked to influential people in the company who were also unsure about the company's future. Because Tom was getting the same message consistently, he felt confident that he was making the right choice in leaving the company.

Exploratory Career Decisions: Trying Out Jobs

In making a career decision many people feel that the decision is final—that it is a terminal decision. If they go in one direction, they assume they cannot go in another. This assumption is true, in many cases. For instance, once a student embarks on a course of study in the humanities, it is difficult, although not necessarily impossible, to go into medicine. However, other career decisions can lead to multiple paths. An undergraduate major in the social sciences can lead to a career in business, law, teaching, or research, to name a few possibilities.

Sometimes people have the luxury of exploring a job or a career opportunity. For example, a college professor who takes a year's leave of absence to teach elsewhere or who tries a job in business can return to the college.

Tom Fenton's decision to leave his employer of twenty years was a terminal decision; it is unlikely that he could go back to work for that company. Because he initially anticipated working for the company for his entire career, this was a big shift in his mental set. After all, his identity was tied to the firm. Leaving would destroy this corporate bond. Although leaving the company was a terminal decision for Tom, he viewed his next job as exploratory. Even before he started the job, he was preparing himself for the possibility of failure or moving on to a better opportunity. He was considering how much he would learn and how the experience, whether successful or unsuccessful, would be valuable in finding his next position.

Harvey Monroe took his present job to tide him over as he paid back his debts. The job gave him a chance to explore the business world and possibly enter corporate legal work through the back door. Now realizing that he would not be able to use his legal education in the company, he was facing a decision—leave for an uncertain environment or stay where he was. When we last spoke to Harvey, he was avoiding the terminal decision. He could stay and start a law practice on the side. He was already doing some legal work for friends and relatives. He could continue exploring.

Patricia Stewart saw her decision to take the new job as terminal until she realized that she was not giving up much by turning down the offer. Staying in her current job was financially beneficial, and she could explore career opportunities and take the time to think about what was important to her in a job.

A study that followed ninety-five men from their adolescence into their mid-thirties examined the series of career decisions they made during those eighteen years (Phillips, 1982). The results showed that decisions made at the early stages of career development are likely to be exploratory and that decisions made at later stages are likely to be terminal. The exploratory decisions continued into adulthood for many of the

subjects; 37 percent of the subjects were still making exploratory decisions by age thirty-six. Exploratory decisions, particularly early in one's career, are likely to forestall premature closure and reduce decision errors. Also, 19 percent of the subjects made exploratory decisions after having made terminal decisions, although, as Tom Fenton demonstrated, doing so is not always emotionally or economically easy. Arthur S. Harris, Jr., a free-lance writer who specializes in travel, aviation, and skiing, wrote in the *Wall Street Journal* about his experience as a corporate dropout. A former corporate executive, he felt that his career in the corporation had peaked and that he was on a professional plateau. He engineered his departure by degrees (Harris, 1985, p. 30):

> Our leave of absence—I say our because Phyllis and I took our three kids out of school and we all left the city—lasted six months. In a rented adobe house in Puerto Angel on the Mexican coast south of Oaxaca, we read, swam, tanned, slept in hammocks, learned pidgin Spanish. The children, especially the youngest who played with Mexican children, learned Spanish more easily than we did. Altogether they learned so much more than they would have in school. They got into archaeology, astronomy (we were close to the epicenter of the February 1970 total eclipse of the sun), and other subjects seldom touched in school.
>
> We took our leave in December and returned tanned, thin, and converted to vegetarianism (pigs were killed next door to our adobe house; we'd hear them scream just after dawn) in late May.
>
> It would be false to say I was thoroughly recharged and approached my job in the corporation with vigor. While I gave the appearance of renewed energy, I had experienced freedom in mid-life: six months with wife and children twenty-four hours a day; reading philosophy in a hammock in the tropical siesta heat of Puerto Angel, a fishing

village being invaded by a few mushroom-seeking
hippies; musing on life Beautiful.

Back at work, outfitted in the suit I now
called my "costume," discussions of budget esti-
mates and quarterly revenues got to me fast. Even
a new title didn't help. I'd had my leave of absence.
It had cleared my head, but I now knew I would
never last until some young employee, surely my
staff senior, gave a little speech while handing me
a Rolex at a retirement dinner.

Harris's taste of freedom was, in his words, "more than an extended vacation." It was a "door opening." He had made an
exploratory decision. Harris spent three more years as a company man before he "walked through that door to mid-life independence."

An alternative career can also sound better than it is,
however. In 1971 Charles C. Townsend, Jr., a managing director for the Manhattan-based Morgan/Stanley investment bank-
ing company, purchased a farm in Hopewell, New Jersey, with
his wife, Ann, and three partners. Neither Charles nor Ann had
a farming background. One of their partners had a master's
degree in animal husbandry, one had a degree in agronomy,
and one was a family friend. Charles continued commuting full-
time to New York City for six years and then went in only one
or two days a week (Lane, 1985, p. 1B):

"We bought sixty-two bred cows (pregnant
cows) and one bull in 1972," Mr. Townsend said.
"After a couple of years with the cows, we disagreed
with each other's decisions about management, so
we split the herd into four equal parts. Animal husbandry and agronomy went away," he explained.

"And so did our knowledge," added Mrs.
Townsend.

Despite their lack of expertise, the Townsends
continued to tend cattle on their 110 acres and
raised crops on more than 700 acres they leased.

But one season, Mr. Townsend tired of operating a combine, a machine used to harvest corn and grains. He also found that farming required plenty of toil to reap even a small profit.

"I got into the combine October 12, 1979, and I didn't get out until Christmas week. It was then that we made the greatest profit we ever made, which was $88," he said.

It was then too that the Townsends decided to phase out their field crops.

"We kept about 80 to 100 acres to make hay for cattle feed and for sale," Mr. Townsend said.

The Townsends, however, sold their last cow in August 1983 and are presently selling 100 acres of land behind and to the east of their house . . . . The couple is holding on to a ten-acre plot with two small ponds, a barn, and a garage/stable.

Accustomed to a steady income, Mr. Townsend found he could not bank on the unpredictability of farming to make a living.

"You couldn't make a buck. You couldn't predict anything. You had little control over your ability to succeed," he said.

At fifty-seven, Mr. Townsend is retired from Morgan/Stanley, but he is not one for sitting still. Four months after his 1984 retirement, he returned to Morgan/Stanley as a consultant to the company's Conrail Project.

The life that seemed romantic and bucolic to Charles and Ann Townsend turned out to be a lot of work. There were challenges and the farm was a good place to raise their children, but farming was not a dream life. Fortunately, Charles Townsend did not give up his livelihood as an investment banker, although he apparently would have liked to give it up sooner than he did.

Arthur Harris and Tom Fenton both explored alternatives before they made a change. Patricia Stewart realized that a career

move she thought would be a good change was not right for her. Charles Townsend had a considerable investment in his farm, and it provided a good home for his family, but he also had his job as a means of livelihood. As we will see again in Chapter Three, an exploratory frame of mind allows a person to try alternatives without making a final commitment.

Summary

As we saw in Chapter One, personal factors that influence career decisions are one's self-confidence and belief that "I control what happens to me." Having an accurate picture of one's own skills and motivation and knowing what one wants from a career are other important factors. Recall how Patricia Stewart agonized over her decision until she took stock of her motivation and realized there was only one logical choice.

Exploratory decisions are temporary choices people make to see how they will work out. Like living with someone before getting married, exploratory decisions are most common early in one's career, when one does not want to preclude later opportunities. People often continue exploring into their thirties or make an exploratory decision after what seemed to be a terminal one. Companies are probably more receptive today to exploratory decisions than ever before. Some firms offer leaves of absence and even encourage sabbaticals so that employees who feel burned out, such as Arthur Harris, can be refreshed and experiment with alternative career choices. Some people try such experiments on their own without leaving their jobs, as did Charles Townsend. Chapters Three and Four look closely at how career decisions are made and give suggestions for making good career choices.

Three

How Career Decisions
Are Made:
Five Decision–Making Stages

This chapter describes ways to recognize that a career decision must or should be made, explore the environment for alternatives, evaluate those alternatives, make the final choice, and commit oneself to that choice. A good way to begin reading this chapter is to think of two examples of decisions that you or someone you know has made. They may be career or job decisions, but they do not have to be. First, think of a decision you would classify as good—one that held up over time (that is, one the person was satisfied with and did not regret or reverse). Second, think of a decision that was unsatisfactory (that is, one the individual changed his or her mind about later or that the individual has been unhappy with ever since). Now consider the differences in how these two decisions were made. Was there a difference in how the need to make the decision arose, the time available to make the decision, the number of alternatives available, how thoroughly alternatives were investigated, or how carefully they were evaluated?

Decision Stages in Theory

Let's consider the different elements of a decision to understand what makes a good decision and what makes a bad one. We distinguish five decision-making stages (after Janis and Mann, 1977).

Identifying Problems. We discussed this aspect of decision making in Chapter One. The need to make a decision usually stems from information the individual receives. This decision to make a decision may be self-initiated or it may arise because of a sudden opportunity that the individual did not seek but that he or she decides to consider seriously. As people appraise their situations, they ask themselves how serious the risks are if they do not make a change. If there are few risks of staying where they are, then they are likely to avoid a decision, unless the alternatives are highly positive and low in risk.

Exploring Alternatives. Once people decide to decide, they consider the alternatives open to them. In fact, the appearance of alternatives may be the source of the decision. In this stage, the individual attempts to survey the available alternatives. We discuss this stage in detail later in this chapter.

Evaluating Alternatives. Evaluation is the process of weighing and comparing alternatives, of asking which alternative is best or which at least meets the essential requirements. This stage is discussed in Chapter Four.

Making a Choice. This is the point of decision. Once information has been gathered about alternatives and the alternatives have been compared, people make a choice. As we shall see in Chapter Four when we consider decision strategies, choice is not always a matter of simply selecting the best alternative. The best alternative may not be the one a person really wants.

Making a Commitment. This final stage, as we will see in Chapter Four, entails announcing the decision, implementing it, and adhering to it.

Decision Stages in Practice

To see how these stages apply, let's use them to describe Tom Fenton's decision to make a mid-career change. (Tom was introduced in Chapter One.)

For Tom, identifying the problem involved feeling dissatisfied with his job over a period of time. Advancement opportunities were slim because the company was cutting back.

To generate alternatives, Tom spoke to many people inside and outside the company. He learned that the company would be in turmoil for at least another three years and that there would be more layoffs. He also learned that there were many opportunities outside the company.

When Tom started evaluating the alternatives, he realized that if he stayed with the company, he would have three to five frustrating years during which he would feel underutilized and would not be increasing his marketability outside the firm. Because many people would be laid off—possibly even himself— he thought it might be advantageous to be one of the first on the job market. The financial incentive from the company was also an advantage.

The choice seemed obvious once he had collected the information and evaluated it. But making the choice required breaking the psychological bond with the company—a bond that had been built over twenty years. Tom rationalized that the company had weakened the bond by reducing job security and lessening its concern for people.

Once Tom had agreed to the settlement and announced his decision, there was no turning back. However, it is not clear that he was completely committed to the decision because his next step was to start a new decision process to investigate other job possibilities.

In practice, many decision processes are anything but logical, as we will see in the case histories presented later in this chapter. People may repeat several stages more than once before making a decision, for example. Despite these permutations, it helps to think of a decision as a series of stages. Just keep in mind that decision processes do not all occur in the same way.

Consider the decisions you identified earlier. Think about how the individual went through each of the stages. Did the stages occur in the order given here: problem identification, generation of alternatives, evaluation, choice, and commitment? Which stages took longer? Which were the most difficult?

Not thoroughly working through the first three stages of decision making can result in a poor decision (Janis and Mann, 1977). Did you find this in your comparison of the good and bad decisions? For example, not collecting enough information, discounting or ignoring relevant information, or not having accurate data can make one vulnerable to negative feedback when announcing and carrying out the decision. People guard against such criticism by trying to make a good case for their decision once it is made, even if the judgment process was not extensive or entirely rational.

Once the choice is made, people may experience a period of relief. At this point, they commit themselves to the choice—for example, by announcing it to friends or signing a contract. This commitment helps them stick to the decision and reduces the likelihood that they will feel unhappy with the choice (what psychologists call *postdecision dissonance*). They realize that there is no turning back and that it would not fit their self-image to admit that they made a mistake. During commitment, they are likely to discover or invent additional reasons why they made a good choice, or they may focus on the good aspects of the choice and ignore the bad. We return to a discussion of commitment in Chapter Four.

Exploration Stage

Exploration involves four components: where one explores, how one explores, how much one explores, and what one explores (the focus of exploration) (Stumpf, Colarelli, and Hartman, 1983). This information about career alternatives comes from the environment and from oneself. For instance, employees receive feedback from their bosses and peers and gather information about job responsibilities from others who have been in the job before. Employees also ask themselves what they want, what they like to do, and what they are able to do.

Some people gather this information systematically. They make lists of people to talk to for information and advice, or they experiment with different career activities, trying out new roles and new skills. Others are less systematic in their search

process. They pick up bits and pieces of information as they do their jobs, or they speak to people they happen to meet rather than making an effort to talk to people they respect or who are in a position to have accurate and thorough information.

Exploration may be quick or it may extend over long periods of time, possibly even years. Many people do not do much exploring, particularly people who are not used to it. Those in mid-career are likely to do less exploring when thinking of a career change than are those who are graduating from college and thinking about their first job. The amount of information one needs before making a decision depends on how one evaluates information and makes choices. Some people want and use every possible bit of information about each alternative. Others want only the most important information.

The focus of exploration is the job characteristic important to the individual. Relevant elements may include the type of job, advancement opportunities, the type of boss, and the type of organization.

Resource 1 is a career-exploration survey; it may be helpful to employees in making a career decision or in analyzing how they explore alternatives before making a job choice. In addition to questions about where, how, and what they explore, it asks about their satisfaction with the information they obtain.

A study of career exploration using the measures in Resource 1 showed that systematically exploring alternatives leads to acquiring more information and being more satisfied with the information obtained than does not exploring alternatives systematically (Stumpf, Colarelli, and Hartman, 1983). In addition, graduating business students were more likely to explore the environment and obtain more information than were those changing careers. (The career changers in the study were Ph.D.s in the humanities and social sciences who were trying to switch from college teaching to working in business.)

Case Histories: How Carefully
Do People Make Career Decisions?

So far in this chapter we have outlined decision stages and highlighted the value of exploration for alternatives. We

also noted that decisions are not as rational as the logical sequence of stages would suggest. Many important decisions in our lives may be made haphazardly, while comparatively unimportant decisions may be given careful consideration. Consider the following descriptions of how several people made career decisions.

George Hammer changed occupations early in his career. George was a music major in a college and wanted to be a music teacher. But he had trouble finding a job after graduation, so he took the first offer that came along—activities director in a nursing home. In the meantime, he sent out resumes and eventually landed a job as a music teacher to fill in for someone on maternity leave. He loved the job, but lost it after a year when the woman on leave returned to work. He found another teaching job, but the schedule was very demanding. George told the school he would work only until they could find a replacement. By now he was married and his wife was pregnant, so he needed a steady position. His father-in-law worked in the personnel department of a large company, and he wanted George to apply there for a management-trainee job. George did, and he also applied to several other companies. He took the job with his father-in-law's firm—the first offer he received. "It's funny to think about the importance of fate," George said. "If the teacher I replaced on my first job had not returned from maternity leave, I would probably still be teaching in that school today."

Carol Locke found her job by following an impulse. She was walking down the street during the winter break of her senior year in college. She had not done much thinking about what she would do after graduation: she just knew she would get a job somewhere doing something. As she was walking, she passed the employment office of a large nationally known organization. She thought, "Why not go in and ask about the job possibilities?" She took a test and was told she would probably be eligible for a management-trainee job. After an interview several weeks later, she received a formal job offer and took it.

Steve Riley considered several job possibilities but was in no rush to find a job after graduation. He was a history major. During his senior year, he applied to several law schools.

He was accepted at Boston College, but he wanted to attend Georgetown, which rejected him. "It did not really matter," Steve said. "I felt burned out academically. Not that I ever concentrated on my studies. I just wasn't up for more academic work."

Steve had four on-campus interviews with corporate recruiters. A few minutes into the first interview, the interviewer said that he could see that Steve would not be good in the job, but he helped Steve improve his interview skills. This coaching made a difference. Steve's next interview was with Procter & Gamble (P&G), which was followed by a rigorous group-interview process with other P&G recruiters who came to campus. They offered Steve two jobs, both in sales. One was on Long Island. He turned that down because he did not want to live there. Then they offered him a job in Buffalo, which was not any better in Steve's mind. By this time he had decided he wanted to live in Boston with his girlfriend. Another tentative offer came from General Electric, but that did not materialize. A third offer came from a large company in Boston two months after he graduated. By this time, he was traveling through Georgia, Florida, and Mississippi doing nothing in particular. He thought he would eventually work for P&G, so he was not worried. They promised him a job in Portland, Maine, if he wanted it. But when he got back to Boston, P&G was not interested in him any longer. Although he had ignored the letter from the other company, he decided it would not hurt to call them. As it turned out, they were still interested and offered him a job. Steve could stay in Boston, the pay and benefits were excellent, and the training program had a good reputation, although not as good as General Electric's.

George Rutter left a secure job to pursue a dream. Raised in Tennessee, George was a talented tenor. He attended a small music college in New Jersey and took a teaching job in a nearby town after graduation. He reasoned that he could continue with his voice teacher at school and look for temporary opera jobs in the New York/Philadelphia area. George loved teaching music but found it did not help his voice career. After he talked all day in the classroom, his voice was in no shape for rehearsals

in the evening. He noticed that his voice improved dramatically during the summers, when he concentrated on singing, and deteriorated in the fall, when school resumed. After a few years, he decided he had to be careful during the school year to be sure his voice did not suffer. He put less energy into teaching and more into his voice. This method worked for a time, but after seven years of teaching he began to realize that if he was ever going to be a professional singer, he would have to concentrate on it full-time. He began to prepare for this change by saving some money and being sure that he had the material things he wanted, like a good stereo.

Three years later, after ten years of teaching, George quit his tenured position. He and his wife took in boarders to make ends meet. His wife, also a teacher and a part-time portrait photographer, moonlighted as a waitress. George took odd jobs like being a messenger boy. During the day, George practiced, worked out in the gym, and worked on his sports car—another love. He auditioned for a number of singing jobs and got a few. Some days he was optimistic about his future. Other days he was depressed. He was thirty-five years old. If he was going to make it, it would have to be now.

Just before George left teaching, he applied for an administrator's job in the school. He thought that if he got the job, perhaps he would find it too good to turn down, even though it would not get him any closer to a career in voice. However, he did not get the job, and it appeared to others that George was quitting the school in anger. It was as though he were providing a rationale for leaving that others would understand, as though he were afraid others would not understand his desire to be a full-time singer.

George did not plan to return to teaching, but he felt that if he had to, he could always get another teaching job. Even if he could not get a full-time job as a teacher, he could teach privately in his home or at a local conservatory. George did not have a deadline for returning to teaching if he was not a success as a full-time singer. He was ambitious and dedicated. He stated that he was not the type to do anything halfway. When he taught privately, a one-hour lesson stretched to three hours.

He felt that he had always given all his energy to his students, and now it was time to do the same for himself. George's vision of the future was clear. Recognizing that the field was competitive, he wanted simply to be able to make a living singing, not necessarily to be famous or financially successful.

Summary

This chapter described five decision stages: problem identification, exploration of alternatives, evaluation, choice, and commitment. We also described the exploration process, and we provided some questions to help people think about how carefully they explore career alternatives. The case histories showed that people vary in the care they give to making career decisions. Chance and laziness play as much of a part in some decisions as deliberateness and energy. In the next chapter, we continue our discussion of decision stages by considering strategies people follow to evaluate alternatives, make a choice, and commit themselves to it.

Resource 1. Career-Exploration Survey.

Think about a time when you made an important career decision recently, such as choosing a new job. Or think about a career decision you are considering making. Then ask yourself the following questions to evaluate the extent to which you explore alternatives before making a move and how much stress you feel in the process. Your answers should help you understand both how you explore and how much more and in what directions you should explore before you make a career decision.

Environment Exploration

To what extent have you . . .

1.   investigated career possibilities?
2.   gone to career-orientation programs?
3.   obtained information on specific jobs or companies?
4.   initiated conversations with knowledgeable individuals in your career area?

Note: Adapted from the Career Exploration Survey in Stumpf, Colarelli, and Hartman (1983). Copyright 1981 by Stephen A. Stumpf, Stephen M. Colarelli, and Karen Hartman. Adapted with permission.

5. obtained information on the labor market and general job opportunities in your career area?
6. sought information on specific areas of interest?

Self-Exploration

To what extent have you . . .

7. reflected on how your past experiences can be integrated with your future career?
8. focused on your personality characteristics?

Job Exploration

To what extent have you . . .

9. experimented with different career activities?
10. tried specific work roles just to see whether you liked them?

Frequency

11. On average, how many times per week have you specifically sought information on careers?

Amount of Information

12. How much information do you have on what one does in the career area(s) you have investigated?
13. How many occupational areas are you investigating?

Satisfaction with Information

How satisfied are you with the amount of information you have on . . .

14. the specific job in which you are interested?
15. types of organizations that will meet your personal needs?
16. the specific occupation in which you are interested?
17. jobs that are congruent with your interests and abilities?
18. the specific organization in which you are interested?
19. occupations that are related to your interests and abilities?

Focus

How sure are you . . .

20. that you know the type of job that is best for you?
21. that you know the type of organization you want to work for?

22.   that you know the occupation you want to enter?
23.   about your preference for a specific organization?
24.   about your preference for a specific position?

Explorational Stress

How much undesirable stress have the following caused you relative to other significant issues with which you have had to contend?

25.   Exploring specific jobs.
26.   Interviewing with specific companies.
27.   Looking for a job.

Decisional Stress

How much undesirable stress have the following caused you relative to other significant issues with which you have had to contend?

28.   Deciding what you want to do.
29.   Deciding on an occupation.
30.   Deciding on a specific job.
31.   Deciding on a specific organization.

Employment Outlook

How do the employment possibilities look for . . .

32.   the job(s) you prefer?
33.   the organization(s) you prefer?
34.   the occupation(s) you prefer?

External Search

What is the probability that each of the following activities will result in attaining your career goals?

35.   Obtaining information on the labor market and general job opportunities in your career area.
36.   Initiating conversations with friends and relatives about careers.
37.   Initiating conversations with others about their career interviews.

Internal Search

What is the probability that each of the following activities will result in attaining your career goals?

38.   Assessing yourself for the purpose of finding a job that meets your needs.
39.   Learning more about yourself.

40. Understanding the relevance of your past behavior to your future career.
41. Focusing your thoughts on your personality characteristics?

Method

What is the probability that each of the following activities will result in attaining your career goals?

42. Planning your job search in detail.
43. Developing a specific process for investigating firms.
44. Developing questions to ask at interviews.
45. Systematically investigating the key firms in your career area.

Preferences

How important is it to you at this time to . . .

46. work at the job you prefer?
47. become established in a specific organization?
48. work in the occupation you prefer?
49. become established in a specific position?
50. work in the organization you prefer?

Summary

51. What conclusions have you reached about yourself and how you explore career alternatives?

Four

Choosing a Decision Strategy:
Helping Others
Make Better Choices

This chapter considers the different ways people evaluate alternatives, make choices, and commit themselves to them. We will see that logical and rational processes are not always followed and, in fact, may not always be best. We begin by describing ways of making a career decision. Next, we offer a way to identify one's decision-making style. The chapter concludes with a description of how people commit themselves to their choices.

Decision Processes

Optimizing. Decision-making theorists have proposed different models that describe how people make decisions. The optimizing approach is prescriptive—that is, it would be the best way to make a decision if people were perfect. The approach shows how to select one alternative from among many. For each alternative, there are a number of possible outcomes, each with a different probability of occurring. The outcomes vary in value; some are positive, some are neutral, and some are negative. The expected value of an alternative is a combination of the value of its outcomes and the probability that each outcome will occur. Outcomes with a zero probability of occurring are irrelevant. The higher the probability of an outcome and the greater its value (positive or negative), the more impact it has on the overall expected value of the alternative.

The optimizing model allows people to compensate for a low-value outcome with another outcome that has a high value. For example, a job where the salary is low but the type of work is interesting may equal the value of or have a higher expected value than a job with high salary but boring work.

The optimizing model requires that people use their judgment in estimating the probabilities and values associated with outcomes. Sometimes they have objective information about the outcomes. For instance, they know how much salary they are being offered for a particular job, and they can be sure that if they take the job they will be paid that salary. However, if they will be paid on a commission basis, they may have to judge the probability of making a certain amount of money.

If people acted rationally, they would probably follow the optimizing model to make decisions. A decision-making aid such as Resource 2 can help individuals judge the value of each alternative and then pick the alternative with the highest expected value. Theorists argue that people use this optimizing model implicitly. They do not list the outcomes, values, and probabilities, and then perform the calculations on paper or in their minds, but the choice they make may be the same as though they did these calculations. However, research has shown that people neither follow the model nor make optimal decisions. This is not to say that they are irrational. They simply use less optimal models for various reasons: less optimal models are easier to use, some decisions are not that important and so do not demand care, sufficient information is not available, sufficient time is not available, or perhaps the individual does not have the intellectual capacity to optimize.

Satisficing. The term *satisficing* refers to looking for an alternative that is good enough—one that meets minimal requirements. The decision maker does not bother to generate all possible alternatives or to thoroughly compare all the known alternatives. The decision maker simply takes opportunities sequentially, evaluating offers as they come along with no attempt to find viable alternatives for comparison, as one would if one wanted to be sure the offer is as good as it seems or that another job would not be better than the current offer.

Opportunity decisions—settling for the first alternative that seems satisfactory—are examples of satisficing. For instance, a college teacher in his mid-thirties who was denied tenure quickly decided to take a low-paying research job with a state agency. His rationale was that at least he could continue doing research. He investigated other academic positions briefly and applied to a few businesses in hopes of obtaining a position that would allow him to use his knowledge. He spoke to a few people he knew in business who gave him advice and circulated his resume. But he grabbed the first offer that came along. He felt he could continue to explore other jobs, but meanwhile he had a position in his field and he did not have to relocate. Recall that Jim Marsh from Chapter One was in a similar predicament. However, because Jim did not have a job offer, he could not use satisficing to make a decision; he continued with a thorough search of many different alternatives.

Satisficing is more commonly used than optimizing to make career decisions. Many people entering the job market for the first time do not obtain a job that closely matches their career expectations and goals. Rather, they take a job that happens to come their way. Then they change their attitudes and goals to conform with the job. Research results confirm the importance of satisficing in making career decisions. In a study of young British, male workers, Roberts (1968) found that 50 percent of the 196 people interviewed were not doing the jobs they had desired to do after graduating from school. But few wished to change their jobs. Over time, they appeared to have developed ambitions consistent with the jobs they held. As Roberts notes, "Popular common sense conceives individuals as making up their minds about the sort of work they wish to do and then selecting appropriate jobs, yet the typical pattern of interaction seems . . . for ambitions to be adapted to the occupations that young people find themselves able to enter" (p. 174). A study of high school students found that they tend to make career decisions based on the opportunities open to them (Rothstein, 1980). If a student's family was able to afford college, then the student went to college. When jobs were available, students left school for jobs. When the job market was tight, they stayed in school.

According to this opportunity model of career decisions, careers are "a series of responses to a succession of opportunity situations rather than the effort to realize a predetermined occupational goal" (Rothstein, 1980, p. 328). Once a person takes a job and becomes committed to it, he or she is likely to remain with the employer if opportunities present themselves within the organization. But if sufficiently attractive opportunities outside the organization come along, the individual may move in the direction of those opportunities instead of remaining with the first employer. An opportunity may seem satisfactory simply because it is an improvement over the present situation. For example, executive recruiters know that business people who feel underpaid relative to their peers, whether inside or outside their current company, are ripe for an offer from a competitor (Neff, 1985). Also, people may use other decisions, such as the decision to marry or to divorce, as opportunities to make career decisions.

Retrospective reasoning often accompanies a job decision based on satisficing. People make sense of their choices by creating acceptable justifications for them. Such sense-making activity may occur prior to or after making a decision. People accommodate their acts and their attitudes to the choices they make.

Satisficing Strategies. Several strategies for making satisficing decisions are described here. These may be used alone or in combination.

1. *Rely on others.* Tell a qualified expert about the problem and do what he or she says.

2. *Justify an implicit favorite.* Look for an alternative that will not be as good as one's implicit favorite. This procedure will help justify the choice of the implicit favorite.

3. *Eliminate by aspects.* Review alternatives by comparing them on the most important criterion first, and eliminate alternatives that do not meet the minimum requirements. For example, an individual may consider only those jobs offering a certain salary or higher. Then he or she eliminates alternatives that do not meet the next most important criterion—for example, being on the East Coast.

4. *Make a successive limited comparison.* Evaluate and decide on each alternative as it comes along.

5. *Do what worked in the past.* Do what has worked for you, especially if the opposite has not worked.

6. *Muddle through.* Consider a narrow range of alternatives—ones that are similar and happen to be available; then make a tentative choice. Compare this choice with another narrow set of alternatives.

7. *Use mixed scanning.* This is a less systematic version of elimination by aspects. List all alternatives that come to mind, reject those with major objections (not necessarily evaluating each criterion separately), and then evaluate carefully those that remain. Eliminate a few more, then look closely at the rest. Arrange to implement the decision in stages so that costly and less reversible parts of the decision occur later, when the situation seems less uncertain. For example, a person may accept a new job in another city but commute there weekly for a while before moving the family. Meanwhile, the person may continue to explore and evaluate other alternatives.

Examples of Decision Strategies. The people whose decisions we described in the first three chapters used different strategies to arrive at those decisions.

Jim Marsh (Chapter One), the college professor in search of a business career, undertook an extensive exploration process, contacting relatives, former students, and other acquaintances in business. He evaluated and decided on an alternative as it came along—successive limited comparison.

Tom Fenton (Chapter One) made a mid-career change from being manager in a large corporation to executive vice-president in a small company. Tom's decision process was the most elaborate we have seen, coming closest to optimizing. However, it was actually mixed scanning. He explored the environment thoroughly, decided to leave his employer of twenty years, and then uncovered solid job opportunities. He relied on others as a major source of information and weighed all aspects carefully, using several crucial criteria, including location. Tom implemented his decision in stages: accepting his company's separation offer, looking for another job, exploring closest

contacts, and developing a long list of additional contacts in case he needed them in the future. In his mind, the decision he made was an exploratory one. He wanted to keep his options open in case a better position came along later.

Harvey Monroe (Chapter Two), the manager/lawyer struggling for career identity, certainly had an implicit goal. He wanted to be a well-known respected attorney serving his community. He seemed to be searching for a reason to leave the business and pursue his dream. However, he could not justify leaving yet. Money and security kept him in his managerial position. By now it was familiar territory. But he continued to explore and hope.

Patricia Stewart (Chapter Two), the administrative assistant evaluating an unsolicited job offer, struggled with optimizing. Many aspects of the new job (money, vacation time, medical benefits, the cost of the new car she would need) were unfavorable. Because she was also influenced by what others thought she should do, especially the neighbor who prompted her to pursue the job offer, the process was more muddling and relying on others; but, in the end, she had a thorough grasp of the alternatives and seemed to make the most logical choice—her current firm's counteroffer.

George Hammer (Chapter Three), music teacher turned manager, evaluated opportunities as they came along—successive limited comparison. If he had not lost the teaching job, he admitted that he probably would still be a teacher.

Carol Locke (Chapter Three), was the college graduate who became a management trainee. Her only job exploration was walking into an employment office she happened to see—an example of successive limited comparison.

Steve Riley (Chapter Three) muddled through his job search after graduating from college. He considered several alternatives but eliminated them based on one criterion—location. He interrupted his search to travel, assuming that an offer would be waiting when he was ready. He was wrong—at least about the offer he expected. Fortunately for him, another company that had written earlier to express interest was still willing to interview him, and he accepted the offer without further exploration.

George Rutter (Chapter Three), justified his implicit career goal of becoming a professional singer. This was an incremental process. After taking the teaching job, he began to realize that if he was ever to be a serious singer, he would have to devote all his energy to singing. He therefore spent increasingly more time and energy singing and less time in extracurricular teaching activities. Before he left the teaching job, he applied for an administrative position that he did not seriously think he would get and that was far removed from his career goal. When he did not get the job, he seemed to have an excuse to go for his implicit favorite—leaving teaching and trying to be a professional singer.

Advantages of Optimizing and Satisficing Strategies. Recall again the two decisions we asked you to think about at the beginning of Chapter Three. Which decision strategy or combination of strategies was used? The decision maker probably did not think about the strategy being used when making the decision. We believe that a conscious process, while more tedious and possibly more stressful than not thinking about the process, is likely to result in a better decision, one the individual will be happier with. Was one of the two decisions less important than the other? Less important decisions are generally easier to make. Satisficing strategies are often used for less important decisions, while optimizing strategies are used for more important decisions. Although people sometimes spend more time on a less important decision, it generally is not worth our time and energy to search for alternatives and evaluate each extensively when the decision is unimportant.

Using satisficing as a strategy does not preclude using some elements of optimizing. People apply combinations of strategies. Also, a series of satisficing decisions can be more fruitful than looking for every possible choice and then making an irreversible decision. Tom Fenton's mixed scanning and George Rutter's justifying his implicit favorite had elements of optimizing in that both decision makers were prepared for the decisions they made, realizing the risks and planning for contingencies in case they had to reverse the decision or follow another career direction.

Knowing When to Use Different Strategies. Several factors influence which strategy is appropriate: the number of alternatives, the amount of information about each alternative, and the uncertainty of outcomes likely to result from an alternative. In general, satisficing may be the best approach when people do not have the time or the resources necessary for optimizing.

As the number of possible choices increases or the information about them increases, the tendency to use an optimizing decision strategy decreases. Many choices and much information make it necessary to use a strategy that quickly eliminates alternatives—all those, for example, that do not exceed a minimal level on one important criterion. Then, as the mixed-scanning model suggests, the decision maker might switch back to an optimizing model. So, for example, a graduating senior who has had ten on-campus job interviews might use one critical criterion, such as location, to eliminate alternatives. Or a person who has thoroughly explored two or three job possibilities and feels overwhelmed by the amount of information about each may choose two or three critical criteria—such as salary, the nature of the work, and promotion opportunities—and ignore all other considerations in making the decision.

Uncertainty of outcome is another factor that influences decision strategy. When the full range of alternatives and consequences for particular alternatives are unknown or uncertain, then a satisficing strategy is suitable. For example, if a person is fired and needs a job, taking the first acceptable job is more realistic than risking losing the offer while mounting an extensive search for other jobs and investigating each one.

Decision Styles

Some people find it difficult to vary their decision strategy to meet the situation. In fact, many people have favorite strategies they rely on, perhaps because the strategies worked in the past. Decision style is the approach an individual uses whenever he or she makes a decision. One can distinguish three types of decision styles: rational, intuitive, and dependent (Harren, 1979; Phillips and others, 1985). A person's approach to decision

making may be characterized by one predominant style, elements of all three styles, or a variety of styles changing from one decision to the next. Each style is described here.

The rational style involves systematic appraisal and logical deliberation over a period of time. Rational decision makers accept responsibility for decision making, anticipate the consequences of decisions, and gather and weigh information carefully, thoroughly, and objectively.

Intuitive decision makers tend to be emotional and impulsive. These individuals accept responsibility for the decision, as do rational decision makers. However, the intuitive style relies heavily on fantasy, attention to present feelings, and emotional self-awareness. Intuitive decision makers are likely to trust their inner feelings and reactions when they make a decision. Also, they are likely to make a decision without checking it out and getting the facts.

People who use a dependent style assign responsibility for their choice to external events or to other people. These individuals are passive, compliant, and heavily influenced by others' expectations. They have a difficult time making important decisions by themselves and generally need a lot of encouragement and support.

This story illustrates the difference between rational and intuitive decisions. A man in his early thirties telephoned a radio talk show in desperation. The show's host, Dr. Bernard Meltzer in New York City, gives his "radio family" advice on almost anything. "I wish I knew what I'm going to do tomorrow," the caller said. "I have to decide whether to stay with my present job or accept a job offer." The man worked on the staff of a commuter airline that was in financial difficulties. He made $35,000 per year and had been with the company for six years. He said he felt like a big fish in a small pond. His technical expertise was valued, and he had developed a strong loyalty to the company. But he worried that if the company went under, he would have trouble finding a job with the same salary because his expertise was in a narrow area. However, the week before he had received an offer from a larger, well-established airline. He would make $10,000 more but was afraid of being a small fish in a big pond.

His wife was earning $35,000 per year, but she wanted to stop working to start a family, so the higher income would help. The man said he was leaning toward taking the new job.

The talk show host stated that decisions such as this are guided by the head and the heart, and when the two conflict, you have a problem. Here your head tells you to go, and your heart tells you to stay. Meltzer recommended that the caller go with his heart—the airline would not fold, his expertise was needed there, and he liked the company. If he left, he had no idea what hassles he would encounter. However, the radio sage advised that in matters such as this, we are usually guided more by the head, so go ahead and take the job, and call up next year and tell me how you like it.

People may use one predominant style in making decisions, or they may use combinations of styles. They may vary their style from one decision to another. The style they use depends on many aspects of their personality and on how they solve problems in their life. Some people have a positive approach to problem solving (Larson and Heppner, 1985). People who evaluate their problem-solving capabilities positively say they have self-confidence and personal control when solving problems. These individuals are generally confident about their decision-making ability and potential for career success. They are likely to choose an occupation related to their abilities and are not likely to blame others or circumstances for their indecision. Those with a negative self-appraisal of their problem solving lack self-confidence, avoid problems, and feel they have little personal control. They often make poor career decisions and can benefit most from structured career-planning activities and career decision-making aids.

To ascertain one's individual style, one may consider the following questions: Do you make better decisions by going with your instincts or by a careful, perhaps painstaking, decision process? Do you vary in how you make decisions depending on the importance of the decision or other factors? Do you procrastinate in making decisions, or are you decisive, taking prompt and firm action on decisions and implementing them once they are made?

We do not know the decision styles and problem-solving abilities of the people we have used as examples so far. Although we can categorize their decision, we can only guess whether the style demonstrated in the decision is typical of them or whether they vary their style depending on the situation. Tom Fenton's and Jim Marsh's careful decisions demonstrated rational styles and positive problem-solving approaches. Harvey Monroe seemed to have an intuitive way of thinking about shifting from being a manager to an attorney. Patricia Stewart tried a rational approach but depended on others to help analyze her situation. Unlike Tom Fenton, who used others only as sources of information, Patricia was influenced by what she thought her neighbor wanted her to do or expected her to do. George Rutter used a combination of intuitive and rational approaches as he slowly realized what he wanted and prepared to pursue his dream.

In general, dependent decision makers probably tend to be poor problem solvers. Intuitive decision makers tend to make snap decisions that they often do not have confidence in or that do not work out well. Rational decision makers are probably most likely to be positive problem solvers.

Commitment

The last stage in the decision process is commitment. This is the stabilizing force that causes one to stick to the decision even when one's expectations are not met. In other words, commitment exists independently of whether a person is rewarded for his or her choice. There are at least four sources of commitment to a decision: the investment one makes—for example, spending time and effort to make the decision or spending considerable money or making sacrifices to implement it; the reward one receives—for example, being promoted or receiving a sizable pay increase; the fact that one has no other alternatives with higher outcomes; and one's social and personal identity—for example, thinking about oneself as an employee of a particular company.

Consider how committed an employee is to his or her employer. The longer people work for a company, the more probable

it is that they feel committed to it. When people first start working for a company, they tend to seek experiences that allow them to contribute significantly to the organization. If these people are handed assignments that enable them to make important contributions, and if the value of their contributions is recognized by the organization, then they are likely to feel committed.

Organizations also induce employee commitment by furnishing young employees with realistic information about what to expect in the way of job assignments, career opportunities, pay increases, and other outcomes important to the employees. People may stay with an organization if they expect that their future work will be desirable. By creating realistic expectations, the organization is avoiding dissatisfaction, which often results when employees have high expectations that cannot be met. Research has shown that employees with more realistic expectations are more likely to stay with the organization longer than those with expectations that are not met (Wanous, 1980).

Consider some of the examples we have described so far. Tom Fenton's decision to leave his employer was irrevocable, which made this a tougher decision for him than what job to choose. He had to deal with his commitment to his long-term employer in deciding to leave. He felt better about it only as he realized that the company, because of the changes it was undergoing, had violated the implicit contract it had with him. This realization gave him the justification he needed to break the tie. Tom's commitment to his choice of a new job was certainly tenuous at the time we spoke to him. He viewed it as exploratory and even admitted that it might not have been the best choice, although other circumstances entered into the decision, particularly not wanting to relocate for several years until his daughter graduated from high school.

The difficulty Patricia Stewart faced in making her decision about the job offer was that she committed herself to the offer prematurely. Because she had announced she would take the job, she found it difficult to reverse her decision. After thinking it through with her husband, she realized she could give up the commitment in favor of her present company's counteroffer.

Harvey Monroe was torn because he felt committed to his new profession of law and also committed to his managerial position. He sacrificed and worked hard for many years to become a lawyer. Yet he was making a good living as a manager. Staying with the company would be tantamount to admitting that he had wasted his time in law school.

George Hammer, Carol Locke, and Steve Riley had been with their companies for several years when we talked to them. Although they all took their jobs without thinking about them too much, they had all developed a commitment to their organizations. They were well paid, and because of a poor labor market at the time, they reasoned that there were few other opportunities open to them.

George Rutter had committed himself to making a living as a singer. He was responsible for making the choice, although he had set up a situation that provided added rationale for his leaving the school system—applying for the administrator's job, which he knew he would not get. Being rejected for that job seemed to legitimize his decision in the eyes of the community more than he felt would have been the case if he simply announced he was quitting to sing professionally. How long he would remain committed to his present course was unclear. He could not envision what, or how long, it would take for him to admit failure and return to teaching. He ran the risk of being stuck with this commitment, unable to admit to himself that he had failed. If he did not become a success, he might find it possible to rationalize that it was important for him to have tried to make a living by singing and not to regret not taking the chance.

As the examples indicate, careers are often a series of decisions. People take a job and evaluate the extent to which their expectations are met. Even if their expectations are not met, their sense of commitment may tie them to the decision. That is why people such as Jim Marsh feel betrayed when the organization, after several years in Jim's case, rejects them. Everyone, however, does not develop a binding sense of commitment. If a person is dissatisfied, explores the job market, and finds good alternatives, he or she is likely to quit. People are most likely

to leave a job sometime during the first year or two before they feel committed and before they feel locked in by increasing pay, benefits, and pension rights. Organizations keep people by offering these incentives, but these incentives also make it difficult for organizations to get people to leave when they need to reduce their work force. For this reason, some companies, such as the one Tom Fenton worked for, find it necessary to offer lucrative early-retirement incentives.

Increasing one's commitment to a job or company is not necessarily desirable. People who maintain provisional commitment, such as Tom Fenton did in relation to his new job, may have more flexibility to negotiate systematic movement toward a goal than those who become permanently committed. Being provisionally committed makes it easier for the individual to leave the position and find another one that meets his or her needs. The amount of commitment necessary in a job is likely to depend on the nature of the position. Some jobs are so demanding that substantial commitment is necessary to do them well. Commitment may depend also on occupation. Pursuing a degree in medicine does not allow flexibility. The same is now true in many technical fields. One cannot leave the field for a short time to try something else; one must constantly keep up with developments. Other fields, such as business and general management, allow considerable flexibility; people move from company to company or start different businesses, applying their management skills to various areas. We suggest the following guideline: Keep your options open. Express commitment, but at the same time feel free to look for alternatives.

Think again about the two decisions you identified at the start of Chapter Three. How did the individuals adjust to those decisions? How committed were the individuals to them and why? Were the outcomes expected? If not, what was the reaction?

Summary

In this chapter, we described the difference between optimizing and satisficing decision strategies and argued that satisficing works well for most of us most of the time. Satisficing

helps people to avoid dealing with a lot of information and uncertainty. People are likely to vary their decision process depending on the importance of the decision, using a process that approaches optimizing when the decision is important. However, they may use a single style that matches their personality, especially when they are making an important decision such as choosing a job. Once people make the decision, they are likely to commit themselves to it. Some people commit themselves completely, without leaving an opening for reversing their decision if it does not work out. And some decisions are irreversible; we do not have an opportunity to change. But when decisions are exploratory, people can tentatively commit themselves to their choice and keep their options open.

Realizing when it is time for a career change and making a good decision requires being self-confident, being willing to take risks, understanding one's abilities and needs, understanding the environment, and having some definite goals in mind. These characteristics, as we will see in the next chapter, are the foundation for career motivation.

Resource 2. A Guide for Optimizing a Career Decision.

Consider a decision you have to make and the alternatives available. For each alternative, list as many outcomes as you can think of—that is, consequences from choosing the alternative. Some will be negative and some will be positive. Next, evaluate just how negative and how positive the outcomes are by assigning each a number from -10 to $+10$. When values approach 0, the outcome is of little importance. Then for each outcome evaluate the probability that it will happen if you choose the alternative. Probabilities range from 0 (definitely will not occur) to $+1$ (definitely will occur). Now multiply the value of the outcome by its probability of occurring and add these products for a given alternative. This sum is the alternative's expected value. You should select the alternative with the highest expected value.

Try this the next time you make a decision. Chances are you will end up, as Patricia Stewart did in Chapter Two, saying, "Well, I'm still not sure." The problem is that it is impossible to envision all relevant outcomes. And also the values and probabilities are highly subjective. Furthermore, two or more alternatives may be so close in expected value that you are not willing to select the alternative with the highest score.

Five

The Motivation Factors: Career Resilience, Insight, and Identity

The last four chapters described how people make important career decisions. The ways in which they make these choices depend largely on their personalities, needs, interests, abilities, and career goals. People who are self-confident, have a need for achievement, are willing to take risks, and know when and how to act on their own are likely to be positive problem solvers. They will probably make successful career choices—that is, long-lasting job choices from which they derive a sense of satisfaction and fulfillment. People who lack self-confidence, are not achievement oriented, do not take risks, and depend on others for direction are likely to be negative problem solvers. Most likely, they will make unsuccessful career choices.

Dimensions of Motivation

These personality characteristics determine not only how people choose careers but also how they view their careers, how hard they work at them, and how long they stay in them—in other words their career motivation covers a wide range of characteristics. We can group these characteristics into three domains: career resilience, career insight, and career identity (London, 1985). These are defined here.

53

Career resilience is the extent to which people resist career barriers or disruptions affecting their work. People who are high in career resilience see themselves as competent individuals able to control what happens to them. They get a sense of accomplishment from what they do. They are able to take risks. They also know when and how to cooperate with others and act independently. Career resilience determines a person's persistence in attaining career goals.

Career insight is how realistic people are about themselves and their careers and how accurately they relate these perceptions to their career goals. People who are high in career insight try to understand themselves and their environments. They look for feedback about how well they are doing, and they set specific career goals and formulate plans to achieve them. Their career insight is thus likely to affect the degree to which they pursue career goals.

Career identity is the extent to which people define themselves by their work. People who are high in career identity are involved in their jobs, their careers, and their professions, and they are likely to feel loyal to their employers. Career identity reflects the direction of career goals—whether a person wants to advance in the company, to be in positions of leadership, to have high status, to make money, and to accomplish these goals as soon as possible.

Table 1 describes the components of the three career-motivation domains.

Measuring Career-Motivation Components

Each of us has a feel for how self-confident we are, how much we want to advance, how well we understand our work environment, and other elements of career motivation. But we do not necessarily see ourselves accurately. Consequently, psychologists have developed ways to measure these characteristics. One way is in a career-motivation assessment center designed by Manny London and Douglas W. Bray. Bray had developed the first business application of the assessment center in the late 1950s for American Telephone and Telegraph (AT&T). The

purpose was to judge managers' potential for advancement to higher levels by measuring various managerial skills such as decision making, leadership, oral and written communication, organization, and planning. The assessment-center method has since been used in many companies, and it continues to be used today in AT&T. The assessment center lasts one, two, or three days, depending on its complexity and purpose.

Managers being assessed participate in behavioral exercises and written tests. The behavioral exercises in the assessment center are simulations; usually the participants are given some information and are then asked to give a presentation, discuss issues with other participants, play a business game, or review data and make decisions. Several observers, psychologists, or managers take notes and write reports about each participant's performance. After the assessment, the staff meets to read all the reports about each participant on the dimensions of managerial success. Research has shown that performance in an assessment center does not change much over time. Also, assessment-center performance is one of the best predictors of further advancement. (In Bray's studies, the assessment-center results were not used to make promotion decisions, so that the relationship between the results and later success is not due to a self-fulfilling prophecy; Bray, Campbell, and Grant, 1974.)

One two-day career-motivation assessment center used psychological tests , background interviews, and role-play exercises to measure the personality characteristics of career motivation. (See London and Bray, 1984, or London, 1985, for a description of the procedures.) The participants were forty-eight young managers. A team of assessors rated each participant on the career motivation dimensions after reviewing the reports on the tests and exercises. Several of the people described in previous chapters participated in the assessment center. Here are their assessment results.

Harvey Monroe (Chapter Two), the frustrated lawyer, was moderate to low on career resilience. His self-confidence was moderate; he believed in his own abilities. His need for achievement was high, which he demonstrated by pursuing law school. But he was low on risk taking, and he feared failure.

Table 1. Descriptions of the Career-Motivation Dimensions.

Dimensions	Definitions	Behaviors Demonstrating the Dimension
Career resilience	The ability to adapt to changing circumstances, even when the circumstances are discouraging or disruptive	Conveying self-assurance in performing the job Easily adjusting to changes (new procedures, rules, technology) Expressing ideas even if they are unpopular Trying to promote career progress
Belief in oneself	The degree to which one is confident of one's ability to perform	
Need for achievement	The degree to which one desires to excel in one's work	Doing one's best on all tasks Taking the initiative to do what is needed to achieve career goals Seeking projects that require learning new skills
Willingness to take risks	The degree to which one is able to take actions with uncertain outcomes	Expressing ideas even when the ideas are contrary to those of the boss Being unafraid to let others know when they have made mistakes Going out on a limb for something one believes in Being innovative in doing one's job

Working independently or cooperatively as needed	The degree to which one is comfortable working alone or with a group, depending on the demands of the task	Making decisions or working effectively either as an individual or as a member of a team Being able to complete whole assignments independently and being able to contribute to a group assignment
Career insight	The ability to be realistic about oneself and one's career and to put these perceptions to use in establishing goals	
Establishing career goals	The degree to which one has thought about one's career objectives and planned how they can be achieved	Having a specific, realistic career goal and a plan for achieving it Being willing to alter goals as career interests and circumstances change Welcoming job changes and assignments that enhance career opportunities
Knowing one's strengths and weaknesses	The degree to which one has determined one's strong and weak points, especially with respect to career objectives	Seeing oneself as others do Having a clear perception of one's ability to accomplish a task Using feedback from others to learn about oneself
Career identity	The extent to which one defines oneself by work	
Job, organizational, and professional involvement	The degree to which one is willing to immerse oneself in activities related to the job, the organization, and the profession	

Table 1. Descriptions of the Career-Motivation Dimensions, Cont'd.

Job involvement	Working hard, even if it means frequently working long days and weekends
	Treating the job as more important than other activities
	Considering the job to be fascinating
Organizational involvement	Taking pride in working for one's company
	Feeling that if one's company is successful, one is successful
	Thinking many people in the company can have a significant impact on one's career
Professional involvement	Seeing oneself as a representative of the profession
	Being active in a professional organization
	Encouraging others in the field to join the professional organization
Need for advancement, recognition, and a leadership role	The degree to which one desires to be promoted and acknowledged as a leader
Need for advancement	Wanting to advance as rapidly as possible
	Having advancement as a major career goal

Need for recognition

Wanting to earn as much money as possible

Thinking it is important when the boss recognizes one's accomplishments

Looking forward to the prestige that comes with advancement

Wanting to be recognized for good performance

Need for a leadership role

Desiring a position of leadership

Emerging as the leader in group situations

Wanting to hold an elective office in an organization

This accounted for his fairly low rating on overall resilience given by the assessment staff. This fear may have been what kept him in the company and prevented him from trying on his own to be an attorney. He was impressionable and relied on others for approval, as was evident in his concern for what his friends thought about him. Recall that they were encouraging him to give up his relatively well-paying job to start a law practice and possibly try his hand in politics.

Harvey's career insight was on the low side. Although he was realistic enough to know that quitting his job would be the start of a difficult struggle, he was not yet certain about his long-range goals. He was tending in several directions, although he appeared on the verge of making a decision—or being pushed into making a decision by his friends. Harvey was an over-achiever. His low scores on a measure of verbal and math ability and his marginal performance throughout his schooling (he always had barely passing grades) suggested that he had gone further than he should have.

Finally, his career identity was low as far as a job in management was concerned. He was not particularly commit-ted to the company, although he liked the salary and security. He craved recognition, but he did not want to be a leader or advance in the company. Certainly Harvey was not content. Nor was he upwardly oriented, at least in the corporate sense. He was professionally oriented. Harvey was beginning to feel that he was a misfit in the corporate world.

George Hammer (Chapter Three), our music teacher turned manager, was moderate on career resilience. He was moderate on self-confidence, need for achievement, and risk tak-ing. However, he did not have a need to be independent, and he seemed to need the approval of his supervisors and peers, relying on them to help make decisions and set career direc-tion. (Recall that he applied for the job in business because his father-in-law worked for the company.)

George was fairly high on career insight and identity. He now knew that he wanted to stay in management. His expecta-tions for his career were modest and realistic. He seemed to have a good understanding of his own abilities and his work environ-

ment. He wanted to advance to middle management, but he did not see himself as vice-presidential material. He expressed strong loyalty to the company, and he was thankful for the job security. He wanted a well-balanced life and was not willing to devote himself to his career at the expense of his family.

Carol Locke (Chapter Three) walked into an employment office and took the first job she was offered. A black from a poor neighborhood, Carol had attended a special city high school known for its tough college-preparatory curriculum. She excelled and received a full college scholarship. Carol was one of the most resilient people we assessed. She was extremely self-confident and independent, and she took risks. The clinical psychologist wrote in his report about Carol, "She is distinctive and unusual in her way of thinking and presenting herself, and her responses (to the psychological tests) convey a strong sense of spontaneity, self-direction, and assertiveness. The life-style she desires involves adventure, excitement, and a free spirit, and she is attracted to nonconformity."

However, Carol was evaluated as low in career insight despite her certainty about her dissatisfaction with the status quo and despite having an accurate picture of her abilities. The raters were influenced by the unrealistic nature of her dreams for the future. For instance, on one test, she admitted that the things she wanted most "are usually expensive and unattainable." Twenty years from now, she dreamed of being "the second wife of a millionaire living in a villa on Capri."

Carol's career identity was low. She was frank in saying that she could not care less about the company. And job security was the last thing on her mind. Promotion would be all right because it would give her the recognition and money she wanted, but she did not want to advance to be a leader. Carol was not the type to wait around for something to happen. In fact, shortly after the assessment, Carol left the company to work as a waitress at a ski resort. A misfit as a manager in a bureaucratic environment, Carol hoped this move would be the start of an exciting career in the travel and recreation industry.

Steve Riley (Chapter Three), who also took a job without an extensive search, was moderate to high in career resilience.

Perhaps his self-confidence and willingness to take risks contributed to the haphazard way he found his first job. His career insight and identity grew over time. He married his college sweetheart shortly after starting the job, and they had a son about a year later. Job security was becoming important to him. It was particularly important to him because of an experience his stepfather had. His stepfather was fired after ten years with a small company. Steve recognized the benefits of working for a large organization that could promise some security. More advancement oriented than George Hammer, Steve wanted increased responsibility in the company. He felt he had the right skills, and he demonstrated his ability on the job.

Developing Career Motivation

Career resilience is probably fairly well established for most people by the time they start their careers. The components of career resilience stem from reinforcements received during childhood and adolescence. For instance, self-confidence is likely to rise when we are positively rewarded for our decisions and actions. Career resilience is evident early in one's career. For example, a music critic writing about the virtuoso classical pianist Murray Perahia stated that ''right from the beginning of his career, he instinctively knew what he wanted to accomplish as a musician, and he communicated a secure sense of himself and his artistic intentions as well as presenting the audience with a clear, instantly identifiable personal image—all of which, I hasten to add, is a natural extension of himself'' (Davis, 1985). This passage describes the essence of career resilience.

Because career resilience starts early in life does not mean it cannot change. Our work experiences support or discourage career resilience. For instance, managers reinforce their subordinates' career resilience by giving them feedback on their performance, praising them when they do well, providing opportunities for achievement, and rewarding innovative behavior without undue punishment for failure. Working for a boss who does not behave this way eventually will weaken if not destroy career resilience.

Being resilient is probably more important in today's work environment than ever before. Today's companies emphasize taking risks. They value entrepreneurial behavior. Competition and pressure to reduce costs mean less job security. In such situations, understanding one's degree of resilience and knowing how to place oneself in a situation that reinforces resilience are crucial to career survival, let alone career success, and are probably more important than career planning.

Career insight and identity are probably less stable than career resilience. Insight and identity stem from the information people receive about themselves and the environment, what they see others do, and what they are likely to be rewarded for doing. They develop insight as they experiment with different career goals. They explore the environment, make some tentative choices, and see how others react. The five-year-old who says proudly that he wants to be a firefighter gets a laugh and a pat on the head. The sixteen-year-old learns quickly that he will get a more positive reaction from his parents when he says he wants to be a physician than when he says he wants to be a scuba diver.

As we described in the last chapter, exploration often continues into adulthood, when people actually try out different careers, first by taking courses in various fields and then by accepting a job, evaluating how they like it, and later possibly deciding to change companies or occupations.

Career identity develops over time as people commit themselves to a career direction. (See the discussion of commitment in the previous chapter.) The longer people stay in a job or the longer they work for a company, the more likely they are to identify with the work and the organization.

Another element of identity is how much a person wants career success. At the risk of oversimplification, consider the following two types: uppies and contentnicks. The uppy (obviously, a genus of yuppy) is advancement oriented and wants the status, power, influence, and money that go with advancement and being in a leadership role. (The uppy is similar to what Bray, Campbell, and Grant (1974) call the *enlarger*.) While the uppy lives for tomorrow, the contentnick lives for today.

The contentnick's prime concern is a well-balanced life. Family is as important to the contentnick as work, if not more important. Contentnicks try to do the best job possible recognizing their limited goals. (Bray and his colleagues call this type of person the *enfolder*.) People are often combinations of both. Steve Riley and, to a lesser extent, George Hammer were basically uppies—both wanted to advance in their companies. But they were also concerned about security, and they would not devote themselves to their careers at the expense of their families. They probably would be content if they did not advance as high or as quickly as they wanted.

The basis of career insight is being aware of one's abilities, needs, and interests. People obtain considerable information about themselves from others and from doing their work. But they also give themselves valuable information and insight. The exercise in Resource 3 may help people think about their managerial skills and career motivation. The goal of the exercise is to identify one or two areas needing development. We ask respondents to select one or two and then, for each, to list the specific steps they will take to improve.

Resource 4 provides the format for a career-development journal. People can use this form to see how their job experiences contribute to their career development and thus to their career insight and identity.

Summary

Career motivation is important to how people do in their careers. Career motivation includes a range of different personality characteristics, needs, and interests. We organized career motivation into three domains, each with its own components. Career resilience consists of self-confidence, need for achievement, the willingness to take risks, and the ability to act independently and cooperatively, depending on the situation. Career insight consists of developing one's goals and attaining knowledge of oneself in the work environment. Career identity includes job, organizational, and professional involvement and the direction of one's career goals, such as wanting to advance

in the company or profession. The degree to which people want to advance determines whether they are uppies or contentnicks.

The next chapter considers how the components of career motivation combine to form different patterns of development, some of which are functional and some of which are dysfunctional from the standpoint of career satisfaction.

Resource 3. Self-Reflection Guide for Assessing Career Motivation.

Are you making the most of your career? The term *career motivation* refers to your ability to do just that—to make the most of your career. Whether you are searching for and accepting a new job, revising your career plans, seeking further training or new experiences, deciding to stay with the company, or setting realistic goals for yourself, you communicate the extent of your career motivation. The purpose of this guide is to give you a chance to assess your own career motivation. You should find the guide helpful not only as it pertains to your knowledge of your career motivation but also as it contributes to your career development in general.

In going through the guide, you will be looking at your past performance in light of the dimensions of career motivation described in Table 1. At the end of the guide is an action-planning section. Here you will be able to set up some concrete strategies for working on one or more of the dimensions you have selected for development.

Because the main thrust of the guide is your career development, feel free to use it in the way that functions best for you. You are not obligated to write extensive responses to questions that are not pertinent to you or that refer to components that you have already developed well. You can complete several components, then put the guide aside until you are ready to do more.

Please be honest with yourself as you complete this exercise. No one else will see your answers. You have much to gain from identifying strengths and weaknesses, then planning a strategy for change.

For each component, answer these questions:

1. Think about a recent occasion when you demonstrated the component. What was the occasion? How did your actions reflect the component?
2. Identify some areas of work where you feel less confident about your ability to demonstrate the component.
3. Overall, how would you rate yourself on the component? Based on your performance, give yourself a rating on each component ranging from 1 (less developed) to 5 (well developed). A rating of 1 does not mean that you are poor on the dimension. It does indicate that you see a need for improvement. Conversely, a rating of 5 does not necessarily mean that further development is undesirable.

Note: This guide was developed by Nancy Hicks, Rosemary O'Connor, and Mabel Satrape.

Take a few minutes to review your reflections on the eight components of career motivation. List the three components you would most like to develop in order of their importance to you and your career.

Form 1. Action-Planning Guide.

Career Motivation Dimension Needing Development

Action Steps:

How, *specifically*, are you going to develop this skill?

Barriers to development:

Helps to development:

Time line:

You are now ready to do your action planning on Form 1. Begin with the career-motivation component you chose as your first priority. Be specific about how you will develop that component in your work life. These samples give some ideas:

- Belief in oneself
    Every time you complete a project successfully, give yourself a reward.
    Begin to believe other people when they tell you you have done a good job.
    Take a seminar on raising your self-confidence.
    Accept a compliment without discounting it.

- Need for achievement
    Take the time to do the best possible job on a task.
    Set a difficult but not impossible goal.
    Design a better way of doing something.
    Take one or more work-related courses offered within or outside the company.

- Willingness to take risks
    Accept a job assignment for which you have little or no expertise.
    Make suggestions even though others may disagree.
    Look for opportunities to interact with higher-level managers.

- Working independently or cooperatively as needed
  Outline ways of accomplishing jobs without waiting for your boss.
  Help a co-worker with his or her project.
  Evaluate your job performance against personal standards rather than comparing it with what others do.
  Make and maintain friendships with people in different departments.

- Establishing career goals
  Discuss your career with your boss.
  Identify specific career goals.
  Seek a job assignment that will allow you to achieve your career goals.
  Change or revise career goals in light of new information about yourself or your situation.

- Knowing one's strengths and weaknesses
  Ask respected peers for feedback on your managerial performance.
  Make a list of your strengths and weaknesses.
  Have your boss discuss your next performance appraisal with you.

- Job, organizational, and professional involvement
  Spend free time on an activity that will help on the job.
  Take courses toward a job-related degree or join a professional organization.
  Keep current on company affairs such as deregulation legislation and labor-management issues.
  Stay abreast of developments in your field.

- Need for advancement, recognition, and a leadership role
  Learn about company policies and procedures that deal with advancement.
  Volunteer for or assume a leadership role.
  Let a higher-level manager know what you accomplished on your last project.
  Volunteer for an important job.
  Ask your boss for feedback upon completion of any special project or assignment.

Next, list possible barriers to development as well as anything that may help it. Set time lines where possible. Then do action planning for the next dimension.

Resource 4. Career-Development Journal.

How to Use the Journal

This journal is a diary of key business events. Key events are those that are significant in accomplishing goals, completing action plans, and in other ways shaping your career. Starting today, document any key events, such as special assignments, presentations, or self-development activities, that you feel are significant.

Form 2. Journal Entry.

Event:
Developmental gain:
Aids/hindrances:
Outcome:

Each key event will have its own record form (Form 2). In filling out the record form, document the developmental goal, how the event contributes to it, and the time frame involved. For the event you should also document the aids or hindrances you encounter in trying to achieve the goal. Do not forget to date all entries.

When the key event ends, write your own evaluation of its outcome.

At the End of the Quarter

After three months of journal keeping, look back over your entries. Think about the extent to which the events you documented contributed to or detracted from your career goals and action plans. Analyze what happened during the course of the key event. Did your action plans and work assignments lead to the accomplishment of your goals? Make whatever notes you wish in your journal.

What Next?

Journal keeping should be an ongoing process. Therefore, you should continue to make entries and review them quarterly. Use of the journal will provide you with information about yourself, your job, and your career. Form 3 shows some sample entries.

Form 3. Sample Journal Entries.

Event: *2/1/85   Planning Project: Project Leader - Target Date = 5/1/85*

  Purpose: To gather information on recent technological innovations,
  prepare a report and present results to corporate vice-presidents.

Developmental gain: *Demonstrate leadership skills, develop organizing*
  and planning skills, get some experience in report writing.

Aids/hindrances: *2/25/85   Hindrance: Information for report is not*
  readily available.

  4/1/85   Aid: Supervisor's feedback on my writing style was favorable.

Outcome: *4/23/85   Project complete, report submitted. Only minor*
  changes were made to original report format. Boss pleased!!!

Event: *4/14/85   Enrolled for externally sponsored developmental course*
  to be held 5/24/85 through 5/30/85.

Developmental gain: *Improve self-objectivity and develop a strategy*
  leading to more flexible behavior.

Aids/hindrances: *Aid: Corporation will pay enrollment fee and air fare.*
  Hindrance: Course will take me away from the office and my family for
  one week.

Six

Assets and Liabilities: Analyzing Personal and Organizational Career Development Strategies

The previous chapter discussed the components of career motivation. In this chapter, we consider how the components combine to form functional, and sometimes dysfunctional, patterns. We discuss how these patterns influence career decisions and career success and failure.

Pattern Development

Resilience and its components set the stage for developing career insight and identity. Specifically, people with a positive self-concept are likely to interpret information about themselves accurately. They are able to absorb negative feedback and change their behavior appropriately. The insight they gain is likely to contribute to establishing a career identity. For example, people who are high on career resilience are likely to experiment with different career alternatives early in their lives. They will seek feedback, interpret it correctly, and adjust their career goals based on the feedback. They can then develop a career identity that matches their abilities.

Unfortunately, the process does not always work this smoothly. For instance, consider an uppy (an advancement-

70

oriented person) with low resilience. Let's say he is a manager in a large corporation. Perhaps he is following in the footsteps of a successful parent or has internalized the high expectations his family had for him. He is articulate and polished and never reveals self-doubt intentionally. But his fear of failure constrains any spark of innovation. He focuses on day-to-day activities and has trouble establishing long-term plans for himself or the department. He is frequently anxious. An authoritarian, he is unconcerned about subordinates' reactions and does not involve them in decision making. Ultimately, his lack of self-confidence, low desire for achievement for its own sake, and inability to take risks and act independently will be his downfall.

Of course, this is a caricature. But uppies do fail, and often they are emotionally unprepared for the experience (McCall and Lombardo, 1983). Eugene Jennings, a professor at Michigan State University, found so many people like this that he offered a seminar for failed executives and company presidents who were dismissed by their boards (Jennings, 1984). The failure was such a new experience for them that they were stunned and unable to function.

Such failure is not as likely to occur when people begin their careers with a solid foundation of resilience. Resilient uppies are advancement oriented but in a balanced, calm way. They are concerned about achievement for its own sake, not just because it will lead to promotion. They take occasional failures in stride, learning from them and correcting the situation. People sense that their self-assured manner is not just a facade. They do not constantly weigh the reactions of others. They have a good understanding of themselves and the environment. Good judges of people, they are friendly and cooperative and also act independently.

The resilient individual is not necessarily an uppy, however. Contentnicks with high resilience and insight also see events in perspective. They relish the feeling of accomplishment, but, having modest career goals, they are content with the status quo. Contentnicks who lack resilience, however, feel they are doing their best but are resigned to mediocrity, to not accomplishing much. Failure becomes a way of life, and they never have the

positive experiences that contribute to resilience. Also, they do not develop the insight required for pursuing a goal that can give them a feeling of self-fulfillment.

Thus, different combinations of personality and goal direction suggest different patterns of career motivation. We identify four patterns: healthy development, redirection, intervening self-doubt, and breaking away from an ineffective pattern. These are described here.

Healthy development occurs in people who start their careers with reasonably high resilience. They experienced success as they grew up. They had positive educational experiences, which gave them a sense of pride and accomplishment. They believe in themselves and know that if they set a difficult, but not impossible, goal, they can accomplish it. This does not mean that they have done everything well or that they are intellectually brilliant. They may have experienced some failures that made them aware of their limitations without destroying their belief in themselves. This type of background provides the foundation for accepting information about themselves, for realizing what they like to do and what they do well. They explore career alternatives and perhaps try several directions before establishing concrete career goals.

Redirection occurs when people make adjustments in their careers because of barriers they face. They may become bored or feel that they can accomplish more than they now do. They may lose a job or work in a company that has few opportunities for advancement. Uppies who are not successful in moving up the organizational ladder may begin to feel like runners-up. Such individuals may begin to explore alternatives again and perhaps try one or more, as did Arthur S. Harris, Jr., described in Chapter Two, who took a six-month break from his work to live in Mexico. Or they may adjust their career expectations to match reality and be content with modest goals.

Intervening self-doubt also occurs when people experience failure, but here the negative feedback is so severe that they question their ability. They begin to wonder whether they are as competent as they thought they were. George Rutter, introduced in Chapter Three, often had this experience when he auditioned

for singing parts he did not get. For some people, like George, the resulting depression is short-lived. They regroup and try again. They have enough successful experiences to restore their belief in themselves. Their foundation of resilience is solid, waivering only temporarily. Some people experiencing self-doubt may make a major change, such as switching jobs or quitting work to return to school. Such a change may restore their belief in themselves. But others become mired in self-doubt and depression, unable to see themselves in a positive light.

Breaking away from an ineffective pattern occurs in misfits, people who lack insight into their true abilities and what they could accomplish in the right setting. Consider people low in resilience who became that way because of a rash of failures. Their career goals are likely to be unrealistic, either so ambitious that they could never be accomplished or so meager that they are meaningless. These individuals are good candidates for career or psychological counseling. Probably the only way for them to reverse the pattern is to experience some small successes. Over time, they begin to feel better about themselves. They establish new, realistic career goals. (Chapter Seven considers how the support people receive from others and the successes they experience bring about changes in their career motivation.)

Impact of Career-Motivation Patterns

One's pattern of career motivation affects how one feels about one's career and the decisions one is likely to make. Harvey Monroe (Chapter Two) and Carol Locke (Chapter Three) were misfits. Harvey was a person with moderate to low resilience who found himself in a position that did not match his goals. He was on the verge of a decision to stay where he was or to give up security and income for a risky alternative. Carol was highly resilient but a misfit, at least when she participated in the study. She was still exploring career alternatives and life-styles. At this point, she was willing to try different career directions. She was not willing to settle for second best. She did not hesitate to make a career move.

George Hammer and Steve Riley (both introduced in Chapter Three) were a mix of uppy and contentnick. George was moderate on resilience. He needed support and reassurance from others. He understood the opportunities that were available to him, and he set modest career goals. He had already made a major career shift from music teacher to manager. He had adjusted well to this change, evaluating his opportunities accurately and establishing a new career identity. Steve was higher on resilience and had somewhat more ambitious goals for advancement than did George. Both George and Steve had sufficient insight and resilience to adjust their career goals depending on opportunities and experiences. They may one day realize that their career opportunities are limited. George, because of a moderate resilience, will probably be content with his fate, while Steve will probably not be as accepting of slow advancement opportunities and may end up feeling like a runner-up, although he too was concerned about job security. These are just guesses at this point because we do not know what will happen to George and Steve. We do know from other research that many people who start a career in management with great expectations for advancement adjust their ambitions downward within the first five years (Howard and Bray, 1981). Thus, uppies may become runners-up and runners-up may become contentnicks or misfits. In Chapters Seven and Eight, we will address the factors that lead to changes in career motivation and ambitions.

Patterns in Early-Career Experiences

The first five years in one's career are formative; they are a time for exploration and establishment of goals—a time of transition and adjustment. People learn about their strengths and weaknesses and about their willingness to seek and take advantage of career opportunities. The foundation of resilience is solidified or weakened during one's early career, often in permanent ways (Lorsch and Takagi, 1986). The following two cases show the impact of patterns of career motivation on early-career experiences and decisions.

Early-Career Success. A few young managers in the study conducted by the career-motivation assessment center were high on both ability and motivation. They had outstanding academic backgrounds, having earned excellent grades at top schools. They were sociable, articulate, and seemed to have everything going for them. They were placed in jobs that allowed them to use their talents to the fullest, and their early-career success was already evident.

Donna Grant was such a person. When we met her, she was twenty-four years old and had been with her company for about two years. She had been promoted to second level just two weeks before the assessment. She already had several job assignments but all in the same department, corporate planning. Her work involved economic analysis and forecasting. It required technical expertise and managerial ability in working with others and supervising her two administrative assistants. The interviewer described her as assertive and independent as well as bright.

We classify Donna as an uppy. Married to a physician, Donna wanted to pursue a long-term career with the company. She said that she intended to advance in the company through her own efforts. She contended that she was in control of her career. She did not believe that as a management trainee it was her right to advance to middle management in five to seven years, the average time. She knew it would require hard work. She was also aware of the value of visibility and said she had excellent relationships with third- and fourth-level managers as well as contacts at the vice-presidential level.

Donna's bosses seemed to test her by giving her special assignments. Several times she took the initiative to suggest a new procedure or a different source of information, and these ideas were adopted. She believed that all her bosses were supportive of her. She worked with managers at all levels, and in completing one particular project, she was in the fourth-level manager's office as much as she was in her own. She was assigned to what she called "exciting, dynamic projects." She believed that she would not have been as satisfied with a field assignment because she loathed the idea of working on routine, day-to-day tasks.

The assessment staff evaluated Donna's career identity as very high. She wanted to advance, and she was involved in her job and committed to managerial work. Also, she identified with the company. Her career insight was also high. She had clear career goals, seemed to understand the political and social environment, and had a good grasp of her own strengths and weaknesses. Although she had great expectations for her career, they seemed realistic. She performed well on her job and was aware of the effects that her current behavior could have on her future.

Donna was rated moderate on career resilience. She was high on self-confidence, need for achievement, initiative, and the desire to do a good job for its own sake. However, she had a high need for supervisor approval. Despite her assertion that she intended to control her career, she seemed to require continuous reinforcement from others at high levels. She looked to her boss and to her husband for considerable support. Yet she did not recognize this dependence, regarding herself as self-reliant. She also had a fairly high fear of failure. Many pressures seemed to be self-imposed, and, perhaps related to this pressure, she reported having frequent headaches. The assessment staff believed that either her career with the company would be quite successful or, because of some emotional reaction, she would leave.

Seven months after the assessment, when Donna was interviewed again, she was still in the same position. She complained about feeling frustrated by the civil-service mentality of her fellow managers. She felt they were not as committed as she was to doing the best job possible. She wished there could be a closer relationship between a manager's performance and his or her salary in that some employees seemed to be overpaid given their low contribution. She, however, did not feel overpaid.

A year later Donna was interviewed again. She had been promoted to the top grade of second level and had been transferred to another position within the corporate-planning department. She recognized that all her experience had been in this staff organization and that if she were going to be promoted to third level, she would need some line experience. She was

working with her boss to determine her next position. His advice was that she take a line job in another department and after several years hope to be promoted to third level, at which point she could return to her current department. She rationalized that a line position would be like having a ticket stamped. She would not enjoy it, but it was necessary.

We talked to Donna's boss, and he was extremely complimentary of her performance. He compared her to a more experienced second-level manager in his group and felt that Donna demonstrated considerable initiative and insight into her work. He felt that her career prospects were excellent, and he hoped to be influential in her career development as far as helping her plan for her next several positions in the company.

Donna Grant was an almost perfect case of healthy career motivation. She understood her strengths and knew how to fend for herself. But despite her self-confidence, Donna wanted the approval of others, particularly those in authority. This may be true of many people who, despite self-confidence, need feedback from others to confirm their abilities.

Early-Career Failure. Mark Forrestal, another young manager in the assessment-center study, had been with the company for only one year when he was assessed; he was working in sales. He was having trouble adjusting to the work world. His undergraduate degree was from an Ivy League school, and he had an M.B.A. from a large state university. He was evaluated as moderate on the three career-motivation domains. He impressed the assessment staff as a status climber concerned with making an impression. He talked about the importance of getting to know the right people, yet there was a naivete about him that suggested he misperceived the social situation. He tended to externalize the reasons for many occurrences, yet he had an inner drive. His need for recognition was high, and he was impatient because he found it difficult to meet this need in his job. He looked to others to propel him up the organizational hierarchy. But, at the same time, he was extremely critical of his bosses.

He found his sales job frustrating and in a sense demeaning because he viewed it as merely delivering to customers what

other people developed. He felt outside the mainstream, which was strange because sales was clearly an area of importance to the company. He complained that he had little contact with his boss. He admitted that he fell apart on this job because he was assigned to a saturated market. His clients simply did not have much call for his products.

Mark's next assignment was in a staff job in corporate planning. He felt he was doing much better in this job but was afraid he was burning out. He said the job was draining. He wished for more direction from the boss than he got. When we spoke to the boss, he admitted that his department lacked a definite mission. Because the job was highly unstructured, it made it difficult to set goals for Mark. Also, the job had changed several times, making it difficult to maintain Mark's motivation. The boss hoped that Mark would exert initiative in setting his own goals, but he did not. Mark had difficulty moving to the next step on the project. In exasperation, the boss established procedures to help Mark progress, but the job was still taking Mark too long. The boss concluded that Mark was not a decision maker. He thought Mark was a procrastinator who got hung up on details. He could be inflexible and sometimes failed to assess his environment. On the positive side, he evaluated Mark as creative and resourceful. He showed good communications skills and logical thinking.

The boss stated that the project would be ending in several months and that Mark would have to be assigned to another position. He felt that Mark had not thought about his career plans very much; he was not asking many questions, and was not determining a career course for himself.

Although he was competent intellectually, Mark had not yet had a job experience that was positively reinforcing. However, he finally had a supportive boss who was concerned about his career development. It was becoming increasingly difficult for Mark to attribute his lack of success to the situation. Mark's sense of self-confidence was undermined by his inability to handle the job, and he was beginning to feel like a misfit, asking himself whether he was suited for a career in business. He dreamed of leaving the company to open a small store of his own.

Mark kept trying but was not learning much from his failures. He faced some tough assignments, but he did not have the ability to make the best of them. His self-doubt, lack of initiative, and inability to set realistic goals may make it difficult for him to break away from this ineffective pattern.

Assessing Motivation Patterns

Resource 5 is an exercise to help people think about their motivation patterns as a basis for establishing a career strategy or for fine tuning their current strategy. We already emphasized the importance of knowing oneself and the environment. Resource 4 was a self-reflection exercise that helps people think about their career motivation. Resource 5 is more extensive than Resource 4. It asks respondents to think about themselves in financial terms (assets, liabilities). These concepts are particularly meaningful to people in business (although the terms are defined in a simple enough way to be valuable to readers in other fields). Our goal was to make this an engaging, thought-provoking process. Try the self-assessment yourself. Do not hesitate to fit your needs by revising the definitions, adding to our list of concepts, or clarifying strategies to make them more applicable to you or your organization.

Before trying the exercise, read the example to see how this career assessment works. Then ask your boss or a co-worker to use the process to describe you. Discuss the results and likely strategies. Do this several times at, for example, three-month, six-month, or one-year intervals, to evaluate your progress and redirect your career if necessary. This type of self-assessment is probably more important than planning for your next job, which may or may not be available when you are ready for it.

Summary

As we have seen in this chapter, people with a solid foundation of career resilience are likely to benefit from information and develop career insight, which, in turn, is likely to lead to establishing a realistic career identity. In Chapter Five, we

described patterns of career motivation change over time. Some uppies become runners-up and eventually resign themselves to modest career goals, that is, they become contentnicks. People without a foundation of resilience may find themselves in a situation where the job does not match their abilities. We call these people misfits.

This chapter focused also on early-career experiences because they are formative; what happens to people early in their careers affects what happens later. Although the career-motivation study assessed only young managers, career motivation is important also at other stages of one's career. We have already seen some cases of important mid-career decisions. (Recall Tom Fenton and George Rutter from Chapters Two and Three.)

The examples in this chapter showed the importance of ability and motivation for career success, but they also suggested the importance of the situation. Donna Grant was in a supportive environment, while Mark Forrestal initially had a succession of difficult assignments. The next chapter considers elements of the work environment that support career resilience, insight, and identity, and what happens when these elements are not present.

Resource 5. Self-Assessment Audit.

If you are financially minded, you may enjoy this exercise. It uses financial concepts to help you understand how well you are using your strengths and minimizing your weaknesses in your career. We define the concepts you need, use the concepts to outline career strategies, and provide formats for a career balance sheet and income statement. We then offer an example to show how this approach to self-assessment can be used.

Financial Concepts Applied to Career Analysis

These definitions will help in your self-assessment. Terms with asterisks are levers for growth.

Assets	What you have to offer, your strengths
Receivables	Career rewards you should receive but have not yet received
Liabilities	Your weaknesses and the resources you deplete
Revenues	Career rewards (financial and psychological)
Costs	Energy, time, money, and other resources expended

Net income	Revenues minus costs
Equity	Your employer's faith in you
Dividends	What you pay to others (for example, your family) in energy, time, and money from the fruits of your career in return for their trust and investment in you
Debt	What you owe to others
Asset turnover	The use of your assets; ratio of revenues to assets (revenues/assets)
Net margin*	Ratio of net income or costs to revenue (net income/ revenues or costs/revenues)
Return on assets	Ratio of net income to assets (net income/assets = net margin × asset turnover)
Assets/equity	Your assets relative to the faith your employer has in you
Return on equity	What your company receives from its trust and investment in you (net income/equity)
Retention (earnings retained)	What you retain; energy you plow back into your career; net income minus dividends
Retention rate*	Proportion of net income you retain (retention/net income)
Sustained growth rate	Proportion of equity retained (retention/equity)
Debt ratio	Leverage (debt (short and long term)/(debt plus equity))
Risk: to you	Variability in net income
to your employer	Variability in operating revenues

Career Strategies

1. Assess the possibilities for career growth, such as a strong rate of sustained growth.

2. Increase return on assets by reducing costs or increasing revenues. This strategy is especially important when competition for advancement is great (for example, if you are in a management-development program from which you will be fired if you do not show potential for promotion).

3. Regular information about your performance is critical. You must track the indices that tell you about your career growth. Complete a career income statement and balance sheet every quarter. Do the analysis separately for each major activity if you have several distinct job responsibilities (for example, if you work on several different projects).

4. Do not spread your equity too thin relative to your assets—that is, do not try to do too much too quickly or promise too much to others. (Remember, equity in this context is the faith others have in you.)

5. Monitor your assets realistically. Know when you are doing well and when you are not. Assess the contribution of your job assignments, training, and other experiences to your career goals. This procedure might be termed *unit-based asset management*.

6. Ask for feedback or your activities may bring little return.

7. Take control of the situation. Use information about yourself to make decisions about different career directions and the best ways to acquire and utilize new resources (new skills).

8. Make your costs variable, rather than fixed, and as low as possible to maximize your assets. Keep your performance as high as you can for each unit of energy expended.

9. Plow extra energy into your career when you can expect a good return. Some young people (our uppies) do that by devoting most of their energy to their careers. But later in life (as they move perhaps from being runners-up to contentnicks), they may maximize their return on assets by reducing their costs (energy devoted to work) while still getting as much revenue in return as they can. They may also reduce their debt by using their extra energy on aspects of their lives they had neglected earlier (for example, home and family).

10. Do not take out too much debt at any time—for example, by relying too much on others—even though it is an easy way to increase your return on assets. This tactic can give a false sense of job security and nothing to fall back on.

11. Know your points of leverage—costs, assets, liabilities—and use them to select the best strategies for achieving your objectives.

12. Develop a career plan, similar to a business plan, by identifying key activities and considering costs (psychological, physical, behavioral, and financial) and income resulting from expected career growth.

13. Balance short-run and long-run objectives. Strategic long-run goals, such as going to graduate school for an M.B.A., may pull you down in the short run. Most young people can afford the investment of time, energy, and money. However, as people get older, short-run objectives become more important than long-range ones.

Filling Out Your Career Balance Sheet and Income Statement

There are two ways to fill out the career balance sheet and income statement—one simple, the other complex. Both are highly subjective—that is, they are based solely on your opinion and the opinion of others. You can also create your own method for applying these ideas; the instructions are just suggestions. This exercise is not intended to be precise but to help you think about ways you can improve your career success. Experiment with different ways of filling out the forms. Ask others—your boss or co-workers—to use them to describe you, and review the results with them. Fill out the forms at regular intervals to assess your progress.

To use the simple method, list categories under assets, receivables, liabilities, debt, equity, risk, revenues, costs, and dividends that are important to you today. Those listed on the following sample balance sheet and income statement are suggestions; use others if they are pertinent to you or break up some categories into finer ones. Then rate yourself for each category as low, medium, or high. This method avoids numbers, which can be misleading with a subjective method. Numbers give the impression that objective values can be attached to the categories and that these values can be used to calculate reliable ratios. To generate overall measures for assets, receivables, liabilities, debt, equity, risk, revenues, costs, and dividends, review your ratings and judge whether the most appropriate overall rating is high, medium, or low. To estimate ratios, try using these calculations: $H/L = H$; $L/H = L$; $L/L =$ even; $H/H =$ even; $H/M = M$;

M/L = M; M/H = L; L/M = L. These are not a rigid set of accounting rules but a matter of judgment. For instance, an even value, that is 1, divided by a low value would be higher than an even value divided by a high value. But to the rater, 1/L may be L, despite the fact that this value might be high in comparison to 1/H, which would be judged as low.

Some people are more comfortable with numbers. In all likelihood, people who like this financial approach to self-assessment will also want to quantify it. To use this complex method, rate each component on a scale from 1 (low) to 3 (high); or use a five-point scale for increased flexibility if you wish. To generate overall measures, average the ratings under each group and round to the nearest whole number. Just remember that the numbers you or others generate are simply guides for self-understanding; they are not objective scores.

Career Balance Sheet
Date:

Assets
    Skills and abilities
        Decision making
        Organizing and planning
        Interpersonal skills with peers
        Leadership
        Technical expertise (knowledge)
        Creativity
    Experience
    Education
    Motivation
        Energy
        Resilience
            Self-confidence
            Need for achievement
            Risk-taking tendency
            Independence
            Ability to cooperate
        Insight
            Goal clarity
            Goal flexibility
            Self-awareness
            Knowledge of work environment
        Identity
            Commitment to company
            Commitment to profession
            Need to advance

    Other   _____

               _____

               _____

Receivables
    Money
    Promotion

Accolades or recognition
Favors people owe you
Other _____
_____
_____

Liabilities
Resources depleted
Time
Energy
Weaknesses
Reliance on others
Other _____
_____
_____

Debt
Obligations to the organization
Obligations to the profession
Obligations to supervisor
Obligations to job

Equity
Faith the organization has in you

Risk
Risk to you
Risk to the company

Career Income Statement
Date:

Revenue
Income
Challenge
Achievements
Extent to which expectations were met
Other _____
_____
_____

Costs
Financial expenses
Stress at work
Stress at home caused by work
Energy expended
Other _____
_____
_____

Dividends

Example

As an example, we completed a balance sheet and income statement using the simple method as Harvey Monroe and his boss might have filled them out at the time we talked to them. (See Chapter Two for the introduction to Harvey Monroe.) Unfortunately, we had not developed the method when the interviews were conducted, so we could not obtain their actual responses. We include the boss's judgments on the same sheet for easy comparison. You would probably do them separately.

Career Balance Sheet
for Harvey Monroe

	Self-Rating	Boss's Rating
Assets	H	L
Skills and abilities	H	L
Decision making	H	L
Organizing and planning	H	M
Interpersonal skills with peers	H	M
Leadership	H	L
Technical expertise (knowledge)	H	L
Creativity	H	L
Experience	L	L
Education	H	M
Motivation	H	M
Energy	H	H
Resilience	H	M
Self-confidence	H	H
Need for achievement	H	H
Risk-taking tendency	M	L
Independence	M	L
Ability to cooperate	H	M
Insight	M	L
Goal clarity	H	L
Goal flexibility	L	M
Self-awareness	M	L
Knowledge of work environment	M	L
Identity	M	L
Commitment to company	L	L
Commitment to profession	H	M
Need to advance	M	L
Receivables	H	L
Money	M	L
Promotion	M	L
Accolades or recognition	H	L
Favors people owe you	H	L

Liabilities	M	M
Resources depleted	M	M
Time	H	L
Energy	H	L
Weaknesses	L	H
Reliance on others	L	H
Debt	M	H
Obligations to the organization	L	M
Obligations to the profession	H	H
Obligations to supervisor	H	H
Obligations to job	L	H
Equity	M	M
Faith the organization has in you	L	H
Risk		
Risk to you	H	L
Risk to the company	L	M

*Career Income Statement
for Harvey Monroe*

	Self-Rating	Boss's Rating
Revenue	M	M
Income	M	M
Challenge	M	M
Achievements	H	L
Extent to which expectations were met	L	L
Costs	M	L
Financial expenses	M	M
Stress at work	M	L
Stress at home caused by work	M	L
Energy expended	L	L
Dividends	H	L

Summary for Harvey Monroe

	Self-Rating	Boss's Rating
Assets	H	L
Receivables	H	L
Liabilities	M	M
Debt	M	H
Equity	M	M
Revenues	M	M
Costs	M	L
Risk to you	H	L
Risk to the company	L	M
Dividends	H	L

Net income (revenues minus costs)	L	L
Asset turnover (revenues/assets)	L	M
Net margin (net income/revenue)	L	L
Return on assets (net income/assets)	L	even
Assets/equity	M	L
Return on equity (net income/equity)	L	L
Retention (net income minus dividends)	L	L
Retention rate (retention/net income)	even	even
Sustained growth rate (retention/equity)	L	L
Debt ratio (debt/(debt plus equity))	L	M

Harvey and his boss disagree about Harvey's assets. In particular, Harvey has a higher view of his skills and abilities and the value of his education than does his boss. They are somewhat closer in agreement on Harvey's motivation, although the boss's evaluation is lower than Harvey's on risk taking, independence, ability to cooperate, goal clarity, self-awareness, knowledge of work environment, and need to advance. Harvey also has a higher view of his receivables than does his boss.

Both Harvey and his boss evaluate Harvey's liabilities as medium, but they arrive at the conclusion in different ways. Harvey says that he is depleting more of his resources (time and energy) than his boss sees. However, his boss says Harvey's weaknesses are greater and Harvey relies on others more than he realizes. Harvey sees his overall debt as lower than the boss sees it, especially when it comes to obligations to the company and the job. Regarding equity, Harvey's boss believes that the company has more faith in Harvey than he realizes, given that Harvey is in the company's management-development program. Harvey's perception of the current risk to himself as an employee of the company is much higher than his boss's perception. However, Harvey sees the risk to the company as low, whereas the boss sees it a bit higher.

Harvey and his boss agree on his revenue, except that Harvey has a higher view of his achievements than does his boss. Harvey sees his costs as moderate, and his boss sees them as low. Harvey's boss does not see him expending much energy or showing much stress. Harvey believes he gives many dividends to others in return for their investment in him. His boss does not see it this way, although his boss may not be in the best position to know.

Turning to the ratios, the information for career strategies, both Harvey and his boss see Harvey's net income as low. Harvey believes he is not using his assets (asset turnover and return on assets) as much or as well as his boss believes he is. Harvey sees his assets as higher than his equity (asset-to-equity ratio), in part because Harvey thinks the company's faith in him is low while his boss sees it as high; but both Harvey and his boss believe Harvey's return on equity is low. Both Harvey and his boss see Harvey retaining little of his net income. In fact, Harvey feels he is paying out more in dividends than his net income. Both Harvey and his boss see low sustained growth (income retained relative to equity), although Harvey is probably more negative about the possibility of growth in his current position than is his boss. Harvey sees a lower debt ratio (debt relative to dept plus equity) than his boss because the boss believes Harvey's debt is higher than Harvey realizes.

The career strategies for Harvey are given here in the order of the general strategies suggested previously.

1. If Harvey and his boss have a frank discussion about their perceptions, Harvey may come to understand why his boss thinks Harvey is not devoting enough energy to his job. His boss could also assure Harvey that, despite his flaws, the organization has faith in him and that although his growth potential in the company is not high, it is somewhat better than Harvey realizes.

2. Harvey's strategy would probably be to lower his costs rather than to devote energy to what he perceives to be a losing cause. His boss would probably say that Harvey should increase his revenues by developing his assets—specifically, by improving his managerial skills and abilities. This task might be easier than it now is for Harvey if he increases his feelings of commitment to the company and to his job (his debt). The result may be increased revenues in the form of more challenges and met expectations.

3. Tracking is necessary for risk analysis. Harvey needs to complete a balance sheet and income statement perhaps every three months at first and then semiannually or annually to evaluate how well he is doing and whether he and his boss continue to disagree. Obviously, if his boss continues to see Harvey reducing his costs and effort rather than increasing his assets and hence his value to the organization, Harvey's revenues (specifically, his financial compensation) are likely to decline or at least not increase as fast as Harvey would like.

4. At this point, Harvey needs to make the most of his organization's faith in him. He needs to show that the organization's trust in him is deserved.

5. Harvey needs to think whether his judgments about himself are correct. His boss's evaluation should be a good stimulus to his thinking as long as he is not defensive and does not deny the boss's perceptions. If Harvey were to have one of his attorney friends complete the forms, the picture would likely confirm Harvey's view of himself. Ultimately, Harvey needs to decide who is right.

6. Obtaining his boss's feedback should be invaluable to Harvey in obtaining a perspective about himself that he would not otherwise have.

7. Ultimately, Harvey is the major barrier to his own career success. He might not be the brightest star in the company, but his boss believes that the organization was and is committed to him. Harvey needs to reduce his liabilities (flaws and weaknesses) and be sure his equity (the organization's faith in him) does not falter.

8. Harvey should keep his costs variable rather than fixed—that is, he should put in more energy when it is needed. In doing so, he may be able to reduce other costs, such as the stress he feels, because his revenues will increase and the support from his boss will grow.

9. The message from his boss is that Harvey can expect more from his career in the organization if he devotes more energy to it. He might experiment by following the strategies emerging from his boss's ratings: increase revenues, decrease liabilities, and increase assets that are valuable to the organization, even though doing so may increase costs. Harvey has already devoted considerable time and effort to the company, and he has a good job; he has little to lose by trying to make the most of it.

10. Harvey must be wiser about his net income, plowing more of his revenues back into the organization rather than devoting energy to outside interests. He should also psychologically restructure his debt by realizing his obliga-

tions to the organization and the job and diminishing his obligations to the profession of law.

11. Harvey should learn to control his points of leverage (his assets, liabilities, and costs) and understand how varying them can affect his revenues and his equity.

12. Harvey must decide to increase his growth potential in the company or devote his assets to nonwork pursuits, reduce his work-related costs, get what he can from the company, and then leave, presumably for a career in law and politics. If Harvey continues as he is, the faith the organization has in him will probably decline, reducing the possibility for growth. Harvey should make the most of the situation one way or the other.

13. However, if Harvey were to balance short- and long-term goals, he would not let his chances in the organization suffer even if his long-term goals are elsewhere. Point 9 suggests that Harvey experiment by doing more than he now is to increase his chances in the organization. If the rewards are forthcoming, then he may want to alter his long-term goals in law and politics. He may find it possible to stay with the company and try his hand at politics or law. But at this point, he could benefit by investing more of himself in the company and evaluating the return. Otherwise, his belief that the organization is not doing enough for him will become a self-fulfilling prophecy.

Seven

Sources of Support
for Career Motivation

Career motivation and its dimensions—career resilience, insight, and identity—are the cornerstones for a satisfying, successful career. How people make career decisions and deal with career situations depends on their resilience, insight, and identity. In the previous chapter, we discussed how the three dimensions of career motivation are likely to develop and form patterns that change over time. In this chapter, we consider how managers, companies, jobs, and other people affect motivation.

Which is more important to career success, the individual characteristics and needs a person brings to the job or the job environment? The answer to this chicken-and-egg question is both. Our needs develop over time and change slowly. At the same time, we are products of our past environments, and we are also influenced by present conditions.

Many factors support or weaken career resilience and help establish career insight and identity. Consider the following guidelines. They suggest how to develop career motivation in others.

To support *career resilience*: Provide positive reinforcement for a job well done, generate opportunities for achievement, and create an environment that is conducive to risk taking by rewarding innovation and reducing the negative consequences of failure. Also, show concern for others and encourage group cohesiveness and collaborative working relationships. Positive reinforcement is likely to develop self-confidence. Opportunities

for achievement and risk taking contribute to a need for achievement and a willingness to take risks. Supportive work climates promote cooperation or independent action, depending on which is needed.

To support *career insight*: Encourage goal setting and give career information and performance feedback. Encouraging goal setting, giving feedback on performance, and providing information about career opportunities foster the establishment of career plans and knowledge of oneself and the environment.

To support *career identity*: Encourage involvement with work through job challenges and encouragement of professional growth, provide opportunities for leadership and advancement, and offer rewards such as recognition and bonuses. Job challenges, encouragement of professional activities, and opportunities for leadership and advancement result in job involvement and a desire to advance.

One's work, the boss's style of management, the company's policies and procedures, and the people with whom one works and lives all have an impact on one's career. Many people look to their company and their boss for support for career development. However, they often expect too much. The boss and the company should provide the resources that facilitate development. These resources include identifying people with talent, giving them special job assignments, offering training experiences to everyone who needs them, and providing opportunities to transfer into other jobs when such transfers are in line with business needs. The boss also should help subordinates set goals and give regular feedback to subordinates. Employees, however, are responsible for taking advantage of these resources.

The Boss

The boss influences subordinates' job assignments and the rewards they receive for taking risks. The boss is also an important source of feedback for subordinates. The boss's influence in the organization is likely to affect subordinates' career opportunities.

The boss's support for an employee is often crucial in promoting motivation. Many managers seem to divide subordinates into an in-group and an out-group. Supervisors have confidence in the in-group to carry out assignments without extensive structure or involvement on the supervisors' part. They allow these subordinates to use their own judgment without consulting supervisors every step of the way (Graen, 1976). These subordinates also have more influence with the boss than those in the out-group. The boss gives information to the in-group members that helps them keep track of the pulse of the organization, while the out-groupers are often left in the dark.

The boss can also promote motivation by being a role model. Subordinates learn from their supervisors how to do things and how not to do things. By observing the supervisor, the subordinate learns what behaviors result in positive and in negative outcomes. This is a way for the subordinate to prepare for being promoted to the supervisor's level.

In addition, a boss's style of management can have an impact on employees' motivation. There are probably as many styles of management as there are supervisors. One way to think of management style is as a continuum from autocratic to participative. Some managers are controlling and even dictatorial. Others are open and democratic. And there is a large range in between. Some managers are able to vary their behavior to fit the needs of the situation. For instance, they involve their subordinates in making decisions when the subordinates have important information to contribute and when the subordinates are affected by the outcome of the decision. Other managers involve subordinates in making trivial decisions but maintain tight control over important ones.

One aspect of management style is how much attention the boss gives to developing subordinates' skills and preparing them for responsible positions. Some managers feel uncomfortable as developers because it is not a formal part of their jobs. The boss's support for subordinates' career development thus depends partly on the extent to which the organization encourages this behavior in the boss. One way companies encourage managers to be career developers is to evaluate and reward

bosses for developing subordinates. Another way is to provide tools and assistance for developing subordinates. These include training courses for managers to help them learn what they can do in the way of development. Resource 6 outlines a course on the manager as a developer. Companies that offer such courses and have mechanisms for transferring subordinates to new jobs are signaling bosses that development of people is encouraged.

A boss's commitment to career development is not totally dependent on organizational support. For example, one company (which we describe later) discouraged the movement of people for developmental purposes. It gave little attention to increasing employers' capabilities and focused on meeting current business needs. Nevertheless, some managers in this company were participative and developmental in their management style. They were as concerned about their subordinates' personal and professional welfare as they were about meeting the performance goals of the work unit. It is also possible to have autocratic bosses in organizations that give managers considerable latitude and that encourage developing people.

As should be evident by now, the boss can affect career motivation in various ways. The boss is probably the most important source of feedback and reinforcement. Bosses support and enhance subordinates' career resilience by treating them with respect, giving them important and challenging job assignments, allowing them to make their own mistakes, and encouraging them to use others as resources and to be resources for others. Subordinates are likely to develop career insight when bosses encourage them to set career goals, give them information about events and opportunities in the organization, and give them feedback about their performance. Bosses encourage career identity by giving subordinates challenging assignments and providing different career directions (assigning them to leadership roles, recommending them for promotions). In all these activities, the boss's role is not one of controlling subordinates but of enabling them to perform well by providing resources.

Here are a few questions you can ask about supervisors to determine how supportive they are of their employees' career motivation.

Does the boss reward subordinates for good performance?

Does the boss value each subordinate's contribution to the group?

Does the boss expect a lot from subordinates (but not the impossible)?

Does the boss ask for subordinates' ideas and involve subordinates in making decisions?

Is the boss likely to back subordinates when they do something that could be of value to the company even though it is uncertain whether it will work?

Does the boss threaten dire consequences for those who do not live up to the boss's expectations?

Does the boss reward cooperative behavior?

Does the boss let subordinates know how well they are doing, and how often does the boss give this feedback?

Does the boss provide subordinates with realistic information about career opportunities?

Is the boss a good role model to follow?

Does the boss give good performers increased responsibility?

Does the boss help or encourage subordinates to set career goals?

Does the boss support subordinates' involvement in professional activities?

Does the boss try to promote good subordinates?

Do subordinates have the freedom to do the work they want to (for example, to establish their own work methods and procedures)?

Does the boss help to make subordinates' jobs challenging (for example, by assigning subordinates to important projects that require using a variety of skills)?

Several examples from our case histories give an idea of the boss's role in career development—and of subordinates' responsibilities. A boss's concern about a subordinate's career

development will not do the subordinate much good if the subordinate does not have the ability to succeed. Consider Mark Forrestal, described in Chapter Six. Mark had had several difficult jobs, but his current boss was supportive and concerned about his career development. Mark wished for more direction from the boss however, direction that Mark was unable to generate for himself.

Bosses can be discouraging. Recall Steve Riley, from Chapter Three. Steve had been promised a promotion that did not materialize. His boss had been transferred, and the new boss felt that Steve had to prove himself all over again. Steve felt that this requirement was unfair because he already had put in considerable time on the job and had done well. So he began to look for a transfer to another department where the opportunities for promotion might be better. The boss saw this move as disloyal, and he refused to release Steve from his job. After another year in the position, Steve was finally transferred to a job at the next level, but this was a temporary assignment and not an official promotion.

Harvey Monroe, whom we first met in Chapter Two, could have used the support of a boss to help him sort through the pros and cons of staying with the company and understand how he could apply his law degree to his work as a manager. Harvey's boss did not believe that bosses should be involved in these matters, viewing a subordinate's career objectives as personal. As a result, Harvey had little information about career opportunities in the company. The personnel department staffer told him it would be impossible to move into the legal department. When we interviewed Harvey, we asked him whether it might be possible for him to apply his knowledge of law to other departments and functions in the company, maybe even his current job. Harvey gave this idea some thought, and the next time we talked, about seven months later, he felt much more positive than he previously had about staying with the company. However, he had not given up his dream of community service and politics.

Donna Grant, introduced in Chapter Six, had the right boss at the right time. Donna was considering the types of job

moves she should have to put herself in a favorable position for future promotions. Her boss wanted to be influential in her career development by helping her plan her next few jobs and find her next position. Also, Donna had a good relationship with a manager who was several levels above her; she viewed him as a sponsor. She mentioned that her first boss seemed threatened when she said that she intended to move up in the company. In general, though, she thought that all her bosses were supportive of her career development. She was assigned important projects that required her to work with higher-level, influential managers, and this exposure helped her career prospects.

The Company

The career-motivation assessment, referred to in Chapter Five, was administered in two companies with twenty-four managers participating from each company. Both companies had about the same number of promotional opportunities available. The results, combined with in-depth case information and attitude-survey data from representative samples in each company, allowed us to compare the two companies on the dimensions of career motivation. The study also allowed us to explore the impact of organizational policies and procedures on managers' career motivation.

One company had a management-development program. This company treated young managers as corporate resources for the future. The company attracted highly motivated managers, and its policies were aimed at sustaining and enhancing their motivation. The development program trained the managers as generalists, moving them from job to job, often between departments, to give them a broad view of the business and a variety of line and staff experiences. The young managers from this company who were part of the study were higher on many personality characteristics that reflect career resilience, insight, and identity than those in the other company. Specifically, they were higher on need for advancement, need for recognition, being enterprising and extroverted, and expecting a favorable career. They aspired to higher levels in the organization and had a higher commitment to work.

The other company treated its managers as resources for meeting current business needs. They would not transfer a manager solely because the manager needed experience in a new job for career development. A young manager was hired to do a specific job, not to be prepared to make a contribution to the company at a later time at a higher level. People in this company were promoted as they demonstrated their ability on the job. The young managers from this company who were in the study were less advancement oriented, less desirous of being leaders, more concerned with social than with business relationships, less flexible in their goals, and less committed to managerial work than those in the developmentally oriented company.

Data from attitude surveys administered to broad, representative samples of managers in both organizations indicated that perceptions of career opportunities and the desire to advance were higher in the developmentally oriented company. In other words, the findings did not apply only to the twenty-four managers from each company, who were part of the career-motivation assessment.

Because there were no differences between companies in the intellectual ability of the participants in the study, the results were probably a function of both the companies' policies and the people attracted to the companies. The policies of the organizations influenced the young managers' career ambitions. The developmentally oriented company led its young managers to expect a lot from their careers. In the other company, bosses were not rewarded for developing their subordinates, and the policies of most departments regarding job assignments and transfers made it difficult to move people.

Several of our case examples were from these companies. Harvey Monroe, George Hammer, Mark Forrestal, and Donna Grant were from the developmentally oriented company. In George Hammer's case (Chapter Three), his career expectations matched reality. He wanted to advance to at least middle management, and the company's development program was geared to preparing him for that level. George realized the difficulty of moving beyond middle management because of the competition and the fact that there were fewer openings as one moved up the hierarchy. George was also aware that there were

fewer openings at middle management than there had been in the past because of pressures on the company to reduce its costs by reducing its work force. Nevertheless, George felt that he was being groomed for middle management, and while it might take longer than he had initially hoped, he would reach that level in a few years. He anticipated then having responsible positions in middle management and hoped to move up in salary grade.

Donna Grant, our prime example of a corporate uppy, felt that the company's development policies were in line with her career interests. Donna was doing well in her job and had the support of her supervisors. They helped her understand what career moves she should make to become a successful general manager.

Mark Forrestal was finding it difficult to make the most of the company's policies. Because young managers were moved fairly frequently to give them interdepartmental experience, he had had several jobs in two years. Unfortunately, he seemed to lack the ability to make the most of these opportunities. He was always hampered by barriers on the job, unable to exert the initiative required to structure his work and make a contribution.

Harvey Monroe's goals did not match the purpose of the company's development strategy. The program focused on general managerial experience, not specialist positions, which explains why Harvey did not receive much sympathy or support from his boss for pursuing law.

Carol Locke (Chapter Three) and Steve Riley were in the company that focused on immediate business needs to the exclusion of management development. For Carol Locke, development and advancement were not major concerns anyway, nor was being a manager a career goal. In fact, when the company learned that Carol intended to leave, it offered her a promotion. The company was dedicated to equal opportunity for minorities and did not want to lose a talented black female. Carol took the promotion, but left a few months later for what she hoped would be exciting work.

Steve, however, was irked by the company's lack of interest in his progress. When he pushed the issue with higher-

level managers, they promised him advancement, but the promotion was slow in coming because of the attitude of a new boss. In this case the company did not provide the resources Steve needed to enhance his motivation.

Several factors indicate a company's developmental orientation. The number of projected job opportunities at a higher level is an important indication of growth opportunities, but having many opportunities does not mean that the company will prepare everyone for them. Similarly, just because a company has few promotional opportunities, perhaps because it is shrinking in size or because there are many long-tenured people, does not mean that there will be no opportunities. Being recognized as an up-and-comer in such an organization could be highly desirable.

But development is not only for advancement. It is also preparation for having a more challenging assignment, more supervisory responsibility, and work that is more important to the organization. Such jobs may be at a higher pay grade, but not necessarily at a higher organizational level. Achieving this type of development does not always require changing jobs. Most jobs have room for considerable growth, depending on the initiative and the ingenuity of the person in the job and on the boss's support.

An organization's philosophy of employee development comes down to whether the organization treats its employees as assets or merely as resources to meet immediate business needs. It takes more than reading company brochures to discover an organization's orientation. The best way for current or prospective employees to investigate a company's philosophy is to talk to people who are in the company and those who have left. They should talk to people at their career stage because they will have a similar perspective. Here are some questions they could ask:

> Does the organization develop generalists with the ability to manage people regardless of the department or specialists or both?
> If the focus is on specialists, what are the prospects for people in the individual's field?

What is the role of the boss in making job
assignments and promoting people?
Are supervisors rewarded for developing
subordinates?
Does the company fill vacancies from within or does
it go outside?
Does the company have a fast-track advancement
program? If so, is it detrimental not to be in it?
Does the company have definite career paths? How
flexible are these paths?
Does the company provide mechanisms for career
planning?

Even if the answers to these questions are positive, an
employee may not be satisfied with the environment. Development programs are usually highly competitive. People in them
have high expectations for themselves, and they complain when
the organization does not help fulfill these expectations. Developmentally oriented firms often leave a lot of casualties along the
way to identifying and developing the best people. If the answers
to these questions are generally negative, or perhaps a mix of
positive and negative, the environment may be more relaxed.
A person's reactions in either case will depend on what he or
she wants. Also, there are exceptions or unusual cases in every
organization. Companies that do not do much to develop people
still may have bosses who are concerned with subordinates' career
development. (The next chapter offers in-depth information on
the role of the company in supporting career development.)

The Job Itself

The actual work a person does is also important to career
motivation, especially having a meaningful assignment. A job
with motivating potential is one that gives employees feedback
and autonomy, allows them to use a variety of skills, and gives
them the responsibility for a complete task (Hackman and
Oldham, 1980). An important assignment is also likely to give
employees exposure to top management. But this type job is

important not just for advancement prospects but also because it helps employees gain a feeling of achievement.

Recall Mark Forrestal's complaints. He described the sales job as demeaning because he only delivered what other people developed. He also complained because the clients to whom he was assigned did not have much need for his services. Mark had difficulty with his next job because it lacked structure and he could not supply his own. Mark's self-confidence was waning because he was unable to gain a sense of accomplishment and positive reinforcement from his work.

While Mark was floundering and perhaps on the verge of burn-out, George Hammer was succeeding on a job assignment that was extremely unstructured and required independent action. One of George's first assignments was in the marketing department. He was responsible for opening the company's first retail store in a shopping mall. George had to find the site, negotiate the rental agreement, arrange for fixtures, supervise construction and installation of the store interior, order the first inventory, and hire the salesclerks. One of his bosses during this time was extremely critical. He came to the store and criticized, without ever acknowledging any of George's accomplishments. Finally, George told the boss to get out of the store and not to come back unless he had something good to say. George's forthrightness had a positive influence on the boss's behavior toward him.

George opened the store in less than a year. He was asked to write up the methods he followed, and this manual became the standard for the company, which later opened many such stores. This job was far from what George had been trained to do as a music teacher. There were no standards for him to follow and no one to guide his efforts, although there were many people from whom George sought advice. George set goals for himself as he went along and could tell how closely he was meeting them. This assignment was important to the company, and George received considerable attention from top management. George ran several other stores during the next year. He said that he thrived on the challenge and responsibility, and he liked the idea of being in charge. He was then moved to a totally

different assignment in another department. His job was supervising a group of about ten people responsible for equipment installation and repair. Again, he was thrilled with the job.

Here are some questions employees can ask themselves about how their job contributes to their career motivation:

Can you tell when you have done a good job?
Does the work give you a sense of achievement?
Is it obvious if the job is not done right?
Are co-workers on this job cooperative?
Does the job require working on your own? How often?
Does the job require long-term planning?
Is the job a stepping stone to other career moves?
Will the job prepare you for more responsibility?
Does the job require interacting with higher-level managers?
Does the job make it easy for someone to tell who does the best work?
Does the job require supervising others?
How well does the job pay, and is there an opportunity to earn more money?
Is promotion likely?
Is the job challenging—for example, does it require using a variety of skills, does it offer feedback on how well you are doing, is it important to the organization, and are you responsible for a complete piece of work?

Other Factors

So far we have considered how one's boss, company policies and procedures, and the job affect career motivation. Other factors play a role as well, including one's peers. Peers are often the most accurate judges of one's behavior. They have a good view of what one does, and they view one's work from the same perspective, unlike subordinates or bosses, who are likely to have different views. Peers are often willing, sometimes

too willing, to give feedback on how well one is doing. Family members, friends, and co-workers are important to an employee's career motivation in a number of ways. Positive feedback strengthens one's self-confidence and gives a feeling of accomplishment. Peers can encourage one to take a risk and do what one believes is right. They may help set career goals and discuss how realistic these goals are. Remember how Harvey Monroe valued the opinions of his friends, who encouraged him to pursue a career in law. Peers also influence the direction of one's career goals. For example, if co-workers value advancement and leadership and are constantly talking about what they can do to get promoted, one is likely to adopt the same attitude and values. It is natural to want to feel part of a group and be the same as others.

In addition, peers' concerns have influence simply because they make the issues salient. We pay attention to whatever is around us, although we do not always conform. If co-workers are frequently talking about promotion, the issue of advancement becomes salient. If advancement is not one of our goals, and we feel strongly about it, then we may pay even more attention than we would otherwise to rejecting the need to advance and highlighting what is important to us, such as spending more time with our families.

Peers and families can be barriers to as well as facilitators of career motivation. Husbands and wives who both work are forever trying to balance their job and family responsibilities, especially when they have children. When our career decisions influence other people in our lives, we must involve these people when we make such decisions. Consider Mel Foreman. Mel was a talented engineer in the computer industry in Boston. When his firm moved its East Coast facilities to its California headquarters, Mel had to make a decision to quit or move to California. His wife, a New Englander by birth, refused to consider the move. Finding another job would be no problem for Mel, but he would have to prove himself to his new employer, and he might not be able to find a company with the same advancement opportunities and pay level. In fact, no firm in the area was as attractive as the one he was leaving. His solution

was to compromise with his wife. She was willing to relocate as far as New York or Philadelphia, but she wanted to stay within driving distance of Boston. Fortunately for Mel, a company in Connecticut fit the requirements.

Summary

This chapter offered guidelines for enhancing career resilience, insight, and identity. It discussed the role of the boss, organization, and job in maintaining and enhancing these dimensions of career motivation, offering examples and questions to help people evaluate their situations. The next chapter contains additional information about how companies support career development. It describes a number of programs and policies for enhancing career resilience, insight, and identity. Chapter Nine then shows how people can lose support for career motivation and what they can do to regain that support.

Resource 6. Outline for a Manager-as-Developer Workshop.

This outline is for a one-day workshop for mid-level managers on career development. The goal is to increase managers' awareness of their role as a key resource in their subordinates' career development.

The workshop focuses on *why* the role of developer is so important to good management. Participants identify *who* is developed and in *what* way—that is, the meaning of development for different types of subordinates (mid-career plateaued managers, young fast-trackers, supervisors newly promoted from occupational ranks). The workshop then explores the *when, where,* and *how* of career development. Participants also consider their own situations—the barriers to and motivations for their spending time developing their subordinates and their competence to be developers. The participants identify resources that support career development (for example, assessment centers to evaluate subordinates' strengths and weaknesses and staffing mechanisms to help move people into different positions). Finally, the participants set goals and plans for developing members of their work groups.

8:30–8:40   Announcements

8:40–9:15   Get acquainted
             To build group cohesion, promote sharing, and focus the direction for the day. Participants interview each other about their career

Note: Sharon Greenfield of Rutgers University made a valuable contribution to the development of this workshop.

histories (10 min.) and then take turns introducing the person they interviewed (25 min.). (Times listed are approximate and can be adjusted as needed.)

9:15–9:35   Agenda clarification
To give participants an opportunity to express their expectations and react to the intended purpose of the day. The instructor presents the broad agenda (5 min.) and then asks for additional goals the participants hope to accomplish or issues they wish to address (5 min.). The instructor discusses which of these issues are already incorporated in the agenda, areas where the agenda can be adapted to accommodate participants' needs, and areas that are beyond the scope of the workshop and how they can be addressed in other ways (other courses, discussions with top managers, investigation of corporate policies) (10 min.).

9:35–10:30   "Why" be a career developer
To establish the rationale for the manager's role as developer in relation to business needs and changing company cultures. Instructor lecture and large-group discussion.

10:30–10:45 Break

10:45–11:30 The "who" and "what" of career development
To understand the needs of different types of employees (for example, early-career managers, newly promoted managers, advancement-oriented managers, those who view themselves as specialists and professionals in a particular discipline, plateaued managers, mid-career managers, and those approaching retirement). Instructor leads a brain-storming session in the large group to identify these different types (10 min.). The focus then turns to what career development means for these subordinates (10 min.). Working individually, participants prepare a matrix of subordinate types and career-development activities (10 min.). The instructor then creates a matrix on easel paper with participant input (15 min.). See Table 2 for a sample matrix.

11:30–11:45 The "where," "how," and "when" of career development
To clarify where career-development activities take place—in the boss's office, at a career-planning seminar, on one's own. To outline different styles of management—the boss merely provides information about career opportunities, the boss tells subordinates about their potential, the boss discusses career possibilities and counsels subordinates. To ascertain the frequency of these activities—once a year, whenever the boss feels a discussion is relevant, whenever the subordinate feels the need for a discussion. The instructor leads a brain-storming presentation of these different possibilities.

11:45–12:00 Applying the career-development concepts
To further acquaint participants with these concepts and encourage them to think about their own career-development needs as well

Table 2. Sample Matrix of Subordinate
Types and Career-Development Activities.

Career-Development Activities	Early-Career Managers with High Potential for Advancement (Fast Trackers)	Manager Specialists	Plateaued Managers	Newly Promoted Managers
Setting career goals	X	X		X
Setting performance goals	X	X	X	X
Obtaining performance feedback	X	X	X	X
Attending courses on management	X	X		X
Attending conventions in one's field		X	X	
Attending a career-planning seminar	X		X	
Attending an assessment center to evaluate advancement potential	X			
Taking special job assignments to expand one's skills, knowledge, and corporate perspective	X	X	X	
Transferring to a job in another department	X		X	

as those of their subordinates. Participants complete a self-assessment sheet on their own work groups and themselves, describing needed career-development activities and when, where, and how they should occur. Participants also describe the extent of support for development they would like from their supervisors.

12:00–1:00   Lunch break

1:00–1:05   Reviewing and clarifying previous discussions and outlining work for the afternoon.

1:05–1:20   Reactions to self-assessment
To discuss how participants feel about putting themselves in the role of subordinates. To deal with the boss's motivation in supporting employee development. Instructor leads large-group discussion of subordinate, self, and supervisor expectations and roles in career development.

1:20–1:55   Motivation for being a developer
To identify the reinforcements from being a developer and to identify barriers. The large group breaks into two or three subgroups to brain-storm about motivators (improved productivity, reputa-

tion as a department for the best people) and barriers (managers are not evaluated on how well they develop their people, time spent with employees on career issues takes time away from achieving the basic goals of the unit) (20 min.). Each group then reports its findings to the large group for discussion (15 min.).

1:55–2:35   Competence in and comfort with the career-development role
To have participants consider their competence in engaging in a full range of career-development support activities and their degree of comfort with those activities. Participants complete written descriptions of their support behaviors (15 min.). In the large group, participants report their reactions, feelings, and conclusions (25 min.).

2:35–3:00   Available resources
To review and discuss internal and external resources available to support the career-development role. Instructor hands out and reviews a resource guide (10 min.). Resources include ways to learn and improve skills related to supporting development, such as giving feedback. Participants are encouraged to use each other for practice—for instance, by being helpful to peers in career planning and development and giving each other reinforcement for help. (15 min.).

3:00–3:15   Break

3:15–4:30   Action planning
To move from learning to planning action steps. To emphasize the need to plan if participants are to spend time and energy on career-development activities for subordinates, peers, and themselves and to engender support from their bosses. Participants individually write their action plans (30 min.) and then discuss and revise them (45 min.).

4:30–5:00   Wrap-up
To review the day's work, solicit reactions, and discuss ways to meet needs that were not met by the workshop. Participants discuss each other's career plans, ways to increase support from higher organizational levels for working with subordinates on their career planning and development, and ways to increase higher managers' involvement in the careers of their immediate subordinates.

Eight

Human Resource Programs and Policies for Building Career Motivation

This chapter reviews corporate career-development programs and related processes and suggests their effects on employees' career ambitions. The chapter also emphasizes the importance of making human resource programs consistent and of designing them to fit changing corporate climates. In addition, two cases describing corporate strategies are presented. The first is a comprehensive effort to enhance employees' competence and professionalism. The other is a way one corporation tied together the career programs and policies of different departments.

Designing Programs to Enhance Career Motivation

We describe here how different company programs and policies contribute to employees' career resilience, insight, and identity. Some of the programs provide direct support for career management—for example, a career-planning workshop to help employees evaluate their opportunities in the company and set goals. For other programs, such as performance appraisals and job redesign, development is a by-product.

Several of the programs are geared simply to providing employees with information about career opportunities or communicating information about how policies and procedures, such as job-transfer policies, affect careers. Clarification of career

opportunities and related organizational processes improves employees' insight into the match between their career goals and the likelihood of their meeting their goals in the organization. People who see a mismatch, especially people whose career resilience is high, are likely to resolve the discrepancy. In such cases, the company may lose people who are doing a good job but who feel their advancement prospects are elsewhere. Although some companies naturally shy away from actions that may increase dissatisfaction and turnover, other companies view it positively. They believe it is valuable to have people who are familiar with their product join another organization, which may be a customer or supplier. This policy has worked well for IBM. Time, Inc., fosters these ties by sponsoring reunions of former employees, both those who retired and those who quit.

Information that tells employees that there is a match is likely to increase employees' motivation and performance and reduce their uncertainty and anxiety. Such information also helps employees know what to do to enhance their career prospects and attain their goals. For instance, assessment centers and performance appraisals highlight aspects of performance that are important for success in the organization. Communication of the company's human resource needs and plans helps employees locate opportunities for promotion. Feedback on performance lets employees know what skills need improving and in what areas of the business they need increased experience.

Building Career Resilience. The following programs strengthen career resilience by rewarding good performance, by providing opportunities for achievement and risk taking without undue punishment for failure, and by offering support for independent action as well as for cooperative behavior.

One way to ensure employees are high in resilience is to recruit and select people who have self-confidence, needs for achievement and risk taking, and the ability to act independently and cooperatively. Organizations that offer positive reinforcement, opportunities for intellectual growth, and supportive leadership are likely to attract such people. To some extent, self-selection plays a role in that people who are not attracted by such

an environment are likely to stay away. This process requires providing an accurate portrayal of the organization to applicants. (Realistic job previews are discussed later.)

Job design (or redesign) can make work meaningful and significant. Jobs can be designed to enhance responsibility, increase opportunities for achievement, and enhance the value of taking risks to improve job performance.

Supervisors should understand how their *leadership style* affects their subordinates' career resilience. Supervisors should help clarify subordinates' job responsibilities, goals, and criteria for evaluation. Supervisors should provide positive reinforcement for goal accomplishment and risk taking, tolerate occasional failure, and encourage independent action and cooperation by making it clear, in words and actions, that subordinates sometimes need to act independently and at other times need to act cooperatively. Companies can encourage supervisors to exhibit this type of leadership through training programs, reinforcement, and role modeling (that is, having higher-level managers behave this way).

Goal setting, appraisal, and reward programs should support the style of leadership described here. Procedures for setting clear goals and standards for evaluating employees on goal accomplishment and comparing employees to each other can be the basis for positive reinforcement. Supervisors must have the discretion to reward subordinates appropriately and meaningfully. Merit-pay treatment must be performance based, significant in amount, and fair. Nonmonetary rewards, such as plaques, extra time off, and special assignments, are other forms of recognition.

Job transfers and assignments with increased responsibility can be rewards for outstanding performance, a way for developing skills, and a means of increasing opportunities for achievement. Such moves do not necessarily require promotion; there is often variation in the importance and responsibility of jobs at a given level. As noted previously, there are ways to improve the challenge of existing jobs, sometimes simply by giving a person difficult and important assignments (for example, chairing a task force or making a presentation to a top executive).

Organizations faced with increased competition, technological change, and uncertain economic conditions are learning, often the hard way, that they must be inventive—on the cutting edge of technology, production methods, and marketing techniques. This realization has given birth to *intrapreneurship* (Pinchot, 1985)—giving employees opportunities to take risks without provoking anxiety about the consequences if they fail. Employees in these organizations are beginning to see that they can take responsibility for running part of the business, just like entrepreneurs in start-up companies.

Intrapreneurship holds small units responsible for new products from design through production and marketing. This strategy both requires and supports employees' career resilience. Although important today, the concept is not new. Companies such as Control Data Corporation and the 3M Company have given employees money, time, and equipment to pursue their ideas for company projects (Berg, 1985). Data General set up two competing research-and-development operations to invent a competitive, small computer (Kidder, 1981). IBM's first personal computer was produced by a separate unit far from corporate headquarters; it had its own budget and even the freedom to ignore long-standing policies, such as not buying parts from non-IBM companies.

While intrapreneurship is a business strategy that gives employees increased freedom and responsibility, other business strategies, such as *employee paybacks*, limit or restrain employees' career moves. For instance, concerned about rising costs and job hopping, some companies now require that new employees repay relocation and training costs if they quit within a certain period (Ward, 1985). American Airlines, for example, requires prospective pilots to sign training payback agreements to protect the company's investment in them.

Building Career Insight. The following programs influence career insight by providing information about the work environment and career opportunities, by encouraging goal setting, and by helping employees understand themselves better.

Realistic job previews help applicants make career decisions that are likely to meet their needs and match their abilities. Also, realistic information helps create accurate expectations that are likely to decrease turnover and increase employee satisfaction (Wanous, 1980). Realistic job previews are important not only for applicants but also for current employees who are transferring to a new job in the company.

Some companies make *self-assessment workbooks* available to employees, although such materials are also readily available in book stores. For instance, we developed a series of self-reflection guides to help managers understand their skills, weaknesses, and career motivation. Several of the exercises from these guides are offered in this book. The exercises include questions to help guide career planning, evaluate goal accomplishment, and refine career goals relative to past successes and opportunities. The guides encourage managers to think about the links between setting career goals and then attaining them—for instance, understanding the extent to which job experiences contribute to goal accomplishment.

Companies often sponsor *career-planning workshops* to help employees explore their career interests, evaluate their strengths and weaknesses, develop job-search skills, understand the company's system for transferring people, improve the way they present themselves (in resumes, in job interviews), and develop practical career plans. (Resource 7 is a questionnaire for evaluating a career-planning workshop.)

Employees' career insight depends on having *feedback* about themselves. Employees may think they know how competent they are, but this view of themselves may not be accurate. Good feedback gives employees the opportunity to adjust their behavior and improve their performance. There are several sources of feedback, including informal feedback from the boss and formal performance-appraisal feedback.

Supervisors should give informal feedback to subordinates any time it is appropriate. Feedback is most likely to be constructive when it is behaviorally based, as opposed to being based on the individual's personality. Supervisors should react to what

the employee did, not to what the employee is like as a person. Also, feedback should be given as soon after the behavior as possible.

Many companies also require supervisors to give performance appraisals annually using a special form. The procedure may also call for a formal feedback session, during which past performance is discussed and, based on that information, future performance goals are set jointly by the supervisor and the subordinate. Supervisors who do not give feedback frequently may have to give a negative appraisal when poor performance has not been mentioned to the subordinate earlier. This situation can make the subordinate defensive. Therefore, a formal appraisal session should not be a substitute for frequent, informal feedback discussions.

Assessment centers are a popular technique used by companies to evaluate the potential of a person to perform at a higher level. (See Chapter Five's description of the career-motivation assessment center.) Note that potential for advancement is not the same as performance. People may perform well at their current level but not have the skills to advance to a higher level. The immediate supervisor should be able to tell whether a subordinate has the potential to advance to the supervisor's level but should not be able to tell whether the subordinate could go higher because the supervisor is not necessarily familiar with the requirements for performance at that higher level. Also, the subordinate may not have had a chance to demonstrate advancement potential because the subordinate's current job does not include the requirements of a higher-level position.

Assessment centers, lasting between one and three days, use behavioral exercises to simulate higher-level job requirements. Several assessors, usually higher-level managers, observe participants' performance and write reports, which are then read at an integration session. All the assessors hear the reports and together make judgments about the participants' skills and abilities. Feedback on assessment-center performance can be extremely valuable in providing the participants with an objective view of their potential. Sometimes companies use the assess-

ment center primarily for developmental purposes rather than to make decisions about the participants. (For more information about assessment centers, see Thornton and Byham, 1982, and Bray, Campbell, and Grant, 1974. See Boehm, 1985, for a description of how assessment centers are used for developmental purposes.)

Business games and other large-scale *simulations* can be valuable in giving employees a chance to practice new skills without the threat of evaluation. One simulation, called Looking Glass, Inc., was designed by the Center for Creative Leadership in Greensboro, North Carolina (McCall and Lombardo, 1978). It includes roles for twenty managerial positions across four hierarchical levels, three divisions, and three functional areas, so there is considerable variation in the requirements for each position. A trained staff observes the participants during the six-hour simulation and provides group and individual feedback on more than a dozen managerial skills. In one company, after a manager has been through an intensive assessment center and has received feedback, the manager participates in Looking Glass to practice skills found to be deficient in the assessment.

Career-management programs take two forms. One type focuses on providing information to employees about career opportunities. For example, company newsletters provide information on promotions and organizational changes (which departments are expanding and which departments are contracting). Also, supervisors can tell subordinates what they know about career opportunities and give subordinates advice. The grapevine is another source of information. Often rumors are employees' most frequent source of information but not necessarily the most reliable basis for making career decisions.

The second type of career-management program does more than provide information. It encourages employees to set career goals, and it requires supervisors to do human resource planning. A number of tools, such as those described in the following paragraphs, may assist in the process.

Career paths establish desirable job sequences that prepare people for advancement by letting them know what they need to do to accomplish their career goals. However, career paths

can become too specific. The more they specify a particular chain of positions, the less likely they can be followed because the jobs are not likely to be available when a person is ready for them. Also, organizations find that there are many ways to attain a particular goal, and career paths may be misleading and inaccurate. A better strategy is using career paths to specify sequences of job families. For example, a career path to middle management within the finance department may specify desirable types of finance jobs and perhaps recommend rotations to related departments, as opposed to listing the exact positions.

Organizations may try to ensure that they have adequate human resources by identifying one or more people who can fill each position should the position be vacated. Such succession plans should be consistent with individuals' career plans. Bosses should coordinate succession planning with the help they give to subordinates in planning their careers. Like career paths, succession plans should be flexible; they should recognize that the most qualified people to fill positions will change over time and that a person may be qualified for, and could benefit from working in, more than one position.

Sometimes computerized job-matching and job-posting systems code job vacancies and candidate characteristics on the same dimensions and attempt to find the best matches of people to openings. Completing and updating the forms should help employees identify the skills needed. Perusing job-vacancy lists can also be valuable in understanding job requirements. Good job matches should help enhance employees' motivation and avoid misfits. A difficulty is that many times supervisors with vacancies consider people they know already or people who are recommended to them by co-workers whose judgment they trust. Because supervisors only occasionally do not have a particular candidate in mind for vacancies (London and Stumpf, 1982), job-matching and job-posting systems, although technologically advanced, have limited success.

Many times, employees in large organizations are not aware of how promotion decisions are made or the criteria used to select people for promotion. Most organizations have for-

mal policies about procedures to be followed, such as circulating a notice of vacancy, allowing nominations (sometimes self-nominations), and involving others in the process (a selection committee). Also, organizations usually have formal procedures detailing how to obtain a job transfer. Awareness of the process should help employees make a career move and should avoid inaccurate perceptions of unfairness and misunderstanding about the criteria used. (See London and Stumpf, 1982, chap. 7, for a description of how managers make promotion decisions.)

A final tool that helps employees set career goals is communicating the company's philosophy of employee development. As we saw in Chapter Seven, some companies treat employees solely as resources for meeting current business needs and ignore the need to develop employees to meet future business needs. Other companies have sophisticated development programs. Recently, we were involved in updating a company's management-development policy and outlining the program for high-potential managers. The finished product, a policy paper, was distributed widely in the company; it clarified what participants in the program could expect and what it meant not to be on the program. This kind of communication can be helpful to employees when they make career plans.

There is little point in providing any of these career-management tools unless the organization supports these activities. For example, the boss should help employees set realistic career goals and should then use information about goals to make staffing decisions and staffing recommendations to others who are filling positions. Otherwise, career planning will be fruitless and frustrating—unless, of course, it extends beyond the employees' current organization to focus on future opportunities elsewhere.

Building Career Identity. The following programs have an impact on career identity by making jobs challenging and involving and by highlighting the value of advancement, recognition, and being in a leadership position.

Most large organizations have some type of *development program*, and a few companies have comprehensive ones. Such

programs are generally aimed at people in their early careers; however, there are also development programs to ensure that mid-career managers maintain their motivation and productivity. Components of development programs include job rotations, assignment to bosses who are good role models and who are concerned about subordinates' development, rewards for bosses for developing their subordinates, meetings with top executives about career issues, opportunities to attend meetings of top managers, opportunities to work with higher-level managers who can be role models and who can be helpful to the developing managers' career progress, and special assignments that grow in responsibility over time. Companies with comprehensive programs may have program coordinators, who track people on the program, run special sessions (for example, orientation meetings), and facilitate developmental job moves. Some companies are careful to keep names of people in the development program secret; in fact, employees may not even know they are in the program except that their job assignments change often and their promotions are frequent compared with those of others. Other companies let people know when they have been appointed to the program—treating the appointment itself as a form of deserved recognition.

Companies also need to *maintain corporate vitality* in order to enhance employees' career identity. Organizations often keep costs down by limiting or decreasing the size of the work force. People who leave are not replaced, thereby cutting into the number of promotional opportunities. Such cutbacks can have a dampening effect on employees' advancement motivation and weaken the credibility of a development program. In these cases, companies may have to make special efforts to create opportunities for promotion and then publicize promotions that do occur in order to show that it values its high-potential managers and takes extraordinary steps to utilize their talents appropriately.

Another way organizations enhance employees' career identity is by *encouraging involvement in professional organizations.* Today, more than ever, organizations recognize the increased specialization in many fields and the importance to people of developing in their specialties. This support is important for

employees who view themselves as professionals in particular areas as opposed to generalist managers, who can move into almost any department in the business.

A challenging job is as important to career identity as it is to career resilience. (See the previous discussion of job design.)

Consistency of Human Resource Programs

A problem some companies have without realizing it is that their human resource programs are out of synch with each other, with employee goals, and with overall business strategy (Von Glinow and others, 1983). Determining the numbers and types of people needed five years from now should affect the people hired today and how they are trained. Programs to identify employees' strengths and weaknesses should be followed by training and also by management support for job moves aimed at developing employees. Career-planning programs and performance-appraisal information will not be valued if they are not used as input for staffing decisions. Promotions will not be valued if the promotion decisions seem to be unfair—for example, if they are based on personality rather than on performance. If the company expects bosses to be career counselors for their subordinates and to take actions that help their subordinates' careers, then the bosses should be evaluated and rewarded financially for good performance in these areas.

Human resource programs also may have unexpected consequences for employees. A career-planning process, for example, may increase competition among employees. Such competition can be good if it improves performance, but it can be bad if it increases anxiety unnecessarily. Other programs may be needed to deal with these kinds of problems.

The firm's human resource philosophy needs to be coordinated also with overall business strategy. For example, firms with little opportunity for growth either internally or by diversification are likely to have more employees who have plateaued and who can be categorized as deadwood than do firms that are adding new products and are in a high-growth market (Slocum and others, 1985). Managers in stable organizations

are generally highly trained in the organization's limited area of operations. Growing firms are less committed than stable firms to market stability and competing in one small niche, and so their managers are more likely to be generalists and have better opportunities for advancement. But stable firms can also provide these opportunities and be concerned about employee development. As we described in Chapter Seven, a career-motivation assessment was conducted in one company with a strong development ethic and in another company that seemed to ignore development and concentrate on using employees to meet current business needs. Both companies were in similar financial condition, and they faced similar markets. However, the development-oriented company was more open to new ideas and to preparing for the future than the other company.

Corporate Change and Career Management

AT&T provides a good example of how corporate change affects career prospects and a company's support for career development. One result of the Bell System breakup was that AT&T had to develop different training for its high-potential managers. Before divestiture, managers were developed by rotating them within operating telephone companies, such as New York Telephone, and between operating companies and the company's headquarters in New York and New Jersey. After divestiture, when the operating companies became independent, this system was no longer possible. However, AT&T still has a number of lines of business that differ considerably from each other (long-distance telephone service, research and development, computer manufacturing and sales). Although these operations existed before divestiture, there was no tradition of moving people between them for the purpose of development. Moreover, AT&T's new corporate headquarters is much smaller than previously, with fewer rotational assignments available. (The operating companies separated from AT&T by divestiture do not have this problem because they rarely rotated people between the operating companies, only within the companies and between the companies and headquarters. Also, the new oper-

ating companies jointly own Bell Communications Research, which continues to allow development rotations to gain an industrywide perspective.)

Aside from the lack of rotational opportunities, another major difficulty is fewer promotional opportunities within AT&T. After divestiture, the company had too many people, and there was tremendous pressure to reduce costs. Early-retirement incentives and layoffs were used to bring the work force down to a reasonable level. Efforts to push decisions downward and reduce the number of management levels were other reasons for fewer promotional opportunities. In addition, there is a question as to whether managers used to operating in a fairly authoritarian environment, with standard practices necessary to maintain high levels of telephone service, can operate successfully in a competitive, often uncertain, and anxiety-provoking atmosphere. Although AT&T's top executives believe that most managers in the company can help the company succeed in a competitive environment, they have moved to hire managers from outside the business at all levels, especially to provide expertise for the company's new lines of business.

However, as the company tries to improve its position in the marketplace, it is reorganizing and in the process creating new positions, thus demonstrating to lower-level, young, high-potential managers that there are opportunities for the best people.

The development program for high-potential managers has also been changed to focus less on group activities, such as meetings with vice-presidents and outside speakers, to redesigning jobs so that they contribute to employees' development. Increasingly, the components of the high-potential development program are tailored to the individual as opposed to being applied in the same way to all participants. For instance, coordinators monitor the progress of participants in the program and ensure that the young managers are transferred to positions that will benefit them. Also, self-assessment materials were developed to help managers understand their skills, set goals, and track their progress. These materials were intended to be used flexibly. Some managers may spend considerable time on self-reflection, writing goals, and keeping a business diary to record events and experiences. Other managers may use the

materials simply as memory joggers and thought stimulators, but they do not keep detailed records.

When we explain career-development programs for high-potential managers, such as this one, people usually ask about those not in the program. Aren't other people capable of handling responsible jobs? Don't they deserve challenging assignments? Isn't it as important to keep them motivated? After all, aren't they the lifeblood of the organization? These questions are particularly important to AT&T, which is reducing size and costs. Of course, the answer to these questions is yes, at least for people who are performing well and are capable of handling increased responsibility but who might not be viewed as capable of advancing to the next level. Or they may have the potential to advance, but there are other people who are more competitive and are more likely to advance more than one level. As promotional opportunities decrease in AT&T, management wants to be sure that the people who are promoted have the potential to advance further so that talent is available for future top-level vacancies. In cases such as this one, we recommend a standard career program for all employees. Such a program includes many of the components of a high-potential manager-development program, but the pace is slower.

Two Organizational Approaches to Career Development

In the remainder of this chapter, we present two cases of organizational career-development programs. In the first, a department designed a program to ensure employee growth and professionalism. Mastery paths were formed for each job, detailing the training and performance levels necessary for job success.

The second case describes how different departments with varying goals and specialties can work together to share information about approaches to career development and to sponsor common programs when needed. The corporate personnel department coordinated a group of department representatives responsible for career development rather than developing general career programs with little or no involvement by the departments concerned.

CASE ONE
*Development of Mastery Paths
to Enhance Employee Professionalism*

Working in complex disciplines requires keeping up with technical advances, as is generally accepted in science, engineering, law, medicine, and other professions. This concept of professionalism is spreading as specialization becomes important in other fields as well, such as marketing, production, personnel, and general management. Being the best in any field today requires keeping abreast of developments, continuously fine tuning one's skills, and being prepared to learn about and implement new technologies. However, unlike recognized, well-defined disciplines, these other fields are likely to be highly organization specific, with skill and output requirements dependent on the organization's business and the philosophy of its leaders. Consequently, fostering professionalism in organizations requires considerable advance work to identify relevant skills and development paths.

These paths are of two types. Many organizations develop career paths specifying job sequences. A problem with these paths is that the specific sequences are difficult to achieve because the recommended jobs may not be available when the person is ready for them. Mastery paths are another type. They are far more comprehensive than career paths. Both types outline job sequences within job families, such as market research, from entry through middle-level management. However, mastery paths recognize the possibility, and even desirability, of movement between paths. Instead of recommending a specific job, mastery paths make explicit the requirements for moving into a job and the training and performance expectations of that job. Mastery paths may also specify the style of management the department wishes to promulgate (for example, supervisors who develop and facilitate self-directed work teams as opposed to supervisors who monitor and make decisions for subordinates).

The authors thank Rosemary O'Connor for her contribution to this project.

Procedure for Generating Mastery Paths

Recognizing the need for increased professionalism in an area is up to the specific department, not the personnel department. However, human resource professionals play an important role in mastery-path development in areas such as job analysis and evaluation, compensation policies, selection criteria and methods, assessment and appraisal, work-force planning, and design and delivery of the management-trainee curriculum.

In this case, the department's goal was to become the best in its field. Top managers in the department believed that they would then be able to recruit and retain the best people, who would make a continuous, significant contribution to the company. The coordinator for this project asked the personnel department to help in generating the necessary human resource systems to accomplish this goal.

Rather than offer the typical bureaucratic response that personnel systems such as job evaluation, compensation, and the training curriculum were fixed, the personnel department realized that there were few actions the personnel department had to prevent the client department from taking because of legal restrictions or corporate policies and few systems that could not be adapted to meet the client department's needs.

In order to be responsive to this client department, the personnel department set up a team consisting of a leader and managers representing relevant personnel-department functions. The team leader and his staff assistant served as one point of contact for the client for any personnel issue that arose during the development process. In early discussions, the personnel and client departments clarified roles and concluded that most of the work on the project would be done by members of the client department who knew their field well. The client "owned" the project. The personnel department staff would be consultants, facilitators, and developers of supporting human resource systems.

Given the need for expert input from the client's line and staff departments, the client formed task forces of subject-matter experts, one task force for each of eight job families. In addition, two staff positions were created by the department to coordinate the project.

Design and Implementation

The project was accomplished in four steps, as outlined here.

Skill and Output Identification. Task-force members held focus groups to ascertain skill requirements and output expectations. The result was extensive documentation for each job. This process was conducted solely by the project leader and the task-force members before the personnel department was asked to participate. However, in other mastery-path projects, this stage offers substantial opportunity for personnel professionals to use reliable job-analysis techniques (perhaps a combination of interviews, observations, and questionnaires). (See Gael's 1987 handbook on job analysis for various methods.)

Mastery-Path Development. Working with the personnel department team as facilitators, the project leader met separately with each task force to outline the mastery paths. We present here an example of a mastery path for a customer-service job family, from service representative through first-line supervisor to second-level manager. This is just an outline. The complete description would be written in detail and presented in booklet form to job incumbents. (This sample was developed for demonstration purposes and is not a mastery path for an actual company.)

Job 1: Service Representative

Prehire Requirements
  Skills
      Basic math and writing ability (level of high school graduate).
      Oral communication.
      Motivation to be sensitive and responsive to customers.
  Validated selection tests
      Basic math and verbal test.
      Assessment of oral communications (candidate role-plays a telephone situation).
      Interviewer judgment of customer orientation.

Job preview
    Description of the job, salary, and benefits.
Early performance objectives
    Understand the company and position, especially the impor-
    tance of the job to the company.
    Learn initial tasks.
    Try new behaviors.
Day 1
        Company orientation.
        Early job training—self-paced computer tutorial about the
        department.
Days 2–5
        Classroom training in telemarketing; on-the-job training.
Months 1–3
        Develop proficiencies in basic tasks.
            Taking and processing orders.
            Selling services over the phone.
            Handling complaints.
        Continuous coaching from peers and feedback from super-
        visor.
End of month 3—first mastery assessment
        Supervisor evaluates newcomer's proficiencies and decides
        next step: salary increase and continued development, return
        to early training to improve in basics, or dismissal.
Months 3–6
        Continued development and evaluation.
        Acquisition of new skills.
        Reassessment at six months with salary increase for successful
        subordinates.
Months 6–12
        Becoming part of the team, sharing tasks and helping peers.
        Obtaining additional telemarketing training.
        Demonstrating skills and finetuning advanced skills—
        particularly selling.
        For those who want, going beyond basic job specification to
        help with scheduling team members, training newcomers,
        contributing ideas for increasing the team's productivity and
        improving the work environment.

Achievement of mastery

The group of supervisors certifies the successful subordinate as having achieved mastery. The successful subordinate receives an additional salary increase and is now eligible for the team gain-sharing plan. (The gain-sharing plan allows employees to profit financially from the team's performance.)

Beyond the first year

Employee continues to contribute to the team.

Any time after one year, high-performing service representatives who demonstrate managerial potential are invited to a one-day assessment center for evaluation of managerial skills. They are then eligible for consideration for promotion.

Job 2: First-Line Supervisor

Prehire requirements

Skills—same as those for service representative plus:

Administrative skills, such as planning and organizing.

Ability to communicate.

Participative philosophy of management (willingness to delegate).

Ability to facilitate interaction.

Good observation skills.

Creativity.

Validated selection methods

Test of basic math and verbal skills.

Interviewer's rating of leadership (based on the candidate's prior experiences that indicate management style).

Additional requirements

College education expected for new, entry-level managers.

Assessment center for nonmanagement employees.

Performance objectives for first three months

Learn the job; attend necessary training programs.

Understand and monitor subordinate's performance.

Attend new-manager orientation.

Spend time with group members to improve their individual performance, coach them, and give feedback to them on their performance.

End of month 3—first mastery assessment

Second-line manager examines the supervisor's knowledge of the job and work-group performance. Directions for additional training are determined, especially management courses offered by the company on such topics as problem solving and decision making, giving feedback, and managing marginal performers.

Months 3–12

Supervisor is expected to devote less time to individual subordinates and more time to the group as a whole. The supervisor is expected to do less work for the group such as scheduling shifts and giving assignments. Such tasks should be delegated to the group as it becomes a self-directed team. (Some new supervisors have the advantage of taking over a cohesive, self-directed team whose members have been working together for some time. Such a supervisor should progress faster in developing the group and would be expected to help maintain the group's progress rather than cause it to regress by close supervision of individual performance and not allowing the group to make decisions affecting its performance.) Supervisor is expected to effectively utilize financial incentives and nonfinancial incentives (theater tickets, plaques) to enhance group performance.

Supervisor is expected to spend increasing time on office activities with fellow first-line supervisors and groups of service representatives from different units on such work as planning for the implementation of new technology.

Month 12—mastery assessment

Second-level managers as a group evaluate a supervisor's mastery of the job functions and group development.

Directions for additional training, developmental work assignments, and goals for the future are discussed.

Achieving mastery is accompanied by a salary increase and, if warranted, a special merit bonus.

Beyond the first year

Supervisor is expected to continue refining management skills. Spot financial awards are given to supervisors and work groups with exceptional performance. Also, there are oppor-

tunities for year-end merit bonuses and increases in the base salary.

High-potential supervisors, as judged by second- and third-level managers, can be considered for promotion.

Job 3: Second-Level Manager

Skills

Similar to those for first-line supervisor with increased attention to advanced management skills and financial knowledge.

Expectations

Work on developing subordinates (appraising mastery, giving feedback, serving as a role model).

Work with fellow managers on ways to accomplish business goals and departmental objectives.

Work with union officials on joint projects to improve quality of work life and productivity.

Clarify business objectives and communicate them to work units.

Mastery evaluation

Manager is judged by third-level management as a group at the conclusion of the first year. Mastery means the manager has accomplished the objectives and has the motivation and ability to continue at a high level of performance.

Salary increases, spot financial and nonfinancial awards, and special assignments are used to enhance the manager's motivation.

A key feature of the mastery path for the first-line supervisor in the example is that the percentage of time spent on different facets of the job is expected to vary as the supervisor progresses. At first the supervisor devotes energy to the immediate work unit. Later, as the work unit becomes self-directing, the supervisor devotes increased time to working with other first-level managers on broad office concerns. The model specifies the expected style of management—a participative approach rather than a bureaucratic approach. Evaluation is based on how the work unit operates as well as on its productivity. The

assumption is that self-directing work groups are more productive and more flexible in adapting to work changes than those
that are not self-directing.

Mastery paths for other job families are totally different
from the one in the example. For instance, the mastery path
for a market-research position specifies different outputs expected
at different points. The newcomer, who usually has a doctorate
in marketing, is expected to produce part of a market analysis
during the first three months. Different types of reports are expected over time, and mastery designation takes two years. In
some cases, a job is split into two levels when the work can be
divided into clearly distinguishable sets of outputs. This procedure offers increased opportunity for promotion and provides
an added incentive for good performance and demonstrated
potential to perform at a higher level.

Program Development. Before the mastery path can be implemented, the components of the model have to be developed—
tests prepared and validated by industrial psychologists, training programs designed and tried out, guidelines developed to
help supervisors give feedback and ultimately assess mastery,
job descriptions evaluated, and compensation policies and procedures (for example, spot financial awards) determined.

Implementation and Integration Within the Company. Mastery
paths are designed with the newcomer in mind. They describe
what someone new to the job would have to accomplish to
achieve mastery. However, when the plan is first implemented,
experienced people are already in the positions. Some will
deserve mastery status immediately. Others will require additional training and job experiences to meet the new standards.
Still others may have to be dismissed or moved into less demanding jobs when mastery is unlikely. Explicit guidelines must be
prepared to ensure fair and accurate evaluation of current
employees. Obviously, this is a threatening process. Involving
job incumbents as subject-matter experts on the mastery-path
task forces contributes to their commitment to the process. One
reason the term *mastery* was used instead of *certification* was to

avoid the threatening implication of having to pass a structured test. Groups of managers (the immediate boss and his or her peers) evaluate an employee's level of mastery, a process that also contributes to a fair and open appraisal.

Achievement of mastery in one job does not guarantee promotion to the next job in the sequence. It does not even imply that the person has the potential to advance. Mastery signifies achievement of company standards in the current job. However, mastery may become a stepping stone to jobs at the same level in other job families. In this continuous learning environment, a person's continued contribution to the business is enhanced because the person learns different aspects of a department or several departments. This experience improves the individual's competitiveness when being evaluated for promotion.

The mastery-path concept enhances employee motivation by providing opportunity for new learning as well as for promotion. Financial incentives beyond mastery allow people to maintain motivation on the current job without requiring movement into new jobs.

CASE TWO
Career Development
in a Changing Environment

Many corporations have reduced their managerial force, particularly mid-level managers, because of the need to reduce costs, because computers now process information previously handled by managers, and because of the desirability of making people at lower levels responsible for decisions (because they are close to the problem or because they know the customer best). The result is that the managers who remain have broader spans of control, more responsibility, and overall more demanding and more challenging jobs. Yet, there are fewer opportunities for advancement.

Traditionally, the purpose of management development was promotion. Development ensured that the corporation had a pool of talented and experienced people to fill vacancies at middle and higher levels. At the same time, the carrot of promotion maintained employee motivation.

The new corporate environment, however, requires changing the purpose of development. The goal becomes ensuring employees' contributions to the business today and in the future. The employees' goals are to expand their skills and thereby increase their value to the organization. Ultimately, this process leads to job security and increased financial benefit but not necessarily to promotion.

Development in this new environment requires continuous learning. Managers must refine their skills, both in a specialty field, such as marketing or finance, and in general management. Therefore, to some extent, development will take different forms in different departments as departments develop their own specific skill and output requirements. These requirements will change over time as the needs of the business change, adding a dynamic quality to career development.

This dynamic nature is increased further as the corporation encourages movement among departments, requiring managers to learn other phases of the business. But unlike fast-track development of generalist managers, this type of lateral movement is slow and is aimed at creating deep knowledge of specific areas. A person might move after five to ten years in personnel to a job in marketing. The individual may prepare for this career change by taking courses in marketing and perhaps experimenting with marketing in the personnel department by, for example, designing and selling personnel products internal to the organization.

These changes in the business environment have necessitated changes in the field of career planning and development. This field gained in popularity in the late 1970s. At that time, the emphasis was on canned programs and how-to books that focused on the individual, helping people answer questions such as "What are *my* interests?", "What do *I* want from *my* career and life?", and "How can *I* get what *I* want?" The individual's needs must now be considered in relation to the corporation's current and future position. Career development cannot be done fruitfully without attention to the expectations of different departments for their employees and to the opportunities that are available today and that are forecasted for the future. In fact, our experience has been that employees today want information

about departments and internal staffing procedures. They have little patience for self-contemplation in a vacuum.

Today's changed corporate environment suggests some goals for personnel professionals building career-management systems. Programs need to help employees understand corporate change and how to react to and cope with change. Programs need to promote an awareness of departmental expectations, climate, and directions, including information about projected vacancies and skill requirements as well as information about declining areas of the business so people can prepare for a job or career change. Programs should help people evaluate their current contribution to the organization and identify areas for future contributions. A career-needs assessment should help employees determine areas for additional training in technical or managerial skills or both. Employees should be informed about corporate policies and procedures, about how to use the system. Ultimately, the career-planning and development process should lead to job moves when appropriate—when the individual wants to move or must move because of force reductions and when there are career opportunities in specific areas.

Because departments differ in their skill requirements, expected performance outputs, and recommended job sequences, employees must be responsible for their own careers, while the company provides the resources. Career-planning and development programs are desirable but certainly insufficient for increasing employees' contributions to the organization and preparing them for the future. Employees must use the information they acquire about themselves and the organization to obtain additional training and new job assignments.

The role of the human resource department is thus to help the client department in its professionalization process (see Case One), to facilitate the sharing of information among departments, and to develop general programs that meet the needs of several departments.

In the case discussed here, we accomplished these goals by establishing a work group of departmental representatives responsible for career development. Meeting several times during the course of a year, the work-group members shared pro-

grams they developed on their own to meet specific departmental needs. One department facing considerable technological change identified technical skills and knowledge it expected its managers to have. The department developed refresher courses and assessment procedures to ensure that the managers achieved the required levels. Another department developed its own career workshop to engender discussions about career opportunities in the department and how to take advantage of those opportunities. This workshop became a model for another department, which designed its own seminar.

Another approach tried by several departments was a career-awareness seminar purchased from an outside company. The seminar focused on self-evaluation of skills and interests. However, the departments refined the seminar by adding information about resources available in the company to help participants achieve their career goals.

The interdepartmental group worked together to develop several general programs that could be administered centrally or, if a department wished, administered by the department in a unique way to suit its objectives. One program was a workshop on organizational and career change. It outlined how people face change and initiate constructive reactions to change. One department thought this workshop fit well into a program developed for all managers on improving management skills. Another department saw it as fitting into a career self-assessment workshop. Still another department used it as a section on training for newly promoted and recently hired managers.

Another general product was a document to be updated as needed on developments in each department. The document offered information about trends and directions in each department, the climate (descriptions of what it is like in each department), areas of growth and decline, skill and experience requirements, and available training inside and outside the company.

A further goal of the work group was to enhance bosses' roles as developers and educators of their subordinates. The boss was viewed as a key resource for information about the department, the subordinate's performance and abilities, and ways to enhance development. After all, bosses would have to support

their subordinates by allowing them to attend training classes, offering them challenging assignments, and allowing them to move into new positions, often helping them find these positions. The performance-appraisal forms required bosses at all levels to consider areas for a subordinate's development; company documents offered suggestions. Yet many employees complained that bosses gave little feedback about their performance and even less attention to career development. Some lower- and middle-level managers wondered why they should develop their people when no one developed them and they were not rewarded for their efforts in developing their subordinates. These complaints gave rise to a one-day manager-as-developer workshop similar to the one outlined in Resource 6.

This workshop was administered by the personnel-department trainers to managers in all departments to help them understand their role in developing subordinates. The premise was that even experienced managers need to be reminded about how important it is to subordinates to have bosses set performance and career goals, give feedback, provide information about career opportunities, and create meaningful work assignments and growth experiences. The workshop also reminded managers that developing subordinates is good for the company.

In this case we thus discovered that career development must not be aimed solely at advancement. Continuous learning to ensure employees' future contributions to the organization is a cornerstone of career planning and development. Also, career development must be tied closely to the needs of individual departments. Our strategy as personnel-department staff was to encourage departments to share information and learn from each other. Moreover, working with the departments, we identified the need for general programs for departments experiencing growth or decline, for self-assessment, and for training the manager to be a career developer for subordinates.

Summary

This chapter explored ways companies can enhance career motivation even in a changing business environment. But a com-

petitive marketplace or declining economy do not mean that the company can afford to ignore employee growth opportunities if it hopes to retain valuable employees and enhance their motivation. The intrapreneurship approach of increasing employees' responsibility for major portions of projects is one way to accomplish these goals. Another is to ensure some vitality by transferring and promoting high-potential people. Standard career programs for all employees support career motivation by providing positive reinforcement for good work, challenging jobs, goal setting, feedback, and rewards.

Case One demonstrated one way to enhance motivation and ensure competence. Case Two acknowledged that career development has different meanings depending on the context; it demonstrated that the role of the personnel department is to facilitate information sharing, consult on projects of client departments, and develop general programs needed by several departments.

In the next chapter, we consider how both situational and individual factors influence career motivation.

Resource 7. Evaluating a Career-Planning Program.

Evaluation should be an important part of any corporate program, including career-planning and development programs. A career-planning workshop, which may last four or five days, represents a significant investment in time and money. Therefore, organizations offering such a workshop should evaluate its effectiveness. One simple and minimal way to do this is to ask participants afterward (for example, one or two months later) to indicate the value of the workshop. Sophisticated research designs can also be utilized—for example, before and after measures and evaluation of control groups who have not yet participated. The following questions might be used in such evaluation work. The questions also give an indication of the topics that might be covered in such a workshop.

1. The following are reasons for taking the career-planning workshop. Please indicate how much each was an important reason for you (1 = strong reason, 2 = moderate reason, 3 = not a reason).
   a. I wanted to learn specific skills (resume writing, networking).
   b. I wanted to learn something about myself.
   c. I wanted to learn about career development.
   d. I wanted specific information about job possibilities in my field.

Note: This questionnaire was developed by Joel Kleinman and James Shilliber.

    e.   I wanted to find a new job within my department.

    f.   I wanted to find a new job within the company.

    g.   I wanted to leave the company.

    h.   Other:

    _____

    _____

    _____

2.   The following is a list of items you might need to develop your career. Evaluate how much each is important to you (1 = great importance, 2 = some importance, 3 = no importance at all).

    a.   Information about emerging careers in new areas of the company.

    b.   Ways of finding out who can provide information about opportunities in my field.

    c.   Information about the organization: what jobs are available now and how to get them.

    d.   Skills such as resume writing, networking, career action planning.

    e.   Knowledge about what jobs would be appropriate for my skills and interests.

    f.   The energy to develop my career actively.

    g.   Other:

    _____

    _____

    _____

3.   Overall, to what extent did the workshop meet your needs (1 = to a great extent, 2 = some, 3 = not at all)?

4.   The following is a list of potential outcomes from the workshop. Check those that apply to you.

    a.   A new job within my department.

    b.   A new job in a different department.

    c.   Increased understanding of myself and my career needs.

    d.   A realization that I am already doing what I like.

    e.   A new job outside the company.

    f.   Increased awareness of my skills and interests.

    g.   Knowledge of job opportunities.

    h.   Knowledge of how to develop contacts to gain information and interviews.

    i.   A resume appropriate for my next career move.

    j.   Identification of a job I can prepare for (a "target" job).

    k.   Contacts in other departments who can help me in my career.

    l.   Contacts in my current department who can help me in my career.

    m.   An improved relationship with my boss about my career (for example, I can talk to my boss about my career plans).

    n.   An improved resume.

    o.   One or more job interviews. (Indicate how many: _____)

    p.   Information about job possibilities.

    q.   Feedback from others about the viability of different careers.

    r.   A career action plan.

    s.   Implementation of my career action plan.

    t.   Enrollment in other career-development programs or training courses.

u.   Talks about career-development plans with my peers.
v.   Increased motivation to work actively toward developing my career.
w.   Increased satisfaction with my job.
x.   Less satisfaction with my job.
y.   Redesign of my job to make it valuable to my career.
z.   Other:

_____

_____

_____

_____

Nine

Guidelines for Enhancing
Individual Employees'
Career Motivation

We have argued that career motivation comes from the support people receive from the environment. Career resilience depends on positive reinforcement and opportunities for achievement and risk taking. Career insight arises when one is encouraged to set goals and is given information about career opportunities and about oneself. Career identity stems from the type of job a person has and the assignments he or she receives as well as the rewards that are available. We have highlighted two career directions: the uppy striving for advancement and the contentnick, for whom a career is not a primary objective. We also briefly described people who have lost support or have little career direction: runners-up and misfits. Here we consider these two categories closely to see how people in these positions react to a loss of support.

Losing Support

Career crises, which can occur at any career stage, often result from a loss of support and an absence of rewards. A person's self-confidence diminishes when he or she lacks positive reinforcement and repeatedly faces barriers to independent action. This can be a self-perpetuating cycle unless the individual receives a boost that propels him or her into a favorable situation.

Runners-up. When uppies lose support, they become runners-up. Loss of support may come when people are passed over for promotion, mentors retire, or younger, more competitive people take center stage. If people who lose support have high resilience and insight, they are likely to recoup quickly and get back on the uppy track. Tom Fenton, introduced in Chapter One, was such a case. Although we did not have measurements of his personality, he did not seem to be the type to give up because the opportunities he hoped for in his company were disappearing. He explored his environment carefully and found opportunities elsewhere for achievement and advancement. Jim Marsh, our college teacher who did not receive tenure (Chapter One), was also a runner-up. He too sought new opportunities.

Constructive behavior in this situation thus is to seek fertile ground elsewhere or do something to enhance one's competitive position. Tom Fenton took such action, although it remains to be seen how successful he will be. He demonstrated that a runner-up can become an uppy again. Another alternative is to change career direction—for example, become a contentnick by settling for lower status, or become an uppy in a different way, such as by adopting a new and different career goal (for example, a teacher could decide to become an administrator).

However, consider runners-up who are not resilient and who do not know themselves or their environments well. Such people may behave in a destructive way by losing self-confidence, taking anger out on subordinates or family, panicking, avoiding future risk at all costs, becoming defensive, blaming others, or denying the obvious.

Misfits. Harvey Monroe (Chapter Two) felt like a misfit. He wanted a career in law and community service, and he increasingly felt locked into his management job. Mark Forrestal (Chapter Five) was also a misfit. He was beginning to wonder whether he was cut out for a career in a big corporation. He dreamed of starting his own business. Both Mark and Harvey had fairly moderate career resilience. Their self-confidence was tenuous and they needed others' support.

Misfits with low resilience attribute failure to themselves and do not know what to do next. When negative feedback occurs time and time again, they neither ignore it nor make constructive changes. They keep repeating the same mistakes; they are frozen in a dysfunctional pattern. For Mark Forrestal, the negative feedback was moving from job to job without a clear success. For Harvey Monroe it was constant badgering from his attorney friends. He identified with them, and they were his only reference group.

Misfits with some resilience seek out the single spark of positive reinforcement. They establish new goals by redefining the meaning of success. This redirection does not come easily. No one likes to be rejected, but failure and rejection can be seasoning experiences. The way out is to find a source of reward. Misfits can find rewards by changing their environment—finding a new situation that values what they have to offer—or by changing the value structure or reward system of their present environment.

Like runners-up, misfits can become uppies or contentnicks. They become contentnicks when they accept themselves for what they are and feel proud of it. They become uppies when they conform, giving up one goal or value in favor of the one that is rewarded in the present environment. For example, if Harvey Monroe does not leave the company, he could change his goals by changing his circle of friends to people who see the value in his management position.

Support from the Environment

The case of Joe Murphy demonstrates how career motivation changes depending on the support people receive. Joe started his career as a contentnick. He became an uppy and then a runner-up. One of the young managers in the career-motivation study, Joe was in the company that was not developmentally oriented.

Joe dropped out of college in his freshman year and spent four years at odd jobs before returning to school. He remained

close to his home and family during most of this time. When he returned to college, he supported himself in a work/study program. He was married during his senior year, and his wife, a registered nurse, helped support him until he finished his degree.

Joe's first job after graduation was in the company's engineering department. He and his wife bought a home near his parents' house, and they started a family. He spent many hours camping, canoeing, playing softball, gardening, and working on the house. He assumed that he would remain with the company for his entire career, doing the same job. He claimed that he got along with almost everyone. In his words, "I learned to shut my mouth before sticking my foot in it." He seemed more concerned with doing a solid piece of work than with where it was going to get him. He was satisfied with his life and was generally optimistic. His life seemed rich, with many leisure interests, a meaningful family relationship, and a good job. He seemed to be a well-balanced individual but not someone who was bent on advancing in the corporate hierarchy.

The assessment staff evaluated Joe as low in career identity. It seemed as though he planned to stay with the company more because it was comfortable than because he had a strong identity with the organization. Both his test scores and his interview report indicated that he was low in need for advancement. He was also low in career insight. His goals did not extend beyond his present job. His strengths and weaknesses and the political situation in the department were not on his mind. His career resilience was moderate. He seemed to have an average level of self-confidence but was fairly dependent on others when it came to making decisions.

But Joe was a person who was in the right place at the right time. Although he did not know it when he was assessed, he was being considered by his department for a promotion to second level after only two years with the company. The person who had the second-level job before had been transferred, and the department was having trouble finding a replacement. Several second-level managers turned down a lateral transfer into the job.

The promotion was to high-band second level, and it meant an immediate jump in salary of over $4000. The promotion also had a profound effect on Joe's motivation. Suddenly, he began to broaden his horizons and think about advancement. He was perceptive enough to realize that there was a certain amount of luck connected with the promotion. Yet the promotion opened up a vista he had not considered before. If he could move to second level so quickly, why not to third level?

Unfortunately, Joe struggled with his new job. He found himself overworked. After a year at second level, his boss took away some responsibilities fearing that Joe was burning out. Joe could not delegate work. He could handle the technical aspects of the job, but he evidently lacked managerial ability. His boss felt that Joe would be lucky if he stayed at second level. Thus, after three years with the company, Joe seemed to be on a career plateau, although Joe did not perceive it that way.

The major reason for his myopia was the lack of direct feedback from the boss. Although everyone in the department had a high work load, the boss felt compelled to take projects away from Joe to lighten his load. Because he did not give Joe reasons, Joe did not see this action as a lack of confidence in his ability but as an opportunity for him to do better with the assignments he had left. He felt that his boss was finally recognizing that no one could be expected to do the job. Unfortunately, the boss did not see it that way because the assignment changes placed a heavy burden on others in the department.

Support from Oneself

One solution to losing support from the environment is to find support from oneself. Such support is the only true insurance for success on one's own terms. Consider the following examples of artists who developed their own support for their careers.

Muriel Franklin was in her late forties when she realized there was more to life than caring for her husband and children. Trained as a concert pianist, Muriel taught music at home and gave concerts in her community before having her first baby.

After that, she kept a few students but found it difficult to schedule them in between the baby's feedings and naps. Her husband thought she was wasting her time teaching. When her second child started first grade, Muriel wanted to take a job teaching part-time. She resented her husband's feeling that if she could not make at least $40,000 a year it was not worthwhile. She was tired of feeling worthless.

Then Muriel was asked to start a music conservatory at a small college near her home. She would be responsible for hiring part-time teachers, advertising the program, and doing all the administrative work. She could teach, and if she wanted, she could give faculty recitals. The pay would be just about enough for one person to live on. Her husband dismissed the idea, and she dismissed him. She found an apartment for herself and the kids, and eventually secured a divorce and child support, and developed an extraordinarily successful conservatory program. Today she is not rich, but she is happy.

An engineer by training, Jerome Mann was a talented oil painter. But he could not make a living as an artist. After graduation in the late 1930s, he became a traveling sales representative for a manufacturing firm and did better financially than most people at that time. One day, he passed a bank window and saw an exhibit by an internationally known potter. Jerome was enthralled by the artist's mastery of his medium. He had never thought of clay pots as art before but found them irresistible. He bought some books, had a potter's wheel built, and taught himself how to throw clay.

Eight years after becoming a salesman, Jerome quit, and he and his wife opened a small clothing store. They were successful and eventually opened two more stores. Thanks to his wife's business sense and support, Jerome was able to work less and less in the business and more and more in his basement studio. During the last ten years they owned the business, he spent only one day a week on the stores' books and the rest of his week throwing and glazing clay. When he was in his seventies, Jerome had two one-man shows in New York City each year. Both shows were sold out before they opened. He was a celebrity in the field and frequently lectured at universities.

Many people, like Jerome and Muriel, are able to create an environment that maintains their career motivation. In Jerome's case, it was a gradual process. In Muriel's case, it was emotionally painful. For others, it is a big risk. (Remember George Rutter from Chapter Three, who left a ten-year teaching career to sing professionally.)

A case of an engineer who turned to his father's craft of woodworking provides some insight into the decision to provide a supportive environment for oneself by shifting careers. Frank Sharp packed away his engineering degree and his fifteen-year career to hang out his shingle as a cabinetmaker. His father had been a woodworker, and Frank had spent many memorable hours as a child in his father's shop picking up the basic skills of the craft. In an interview, Frank explained his job change: "I am often asked why I chose woodwork, especially over engineering. Out here in the shop, the entire product is the result of my actions. I am seeing it through from the concept through to the finished stages. I am not in a pool of some sort—as in a typical engineering firm—contributing in some narrow way. I am completely responsible for the final product. I enjoy that. It was not an easy decision to make. I question it occasionally. I think about it, sort of question it in my mind. But when I get through, I don't have any regrets. I am satisfied" (Sidener, 1985, 18–28). Frank works alone. He prefers that to expanding his business and losing control over the finished product. To make up for working alone all day, Frank is active in community activities.

Guidelines for Self-Support. Here are a few guidelines to help increase one's own career motivation:

> Review your accomplishments and give yourself
>   credit for them.
> Take a moderate risk—one from which there will be
>   some benefit.
> Show others you can cooperate but that you also have
>   your own ideas.

Inquire about how well you are doing.

Ask for information about career opportunities.

Set specific career goals for next year and general goals for the next five years.

Create your own job challenge by redesigning your job and generating new assignments.

If you want to be a leader, try it. Initiate and delegate work.

Take actions toward your goals.

Mind Plays for Increasing Self-Support. Think about yourself in each of the following situations. How would you answer the questions?

You are sixty-five years old and forced to retire. What are your achievements? What are your regrets? What will you do now?

You are forced to choose between a high-pressure job with considerable advancement opportunities but low job security and a low-pressure, secure job with few advancement opportunities. Which one would you choose? What type of job do you have now?

You have worked at the same job for fifteen years. Your pay has been about the same for the last five years except for cost-of-living increases. You are bored, but you have family obligations. You feel you should be retrained in another field, but you do not know which one. What do you do?

Your boss ignores you. She always seems to have better things to do than talk to you. What is keeping you from walking out? What is keeping you from telling her exactly what you think?

Summary

Chapter Seven showed how one's boss, company, job, and peers can influence career motivation. In this chapter, we

saw that losing support for career motivation can have an impact on one's career goals. Uppies become runners-up. Contentnicks and runners-up become misfits. Joe Murphy showed us how reinforcement in the environment can influence career ambitions. However, people are ultimately responsible for their own careers. The trick is to find the needed resources and use them wisely. We saw ways to develop one's own support in the cases of Muriel Franklin, the housewife turned conservatory director; Jerome Mann, the engineer/businessman turned potter; and Frank Sharp, the engineer turned cabinetmaker.

Ten

Understanding the Sources of Career Stress

We have discussed how people make career decisions and the situations they face that prompt a career choice. We have seen several examples of the stress people feel as they make decisions and live through career transitions. Consider a few of the individuals we introduced in the first two chapters. Patricia Stewart, for example, agonized over whether to accept a job offer or stay with her present firm. Tom Fenton took months to investigate all aspects of his mid-career shift. Harvey Monroe was unhappy with his decision to enter business and felt pressured to go out on his own as an attorney. Arthur Harris returned to his job from a sabbatical and found that he no longer wanted to remain in the corporate world. Two people we met in Chapter Three made major career transitions. George Hammer moved from being a music teacher to being a manager in business. George Rutter changed from being a music teacher to being a professional singer.

Work is not the only factor that affects career decisions. Remember Mel Foreman, whose case was described in Chapter Seven. He needed a new job when his company moved because his wife refused to leave the East Coast. Also recall Muriel Franklin, from Chapter Nine, whose husband's constant badgering about her career ambitions pushed her into a divorce and the freedom to succeed in a new job.

This chapter defines career stress and considers the sources of stress. In subsequent chapters, we consider how people react to career stress and examine stress-management methods that can help prevent or reduce stress. Our goal is to examine feelings of career stress, how people react to them, and what they can do to help themselves and others.

What Is Stress?

Psychological stress is a set of interactions between the person and the environment that result in an unpleasant emotional state, such as anxiety, tension, guilt, or shame (Janis and Mann, 1977). As McGrath (1976, p. 1352) explains: "Something happens 'out there' which presents a person with a demand, or a constraint, or an opportunity for behavior. . . . The extent to which that demand [or constraint or opportunity] is 'stressful' depends on several things. . . . First, it must be perceived by the 'stressee.' Second, it must be interpreted by him (or her) in relation to his or her ability to meet the demand; circumvent, remove, or live with the constraint; or effectively use the opportunity. Third, [the stressee] must perceive the potential consequences of successfully coping with (i.e., altering) the demand (constraint, opportunity) as more desirable than the expected consequences of leaving the situation unaltered."

General Causes of Stress

A stressor thus creates an imbalance between the individual (his or her abilities, needs, expectations) and what is demanded of the individual. Stress is positive (sometimes referred to as *eustress*; Selye, 1976) when the individual is motivated or challenged to correct the imbalance. Negative stress arises when the consequences of not being able to meet the demands of the situation are great. For instance, not being able to complete a certain project on time may mean losing a promotion or incurring additional production costs. Negative stress can also arise when the outcome of failure is not known—for example, when one does not know how one's boss will react if a project is behind schedule. Negative stress often results in physical or

behavioral symptoms of strain (fatigue, difficulty sleeping, headaches, ulcers). A person's career resilience, insight, and identity
determine reactions to potentially stressful career situations.
Resilient individuals with insight into themselves and a sense
of career direction are likely to have less negative stress than
those who are low in these dimensions of career motivation.

Stress is largely in the eye of the beholder. What is stressful
to one person is not necessarily stressful to another. For instance,
Patricia Stewart agonized over her career decision, while someone else in the same situation might have made the decision
quickly and without much thought. Some people may think of
Harvey Monroe's situation and wonder, "Why can't Monroe
see that he is better off in management than he would ever be
out on his own?" or "Why should Harvey care what his friends
think?"

Knowledge of oneself and one's values also affect perceptions of stress. Joe Murphy (see Chapter Nine) failed to perceive
the difficulty he had in handling his work load. When his boss
took responsibilities away from him, Joe did not interpret this
move negatively because he did not understand that he did not
have the ability to do the job. George Rutter was not worried
about his income as a professional singer because the amount
of money he made was less important to him than the improvement in the quality of his voice and the favorable reviews he
received from critics.

Other people also can influence how an individual inter-
prets a situation by making the situation more or less salient.
We all care about what others think about us. Other people are
the source of rewards and punishments, and how they react to
our behavior and opinions arouses our attention and concern.
Harvey Monroe probably would not worry as much about his
career as an attorney if his friends were not badgering him.
Jerome Mann (see Chapter Nine) had few qualms about devoting increasingly more time to the art of making clay pots and
less time to his family business because he had the support of
his wife. In fact, his wife became a major organizer of his shows
and held an important position in the state art council. If
Jerome's wife's interests were incompatible with his art, his life
would have been more stressful than it was.

Sources of Stress

This section describes different sources of stress. We begin by examining stress in relation to people's roles. Next, we describe the stress people impose on themselves through their goals and feelings of inadequacy and the stress that is imposed on them by others.

Role Conflict. A common source of stress in the work environment is the individual's role in the organization. Role conflict occurs when people face two or more sets of demands such that compliance with one makes compliance with the other difficult (Kahn and others, 1964). Research has demonstrated that role conflict contributes to emotional strain, which in turn lowers job satisfaction and increases a person's intention to leave the job (Jackson, 1983; Bedeian and Armenakis, 1981; Kemery and others, 1985).

Interrole conflict occurs when two or more roles have conflicting demands. The conflicting demands of work and family are frequent forms. The time required by one role may make it difficult to pursue the other, as when one's work schedule requires being away from one's family for extended periods of time. One role may produce strain symptoms, such as tension, anxiety, and fatigue, which make it difficult to comply with the demands of another role, as when marital difficulties make it hard to concentrate at work. Behavior-based role incompatibility occurs when the behavior required in a role makes fulfilling the requirements of another role difficult, as when the role of parent requires warmth and openness and the role of executive requires objectivity and secretiveness (Greenhaus and Beutell, 1985). Working mothers often feel stress as they try to balance family needs against job requirements and career concerns. (We discuss this type of conflict in detail later.) Interrole conflict can also occur on the job when two or more roles place inconsistent demands on an individual, as when a faculty member is expected to be a researcher, teacher, and administrator.

Intrarole conflict occurs when there are conflicting expectations within a role, as when a manager must reduce labor-force costs while increasing productivity. Inconsistent messages

from the same source are called *intrasender conflict*. Intersender conflict occurs when a person faces inconsistent directives from more than one person, as when a person reports to one boss for administrative purposes and works for one or more other bosses on different projects.

Person/role conflict occurs when one's attributes (a trait, value, need, desire, or moral principle) conflict with the role, as when a person who is promoted to a supervisory position finds it difficult to delegate responsibility or give directives or when an individual wants to advance in the corporation but is not sufficiently aggressive. Person/role conflict may also occur when an individual is given an assignment he or she does not want, as when the corporate psychologist is assigned responsibility for monitoring the personnel-department budget or when a marketing/sales executive is transferred to the public-relations department for a developmental assignment.

In *role or task overload*, stress arises because a person simply has too much to do relative to his or her abilities and resources. This may be an interrole problem, as when a single parent has to take care of the children, do the housework, and maintain a career. It may also be an intrarole problem, as it might be for a mother with three children all under four years of age or for a professional who has too many clients to handle at once.

Role or task underload—having too little to do—can be another source of stress. Role underload occurs on jobs that are insufficiently challenging or where the volume of work does not keep the person busy.

Role ambiguity is uncertainty about what to do, when to do it, how to act, and so forth. Ambiguity can arise about the scope of one's responsibilities, rules and regulations, sources of authority, a boss's evaluation of one's performance, organizational changes, and job security. Ambiguity is likely to occur in large, complex organizations. It also occurs when there are changes in technology or personnel, as when a person changes jobs. Ambiguity can result from a lack of information from upper management. Or subordinates can create ambiguity for supervisors by withholding information as a way of controlling events or as a way of retaliating against unpopular supervisors.

Role conflict and ambiguity generally result in tension, job dissatisfaction, lowered self-esteem, and ultimately absenteeism and turnover (McGrath, 1976). Although ambiguity may result in increased communication to reduce uncertainty, both role conflict and ambiguity are likely to generate dislike for the people who are seen as the cause. Role overload may result in as much interpersonal stress as conflict and ambiguity because overload can decrease the level of one's performance or cause one to ignore some aspects of a role, resulting in complaints and quarrels about meeting deadlines.

How one views the source of role conflict may depend on how one responds. For instance, suppose you feel conflict between your job and your involvement in community activities. Say you have to take a business trip that will mean missing a board meeting of a community organization. You promised people on the board that you would be at the meeting even if it meant canceling the business trip, but you later find that it would be awkward to cancel the trip. The outcome is that you take the trip. You are likely to believe that work interfered with your community activities and responsibilities. If you had canceled the business trip at the expense of your job, you would probably say that your outside commitments interfered with work.

Role conflicts are a particular source of stress for women. Society seems to demand that female managers and professionals be superhuman (Cooper and Davidson, 1982). For example, there is little or no tolerance in corporations, particularly at higher echelons, for childcare concerns. Women who reenter the work force after having children—for example, when the children enter grade school—find that they are at a disadvantage because corporations tend to develop young people to move into top management (Dubois, 1981). Women in management face a number of unique stressors that do not affect men (Nelson and Quick, 1985). These include discrimination, stereotyping, marriage/work conflicts, and social isolation.

Discrimination against women in the work place has been blatant. In 1982, fewer than 2 percent of higher-level business managers were women (Forbes and Pierce, 1983). Women earned 57 to 87 percent of the wages of men in comparable occupa-

tions (Rubin, 1984). In addition, men are much more readily incorporated into work groups and given support and advice than are women.

Stereotyping is a problem especially for women entering male-dominated organizations. In the eyes of both women and men, the stereotype of the successful manager is the same as the stereotype for men: aggressive, highly motivated, confident, and competent (Schein, 1973). Although some female executives have these characteristics (Crawford, 1977), the characteristics do not fit the stereotype for females in general. The successful woman executive with these characteristics does not live up to her social role as a female, yet if she fails on the job, she is not likely to live up to her own standards (Horner, 1972). The potential for this internal conflict is likely to decrease as stereotypes change, but the change is taking substantial time.

Marriage/work conflicts are another source of stress for women. Women who mix children and career often face severe role demands coupled with dual-career conflicts. The psychological and financial costs of working may be too great to outweigh the career benefits. Despite the cooperation of their husbands, women usually retain primary responsibility for the children and the household. Some corporations are trying to ease the childcare burden by establishing childcare facilities or helping employees find adequate facilities close to the home or office. Seminars may be offered to increase supervisors' awareness of the scheduling and other problems women have in caring for children. Flexible work schedules and working at home can be a help without decreasing productivity (Fernandez, 1986).

Social isolation arises when men place a token female executive in a stereotypic role—mother, seductress, or fair maiden (Kanter, 1977). In a work setting, this may isolate a woman because she is not called on to use her work-related skills. Women may avoid this labeling by repressing aggressiveness or other behavior that will call attention to them.

Work/nonwork responsibilities affect men as well as women, especially husbands of managerial and professional women (Greenhaus and Kopelman, 1981). Major events in one area of life have an impact on other areas of life. For instance,

accepting a new job can mean disrupting the family. This is one reason why Tom Fenton, in making a mid-career change, chose a position that did not require relocating, even though he had offers that were favorable to his career but that would have required moving.

In general, work and nonwork affect each other in two ways. The stress of work can spill over to the nonwork sphere, increasing overall stress. Or leisure time and family life can compensate for a poor work environment. Work can also compensate for a negative family situation—for example, people may delve into work to avoid thinking about a personal tragedy. Alternatively, a negative family situation can make it difficult for a person to function at work (Latack, 1984; Near, Rice, and Hunt, 1980). Whether spillover or compensation occurs depends on the circumstances. Spillover is probably more likely if one area of life interferes with another. One area may impose time demands, sap one's energy, or require behaviors that make it impossible or difficult to do anything else. For example, children place demands on parents' time that make it difficult to put extra time and energy into a career. Or business trips take time away from family and create marital friction.

Today's couples must be protean in that they must assume multiple roles and flexibly adjust to different demands posed by work and family (Hall and Hall, 1979). Also, the efforts of dual-career couples with children to coordinate two careers and a family may be described as herculean. As we have shown, both husbands and wives feel this stress, but they feel it in different ways. Women who have to deal with multiple roles often face the brunt of the demands. Men may generate conflict by not readily accepting the added roles of housework and childcare.

Today, we find many different patterns of balancing work and family. Some men become househusbands, taking leaves of absence from their jobs to care for young children while their wives resume their careers. However, few corporations support this role by granting men the same benefits women receive for newborn care.

When the husband and wife are both professionals with good jobs, the daily routine of running the household and caring for the children can be much easier than when they do not have

good jobs. Having substantial incomes makes it possible to afford a full-time housekeeper or an au pair (a young person from another country who is willing to care for the children and do some housework in exchange for passage to and from the United States, room and board, and a small stipend). Also, these couples have the money to pay for the best education and special activities for their children outside of school. The families may take expensive vacations together to compensate for the time that the parents are away from the children. Unfortunately, most couples with children are not so lucky, and they experience much stress in trying to cope with conflicting roles. To avoid this predicament, many couples are delaying having children until they have purchased a home and are fairly well established. Other couples are deciding not to have children in order to maintain their freedom and standard of living.

Another pattern we see today is the single parent. Once the parent has worked out the finances and logistics of childcare, the situation may be easier to handle than living with an unsupportive spouse who increases the conflict rather than helping to manage multiple responsibilities. Some unmarried men and women choose to be single parents by adopting or having children in other ways.

Career Stage. Job stress is likely to vary at different career stages. Early career is a time of uncertainty about which career direction is the best, what types of behaviors are appropriate, and whether one will succeed. Working to fulfill one's needs for achievement, advancement, and friendship imposes stress. (A need is an imbalance or tension between an existing and a desired state. The strength or importance of the need and the difficulty in attaining it determine the degree of felt stress.) Many times in early career, pressure to advance and achieve is self-imposed as people set standards for themselves, compare themselves with others, and establish deadlines for goal attainment. Some people feel comfortable with this pressure; for them fulfilling needs is a driving force.

Whether goals create pressure and strain or whether they are a positive force is likely to depend on how realistic and attainable they are and how committed the individual is to them.

For a goal to be important to a person, it has to impose challenge. Otherwise, it is not much of a goal. But if the person realizes that a goal is impossible or unrealistic, the goal is not likely to affect the person's behavior or emotions. For instance, many of us feel it would be nice to be rich and famous, but this desire is not a driving force. However, for a few people, it may be a driving force, and it may even be an obsession. Then the goal becomes stress provoking. Even realistic goals are stressful when they take years to accomplish and when we are impatient or when we are doubtful about our ability to attain them.

Mid-career often brings evaluation and redirection. At this time, a person's expectations are brought in line with reality. For some, this evaluation occurs within the first five years of starting a career. For others, it takes years. People who revise their expectations downward diminish the energy they put into their careers and look toward other goals. For many, the stress of mid-career is indecision about which direction to take and reluctance to give up old goals, which may be tantamount to admitting failure.

People whose early-career goals are met may enhance their ambitions in mid-career and continue to strive for success. Tom Fenton took positive action when he realized his career goals would be blocked if he stayed with the company he had been with for twenty years. Arthur Harris found a new way of life while taking a sabbatical. This experiment in changing life-style was so attractive to him and his family that they eventually made it permanent. People such as Harvey Monroe and Mark Forrestal (Chapter Six) saw themselves as misfits early in their careers but had not yet resolved their situation and reduced the stress.

Late career is a time for reflection. It differs from early and middle career in that the individual realizes that unfulfilled goals are not likely to be attained. The disappointment may be stressful in itself, or it may be a relief. Unfortunately, many older people face the stress of physical impairment or financial concerns, feeling useless, unneeded, and abandoned.

Career Goals. In previous chapters, we described how different career goals and the extent to which people accomplish

them affect how they feel about their careers, the anxiety they experience, and their level of motivation. We identified several types of people: the uppy, who is constantly striving for career advancement; the runner-up who confronts a major career barrier; the misfit, whose career goals conflict with the opportunities in the organization; and the contentnick, who is satisfied with the status quo. The uppy, runner-up, and misfit are plagued by a dynamic tension between what they want and what they have. Uppies want more; runners-up want what they have been denied; and misfits do not know what they want, or, if they do, they are presently on the wrong track. People move between these states. Opportunities improve for runners-up. Self-confidence restored, they become uppies again. Or the runner-up may lower expectations and settle for the calm life of the contentnick. Misfits have the greatest struggle because they generally lack the foundation of resilience and the self-insight and knowledge of the environment to develop a meaningful career identity. Readily influenced by others, misfits lack the backbone and self-knowledge to take a new career direction.

Uppies, runners-up, and misfits can be found among people in all career stages. Mark Forrestal and Harvey Monroe, two of our misfits, were in their early careers. Tom Fenton was a mid-career runner-up. Jerome Mann, our misfit salesman turned potter, made a slow career shift from occupation to avocation throughout the course of his life. Arthur Harris made a major career change after his sabbatical.

Unfortunately, everyone does not wind up a contentnick or a successful uppy. Being a runner-up, however, is generally a transient stage because the individual has a foundation of resilience. Feeling like a runner-up is incongruent with the individual's self-concept. So the runner-up is likely either to pursue other opportunities or to change career goals and become a contentnick.

Misfits have a greater problem than runners-up because they must first find a way out of their present predicament and then establish a new career direction. Both steps are risky, and taking risks is often foreign to the misfit. Harvey Monroe seems to have a chance. He is ambivalent about his career direction,

but he has created several viable alternatives—start a full-time law practice, stay in business, or stay in business and start a part-time law practice. Mark Forrestal does not have the vision for himself that Harvey Monroe has. Mark had a sequence of unsuccessful job experiences in a short time. He needs a positive experience to get on track. Otherwise, he may be dreaming for years.

Feelings of Inadequacy. Stress comes from feeling an imbalance between the rewards one receives and the rewards one expects to receive or the rewards one sees others receiving. People evaluate how good they feel about their accomplishments or how bad they feel about their lack of accomplishments by comparing themselves with others. Feelings of inequity are often coupled with another source of stress, peer pressure. Harvey Monroe felt peer pressure from his attorney friends, who wanted him to leave business to practice law and enter politics. Because Harvey was influenced by his friends, he felt inequitably treated by the company, which barred him from transferring to the legal department. Also, Harvey felt that he was not being fair to himself after having worked so hard to become a lawyer.

Interpersonal Stress. We have mentioned peer pressure as a type of stress people impose on themselves by their willingness to be influenced by others. Another type of interpersonal stress is due to personality clashes and disagreements about appropriate behavior. A supervisor can create stress by not showing sufficient concern for subordinates' feelings or needs. Interpersonal stress may also arise from race or sex discrimination or harassment.

Discordant Values. A special kind of person/role conflict arises when there is a disparity between what the individual thinks is right and the demands of the job. Employees do not always subscribe to the values of their employers. For example, "there is a growing resistance to managerial authoritarianism, [and] a heightened desire for participation in decision making and a greater demand for satisfaction in work and opportunities for self-actualization. There are also demands for honesty and

openness with regard to company financial data and policy decisions'' (Sager and Kipling, 1980, p. 24). Organizations that do not provide meaningful jobs, that do not involve employees in decision making, or that are not open about business transactions and corporate policies are likely to create stress in the employees who value these things.

Moreover, an organization may expect employees to adopt career goals in line with the organization's structure and rewards. The most valued reward an organization has to offer is promotion and its correlates—money, prestige, power, and status. Yet, many young people today are not impressed with advancing up the corporate hierarchy. They are less advancement oriented than they are achievement oriented. In many cases, however, job challenge and opportunities for achievement are greater at higher corporate levels. Although there are ways to meet achievement needs outside work, people who cannot achieve their personal goals through work are likely to be dissatisfied because work is a central part of life. These individuals are likely to look for other career opportunities, as Arthur Harris did and as Mark Forrestal dreams of doing.

In reality, many people's needs conform to the opportunities available in their particular organizations. People are attracted to organizations that can meet their needs. Also, organizations make certain needs salient to people by emphasizing those needs. Thus, a company that emphasizes management development and early-career advancement hires the brightest and most motivated people and then provides opportunities and rewards that reinforce that motivation. Donna Grant (Chapter Six) worked for a company that gave her experiences in different areas and promoted her early in her career. Employees who find pressures to advance stressful or who do not place the same values on management development are likely to leave. Frank Sharp, the engineer turned cabinetmaker described in Chapter Nine, and Jerome Mann, the businessman turned potter, are people whose values did not match those of their original careers.

Resource 8 is a self-reflection guide to help employees think about their sources of stress.

Summary

Career stress results from the interaction between a person and the environment. Although some stress can be positive in that it is challenging and prompts people to make good career decisions, we usually think of stress in negative terms. Sources of stress include role conflict, ambiguity, and overload. Professional women and women in management feel the stress of discrimination and stereotyping on the job and the pressure of performing multiple roles. Different career stages often bring different sources of stress. Early in our careers, we worry about succeeding in the work world. In mid-career, we adjust to our level of accomplishments. In late career, we prepare for the transition to retirement. Other sources of stress stem from perceived inequities, personality clashes, and discordant values. Resource 8 poses questions to help people identify their sources of stress.

These sources of stress are often most acute when people have to make a decision or when they are in the process of a transition. The next chapter focuses on the stress employees feel when making career decisions and when undergoing major career transitions.

Resource 8. Self-Reflection Guide for Identifying Sources of Stress.

After you complete each of the following sets of questions, ask yourself whether there are other sources of stress in that category. Then, for each source, consider the strength of the stress, whether it is good or bad (motivating or debilitating), and what your reaction to this type of stress is. (Reactions to stress are discussed in Chapters Twelve and Thirteen.)

Interrole Conflict

How often do people seem to expect you to do two things at once (for example, your boss wants you to work late to finish a report and your spouse wants you at home to watch the children)? How do you react to this situation (by sticking with the job and asking your spouse to make other arrangements or by rushing home and telling your boss you will finish the work in the morning)? The answer to this question should tell you something about how you cope with role conflict as well as where your loyalties lie.

Do you wish you had more time to spend with your family or on favorite leisure activities? What is stopping you?

Do you find it hard to relax at home after a tough day at the office?

Does your work suffer after you have had an argument with your spouse or when the kids are acting up?

Intrarole Conflict

Does your job demand that you do routine tasks (for example, some clerical work) that could just as easily be done by someone with less expertise who is paid less?

Do you feel your professional expertise is not valued by your boss?

Do you have to report to higher-level managers other than your immediate supervisor who call on you to do work?

Does being a parent interfere with your marriage?

Does your spouse ever complain that your family needs a vacation or new furniture or that you are not saving enough money?

Does your boss want to impress clients with fancy presentations and also want to impress co-workers by reducing departmental costs?

Person/Role Conflict (Discordant Values)

Have you ever been told that you are not aggressive enough, and you do not like to be aggressive?

Do you want tenderness while your spouse wants friendship?

Does getting ahead in your career require a skill you do not feel you have?

Do you feel it is not right to use personal friendship to get ahead at work?

Role Overload

Do you feel your work never ends?

Is the amount of work you have to do virtually impossible for one person to handle?

Do you feel that just when you finish a project another one comes along?

Are you constantly pushing to get things done?

Does your spouse expect too much from you?

Role Ambiguity

Does your boss ever give you an assignment that is unclear—that is, do you not know exactly what your boss means or wants?

Are you uncertain about what your boss expects from you?

Are you uncertain about what you are supposed to do?

Do you lack deadlines for completing projects?

Are your children difficult to handle and you do not know how to discipline them?

Inequities

Do other people take credit for your accomplishments?
Compared with you, do other people seem to be rewarded more for doing less?
Have you been passed over for promotion by someone you perceive to be less qualified than you?

Interpersonal Stress

Do you have to work with people you dislike?
Are there some people with whom you argue a lot?
Do people with whom you work get on your nerves?

Early-Career Stress

Are you in a hurry to move up the career ladder?
Do you feel that you cannot wait until you are promoted?
Are you constantly comparing yourself with your peers?

Mid-Career Stress

Do you feel time is running out for accomplishing your career goals?
Have you been doing the same job for years with no end in sight?
Are your assignments unimportant?

Late-Career Stress

Are you dissatisfied with your career?
Do you feel useless?
Do you feel others do not respect you?

Eleven

The Stress of
Career Decisions
and Transitions

The previous chapter described different sources of career stress: role conflict (interrole, intrarole, person/role), role ambiguity, and role overload. We examined the stress professional and managerial women feel in juggling work and family roles and the increased pressure they face at work because they are women. We also considered how dual-career couples cope with work/family conflicts. We examined stress at different career stages and how the likelihood of goal accomplishment influences stress. In addition, we discussed the stress resulting from perceived inequities, interpersonal conflicts, and discordant values. These different sources of stress often lead people to make career decisions and career transitions. However, we have not yet addressed the stress that can occur when people make such decisions and experience the resulting transitions.

Stress Arising from Career Decisions

In Chapter Two, we described the case of Patricia Stewart, who agonized over whether to reject a job offer and accept the counteroffer made by her present employer. We saw how her commitment to her employer and to the friend who recommended that she pursue the new job pulled her in different direc-

tions and caused her several sleepless nights. In this section, we dissect the stress of making a career decision such as Patricia's.

How people make a decision depends on the alternatives available to them and, more specifically, on the information they have about the alternatives and the associated risks. A person feels stress when the decision entails a conflict between two or more alternatives, each with positive and negative attributes, and when the decision maker stands to attain or not attain significant goals.

Continuing with Patricia's example, she was presented with two choices, either of which would result in gains and losses: a new job closer to home but with fewer benefits initially or her present job farther from home with a few added benefits. The decision occurred in stages. At first, she did not know about the loss of benefits she would incur if she took the new job. She told herself and her friend that she would take the new job. Then, she received the counteroffer from her present employer and learned that the new job was not as attractive as she had originally thought. But she felt committed to her initial decision. She also felt committed to her present employer.

Patricia therefore experienced stress because she was committed to more than one alternative and because she expected losses—specifically, social disapproval. Patricia's conflicting commitments and anticipation of losses and the accompanying stress caused some initial panic. She seemed to lose sight of what she wanted from her career, and she was influenced mostly by what others would think of her. Talking with her husband moderated the stress of having to make a decision, giving her the time and courage to scrutinize her alternatives and carefully work out a solution. He helped put the situation in perspective so that she could separate her feelings of commitment from what she wanted in her career. In Chapter Two, we said that making a decision is like climbing a hill. When you start up, the difficulty of the climb is affected by your immediate surroundings. You do not gain wide perspective until you reach the top and the barriers you have encountered along the way are no longer important.

Most people probably make career decisions the way Patricia Stewart did. They consider the alternatives that are available at the time, they think about what other alternatives may be open to them, and they are influenced greatly by the commitments they have made and by what other people think. They may feel intense pressure, but they eventually make a choice.

Some decision situations are anxiety provoking because each alternative poses serious risks or losses. Consider the case of John, who has been with his company for four years and has been on the company's management-development program for high-potential managers for the last two years. Since starting with the corporation, he has been in a staff position in the personnel department. John is a good, stable performer who has a knack for handling large-scale projects. Even though he likes his assignment in the personnel department, John is eager to learn about other parts of the business, so he asks for a reassignment. Because he does his best work on challenging projects, his boss works hard to get him reassigned to an operations department known for its demanding jobs in line management. Even though John knows this transfer is important to his career, he is anxious about it. First, he has never worked in operations and has no technical background. Second, he has never supervised or managed a group of people and is worried about his ability to do so. Third, he is concerned that his sponsoring department, personnel, will lose interest in him. In John's case, there is a risk of staying and a risk of moving.

Another type of decision stress occurs when the choices are equally positive or equally negative. The response to this situation is likely to be defensive avoidance. People stop the search, distort the meaning of information, and construct rationalizations to help make the decision. Panic (hypervigilance) ensues when the alternatives are equally negative and there is little time to make a choice. Satisficing is a decision strategy that works well in this type of situation. People may take the first alternative that comes along or select a set of criteria on which to base the decision, ignoring other information. As we

said in Chapter Four, satisficing can be an effective and sane way to make a choice. People do not have to identify all possible alternatives and then evaluate every aspect of each alternative to make a good decision. But if they use criteria that seem important now but are actually irrelevant—for example, basing their decision on feelings of loyalty and friendship—then their choice may not work out.

In general, a moderate amount of decisional stress probably motivates people to make careful decisions. Too little stress makes them cavalier, and too much stress leads to panic or avoidance. Try the following exercise yourself or with an employee or friend.

Consider the stress you felt when making an important career decision. Were you anxious about the decision? Did you have a tough time making up your mind? Did you vacillate—choosing one alternative one day and then changing your mind the next? With hindsight, perhaps you can recall now why the decision was difficult to make. Was it a matter of not being sure what you wanted and what alternative would result in the best outcome? Were you bothered by the uncertainty of not knowing how well you would do? What other considerations were important, such as what your friends would think or your not wanting to leave a situation where people depended upon you?

The Stress Arising from Career Transitions

So far, we have discussed conditions that cause career stress (conflicts, uncertainties, demands) and the stress that may occur when making a career decision. Next, we look at what happens when the decision results in a change in roles or a change in orientation to a role.

A career may be defined as a succession or an accumulation of role-related experiences over time (Hall, 1976). Career progress refers to moving up an organizational hierarchy, staying at the same level but acquiring additional skills, or "spiraling" by taking a succession of job moves through related or different fields (Van Maanen and Schein, 1977). With this definition in mind, we can distinguish two general types of role transitions—

interrole and intrarole (Louis, 1980). Interrole transitions include entering an organization or reentering after a period of absence. Moving between departments within an organization, changing organizations, and changing professions are other interrole transitions; they all involve entering new roles. An often-neglected aspect of interrole change is the dynamics of leaving a role. These dynamics are especially important at retirement, when the focus is on the role that is left behind and the process is one of separation rather than joining. An interrole transition may be forced, as when a person is fired or laid off, or it may occur by choice, as when a mother reenters the labor force after her children have started school.

Intrarole transitions include adjusting to one's present role or accepting a new responsibility. Making the psychological transition to a new career stage or life stage is another intrarole transition. This is a slow process, as people realize, for example, that they are unlikely to advance further in their careers.

The stress of a career transition comes from various sources: from the uncertainty people feel in accepting the new role and the regret they feel in leaving the old role, and from role conflict and change in role demands. The characteristics of change also cause stress. Some change happens quickly; in these cases, people experience stress because they have no time for preparation. Some change is voluntary; in these cases, people must attribute the cause of the change (and hence, the stress they feel) to themselves. Other times, the change is involuntary; in these cases, people experience stress because they blame others (the boss or the organization) for the change. Another important characteristic of change is the extent of the discontinuity it involves. How big a change is it? Does it affect the core of a person—how the individual sees and defines himself or herself? Is the change reversible? Changes that are permanent or irreversible are probably more stressful than changes that are not. Consider the following examples.

The director of a college placement center, Fran Cooper was responsible for working with businesses to arrange campus visits and coordinate interviews with graduating seniors and graduating M.B.A.s. Fran had a graduate degree in education

and had been working within the administration of the university for almost ten years, first as an assistant dean of admissions and then as the assistant director and eventually the director of the placement office. But Fran was not fully satisfied. The students she placed received starting salaries that were higher than her current salary. Also, their jobs sounded more exciting than hers.

A friend employed by a major company convinced Fran that she could do well as a manager in the corporate world. Fran had ample supervisory experience, and her interpersonal and communications skills were excellent. She was active in the state educational association, where she showed her leadership potential, especially her ability to envision changes needed in her field and then coordinate people to make the changes. Her friend was willing to help her get a job in the personnel department of his company as a recruiter.

Fran took the position. However, she soon learned that to get ahead in business she would have to leave the personnel department and work in one of the operations departments, where she would have responsibility for providing customer services. Customer service was the heart of the business. After only one year in personnel, she transferred to the operations staff. And after several months in that position, she moved to a field job. After one year in the field, Fran was promoted to middle management and had over 300 people in her unit.

This transition was not simply a matter of applying existing skills to a new situation. It required that Fran make a psychological transition by breaking away from her former profession and immersing herself in a new professional world. She had to learn the technical aspects of the company's operations and establish a new professional identity. Fran had the self-confidence to know she could be successful. She also had the insight to realize that this transition was necessary for her to be a success in the corporation. In the process, her definition of success, her reference group, and her role models changed. These changes were not easy for someone trained in another discipline and with many years of experience in another field. Other people in Fran's place might have been content with the

job in the personnel department, which offered a good salary and allowed retaining the tie to her profession. But Fran knew that in this company such an attitude would be a dead end. She was able to make the psychological transition of embracing the goals of the business. Recall that George Hammer (Chapter Three) was able to make a similar transition from music teacher to corporate manager. Because George made this transition early in his career however, it was easier than in Fran's case.

Several aspects of the change ameliorated the stress for Fran. Fran's major risk was in giving up her professional identity. But Fran reasoned that doing so was not irreversible. She maintained her contacts in the personnel department as well as at local universities. Also, the change was gradual. Working in the personnel department for a year provided a smooth transition between the academic environment and business operations. The operations department, however, was initially foreign territory to Fran. She had to prove herself over and over, both to herself and to her supervisor. She did not have the technical background most people had in operations, and she was a woman in a predominantly male part of the business. Fortunately, the company had a policy of training generalist managers, and it had found that managers with a liberal arts background often did better than those with an engineering background in supervisory positions. Consequently, Fran had the support of her coworkers and her supervisors, who rewarded her performance and her demonstrated potential to advance.

Moe Grant's transition from a career to early retirement did not proceed as smoothly as Fran's transition. Moe had worked for his company for twenty-two years. He had been employed by several firms as a salesman before starting with this company. He went with the firm because of its reputation as a secure place to work. He might not earn as much money, he reasoned, but he was tired of jumping from company to company with every swing of the economy. Whether business was bad or good, at least he could stay. Moe remained in sales for his first five years with the company and then moved into public relations. He later moved into personnel. Eventually a middle manager, he had a decent salary and interesting, steady work.

About three months before Moe retired, the company went through a reorganization. Consultants were brought in to redesign the organization in order to save money; they accomplished this goal mainly by reducing the number of middle managers. Some people were placed in new assignments, and the company offered financial incentives to encourage early retirement for employees like Moe who were over fifty-five years old and had been with the company long enough to collect a reasonable pension. In addition to the usual retirement benefits, the plan offered a year's salary spread over two years. Moe discussed the options with his wife. The children had finished college, they owned their own home, and they had a summer house with a small mortgage. They also had a good amount of savings. Moe thought that if he left the company, he could pick up some consulting work. His wife had a decent job, and she would be eligible for a pension in three years. This seemed to be an opportunity Moe could not turn down. It would be a relief to leave the firm. If he stayed, he knew he would be relegated to a job with little responsibility until he retired. He felt betrayed by the organization, which once had been known for its commitment to its people. The retirement incentive was lucrative, but the message he received was that he and people like him were deadwood, unable to make a productive contribution to the bottom line.

Two days after Moe accepted the company's offer, he was given a retirement party with other retirees. The next day, he was off the payroll. The first week was like a vacation. His wife went to work every day, and Moe puttered around the house. He worked on projects he had been putting off for years. He painted the porch, fixed the fence, and repapered the guest room. The next week was more of the same, but Moe began to feel uneasy. No one from work called, even to see how he was. He thought about his plans for consulting, but he had not given thought to what he could do for people and who would use his services. His company had banned rehiring early retirees for temporary work. Moe had a few friends in other companies, but he did not know their businesses as well as his own. The more he thought about it, the more worried he got.

The third week of Moe's retirement, he wrote a resume and contacted his friends. He called people in his former company to let them know that he was available in case they knew people in other companies who could use his services. The reception he got from his former co-workers was cool. They were polite, but it was clear that they were busy and could not worry too much about someone who was being paid for not working. He called a few acquaintances in other organizations, and they promised to pass around his resume.

At the end of the week, his mother-in-law broke her hip and had to be hospitalized. Moe was the only close family member who was available every day, and he found himself running errands and chauffeuring elderly family members to and from the hospital. Moe was glad to help at first, but as his mother-in-law recuperated in a nursing home and his errands seemed to be never-ending, Moe began to wonder when he would have time to do something for himself. He could not pursue his business contacts because if a job became available, he would not have time to work now, and it would be detrimental to turn down an assignment, especially his first opportunity.

After nine months of retirement, however, Moe had adjusted and had even learned to enjoy his leisurely pace. He missed work but found other interests and resigned himself to retirement.

Moe's transition into retirement was a sudden and major shift in life-style. Unlike many people who retire, Moe was perfectly healthy and able to work for many more years. Moe felt betrayed by his company, and he felt a sense of personal loss, for himself and his organization. His withdrawal process was similar to grieving, moving from a sense of shock to denial and slowly to acceptance. On the one hand, if Moe had been more self-assured and aggressive, he might have been able to market his knowledge and experience. On the other hand, if he had been more self-deprecating, he might have become withdrawn and despondent. As it was, Moe was able to slowly rechannel his productive energies into personal tasks that gave him a sense of accomplishment, although not the fulfillment he desired.

As these two cases show, career transitions are often accompanied by stress. Here is a set of questions to help a person to think about the stress caused by career transitions: Think of career transitions you have made—starting your first job, changing jobs, taking a new assignment, or becoming a supervisor for the first time. Or consider a nonwork transition that might have affected your career, such as marriage or having your first child. How big a change was it? Could it be reversed? Was your new role clear? Did you disagree with others about your role? Was the decision voluntary? How did these factors combine to make the decision stressful? How did you react? Could you have improved the situation by clarifying roles or slowing down the change? What will you do in the future to prepare for such a career transition?

Summary

This chapter discussed the stress people feel when they make career decisions and experience career transitions. Career decisions are stressful when people are pulled in more than one direction because the alternatives have similarly desirable or undesirable components. Decisions are also stressful when people feel committed to more than one alternative or when they expect losses, such as disapproval from their family. Transition stress stems from role uncertainty, role conflict, new performance demands, and characteristics of the change such as how fast it happens, the degree of change, and the extent to which it is voluntary and reversible. For example, stress will be greater the more the new role is uncertain, involuntary, and irreversible. The self-reflection questions were meant to help people understand the stress they feel when making career decisions and transitions.

Although we have addressed sources of stress, we have not yet said much about the negative reactions people have to career stress and what they do about it. Also, we have not considered the factors that determine how people react to stress. These are the topics of Chapters Twelve and Thirteen. In Chapters Fourteen and Fifteen, we suggest ways to manage and prevent career stress.

Twelve

Individual Strategies
for Attacking
Career Stress Problems

The previous two chapters described sources of career stress. Here we consider reactions to stress, ways of coping with it, and preventing it.

Reactions to Stress

Table 3 lists a number of possible reactions to career stress. Psychological reactions may be emotional (affective). These are feelings of anxiety, tension, frustration, shame, or isolation. Psychological reactions may also be cognitive (interpretive of events and circumstances). Such reactions include a loss of interest in work or in life in general, or a loss of commitment to career goals. Physical reactions include fatigue, ulcers, and other diseases that have been linked to job pressure. Behavioral reactions include turnover, absenteeism, and lowered performance. These reactions often occur together. Also, some reactions, such as alcoholism, are a combination of psychological, physical, and behavioral responses.

We noted in Chapter Ten that the stress a person feels from a particular situation depends on the individual. How a person reacts to stress is also an individual matter. Some people thrive on exercising, playing golf, or watching football on television. Other people, perhaps more adventurous or ambitious, take up sailing, scuba diving, or classical piano.

Table 3. Individual Reactions to Career Stress.

	Curative		Preventive	
	Alter the Situation	*Alter Symptoms*	*Alter the Situation*	*Alter Symptoms*
Behavioral reactions	Obtain information to reduce ambiguity Work harder Do less Leave the situation Take a sabbatical Request and accept a job transfer Redesign the job Present oneself in a positive light		Volunteer for desirable assignments Raise issues and deal with problems when they arise	Get involved in a hobby or leisure pursuit Keep a journal (diary)
Physical reactions		Overindulge in alcohol, drugs, smoking, food, sleep		Stay physically fit
Psychological reactions	Vigilance Hypervigilance Become aware of one's strengths and weaknesses Increase one's understanding of the political and interpersonal environment Get help and advice from friends	Defensive avoidance Rationalization Sense making	Use peer relationships as a support network Become aware of one's strengths and weaknesses Increase one's understanding of the political and interpersonal environment	Meditate Maintain a pleasant, positive attitude Show stress (for example, give the appearance of having too much work to do)

Some people take comfort in support from peers while others who are more introverted find that keeping a diary reduces anxiety.

Impact of Role Stress. Role-based stress has multiple effects. Role conflict generally causes low productivity, tension, job dissatisfaction, and psychological withdrawal from the work group (Van Sell, Brief, and Schuler, 1981). Those in high-conflict roles tend to reduce trust, liking, and respect for those from whom the conflict stems, attribute less power to them than they had previously, and withdraw from them or restrict communication with them. Those in high-conflict roles also experience internal conflicts (McGrath, 1976).

The effects of role ambiguity are similar to the effects of role conflict—lowered job satisfaction, lowered self-esteem, and dislike for others who are associated with the ambiguity. A difference in reactions to the two sources of stress is that ambiguity is likely to increase rather than decrease communication, at least initially, as the individual tries to reduce the ambiguity (McGrath, 1976).

Role overload may be less stressful than role conflict and ambiguity because it is more concrete and under the individual's control. It is not likely to generate poor interpersonal relations except when it has secondary effects, such as low performance because the individual cannot meet all the job demands adequately or because the individual reduces the overload by simply ignoring some demands.

Cost of Stress on Female Professionals and Female Managers. Female managers often report physical and psychological illnesses as reactions to career stress. In one investigation of stress among 135 top female executives in the United Kingdom, more than half reported tiredness, irrationality, and anxiety, and more than one-third reported neck or back tension, feelings of anger and frustration, and sleeplessness (Cooper and Davidson, 1982). Another study of sixty female managers at different organizational levels found that women in senior and junior management reported moderate fatigue (Cooper and Davidson, 1982).

In general, female managers smoked more and took more stress-relieving drugs, such as tranquilizers and antidepressants, than did their male counterparts.

Men in similar positions have similar problems and similar reactions, but, as we stated in Chapter Ten, women must confront additional stressors such as discrimination, harassment, and stereotyping. These stressors occur in all types of occupational and management positions, especially if the job is not traditionally held by women. The result is that women face increased levels of stress. Clearly there is a need for a change in attitude toward and in organizational policies regarding the treatment of women in the work force.

Stress of Balancing Work and Nonwork. Both the work and the nonwork aspects of our lives produce stress, and pressures at work increase pressures at home and vice versa. (We called this *spillover* in Chapter Ten.) Also balancing multiple responsibilities for one's home, children, community activities, career, and oneself generates conflicts, ambiguities, and overloads that can negatively affect physical and mental health. Physical reactions such as suicide, heart attack, drug abuse, alcoholism, high cholesterol levels, and high accident rates, to name a few, have been attributed to lack of career progress, poor supervision, layoffs, the inability to leave a negative job, family relationships, race and sex discrimination, and socioeconomic factors (Martin and Schermerhorn, 1983). Some of these reactions are aimed at alleviating anxiety, but they may have the desired impact only in the short run. Such reactions (drug abuse and alcohol abuse are prime examples) usually make matters worse. In addition, people who make major transitions are most at risk for problems in their personal life (Latack, 1984). Career transitions, such as quitting one's job, as Tom Fenton did (first discussed in Chapter One), may trigger instability in one's personal life.

Coping Strategies

Different strategies for coping with stress are listed in Table 3 and are described here. Coping strategies are ways in-

dividuals and organizations try to reduce or eliminate the negative results of stress.

   Attacking the Situation. One strategy is to act on the stressor itself to reduce the role conflict, ambiguity, or overload. For example, people may improve the balance between their work and their family life, or they may obtain rewards that are more equitable than those they have been receiving. The coping strategy may be an action that alters the stressor directly or that removes the individual from its effects. Quitting a job to get away from a demanding boss is an example. Alternately, the strategy may be psychological, as when people change their opinion about whether a reward is inequitable.

   Table 3 lists a number of situation-oriented strategies for curing (reducing, eliminating) existing stress. Behavioral actions include leaving the situation (quitting, absenteeism), requesting a job transfer, taking a sabbatical, changing work procedures, getting help to do the job, seeking information (which will be helpful only if it can be applied to change the situation), delegating responsibility to others, and working harder (for example, working longer hours to reduce the overload). Which strategy a person uses depends partly on familiarity with the situation. New hires tend to cope with the uncertainty of their jobs by seeking social support and aid from others. People who transfer to another job in the same company try more than new hires do to control and change their job situation (Feldman and Brett, 1983).

   Two psychological strategies are vigilance and hypervigilance. Vigilance means devoting a reasonable amount of attention to a stressful situation, whereas hypervigilance involves devoting an inordinate amount of attention and displaying anxiety. Which of these reactions arises depends on the situation. When a person believes that an alternative with a positive outcome can be found but there is no time to find it, the reaction is likely to be hypervigilance. The reaction is likely to be vigilance when there is time for a careful search and evaluation of available alternatives.

   Another response to stress that has both psychological and behavioral aspects is to change reference groups—change one's friends or the people one respects and models. For example,

if a young manager's idol is a vice-president who advanced quickly through the corporate ranks and the young manager's career is not progressing as rapidly, the young manager may change role models by focusing on another respected individual whose early career is more similar to that of the young manager.

Changing role models is a psychological process. Changing friends has behavioral implications as well. Friends who provide support help to alleviate stress. Also, when they have been through the same situation themselves, they can provide strategies for coping or some encouragement that "this too will pass in time." People bond together for social support in times of stress. People who are hired into a management-development program at the same time, for instance, offer social support to each other just as fraternity and sorority pledges do.

Attacking the Symptoms. Another type of coping strategy ignores the stressor and focuses on the symptoms, such as headaches, anxiety, or fatigue. These are palliative strategies in that they are intended to reduce or eliminate anxiety or tension by distracting the person (Feldman and Brett, 1983). People who experience a large number of transitions are more likely to use a symptom-management strategy as opposed to one that focuses directly on the stressful situation (Latack, 1984). As we stated earlier, a career transition, such as a promotion or relocation, can contribute to other transitions in one's personal life, such as increased difficulty disciplining children or divorce. The more transitions one faces, the greater the negative reactions and the more it is necessary to focus on the reactions rather than on the sources. For example, a person who is promoted into a difficult, unstructured job with political pressures is likely to work harder, spend less time at home, and be more difficult to get along with than before. The psychological strain, time pressures, and the behavioral clash from being aggressive on the job to being mild mannered with one's family are likely to produce symptoms such as exhaustion, short temper, and difficulty in making decisions. Some people in this position find it easier to use escape mechanisms such as alcohol or sedatives than strategies to reduce the stress at work.

Physiological ways to reduce the symptoms of career stress include overindulgence in alcohol, drugs, cigarettes, food, and sleep. Psychological ways to reduce stress symptoms include ignoring or reinterpreting the stressful environment. Defensive avoidance (pretending that nothing is wrong) and rationalization (explaining to yourself that you are not the cause of the problem) are examples of these strategies.

Defensive avoidance and denial occur when all the alternatives open to a person appear to have negative consequences and there is nowhere to turn. This reaction often occurs after one is fired or when one's company is in trouble. In one example, a company in Detroit told all its employees that it would phase out its operations over a two-and-a-half-year period (Petty, 1985). But because attrition rates (the number of people leaving) declined, everybody stayed until the last moment. In interviews employees said that they hoped something would happen to change the situation. Companies foster loyalty in their employees by providing benefits and supervising them in a parental way. It is no wonder under such circumstances that employees disbelieve that their positions are not secure and that the company will no longer take care of them.

Attributing meaning to the stressful situation, *sense making* (Louis, 1980), is another psychological strategy for relieving symptoms such as a sense of failure, frustration, or regret. Sense making is the process we use to interpret and describe experiences in a new role or setting. Sense making is also important for other types of stress—for instance, to understand conflicts, uncertainties, and discordant values.

Many conditions are stressful because we have not been through them before. We may misinterpret the situation, which could lead to inappropriate behaviors or attitudes. Under such conditions, we try to test out interpretations by describing them to others and seeing how they react. When we are new in a situation, we may not know who can provide such information. Even when we have a reference group available, sense-making errors are possible. The example of the company's impending closing showed how people in an unexpected negative situation deluded themselves into thinking that things would be all right despite

the information they received from the company and the signs of declining business.

Another psychological process that does not change the situation but alters the way people feel about it is changing one's opinions to conform with others. This strategy is one way to deal with discordant values—people rationalize why they should change their opinion to match the prevailing trend. Suppose you are expected to keep a record of your work time and expenses. You feel that this type of strict control is unnecessary for a person in a responsible managerial position. You find it demeaning, a waste of your time, and an indication that the company does not trust you. Each time you fill out your time sheet at the end of the day your frustration and anger grow. Your boss explains that this procedure is necessary and that you can conform with it or leave. Then you reconsider. The records help the corporation keep track of costs and hold employees accountable for their time. You can also use the records to manage your time. You can look back at the end of each week and see how you have spent the time and adjust your schedule for the next week to accomplish more than you did before. If you owned the company, you would probably want the same type of records for your employees, you reason. Your anger and frustration disappear and you even convince one of your friends who felt the same way you did that the record sheets are a valuable management tool for the corporation and the employee.

Preventive Strategies

In addition to the coping strategies, meant to be curative, Table 3 lists strategies that prevent stress and its negative reactions before they arise.

Attacking the Situation. Situation-oriented strategies to prevent stress include being aware of one's strengths and weaknesses and collecting information on the environment to understand political and interpersonal aspects of the situation. Another way to avoid stressors is to control the environment by, for example, learning how to present oneself in a positive light, volunteering for desirable assignments, and getting in the habit of step-

ping up to a problem when it arises as opposed to procrastinating.

Maintaining contact with peers as a support network when things go wrong and as a source of information is a valuable stress-prevention mechanism. Consider three types of peers: the information peer, the collegial peer, and the special peer (Kram and Isabella, 1985). These different peers have a variety of functions depending on a person's career stage.

During early career, information from peers helps one learn the job, get it done, gain visibility, and prepare for advancement. Collegial peers demonstrate good performance, define what it means to be a professional, and help a person gain recognition and identify advancement opportunities. Special peers provide positive reinforcement for a sense of self-confidence and commitment. They also provide the emotional support to deal with work and family conflicts.

During mid-career, information peers provide contacts and help maintain visibility. Collegial peers are role models for developing subordinates and passing on wisdom. The special peer offers feedback, support, and strategies for career assessment, redirection, and dealing with threats of obsolescence.

During late career, information peers help maintain knowledge, and collegial peers demonstrate ways of assuming a consultative role and being viewed as an expert. The special peer helps one review the past and assess one's career and life— good psychological preparation for retirement.

Spouses may also play supportive roles. Patricia Stewart's husband gave her support as she struggled through her decision to stay with her present firm (Chapters Two and Eleven). Arthur Harris's family was supportive of his sabbatical and subsequent career change (Chapter Two). Jerome Mann's wife provided the support he needed to move from the world of business to the world of art (Chapter Nine).

Peers and spouses can also be a hindrance. Harvey Monroe's respect for his friends who wanted him to give up business for law made his career conflict a constant source of stress (first discussed in Chapter Two). Muriel Franklin had a husband who failed to support her career, and his nonsupport was the ultimate cause of her divorce (Chapter Nine). Mark Forrestal did not

have friends with whom he could commiserate about his difficulty in managing his job as he moved from position to position (Chapter Six).

Attacking the Symptoms. Symptom-oriented strategies try to make the person resistant to the effects of a stressful situation. Staying healthy and physically fit are ways to avoid the fatigue of a stressful job. Involvement in a hobby or other leisure pursuit can also help. Meditation is another way people try to maintain a calm frame of mind. Several other techniques may help prevent the symptoms of stress. One idea, which admittedly is easier to recommend than to do, is to keep a diary of work activities and thoughts about them. This activity can provide the catharsis some people need and can help them understand how they can control the environment. People can also use various strategies to try to control how others see them, such as expressing a pleasant, positive attitude about life.

Another tactic for preventing the symptoms of stress is showing stress even when it is not present. Employees may act like martyrs giving the impression that they are overloaded with work. Their goal is to gain sympathy and possibly avoid additional assignments. Such a strategy works for only a short time before others catch on, but we all know people who wear this strategy into the ground and us along with them.

Summary

This chapter examined ways people alleviate and prevent stress by attacking the situation or symptoms or both. The more stress a person faces, the more the person is likely to focus on symptoms. Because stressors have a tendency to multiply, the best way to react to stress is to prevent it, and probably the most constructive way to do that is to behave in a way that changes the situation. Doing so requires career resilience and insight. We described these aspects of career motivation in Chapters Five and Six. Later (Chapter Fourteen) we discuss how career resilience affects how people manage stress. The next chapter considers how organizations can try to reduce their employees' stress.

Thirteen

Organizationwide Policies and Programs for Reducing Career Stress

Many of the sources of career stress lie in the organization: its policies and procedures, the nature of the work, the type of supervision, the opportunities for advancement, the rewards. Organizations may cause stress, but they can also provide cures for stress. Table 4 describes how.

Altering the Situation to Reduce Stress

A job can be designed to increase or decrease challenges and responsibility for employees, or employees can be allowed to redesign their own jobs, to take on or decrease responsibilities. This type of self-direction can help individuals eliminate the stress of boredom or overload. For example, George Hammer, the music teacher turned manager from Chapter Three, had the responsibility for opening his company's first retail store. He took this responsibility as a challenge and oversaw every aspect of the operation. He even went so far as to tell his boss, whose incessant questions created stress, to leave him alone until he had something constructive to offer.

A restructuring of the organization can also reduce stress or alleviate existing stress. Although people may worry about how a reorganization will affect them, changes in reporting relationships not only may enhance efficiency but can also be refreshing. They may give the chance for new and improved

183

Table 4. Organizational Reactions to Career Stress.

Curative		Preventive	
Alter the Situation	*Alter Symptoms*	*Alter the Situation*	*Alter Symptoms*
Job transfers	Open forums for expressing emotions	Participative management styles	Health-fitness programs
Job redesign	Information distribution	Mentoring	Courses (for example, smoking cessation, relaxation methods)
Restructuring of the organization	Employee-assistance programs (counseling)	Information distribution	
Supervisor training		Positive reinforcements	
Performance-management techniques (for example, discipline)		Opportunities for achievement and risk taking	
Outplacement counseling		Feedback on job performance	
Sabbaticals		Goal setting	
		Challenging jobs	
		Quality circles and other participative programs	
		Help for employees to understand the link between events and career goals	

working relationships to develop. A reorganization that breaks up cohesive work groups is not necessarily bad because these bonds can enhance relationships between work groups after the reorganization.

Supervisory training programs can help bosses understand how they contribute to their subordinates' stress and how this stress can be dysfunctional not only in increasing absenteeism and reducing performance in the short run but also in creating illness and turnover in the long run, both costly responses for the employee and the organization. Bosses can learn how to judge their subordinates' levels of confidence and needs for structure and concern. Supervisors can learn techniques of performance management that focus on subordinates whose performance is not up to par. The ultimate action may be termination. When done in a way that helps the employee save face, termination can be a relief to the employee as well as to the company. Offering to help the poor performer find a job elsewhere is a technique companies often use.

Job transfers within the company can help subordinates who want a different assignment but do not want to leave the organization and endure the stress of a job search. Job transfers help to reduce stress by providing the opportunity for employees to more effectively utilize their skills and talents, increasing their motivation and self-esteem. Large companies use transfers as a way to increase their employees' worth to the organization. As they move into different jobs often in different departments, employees learn various aspects of the business and increase their understanding of how the different departments work together to improve the firm's operations. Job transfers are developmental for the employee and help the organization meet its changing staffing needs. Job transfers also reduce stress when they result in providing continuous employment. For instance, when one department is reducing force, another department may be in need of people.

Providing for leaves of absence and even providing financial support for such leaves, in the form of sabbaticals, can be a way for organizations to help employees cope with stress. Leaves are especially valuable when the job is physically or mentally wearing, such as teaching in an inner-city high school.

Sabbaticals are offered by companies and universities to give employees a break and a chance to develop a fresh or broad perspective, which will help on the job. A sabbatical may mean moving from a comfortable job to one that is extremely difficult. For instance, some corporations, such as Polaroid, loan executives to community organizations for fund-raising or other projects that need people with business acumen. For the employee, the change may be difficult, but it is a chance to manage different types of people and different relationships and to have meaningful impact in another area. Such leaves can be both a learning experience and a good break from routines.

Sabbaticals may not have positive results for the company however. We described how people like Arthur Harris (Chapter Two) may get a new lease on life from a sabbatical. Harris not only had a break but liked it so much he found it impossible to return to work; he embarked on another line of work that gave him increased freedom. Sabbaticals also may be detrimental to employees, as Apcar (1985, p. 1) points out:

> Taking a sabbatical, a few months off from work with full pay and benefits, sounds to many like the ultimate. Well, it is—and it isn't.
>
> Penny LeVasseur, a field-service representative at Rolm Corp., says she had a "marvelous" time on her twelve-week break but would be "terrified" to take another. She believes that three of her co-workers were demoted after their sabbaticals. Rolm, a unit of International Business Machines Corp., denies that, but says its policy is to return workers to "comparable" rather than identical posts.
>
> But many who return from sabbatical find it hard to readjust to the job. Ross Morgan, a technical-marketing manager at Intel, used his six-month leave to add a room to his house and to design and install a science exhibit in San Francisco. But his return to work drained his enthusiasm. "There's this depression that hits you," he

says, as well as the feeling "that this workaday world is the pits."

And returnees can be thrown off by changed business conditions. At Blass, Valentine & Klein, a small law firm in Palo Alto, partner Lawrence Klein found that one of the firm's clients took a chunk of business elsewhere during his six-month absence.

For these reasons and others, companies say not all eligible employees take a sabbatical.

Altering the Situation to Prevent Stress

Company reorganizations are an obvious and powerful source of stress. The amount of stress people feel and how they are likely to cope with it depend on how the organization handles the situation. Keeping employees informed and involving them in the decision-making process may be the best way of keeping stress to a minimum. When people have control over a situation, they are less likely to feel role ambiguity. Workshops on anticipating change are one way to provide information to employees and help them deal with the stress of change. Such a workshop is outlined in Resource 9.

One company that has experienced more change than most is the Bell system. During the almost two years between the time divestiture was announced and when it occurred, employees gathered information and held numerous discussions about whether it would be better to stay with the local operating company or move to AT&T. The company provided an unending stream of news and data, and business periodicals offered abundant information. The experts disagreed about the potential viability of the different companies, and they changed their opinions over time. The uncertainties and anxieties were tremendous, and they still are as the companies undergo further reorganizations to streamline and improve their competitive positions.

The Bell employees faced extreme upheaval. Some were offered financial incentives to retire early. Others faced layoffs. Thousands of operators moved from the local companies to

AT&T and then back to the local companies. In many cases, the company allowed employees some control over what happened to them. Employees' preferences were taken into account in making job reassignments. Employees could take early retirement or stay with the organization. (Recall that Moe Grant from Chapter Eleven faced a similar decision.) In the case of layoffs, the company usually tried to find alternative positions elsewhere in the organization, especially for employees with the most seniority. Despite the company's efforts, many people still felt cheated and without control. Many believed that the company could have done more to avoid some changes, to keep employees better informed, and to involve them in the decision-making process.

The style of management has a major impact on employee stress that arises for reasons other than major change. A participative style of management can reduce role conflict and ambiguity and increase the influence people feel they have in the organization. Employee-involvement programs, quality circles, and related efforts to involve employees in decision making help alleviate anxiety. Quality circles are meetings of work groups to identify ways to improve productivity or the environment. A group can focus on whatever issues it feels are appropriate: smoking areas, decorating the employee lounge, and new ways for the company to notify groups of work progress. All members of a work group participate in the meetings, and then a representative from each group attends meetings with representatives from other groups to discuss issues of broad concern. The representatives then return to the local groups to share these concerns. In this way, everybody is kept informed and has a chance to express opinions.

Bosses have a major impact on their employees' level of stress. In Chapter Seven, we presented guidelines supervisors can follow to enhance subordinates' career motivation. These guidelines are also likely to reduce subordinates' career stress, and so they bear repeating briefly here: Increase subordinates' career resilience by rewarding good performance and providing opportunities for accomplishment and risk taking without undue fear of failure. Increase career insight by encouraging goal

setting and providing feedback on job performance. Increase career identity by providing a challenging, involving job.

In addition to affecting employees' current work assignments, bosses can influence employees' future assignments. Supervisors who act as mentors advise their proteges and influence organizational decisions to be sure the proteges have desirable career opportunities. (See our discussion of the boss's role in career development in Chapter Seven.) The mentor may not be the protege's immediate supervisor but is generally someone at a higher level than the protege. Mentoring implies a close personal bond between the mentor and the protege. Less involving relationships are sponsorship or simply role modeling.

Helping employees understand the links between various events and their career goals can also be a way to reduce ambiguity. Supervisors can explain how new job assignments and training courses contribute to employees' career goals. Resources 3 and 4 can help by encouraging employees to focus on their abilities and their goals and to evaluate their goal accomplishments. Employees then have a sense of control over their own accomplishments.

Reducing and Preventing Stress Symptoms

Many organizations sponsor programs to help employees reduce and prevent stress symptoms. Open forums for distributing information and giving employees a chance to express their feelings may reduce anxiety in the event of impending layoffs, for example. Employee-assistance programs provide trained counselors to aid employees with emotional problems or drug or alcohol dependencies. Supervisors may recommend that subordinates who have performance or absenteeism problems see a company counselor, or employees may do so on their own. The counselor may help the employee with the problem or refer the employee to a social worker, psychologist, or psychiatrist, depending on the nature and severity of the problem.

Health-fitness programs aid employees by providing an exercise program after thorough physical tests. A fitness program should lessen the physical impact of stress. Staying fit

may also be a way of coping with emotional stress, just as a hobby or a leisure activity helps escape one's problems, at least temporarily.

Some companies offer comprehensive programs to help employees with a variety of work and life issues. This "total life concept" may include seminars on smoking cessation, relaxation methods, weight control, nutrition, and exercise.

Managing Organizational Decline

The Atari Corporation is now well known for both its phenomenal success and its phenomenal failure in the home video game industry. After the introduction of the world's first programmable home video player in 1976, Atari's success continued through 1982. In that year its sales were $2.7 billion, and the company employed more than 7,000 employees. But the environment began changing in 1982, with many aggressive firms entering the video game business and consumer preferences changing to home computers. Sales dropped in 1983 by 30 percent, and the company was sold a year later after its labor force had declined to only 1,000 people.

In an analysis of Atari, researchers at Stanford University observed that Atari executives did not attempt to redirect their market strategy away from video games toward minicomputers. Moreover, they did a poor job of managing the decline of the organization (Sutton, Eisenhardt, and Jucker, 1986). The dilemma Atari faced was how to reduce the size of the company while maintaining a productive and high-quality work force.

The Stanford study found that Atari made some significant errors in management. Executives were reluctant to lay off top-level managers. Instead, the layoffs focused on lower-level employees, leaving the remaining middle managers with few subordinates and few responsibilities and leaving the company with high overhead for unnecessary higher-level managers. The message to employees was that managers would not share equally in the painful force reductions.

A class action suit filed by former Atari employees against the company asserted that the layoff process was humiliating.

Laid-off production workers were given no prior notice and were escorted off the premises by security guards. In addition, little was done to help displaced employees find new jobs. The employees who left were belittled. Although the layoffs were made to drive costs down, not to identify and fire poor performers, top management apparently wanted to convey the idea that they had removed the deadwood. Instead, the message was that the company was insensitive to employees.

Atari made other mistakes, such as hiring new executives who did not understand the business. Employee stress was increased by continuous uncertainty. Rumors abounded, and expectations were unrealistic, fed by promises for improvement in business conditions that never materialized. Employees were unable to plan for the company's future or their own.

In general, companies are beginning to recognize the importance of managing decline from the standpoint both of those who are losing their jobs and of those who are not. Job loss is likely to be more stressful the less the individual controls and desires the change (Holmes and Rahe, 1967). Job loss can be less devastating when the individual views it as a career transition that requires recognizing the need to change, searching for alternatives, possibly exploring different possibilities, and making a decision. Career growth may result from job loss when financial resources are adequate, family and friends are supportive, unemployment is not prolonged, and the individual is actively engaged in controlling the process (Latack and Dozier, 1986). Companies can smooth the way for terminated employees with financial settlements, employment counseling, retirement planning, and experience-sharing sessions to help people cope.

The Atari case described above led the Stanford researchers to suggest better strategies (Sutton, Eisenhardt, and Jucker, 1986).

- Be even-handed in implementing layoffs; spread layoffs throughout the organizational ranks, not just at lower levels.
- Allow employees to leave with dignity. They should be given time to plan their futures, and they should not be the subject of derision.
- Help those displaced find new jobs. This bolsters the em-

ployees' sense of control and suggests to the survivors that the company is concerned about their welfare.

- Set realistic expectations. Giving too much hope or false hope is dangerous. It undermines trust when things get worse, and it prevents employees from taking realistic actions that could save jobs.
- Be cognizant of the messages conveyed by decisions and actions. Having a business meeting at a lavish restaurant, business trips to exotic places, and other frills are demoralizing when people are losing their jobs.

Layoff policies that are fair, help displaced employees find new jobs, and treat these employees with dignity and respect signal all employees that the company values their contribution. Companies that ignore the problem, keep information from employees, hire some people while others are being laid off, and belittle employees who are dismissed threaten the commitment and loyalty of the survivors and damage the company's reputation as an employer.

Managing the Stress of Corporate Mergers

Mergers are occurring more frequently today than ever before. Examples include Chevron's merger with Gulf, General Electric's acquisition of RCA, Standard Brands' merger with Nabisco, and Reynolds' acquisition of Nabisco Brands. These mergers are a form of corporate growth and a way to increase financial power. Yet many mergers fail to realize the expected economic benefits, often because of a clash of corporate cultures, the uncertainty of how the take-over will affect employees, and ultimately the painful process of laying off employees. The "we—they" mentality can persist years after a merger. For instance, polarization occurred early in the Chevron-Gulf merger with Gulf managers accustomed to broad authority and liberal perks and Chevron managers accustomed to a lean, centrally run company. "Chevron kept saying it was going to choose the

The authors thank Linda Streit and Rosemary O'Connor for their ideas on this section.

best and the brightest. But these were always Chevron people,''
one Gulf executive stated (Hymowitz and Schellhardt, 1986).

Employees in a company that is merged with another are
likely to experience a loss of corporate identity. Also, their careers
are in jeopardy. The psychological impact is likely to include
feelings of insecurity, uncertainty, suspicion, vulnerability, lack
of control, fear, anxiety, and depression. Time is spent discussing
rumors. Uncertainty leads to inaction, and employees are less
willing to make decisions or take risks. Self-interest becomes
paramount. Corporate goals become obscure, and a weakened
sense of direction diminishes employees' commitment. Some
employees bail out in the anticipation of termination or as a
way to escape the ambiguity and anxiety.

On the positive side, mergers can be invigorating, stimu-
lating a closer look at employee performance and allowing for
the removal of people who are dull, dependent, and a drag on
the corporation (McDowell, 1985). When the PCN Financial
Corporation, owner of the Pittsburgh National Bank, acquired
Philadelphia's Provident National Corporation, PCN executives
tapped Provident managers to head committees planning the
combination. The best-performing managers at both banks were
identified and rewarded with top duties. Frequent meetings were
held at all levels to explain changes and assure employees that
while some might be assigned to new jobs, few would be let go
(Hymowitz and Schellhardt, 1986).

Earlier in this chapter, we described the effects of the Bell
System divestiture on its employees. Three years later, AT&T
employees experienced another dramatic change as two parts
of the company were merged, the regulated long-distance network (AT&T Communications) and the unregulated telephone
equipment and computer side of the business (AT&T Information Systems). The Federal Communications Commission (FCC)
had previously required these units to be totally separate to ensure that the regulated portion of the company did not subsidize
the unregulated portion. After divestiture, as competition increased in the long-distance market, the FCC relaxed its restrictions, allowing AT&T to have a single sales force to jointly
market long distance services and telephone equipment. While
this was what AT&T wanted from the standpoint of providing

better customer service and saving cost, separate cultures had evolved in the two separate companies. AT&T Information Systems had experienced considerable work force reductions and continuous cost control. AT&T Communications had experienced other problems as it improved responsiveness to customers, began establishing its own billing department (a mammoth task given the millions of customers billed for long distance through the local telephone companies), and began managing the regulatory environment and the high costs of linking the long distance network to the local companies' networks.

This change was similar to other corporate mergers in that it entailed the combination of two distinct entities. However, there were differences. Many employees shared a common history. This was not a takeover but an integration. Whereas before there were two separate marketing, personnel, and public relations departments, these line and staff departments would now be one. The merger required a high degree of integration for the efficiencies and effectiveness of the merger to be realized.

Mergers are opportunities for managing change. The AT&T internal merger entailed downsizing, redesigning organizational structures, and changing job responsibilities. In addition, the company was attempting to establish a renewed corporate mission focusing on its strength in the long distance market and relying on equipment manufacturing and sales to support the network capabilities it could offer to customers, rather than marketing equipment separately.

These changes imposed tremendous demands on employees. A manager who had been with the company for only ten years had experienced the bureaucratic, by-the-book management of the predivestiture era and the entrepreneurial spirit required in the emerging competitive marketplace. Such a manager went from the certainty of standardized Bell System practices aimed at ensuring uniformity and constancy of service to the ambiguity and complexity of new markets, new organization structures, and continuous change.

The AT&T employees learned how to manage a changing environment. They learned how to downsize the corporation while maintaining productivity and quality service. How

ever, this was not without pain. Thousands of managers took advantage of financial incentives to leave the business. Others were forced to leave because the company needed fewer people. The environment was filled with rumors, turf battles, perceptions that one part of the business was usurping the other (with employees from both sides feeling the other side had the upper hand), and low morale. The challenge was to demonstrate that the new business created opportunities for career growth. Managers had to learn from experience how to handle ambiguity and to maintain productivity when people felt the company's commitment to employees' welfare and job security was disappearing. In addition, the company had to show good performers that there were opportunities for career movement such as transfers to learn new parts of the business and promotions to positions of increased responsibility. A special management development committee of vice-presidents was set up to make that happen.

Effective communication can reduce the ambiguity and help merge differing corporate cultures. Communication from the top of the company should be honest and open, full and complete. It should include both positive and negative information, and it should be timely. Bottom-up information should be encouraged. Attitude surveys provide a way for employees to voice their opinions. When the results of these surveys are announced and discussed, they can provide a stimulus for handling employee concerns. Surveys also allow management to monitor the integration process. Moreover, they send a message that employees' opinions are valued. An employee survey was used by the AT&T management to highlight employee concerns and serve as a benchmark for evaluating the long-term effects of the change.

Summary

Organizations have considerable influence over how their employees feel. Organizations can create stress, but they also have the potential for reducing and preventing it. This chapter reviewed stress-reduction programs that alter the situation or

help employees with their symptoms. Employees should understand how organizational actions and events influence their feelings of stress, and they should understand ways they can control the situation to influence their own stress and that of their
subordinates. Some people are better at managing stress than
others, and stress-reduction strategies may not always work.
Constructive action to reduce stress requires career resilience.
The next chapter describes how resilience influences responses
to stress and suggests ways employees can be effective in their
responses to the organizational environment.

Resource 9. A Workshop on Anticipating Change.

The purpose of this workshop is to help managers understand their feelings about and reactions to corporate change and to understand their role as
managers of change. Timing for each phase of the workshop is not provided;
it will depend on the difficulty of the change issues faced by the organization.
One possibility is a one-day workshop with each phase taking about one and a
half hours.

Outline

1. Participants discuss how change affects them (emotions, behaviors).
The instructor puts responses on the board. Dimensions of change are summarized
(extensiveness, suddenness) as are personal dimensions (degree of control, uncertainty, degree of involvement, likelihood of positive or negative outcomes, impact of others' reactions, degree of acceptance).

2. The stress of change is discussed, with attention to the difference between anticipatory stress and situational stress. The instructor outlines typical
reactions to good news (excitement, optimism) and bad news (immobility, depression, denial, search for alternatives). The concept of resistance is introduced. Actual organizational changes faced by the participants and their reactions are
elicited. Key people in the change effort are identified: initiators, catalysts, imple-
mentors. These roles are elaborated by the instructor and participants.

3. Transition stages are described with examples of facing endings and
moving to new beginnings. Patterns of managing change are identified, including
ignoring the problem, trying to protect the status quo, being responsive to the
need for change, and anticipating needed actions. Autocratic versus participative
approaches to the management of change are reviewed. The value of providing
information to reduce anxiety is acknowledged. Ways of increasing employees'
understanding, acceptance, and control are discussed.

4. Attention is now turned from generalities to specifics by reviewing
the corporation's recent past, current state, and anticipated changes. Upcoming
changes are reviewed one by one. Possible outcomes are outlined for each change
along with likely alternatives for what the change will mean to the participants

and what their role will be in the change effort. Subgroups may address different changes and later share their perceptions with the larger group. Some of the changes should be large in scope (designing a major reorganization, laying off people, eliminating a layer of management, starting a new venture or eliminating an unsuccessful one, preparing for the growth of a major part of the business, changing top management). Other changes discussed should be less momentous to the corporation as a whole but still important to the people involved (redesigning jobs in a work unit, shifting assignments, changing work schedules, increasing demands for outputs, making do with fewer people, changing bosses, introducing a new technology). If everyone in the group faces a common change, several outcomes could be outlined by subgroups working independently on the same change. The larger group could then share the subgroups' perceptions and attempt to build a unified model of anticipated outcomes. The model should include not just what is likely to happen but also, and more importantly, what the participants' roles will be and what would constitute productive reactions. In line with the first three phases of the workshop, the model should include the dimensions of the change, likely reactions, key people, transition stages, and management approaches.

Example

In one case a department head worked with his group to consider the implications of an upcoming merger between their company and another one. The details of the merger had not yet been announced, and there was considerable anxiety within this staff department because the merger would combine departments from the two companies and would necessitate fewer people. Also, the new combined company would probably need different services or new ways of providing the services to meet new needs.

The department head began building the model by asking group members to think about what the organizational structure of the new organization might look like. Using an easel, the department head used the group's suggestions to construct a logical organization chart. Although everyone recognized that the chart was hypothetical, having a shared vision of what they may be dealing with seemed to reduce the group's anxiety. They continued their model building, trying to be specific about how their department might be reorganized and what they might do in the new environment; they created several possibilities for reorganization and considered what they would need to do to prepare for them. Sharing their concerns and ideas with the department head and acknowledging logical outcomes reduced the uncertainty and showed them where they would have control over their future.

Fourteen

Career Resilience:
The Key to Overcoming
Career Stress

Some strategies for overcoming stress are positive and constructive. People alleviate stress by behaving in ways that alter the stressful situation. Or they try to prevent stress by controlling the situation. Other strategies are nonconstructive. People ignore or avoid the stress and focus on the symptoms. Sometimes the stressful situation goes away on its own. Other times, the stress lingers and is ultimately the victor.

Resilience determines whether people react to stress in constructive or nonconstructive ways. In Chapter Five, we described career resilience as an important component of career motivation, along with career insight and career identity. We defined resilience as the extent to which people keep their spirits up in adverse circumstances, how resistant they are to barriers or disruptions affecting their work.

In this chapter, we see that resilience determines not only how people react to stress but also how they take positive action to prevent stress. Career resilience is a disposition that is essentially established fairly early in life, at least by the time a person starts his or her career. Resilience is not simply reacting to barriers; it is controlling and managing one's career and life. Understanding one's own resilience and how to enhance it should help one prevent stress.

198

Components of Resilience

Chapter Five described people who are high in career resilience as competent individuals able to control what happens to them. They get a sense of accomplishment from what they do, and they are able to take risks. They also know when and how to cooperate with others and when and how to act independently. You can probably add other components that fit your personal definition of resilience, such as autonomy, adaptability, ability to take the initiative, ability to control the environment, creativity, need for personal and career development, and adoption of inner work standards (trying hard even when second best will do). In addition to willingness to take risks, resilience implies a low fear of failure, a low need for security, and a high tolerance for uncertainty and ambiguity. Resilient people are not likely to rely on others to meet their needs and guide their career. They do not wait for the job fairy. They are competitive, and although they appreciate others' approval of their behavior, they do not need it to function.

One does not need all these characteristics to be resilient. For instance, some resilient individuals may be higher on self-confidence than on risk taking. But generally, self-confidence, risk taking, and independent action go together.

Correlates of Resilience

Vulnerability. The opposite of resilience is vulnerability. Vulnerable people blame themselves for negative events, even when they are not to blame. As you might guess, they are frequently depressed. When they make a mistake, they are likely to attribute it to a stable characteristic rather than a momentary lapse. They are like a child who misbehaves and cries, "I can't help it; I'm a bad kid." Resilient individuals may blame themselves when justified, but they can also attribute negative events to a temporary condition such as not paying attention (Metalsky and others, 1982).

Alienation and a sense of failure are also associated with vulnerability (Korman and Korman, 1980). People who are personally alienated are out of touch with themselves. They do not use their interests and needs to make choices. They see themselves as isolated from those around them. Alienation happens to people when their expectations are not met, when they are around strong people who control their lives, and when they do not have close friendships.

Type-A Personality. The Type-A behavior pattern (Friedman and Rosenman, 1974) is similar to the vulnerability pattern. Type-A behavior can be observed in people who are involved in a chronic, incessant struggle to achieve more and more in less and less time, often against the efforts of others. Type-A behaviors include extreme competitiveness, striving for achievement, aggressiveness, haste, impatience, restlessness, hyperalertness, and feelings of being under the pressure of time and the challenge of responsibility (Cooper and Davidson, 1982).

Type-A individuals are subject to heart attacks (Matthews, 1982), and Type-A behavior tends to increase as people face stress. It may be a particular problem for career women because they face more stresses than men do in managerial positions (see Chapter Ten). They risk enhancing Type-A behavior and subsequently risking the stress-related illnesses that have plagued many men (Cooper and Davidson, 1982).

Type-B Personality—Hardiness. Hardiness is the opposite of vulnerability and similar to resilience. Hardiness involves a strong commitment to oneself, a vigorous attempt to control the environment, a sense of meaningfulness, and a belief in one's ability to control one's own destiny (Kobasa, 1979). Hardiness includes dispositions toward commitment, control, and challenge. Here commitment refers to finding meaning in events, not giving up under pressure, and generally taking an active approach toward life (similar to the risk-taking and self-confidence components of resilience). Control is the tendency to feel and act as if one can influence events in one's life (similar to the ability to act independently when appropriate). Challenge refers to thinking of changes as incentives for growth rather than

as threats to security (similar to the need-for-achievement and self-confidence components of resilience).

Hardiness decreases the likelihood that symptoms of illness will result from stressful events. People who are high on personality dimensions indicative of hardiness are likely to show few symptoms of illness when confronted by stressful events compared with people who are low on hardiness (Kobasa, Maddi, and Kahn, 1982). To remain healthy, it is especially important to be hardy if one is in intensely stressful circumstances. Possibly, hardy people, because they are generally disciplined and realistic, might be conscious of positive health practices. Those low in hardiness might engage in poor health practices, such as overeating and overdrinking. Another explanation is that hardy people seek out social support that helps manage stressful events. For instance, when hardy people are laid off from their jobs, they may talk over the situation with friends and discuss ways to find another job. They may seek job counseling to help them reformulate their career ambitions. In contrast, those low in hardiness are less likely to seek social support and help from counselors (Kobasa, Maddi, and Kahn, 1982).

Integrating the Concept of Resilience. Whether we call it resilience or hardiness or focus on their opposites, vulnerability and Type-A behavior, we are basically talking about inner strength—confidence in oneself and a desire to achieve because the task is challenging and exciting. The resilient individual would rather take a reasonable risk to obtain an important goal than avoid the risk and settle for a lesser goal. Resilience is having the confidence that one's independent actions will have the intended results, and it is also knowing when cooperation and attention to a group goal are important. Therefore, resilience is not just how a person reacts to a negative environment. It is also taking a proactive stance by, for example, avoiding career barriers and creating career opportunities.

Acquiring Resilience

Resilience is a disposition that develops early in life. Resilient people have considerable breadth and variety of experi-

ences, and they have been reinforced for exercising their judgment; they have received approval and admiration for acting independently (Kobasa, Maddi, and Kahn, 1982). Career resilience develops during the adolescent years and during the early twenties, as people experiment with different fields by taking courses and holding summer and part-time jobs. It also develops as people get older and continue to explore the best uses for their talents.

Sex Differences in Self-Confidence. As described in Chapter Ten, women face substantial barriers that make it difficult for them to seek full-time employment in previously male-dominated organizations (Terborg and others, 1977). One barrier is that women are more likely than men to express low self-confidence in achievement situations (Maccoby and Jacklin, 1974). They tend to underestimate their potential to excel and to give lower evaluations of their performance than men do (Lenney, 1977). One explanation is that differential sex-role socialization in childhood and adolescence results in women having certain personality traits or behavior patterns (or both) that are contrary to the demands of success. Because women have not been encouraged to participate in team sports, for example, they fail to develop certain skills that later lead to effective managerial performance (Hennig and Jardim, 1977). They do not learn how to view risk as an opportunity for success as well as for failure. They do not aim to win as a team, and they accept loss by distancing themselves from it instead of attributing it to their own failures.

Low self-confidence can be debilitating in a work situation because it reduces the effort expended on the task, makes one susceptible to the influence of others, and inhibits performance. These correlates of low self-confidence can further the trend to discriminate against women in the work force. Because of this discrimination, women who are in managerial jobs may face different work environments than men in similar jobs, which may limit the opportunity of women to reach their full potential.

One important characteristic of the work environment that may affect self-confidence is feedback on job performance. Feed-

back increases a person's expectation that he or she will succeed on a task. Women may not be told as frequently as men when they are doing well or when they are doing poorly. Such feedback, when present, may increase women's self-confidence. Without feedback on performance, a woman's self-confidence is likely to be low. Research has shown that women tend to be equal to men in confidence to perform a task when feedback is provided—either because it is obvious from the task how well the person is doing or because someone (a supervisor or a co-worker) gives some feedback (Lenney, 1977).

Career Opportunities. We argued in Chapter Nine that the components of career resilience are affected by the work environment. Positive reinforcement for a job well done enhances self-confidence. Opportunities for achievement increase the desire to achieve. Opportunities for risk taking without severe negative consequences for failure increase risk taking. A supervisor who shows concern and support for subordinates can increase their willingness to act independently or to be cooperative depending on the demands of the situation.

Although environmental conditions can make a difference in career resilience, organizations do not provide the environment needed for the development of career resilience. Early dispositions are important here. One's self-confidence and general resistance to stress at the start of one's career are related to success (promotions received) eight and twenty years later (Howard, 1984). People are attracted to organizations that match their early dispositions. People high in career resilience may be attracted to environments that reward independent behavior, risk taking, and achievement. When such people find themselves in an environment that does not provide this support (for example, they suddenly have a boss who does not reinforce their good performance), they are likely to leave. People who are low in resilience are not likely to look for these characteristics in an organization. In fact, they may seek environments that are consistent with their low self-confidence, a characteristic that goes along with their low resilience. Although this is speculation, we do know that the components of career resilience do not change

easily over time and that early dispositions toward resilience are important to later success. We also know that the environment can enhance components of career resilience, strengthening it, encouraging the individual to set difficult goals, and paving the way for increased achievements (Hall, 1976).

How Resilience Affects Reactions to Stress

Table 5 gives some examples of how people with high and low resilience respond to different types of career stress. These responses are determined also by people's career goals. *Contentnicks* experience low stress. They are satisfied with the way things are, and they do not constantly look toward tomorrow for something better. We described several contentnicks, or at least people who seem to be content for the time being. Arthur Harris (first discussed in Chapter Two) was such a person. Tired of his work and refreshed by a sabbatical, Arthur and his family felt they could prevent future stress by turning to a new way of life. Although we did not have an opportunity to measure Arthur's personality, as we did for some of the others we have described, we would guess that Arthur is high in resilience. He believes in himself and seeks challenges even if it means taking a risk.

For *uppies*, wanting to advance can be stressful, challenging, or both. The moderate-resilient uppy, such as Donna Grant (Chapter Six), finds stress challenging. Donna wanted to advance in her company, and she let others know her career goals. She performed consistently well enough to make those goals realistic. She was willing to make the job moves that would prepare her for promotions.

Steve Riley (Chapter Three) was a moderately resilient uppy. Unlike Donna, Steve was in a company that did not seem to value talent or reinforce career ambitions. While Donna's potential for advancement was nurtured, Steve was viewed by his supervisors as meeting a current business need. He did not advance as quickly as he hoped. Although he stayed with the company, he felt depressed and rejected. He had enough resilience to tell himself the problem was not him but the company—the lack of opportunities for advancement and the need to solve

Table 5. Factors Affecting Reactions to Stress.

Level of Stress	Career Goal	Examples of Stress Sources	Reactions to Stress	
			High Resilience	Low Resilience
Low	Contentnick	Discordant values Decision making Role conflict	Prevent stress Focus on situation Change behavior	Use negative problem-solving methods Be reactive, not proactive
	Uppy	Role conflict Interpersonal relationships Nonwork conflicts	Use positive problem-solving methods Prevent stress; seek challenge	Focus on symptoms Rationalize
High	Misfit	Role uncertainty Role demands	Use positive problem-solving methods Do not act until ready Focus on the situation	Use negative problem-solving methods Dream about the future
	Runner-up	Unmet expectations Inequity	Cure stress through positive action; change the situation	Ignore stress Focus on symptoms

immediate economic concerns. Steve craved secure employment and was unwilling to take the risk and independent action needed to leave the company for more challenging assignments and better opportunities for advancement elsewhere. However, promotion was still a possibility in his company, enough to make him continue to feel like an uppy.

For *misfits*, the level of stress is high. We have come to know Harvey Monroe quite well since he was introduced in Chapter Two. He may have expected too much from himself, considering the fact that he had only average ability. He was pulled in several directions at once. His reaction to stress was psychological; he rationalized why he stayed with the company. Still he promised himself that one day he would be a successful attorney and an admired politician. His dreams kept him going; he believed in himself enough to keep them alive but not enough to make them a reality, at least not yet.

Carol Locke (Chapter Three) was another misfit in the corporate world. Her high career resilience led to positive action. She left a well-paying position in management for a more uncertain, less staid job in the travel business.

Mark Forrestal (Chapter Six) was not so confident. His resilience was moderate, and he needed some evidence that he was competent. He just could not seem to make it in business, finding it difficult to structure his work on his own and accomplish things. After a series of jobs where his performance was low, his reaction to the resulting stress was to dream of going into business for himself one day.

Runners-up also often experience a high level of stress. Tom Fenton and Jim Marsh from Chapter One were runners-up. Their careers were stymied, and they had to look elsewhere for success. Although we did not measure their resilience, we guess it was high. They believed in themselves, wanted challenging positions, and were not content to remain runners-up. They took calculated risks, exploring the environment thoroughly for new opportunities.

Joe Murphy (Chapter Nine) was another runner-up. His resilience was moderate. He started out as a contentnick, happy with life and not expecting much from his career other than being

able to earn a good living to support his family and pursue his hobbies. Promoted to second-level management, he found he liked the money and prestige and saw no reason why he could not continue to advance. Yet he was overburdened by the work to the point that his boss found it necessary to lighten his responsibilities even though doing so increased the demands on the others in the group. But Joe avoided stress by attributing his difficulties in handling the job and the change in assignments to his boss's realizing his true talents and giving him the opportunity to succeed. Joe's self-confidence was precarious. He was neither a high risk taker nor independent. His reaction was to wish the problem away as quickly as his newfound ambitions had materialized.

Resilience and Career Success

In Chapter Six, we described career resilience as the foundation for career insight and identity. To a large extent, resilience brings certain results. Resilient people are not likely to be misfits or runners-up, or if they are, they are not likely to be misfits or runners-up for long. Tom Fenton and Jim Marsh are likely to get back on track as uppies or eventually settle down as contentnicks. Carol Locke already escaped being a misfit to continue her search for success and happiness. Harvey Monroe may have a difficult time redirecting his career, but he could still alter his goals. Or he may resign himself to stay where he is.

Vulnerable people are not likely to be uppies or contentnicks, or if they are, they are not likely to be uppies or contentnicks for long. Steve Riley will probably feel more like a runner-up as time goes by. Patricia Stewart may always have trouble feeling truly content. Every time an opportunity arises, she may struggle with it, not quite sure what she wants.

You might apply these concepts to yourself or test them with a friend or employee to see how meaningful they are. The exercise in Resource 10 ties together exercises in the preceding chapters to help you understand how your resilience affects your reactions to stress.

Finding Supportive Environments

To some extent, people seek environments that meet their needs and expectations. When they make a mistake, as runners-up and misfits do, they try to change the situation (if their resilience is high) or they suffer through it (if their resilience is low).

People have substantial control over their environments, perhaps more than many of them realize. We have seen several people who found environments to suit their needs. Fran Cooper, described in Chapter Eleven, left university administration for business, changing her goals and professional identity for a career that was challenging and supportive (from the standpoint of financial compensation and skill development) and that offered opportunities for advancement. She was willing to take a risk in leaving secure employment for a company that was willing to believe she had the general managerial skills needed in business even though she lacked the technical background.

Moe Grant, also described in Chapter Eleven, faced a hostile organizational environment. In his case, the company changed, and he was unable to meet the demands of the new situation, which led him to early retirement. Charles Townsend, described in Chapter Two, was an investment banker who turned to farming. However, he found it disappointing; it sapped his energy and produced little profit. He eventually returned to a more hospitable environment.

In previous chapters, we saw the value of careful career exploration for identifying jobs and organizations that suit our needs. Donna Grant (Chapter Six) found a management-development program that offered an opportunity for her to demonstrate her talent as a manager and that rewarded her appropriately. Steve Riley (Chapter Three) may have had high managerial potential as well, but his work environment was not so supportive. Our misfits, Harvey Monroe (Chapter Two) and Mark Forrestal (Chapter Six), missed the mark entirely in finding an environment suitable to their abilities and career motivation. Career exploration worked well for people like Arthur Harris (Chapter Two) and Fran Cooper (Chapter Eleven), who were well into their careers at the time they made a shift.

Interaction Between Employee
and Organizational Characteristics

Determining whether the individual's disposition or the situation is more important to career success is probably a fruitless exercise. In some cases, the individual's characteristics are more important. In other cases, the environment predominates—for example, when the work is stressful for everyone regardless of ability or motivation. An organization's selection errors, poor supervision, and changing job demands all can induce career stress. In still other cases, situational and individual characteristics interact (Staw and Ross, 1985; Terborg, 1981). A positive environment may increase career resilience for those predisposed to high resilience but will do nothing for people who have low resilience. A negative environment may increase career stress for those with low resilience, whereas individuals with high resilience may be able to withstand the stress, perhaps viewing it as a challenge and possibly trying to change the environment (or withdrawing from it).

Also people bend to fit the environment. Harvey Monroe seemed flexible, and that may have been part of his problem. Influenced by others, he was searching for a career direction that matched his identity as an attorney. However, he could still alter his career identity to match his current position as a manager.

Relationship Between Resilience and Ability

We have not said much about how a person's ability is related to career resilience. Resilience and ability generally go together because they are mutually reinforcing. Competent people tend to be reinforced for their outstanding work and this reinforcement enhances their self-confidence, which in turn encourages them to set higher goals and achieve even more. Incompetence prompts lower self-confidence.

Although ability and resilience are closely tied, they are not always related. Some people are highly able and have found their way to a career that matches their abilities, yet they lack resilience. Moreover, some people with low or average ability

have an inflated sense of self-confidence. These individuals often pass muster because they believe in themselves. Also, if they are articulate, they can convince others to believe in them. Such people talk well about their ambitions and abilities but look different when you see an example of their work.

A career goal should be in an area where one excels. Experimenting and exploring career options can help one discover such a match. This process can enhance career resilience and eventually lead to high career insight and identity.

Summary

Career resilience is an individual disposition that moderates how one responds to career stress. People who are high in career resilience often take a proactive stance to alleviate and prevent job stress, whereas those who are low in career resilience often take a passive, reactive stance to stress, focusing on the symptoms rather than on changing the situation. A positive organizational environment, one which provides good reinforcement, opportunities for achievement and risk taking, and support for individual action and cooperation as necessary, strengthens employees' career resilience. A hostile environment, one that ignores good performance and focuses on the negative consequences of failure while discouraging initiative and independent action, weakens career resilience. People with high resilience are likely to seek positive organizational environments and escape from negative situations. People with low resilience are not likely to be active in improving their environments. The low-resilience person lacks a solid foundation for developing insight into himself or herself and the organization. If the boss happens to be supportive or the task is challenging, the low-resilience person may benefit. However, a person with low resilience is likely to be stuck in an organizational climate with little support.

These conclusions are based on logic and examples. Research is needed to measure career resilience before one's career begins and then examine changes in career motivation and its impact on career decisions, on adjustment to career transitions,

and on reactions to career stress over time. Although the results of such a study are not available, the ideas presented here can be useful in understanding employees' behavior and reactions and how they can have satisfying careers.

The human resource professional plays an important role in career development. Corporate programs may smooth the way for satisfying career decisions, increased motivation, and reduced stress. This book provided some ideas to help the professional understand career decisions, motivation, and stress. The Resources, techniques to aid employees in understanding themselves well, may be adapted to suit individual needs. We believe that people who accurately assess their interests, needs, strengths, weaknesses, and job and career prospects will be successful in their careers. However, we also recognize that insight is not enough. Efforts to reinforce career resilience are necessary. We have emphasized the role of the boss, company, and job in enhancing motivation and reducing stress. Personnel professionals must recognize the resources they have to help employees survive and succeed.

**Resource 10. Self-Reflection Exercise for
Assessing How Resilience Affects Reactions to Stress.**

Think about your sources of stress. (See Resource 8.) Are your career goals a source of stress? For instance, do you worry about the degree to which your career goals are met?

Next, review your career motivation. (See Resource 3.) In particular, how did you evaluate your career resilience? Now, how do you react to career stress? Do you see yourself as preventing stress or reacting to it? When you experience career stress, do you focus on the situation or on your symptoms? Are your responses psychological, physical, or behavioral?

How does your resilience affect the type of career stress you feel? Is there a relationship between your resilience and the sources of your stress?

Think about your reactions to stress. What can you do in the future to respond to career stress constructively? Also, think about what you can do to increase your career resilience. If we understand ourselves and are able to put ourselves in a position that reinforces our self-confidence and rewards us for our achievements and risks, our goals will be realistic, and we will have a chance for career success.

References

Apcar, L. M. "More Firms Offer Sabbaticals from Jobs, but Sometimes Workers Hate to Return." *Wall Street Journal,* Mar. 26, 1985, p. 1.

Bedeian, A. G., and Armenakis, A. A. "A Path-Analytic Study of the Consequences of Role Conflict and Ambiguity." *Academy of Management Journal,* 1981, *24,* 417–424.

Beehr, T. A. "The Process of Retirement: A Review and Recommendations for Future Investigation." *Personnel Psychology,* 1986, *39,* 31–56.

Berg, E. N. "Now 'Intrapreneurship' Is Hot: New Ventures in a Company." *New York Times,* Apr. 4, 1985, pp. D1, D25.

Boehm, V. R. "Using Assessment Centers for Management Development—Five Applications." *Journal of Management Development,* 1985, *4,* 40–53.

Bray, D. W., Campbell, R. J., and Grant, D. L. *Formative Years in Business: A Long-Term AT&T Study of Managerial Lives.* New York: Wiley, 1974.

Clecak, P. *America's Quest for the Ideal Self: Dissent and Fulfillment in the 60s and 70s.* New York: Oxford University Press, 1982.

Cooper, C. L., and Davidson, M. J. "The High Cost of Stress on Women Managers." *Organizational Dynamics,* Spring 1982, pp. 44–53.

Crawford, J. S. *Women in Middle Management.* Ridgewood, N.J.: Forkner, 1977.

Davis, P. G. "Power Play." *New York Magazine,* May 13, 1985, p. 107.

"Despite the Expansion, Many Companies Trim Their Labor-Force Size." *Wall Street Journal,* Oct. 26, 1984, p. 1.

Dubois, L. "Career and Family in Midlife Men and Women." Unpublished doctoral dissertation, Department of Psychology, Adelphi University, 1981.

Feldman, D. C. "The New Careerism: Origins, Tenets, and Consequences." *The Industrial and Organizational Psychologist,* 1985, *22,* 39–44.

Feldman, D. C., and Arnold, H. J. "Position Choice: Comparing the Importance of Organizational and Job Factors." *Journal of Applied Psychology,* 1978, *63,* 706–710.

Feldman, D. C., and Brett, J. M. "Coping with New Jobs: A Comparative Study of New Hires and Job Changers." *Academy of Management Journal,* 1983, *26,* 258–272.

Fernandez, J. P. *Child-Care and Corporate Productivity: Resolving Family/Work Conflicts.* Lexington, Mass.: D. C. Heath, Lexington Books, 1986.

Forbes, J. B., and Pierce, J. E. "Rising to the Top: Executive Women in 1983 and Beyond." *Business Horizons,* 1983, *26,* 38–47.

Friedman, M., and Rosenman, R. *Type A Behavior and Your Heart.* New York: Knopf, 1974.

Gael, S. *Job Analysis Handbook.* New York: Wiley, 1987.

Graen, G. "Role-Making Processes Within Complex Organizations." In M. D. Dunnette (Ed.), *Handbook of Industrial and Organizational Psychology.* Chicago: Rand McNally, 1976.

Greenhaus, J. H., and Beutell, N. J. "Sources of Conflict Between Work and Family Roles." *Academy of Management Review,* 1985, *10,* 76–88.

Greenhaus, J. H., and Kopelman, R. E. "Conflict Between Work and Nonwork Roles: Implications for the Career Planning Process." *Human Resource Planning,* 1981, *4,* 1–10.

Hackman, J. R., and Oldham, G. R. *Work Redesign.* Reading, Mass.: Addison-Wesley, 1980.

Hall, D. T. *Careers in Organizations.* Santa Monica, Calif.: Goodyear, 1976.

Hall, F. S., and Hall, D. T. *The Two-Career Couple.* Reading, Mass.: Addison-Wesley, 1979.

Harren, V. A. "A Model of Career Decision Making for College Students." *Journal of Vocational Behavior,* 1979, *14,* 119–133.

Harris, A. S., Jr. "Sorry, No Number: The Corporate Drop-outs." *Wall Street Journal,* Apr. 16, 1985, p. 30.

Hennig, M., and Jardim, A. *The Managerial Woman.* Garden City, N.Y.: Doubleday, Anchor Press, 1977.

Holland, J. L. *Making Vocational Choices: A Theory of Careers.* Englewood Cliffs, N.J.: Prentice-Hall, 1973.

Holmes, T., and Rahe, R. "The Social Readjustment Rate Scale." *Journal of Psychosomatic Research,* 1967, *11,* 213–218.

Horner, M. S. "Toward an Understanding of Achievement Related Conflicts in Women." *Journal of Social Issues,* 1972, *28,* 157–175.

Howard, A. "Cool at the Top: Personality Characteristics of Successful Executives." Paper presented at the annual meeting of the American Psychological Association, Toronto, Aug. 1984.

Howard, A., and Bray, D. W. "Today's Young Managers: They Can Do It, but Will They?" *The Wharton Magazine,* 1981, *5* (4), 23–28.

Hymowitz, C., and Schellhardt, T. D. "Merged Firms Often Fire Workers the Easy Way—Not the Best Way." *Wall Street Journal,* Feb. 24, 1986, p. 1.

Jackson, S. E. "Participation in Decision Making as a Strategy for Reducing Job-Related Strain." *Journal of Applied Psychology,* 1983, *68,* 3–19.

Janis, I. L., and Mann, L. *Decision Making.* New York: Free Press, 1977.

Jennings, E. "Leadership and the Exceptional Executive." Paper presented at the Institute for Management Studies meeting, Hopewell, N.J., Apr. 1984.

Jurgensen, C. E. "Job Preferences (What Makes a Job Good or Bad?)." *Journal of Applied Psychology,* 1978, *63,* 267–276.

Kahn, R. L., and others. *Organizational Stress: Studies in Role Conflict and Ambiguity.* New York: Wiley, 1964.

Kanter, R. M. *Men and Women of the Corporation.* New York: Basic Books, 1977.

Kemery, E. R., and others. "Outcomes of Role Stress: A Multisample Constructive Replication." *Academy of Management Journal,* 1985, *28,* 363–375.

Kidder, T. *The Soul of a New Machine*. Boston, Mass.: Little, Brown, 1981.

Kobasa, S. C. "Stressful Life Events, Personality, and Health: An Inquiry into Hardiness." *Journal of Personality and Social Psychology,* 1979, *33,* 1–11.

Kobasa, S. C., Maddi, S. R., and Kahn, S. "Hardiness and Health: A Prospective Study." *Journal of Personality and Social Psychology,* 1982, *42,* 168–177.

Korman, A., and Korman, R. W. *Career Success/Personal Failure: Alienation in Management.* Englewood Cliffs, N.J.: Prentice-Hall, 1980.

Kram, K. E., and Isabella, L. A. "Mentoring Alternatives: The Role of Peer Relationships in Career Development." *Academy of Management Journal,* 1985, *28,* 110–132.

Lane, S. "Banker Turns Farmer and Back to Banker." *Princeton Packet,* June 28, 1985, p. 1B.

Larson, L. M., and Heppner, P. P. "The Relationship of Problem-Solving Appraisal to Career Decision and Indecision." *Journal of Vocational Behavior,* 1985, *26,* 55–65.

Latack, J. C. "Career Transitions Within Organizations: An Exploratory Study of Work, Nonwork, and Coping Strategies." *Organizational Behavior and Human Performance,* 1984, *34,* 296–322.

Latack, J. C., and Dozier, J. B. "After the Ax Falls: Job Loss as a Career Transition." *Academy of Management Review,* 1986, *11,* 375–392.

Lenney, E. "Women's Self-Confidence in Achievement Settings." *Psychological Bulletin,* 1977, *84,* 1–13.

London, M. *Developing Managers: A Guide to Motivating and Preparing People for Successful Managerial Careers.* San Francisco: Jossey-Bass, 1985.

London, M., and Bray, D. W. "Measuring and Developing Young Managers' Career Motivation." *Journal of Management Development,* 1984, *3,* 3–25.

London, M., and Stumpf, S. A. *Managing Careers.* Reading, Mass.: Addison-Wesley, 1982.

Longman, P. "The Downwardly Mobile Baby Boomers." *Wall Street Journal,* Apr. 12, 1985, p. 28.

Lorsch, J. M., and Takagi, H. "Keeping Managers off the Shelf." *Harvard Business Review,* 1986, *6* (4), 60–65.

Louis, M. R. "Career Transitions: Varieties and Commonalities." *Academy of Management Review,* 1980, *5,* 329–340.

McCall, M. W., Jr., and Lombardo, M. M. *Looking Glass, Inc.: An Organizational Simulation.* Technical Report no. 12. Greensboro, N.C.: Center for Creative Leadership. 1978.

McCall, M. W., Jr., and Lombardo, M. M. "What Makes a Top Executive?" *Psychology Today,* Feb. 1983, pp. 26–31.

Maccoby, E. M., and Jacklin, C. N. *The Psychology of Sex Differences.* Stanford, Calif.: Stanford University Press, 1974.

McDowell, J. D. "Job Loyalty: Not the Virtue It Seems." *New York Times,* Mar. 3, 1985, sec. 3, p. 1.

McGrath, J. E. "Stress and Behavior in Organizations." In M. D. Dunnette (Ed.), *Handbook of Industrial and Organizational Psychology.* Chicago: Rand McNally, 1976.

Martin, T. N., and Schermerhorn, J. R., Jr. "Work and Nonwork Influences on Health: A Research Agenda Using Inability to Leave as a Critical Variable." *Academy of Management Review,* 1983, *8,* 650–659.

Matthews, K. A. "Psychological Perspectives on the Type A Behavior Pattern." *Psychological Bulletin,* 1982, *91,* 293–323.

Metalsky, G. I., and others. "Attributional Styles and Life Events in the Classroom: Vulnerability and Invulnerability to Depressive Mood Reactions." *Journal of Personality and Social Psychology,* 1982, *43,* 612–617.

Near, J. P., Rice, R. W., and Hunt, R. G. "The Relationship Between Work and Nonwork Domains: A Review of Empirical Research." *Academy of Management Review,* 1980, *5,* 415–429.

Neff, T. S. "How to Keep the Headhunters at Bay." *Wall Street Journal,* May 13, 1985, p. 22.

Nelson, D. L., and Quick, J. C. "Professional Women: Are Distress and Disease Inevitable?" *Academy of Management Review,* 1985, *10,* 206–218.

Petty, P. "Men, Too, Want Rescue When Facing Loss of Job." *Courier News* (Somerville, N.J.), July 9, 1985, p. D-3.

Phillips, S. D. "Career Exploration in Adulthood." *Journal of Vocational Behavior,* 1982, *20,* 129–140.

Phillips, S. D., and others. "A Factor Analytic Investigation of Career Decision-Making Styles." *Journal of Vocational Behavior,* 1985, *26,* 106–115.

Pinchot, G., III. *Intrapreneuring.* New York: Harper & Row, 1985.

Roberts, K. "The Entry into Employment: An Approach Towards a General Theory." *Sociological Review,* 1968, *16,* 165–184.

Robinson, J. P., and Shaver, P. R. *Measures of Social Psychological Attitudes.* Ann Arbor, Mich.: Survey Research Center, Institute for Social Research, 1974.

Rothstein, W. G. "The Significance of Occupations in Work Careers: An Empirical and Theoretical Review." *Journal of Vocational Behavior,* 1980, *17,* 328–343.

Rubin, D. K. "Fifth Annual Salary Survey: Who Makes What, Where?" *Working Woman,* 1984, *9,* 59–63.

Sager, L. B., and Kipling, R. E. "The Alchemy of Career Changes." *Business Horizons,* 1980, *23,* 23–30.

Schein, V. E. "The Relationship Between Sex Role Stereotype and Requisite Management Characteristics." *Journal of Applied Psychology,* 1973, *57,* 95–100.

Selye, H. *Stress in Health and Disease.* Boston: Butterworths, 1976.

Sidener, J. "Engineer Turns to Father's Craft." *Princeton Packet,* May 24, 1985, pp. 1B–2B.

Slocum, J. W., and others. "Business Strategy and the Management of Plateaued Employees." *Academy of Management Journal,* 1985, *28,* 133–154.

Staw, B. M., and Ross, J. "Stability in the Midst of Change: A Dispositional Approach to Job Attitudes." *Journal of Applied Psychology,* 1985, *70,* 469–480.

Stumpf, S. A., Colarelli, S. M., and Hartman, K. "Development of the Career Exploration Survey (CES)." *Journal of Vocational Behavior,* 1983, *22,* 191–226.

Stumpf, S. A., and others. *Financial Services Industry (FSI): A Strategic Decision Making Simulation.* New York: School of Business Administration, New York University, 1984.

Sutton, R. I., Eisenhardt, K. M., and Jucker, J. V. "Managing Organizational Decline: Lessons from Atari." *Organizational Dynamics,* Spring 1986, pp. 17–29.

Terborg, J. R. "International Psychology and Research on Human Behavior in Organizations." *Academy of Management Review,* 1981, *6,* 569–576.

Terborg, J. R., and others. "Organizational and Personal Correlates of Attitudes Toward Women as Managers." *Academy of Management Journal,* 1977, *20,* 89–100.

Thornton, G. C., III, and Byham, W. C. *Assessment Centers and Managerial Performance.* New York: Academic Press, 1982.

"To Reduce Their Costs, Big Companies Lay Off White-Collar Workers." *Wall Street Journal,* May 22, 1986, p. 1.

Van Maanen, J., and Schein, E. H. "Career Development." In J. R. Hackman and J. L. Suttle (Eds.), *Improving Life at Work: Behavioral Science Approaches to Organizational Change.* Santa Monica, Calif.: Goodyear, 1977.

Van Sell, M., Brief, A. P., and Schuler, R. S. "Role Conflict and Role Ambiguity: Integration of the Literature and Directions for Future Research." *Human Relations,* 1981, *34,* 43–71.

Veiga, J. F. "Mobility Influences During Managerial Career Stages." *Academy of Management Journal,* 1983, *26,* 64–85.

Von Glinow, M. A., and others. "The Design of a Career Oriented Human Resource System." *Academy of Management Review,* 1983, *8,* 23–32.

Wanous, J. P. *Organizational Entry: Recruitment, Selection, and Socialization of Newcomers.* Reading, Mass.: Addison-Wesley, 1980.

Ward, J. L. "Firms Forcing Employees to Repay Some Costs If They Quit Too Soon." *Wall Street Journal,* July 17, 1985, p. 35.

Index

DATE DUE

JUL 2 5 '90	
DEC 1 5 '91	
APR 1 5 '92	
MAR 2 4 '93	
APR 1 5 1996	
APR 0 6 1998	

BRODART, INC.   Cat. No. 23-221

And they brought young children to him, that he should touch them: and his disciples rebuked those that brought them. But when Jesus saw it, he was much displeased, and said unto them, Suffer the little children to come unto me, and forbid them not: for of such is the kingdom of God. Verily I say unto you, Whosoever shall not receive the kingdom of God as a little child, he shall not enter therein. And he took them up in his arms, put his hands upon them, and blessed them.

Mark 10:13–16

As depicted in this painting by George Hinke, in which Jesus is surrounded by young boys and girls and their mothers, Christ often reached out to little children. In their innocence and humility, He found a perfect model to teach us how to approach God. The lesson was clear: God was a loving and all-forgiving father.

On the Road

For road-mates and companions he chose twelve,
All, like himself, of homeliest degree,
All toilers with their hands for daily bread,
Who, at his word, left all and followed him. . . .
He taught a new sweet simple rule of Right
'Twixt man and God, and so 'twixt man and man—

That men should first love God and serve Him well.
Then love and serve their neighbours as themselves.
They loved him for his gentle manliness,
His forthright speech, his wondrous winning ways,
His wisdom, and his perfect fearlessness,
And for that something more they found in him
As in no other.

For through the mortal the immortal shone—
A radiant light which burned so bright within
That nought could hide it. Every word and look,
And a sweet graciousness in all he did,
Proclaimed him something measurelessly more
Than earth had ever seen in man before,
And with him virtue went and holy power. . . .

Through all the land he journeyed, telling forth
The gracious message of God's love for man—
That God's great heart was very sore for man,
Was hungering and thirsting after man,
As one whose dearly-loved have gone astray,
As one whose children have deserted him.

The people heard him gladly, flocking round
To catch his words, still more to see his deeds,
The men all hopeful, and the women touched
By this new message and the messenger;
And everywhere the children drew to him
And found in him a sweet new comradeship.

Strange was his teaching, stranger still his deeds—
He healed the sick and gave the blind their sight,
With his own hands cleansed lepers of their sores,
And raised the dead—all in the name of God,
And for the love God's great heart held for them.

JOHN OXENHAM
1861–1941

Political Leaders of Israel

"And it came to pass in those days, that there went out a decree from Caesar Augustus, that all the world should be taxed. . . . And Joseph also went up from Galilee . . . unto the city of David, which is called Bethlehem" (Luke 2:1, 4a). Bethlehem of Judea was conquered by the Romans in 63 B.C. and became part of the massive Roman Empire, which stretched from the northwest corner of Europe to Egypt and from Mauritania to the Black Sea. More than fifty million inhabitants lived under the relatively stable rule of Augustus Caesar, the first Roman emperor. Augustus organized this vast region and brought peace to the diverse peoples, a peace which would prove crucial to the spread of Christianity since Jesus' disciples were able to travel unimpeded to the far corners of the Roman Empire.

Under the Romans, the Jews could practice their religion and were granted some special rights; but the Empire was still pagan, and conflicts with the monotheistic Jews were frequent and often violent. The Jews resented the influences of a foreign culture and the taxes Rome imposed. Roman occupation brought improvements in daily life, such as better roads, increased trade, and beautiful architecture; but as long as the Romans remained, the ancient land of Palestine remained in bondage.

"Where is he that is born King of the Jews? for we have seen his star in the east, and are come to worship him" (Matthew 2:2). This question, asked in Jerusalem by the Magi, troubled no one more than Herod the Great, reigning king of the Jews. Herod ruled Judea from 37 to 4 A.D. (the year of Christ's birth) and was, at times, an effective, although irrational, leader. Under his rule, Judea prospered and built a magnificent array of palaces, parks, theaters, and fortresses. Herod's most ambitious project was the transformation of the five-hundred-year-old, decaying temple in Jerusalem into a magnificent house of worship.

Powerful as he was, however, Herod was also probably mentally ill. A half-Jew by birth, yet a Roman citizen as well, he imagined threats in every corner, even among his family. He had one of his wives, his mother-in-law, a brother-in-law, and three sons assassinated. By the time the Magi came to Jerusalem, Herod was so irrational that he decreed all male children in Judea under the age of two be killed; Jesus, however, was already in Egypt. Within three years,

Emperor Augustus Caesar, pictured above, then known as Octavian, came to power in Rome after the assassination of Julius Caesar in 44 B.C. He ruled first as a part of a triumvirate that included Mark Antony, but eventually came to hold sole power over the vast Roman Empire.

Herod the Great was dead and his kingdom divided among his three surviving sons.

The Sanhedrin, whose name comes from the Greek *synedrion*, meaning counsel, was the highest ruling body of the Jewish people. Composed of priests, elders, and scribes of the Jewish synagogue, the Sanhedrin was presided over by one ruling high priest and controlled most of the day-to-day business of the Jewish courts of law. Historians are not certain as to the exact jurisdiction of the Sanhedrin; but they do know that in certain matters, court cases were taken to the Roman governor for sentencing, which is why Jesus was brought before Pontius Pilate.

The Sanhedrin convicted Jesus of blasphemy for His teachings; but when they delivered Him to Pilate, they told the Roman governor that Jesus was guilty of "perverting the nation, and forbidding to give tribute to Caesar." Led by the high priest, Caiaphas, and the former high priest Annas, the Sanhedrin urged Pilate to sentence Jesus to death.

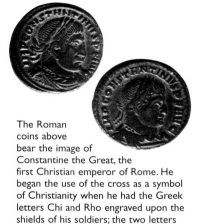

The Roman coins above bear the image of Constantine the Great, the first Christian emperor of Rome. He began the use of the cross as a symbol of Christianity when he had the Greek letters Chi and Rho engraved upon the shields of his soldiers; the two letters together form the shape of a cross.

As Roman governor of Judea from A.D. 26 to 36, Pontius Pilate had judicial authority over the Jewish people. His overriding concern was protecting his position within the Roman government, and his insensitivity to the religious beliefs and traditions of the Jews resulted in periodic uprisings. After one such riot, Pilate momentarily lost his political instincts and ordered a group of Samaritans executed. For this rash act, he was finally called back to Rome.

But Pontius Pilate will be forever known as the man who condemned Jesus to death. Pilate hesitated in his condemnation, probably because of political concerns with the Sanhedrin; but when he turned to the crowd, which was probably assembled by the Sanhedrin for political purposes, he threw the question of Jesus' fate to them. The mob, incited by the priests of the Sanhedrin, called for Jesus' death. Pilate, ever the politician, obliged and sentenced the Son of God to die.

The stone above bears the inscription *legia x fretensis*, signifying the Roman legion that destroyed Jerusalem in A.D. 70.

At right are the remains of an architecturally graceful Roman aqueduct where Caesarea once stood. Built by King Herod in the first century B.C., Caesarea was a city with no Jewish roots and a distinctly Roman character. Pontius Pilate lived there, and the city was the headquarters for Roman soldiers sent to crush the Jewish revolt that began in A.D. 66.

And it came to pass,
that, as the people
pressed upon him to
hear the word of God,
he stood by the lake of
Gennesaret, And saw
two ships standing by
the lake: but the
fishermen were gone out
of them, and were
washing their nets. And
he entered into one of
the ships, which was
Simon's, and prayed
him that he would
thrust out a little from
the land. And he sat
down, and taught the
people out of the ship.
Luke 5:1–3

ne of the two was Andrew, the brother of Simon; the other was John, son of Zebedee. . . . What did Jesus do to keep them? "Jesus turning around and seeing that they followed him, saith to them, 'What seek ye?' They said to him, 'Rabbi . . . where abidest thou?' He saith to them, 'Come, and ye shall see.' They went therefore and saw where he abode, and they abode with him that day; it was about the tenth hour."

The text of the gospel narrative is as moving as any direct words of Christ. . . . That which passed between them at that first meeting, in the dawn of Bethany, was the secret of a more than human love, love inexpressible. Already the lighted fire was catching from tree to tree, from soul to soul. Andrew told his brother that he had found the Christ and brought back to the desert with him Simon, who from that day forward Christ called Kephas.

The next day the conflagration spread, reached Philip, a native of Bethsaida, as were Andrew and Peter. The words and acts which attached him to Christ are not known to us. But the flame spread from Philip to Nathanael. This new tree did not take fire at once, for Nathanael was versed in the Scripture and protested that nothing good could come out of Nazareth. His friend answered simply: "Come and see."

Was it enough for each of these chosen souls to see Jesus in order to recognize him? No, Jesus gave each a sign; and the sign he gave Nathanael was the same he was soon to use to convince the woman of Samaria. "Whence dost thou know me?" Nathanael had asked in a distrustful tone. "Before Philip called thee, when thou wast under the fig tree, I saw thee." Nathanael at once replied: "Thou art the Son of God."

It matters little that the secret act which took place beneath the fig tree was never revealed. What Nathanael discovered was that the very depths of his being were known to this man; he felt himself open before him, as do the least of us today, kneeling for the avowal of our sins or with our faces turned toward the Host. During his mortal life Christ was prodigal of that sign which caused many a simple and unaffected being to fall with his face against the earth. He replied even to the most secret thoughts of the scribes and the Pharisees, but they, far from striking their breasts, saw therein but a ruse of Beelzebub. The faith of the humble Nathanael surprised Christ more than their incredulity, and we may imagine his smile as he said: "Because I said to thee, 'I saw thee under the fig tree,' thou believest. Greater things than these shalt thou see."

Perhaps when this encounter with Nathanael took place, Jesus had already left the desert, where during forty days he had fasted and suffered the attacks of the Prince of Evil. Going up to the Jordan by Archelais and Scythopolis, he had reached the Lake of Tiberias and Bethsaida, the native country of the disciples who had left John to follow him. Not that the hour of total abandon had as yet sounded for them. Their nets and their barques were still to hold them for a little while; they had had only the first call. . . .

Jesus with his followers went to Capharnaum, to the shores of the lake where Simon, Andrew, James, and John found once more their boats and their nets. His grip on them loosened for a little while; they would never escape him again. We have read the story so often it seems simple to us that Jesus, passing along the shores of the lake and seeing his friends cast down their nets, had need of only the words, "Come, follow me and I will make you fishers of men," for them, without so much as a turn of the head, to leave all and follow him. However, it was not without his having given them a new sign of his power, chosen from among all those which might most surely strike these simple minds.

He had first borrowed their boat in order to escape the people who pressed too closely upon him. Simon had rowed out a little way, and Jesus, seated in the stern, spoke to the multitude grouped around the water's edge, to a multitude in which feeling ran high, for already there was great division of opinion concerning him. In Nazareth, in the synagogue (where, like any other pious Jew, he had the right to speak) his commentaries on the prophecies had irritated the people who had known him from his earliest years. To them the carpenter Yeshua was of little importance, despite the cures which were beginning to be laid at his door. Their irritation had reached its height when he had let them understand that the Gentiles would be preferred to them, and it was only by a miracle he had escaped their fury.

Now he no longer risked being alone: here he was in the boat with Simon and the sons of Zebedee. Since that day in Bethany, these boatmen knew that he saw into the secret life of each one of them; they had seen with their own eyes the miracle of Cana; Jesus had cured Simon's mother-in-law of fever. It remained for him to touch them in that which counted for most in their eyes: to catch as many fish as they wished— it was their job to know that was extremely difficult.

Indeed they had worked all that night without catching anything. And now Simon had to call James and John to his help to draw in the nets. The two boats were so full of fish they were almost sinking. Then Kephas fell to his knees. "Depart from me, for I am a sinful man, O Lord." Jesus' answer, like many of his words, contained a prophecy which we are still seeing fulfilled before our eyes: "Henceforth thou shalt catch men."

FRANÇOIS MAURIAC
FROM *LIFE OF JESUS*

Now when he had left speaking, he said unto Simon, Launch out into the deep, and let down your nets for a draught. And Simon answering said unto him, Master, we have toiled all the night, and have taken nothing: nevertheless at thy word I will let down the net. And when they had this done, they inclosed a great multitude of fishes: and their net brake. And they beckoned unto their partners, which were in the other ship, that they should come and help them. And they came, and filled both the ships, so that they began to sink. When Simon Peter saw it, he fell down at Jesus' knees, saying, Depart from me; for I am a sinful man, O Lord. For he was astonished, and all that were with him, at the draught of the fishes which they had taken: . . . And Jesus said unto Simon, Fear not; from henceforth thou shalt catch men.
Luke 5:4–10

And he said unto another, Follow me. But he said, Lord, suffer me first to go and bury my father. Jesus said unto him, Let the dead bury their dead: but go thou and preach the kingdom of God. And another also said, Lord, I will follow thee; but let me first go bid them farewell, which are at home at my house. And Jesus said unto him, No man, having put his hand to the plough, and looking back, is fit for the kingdom of God. After these things the Lord . . . sent them two and two before his face into every city and place, whither he himself would come.
Luke 9:59–62; 10:1

Obedience

I said, "Let me walk in the fields."
He said, "No, walk in the town."
I said, "There are no flowers there."
He said, "No flowers, but a crown."

I said, "But the skies are black;
There is nothing but noise and din."
And He wept as He sent me back;
"There is more," He said; "There is sin."

I said, "But the air is thick,
And fogs are veiling the sun."
He answered, "Yet souls are sick,
And souls in the dark undone."

I said, "I shall miss the light,
And friends will miss me, they say."
He answered, "Choose tonight
If I am to miss you, or they."

I pleaded for time to be given.
He said, "Is it hard to decide?
It will not seem hard in heaven
To have followed the steps of your Guide."

I cast one look at the fields,
Then set my face to the town;
He said, "My child, do you yield?
Will you leave the flowers for the crown?"

Then into His hand went mine,
And into my heart came He;
And I walk in a light divine,
The path I had feared to see.

GEORGE MACDONALD
1824–1905

Artist Richard Hook portrays Jesus as the compassionate friend and kind leader described in biblical accounts.

Peter

Peter saith unto him, Thou shalt never wash my feet. Jesus answered him, If I wash thee not, thou hast no part with me. Simon Peter saith unto him, Lord, not my feet only, but also my hands and my head.
John 13:8–9

alled from the shores of the Sea of Galilee, the fisherman Simon would become the leader among Jesus' apostles. Simon was emotional and impulsive, but he first recognized Jesus' divinity. When Jesus asked His disciples who they said that He was, Simon alone replied, "Thou art the Christ, the Son of the Living God." For this declaration of faith, Jesus renamed Simon, Peter—the Greek word for rock—and declared that it was Peter's statement upon which Christianity would be built (Matthew 16:18).

Yet those strong feelings that drew Peter to Jesus made for a tumultuous relationship with his beloved Lord. Peter's overwhelming love for Jesus prevents him from accepting Jesus' explanation of His upcoming death. As Jesus is arrested and led away, Peter bravely follows Him to the garden of the chief priests, only to collapse in fear and to lie under questioning about Jesus of Nazareth. After these trials, or perhaps because of them, Peter is strengthened.

After Jesus' resurrection, on the day of Pentecost, Peter dramatically becomes an articulate spokesman and carries the Gospel to Antioch, Asia Minor, and Rome. It was Peter who insisted Jesus' message was universal and open to all who confessed their faith, and it was Peter who first preached the Gospel to the Gentiles.

According to tradition, Peter was martyred in Rome in A.D. 61. The story is told that Peter—in a moment of fear and weakness—tried to flee the city when his arrest appeared imminent, but a vision of Jesus entering Rome to be crucified again, this time in Peter's place, convinced the disciple to return to his own death. Peter requested that he be crucified head down, as he felt unworthy to die in the same position as Jesus. To the end, Peter was guided by his emotional, yet passionate devotion to his Christ.

John

And when his disciples James and John saw this, they said, Lord, wilt thou that we command fire to come down from heaven, and consume them, even as Elias did? But he turned, and rebuked them, and said, Ye know not what manner of spirit ye are of. For the Son of man is not come to destroy men's lives, but to save them.
Luke 9:54–56a

John, with his older brother James, was a fisherman on the Sea of Galilee; and he also became a disciple of Jesus. A member of the inner circle of disciples, John was perhaps the closest of all the apostles to Jesus. His life is an illustration of the power of Jesus to transform ordinary men.

Typical of the Galilean fisherman of his day, John was rough and emotional, given to violent temper. At one point, when Jesus and His disciples were on the road to Jerusalem, the Samaritans refused hospitality; John became angry and was moved to violence. His Master's calm rebuke reminded John that, in following Jesus, he had chosen the way of peace and love.

Traditional stories give us further information about John's life. It is generally believed that John was the "beloved disciple" into whose hands Jesus committed His mother's care as He was dying on the cross. Legend holds that John was faithful to this charge and remained in Jerusalem with Mary until her death. Then he traveled to Rome and suffered great persecution, but he remained true to the teachings of his Lord.

In his later life, on the island of Patmos and in the town of Ephesus, legends emerge of John as a man of peace and quiet devotion. One legend is particularly telling. Extremely old and physically weak, John was a beloved teacher in the church at Ephesus. He became almost too weak for speech and answered all questions put to him by reminding the faithful of Jesus' instruction that they love one another. When finally questioned as to why he uttered only these words, John found the strength to reply that love was the heart of Jesus' message. One of the "sons of thunder," who in his youth had been so quick to anger, had come to believe in love above all else.

Andrew

One of his disciples, Andrew, Simon Peter's brother, saith unto him, There is a lad here, which hath five barley loaves, and two small fishes: but what are they among so many?
John 6:8, 9

Andrew brought the young boy with the loaves and fishes to Jesus in the same spirit of optimism that he had brought his brother, Simon, to meet the Lord, and that he would later bring the Greeks who searched for Jesus in Jerusalem. Andrew understood that Jesus would accept and make use of all who sought Him in good faith.

A fisherman from the village of Bethsaida, Andrew, according to the Gospel of John, was a disciple of John the Baptist when he heard John acknowledge Jesus of Nazareth as the Lamb of God. From that moment until his death, Andrew was a devoted missionary for Jesus. The Gospels depict a quiet man—nearly always in the shadow of his brother—who happily accepted his often anonymous role.

In tradition Andrew emerges, after Jesus' ascension, as an active and devoted disciple. In Greece he converted several prominent citizens but angered the governor, who ordered Andrew arrested and crucified. Legend tells that Andrew requested an X-shaped cross. Like his brother Peter, Andrew felt himself unworthy of a death that mirrored that of Jesus. Andrew's death inspired many Greeks to faith in Christ.

Centuries after his death, Andrew's memory continues to inspire people. One legend tells of an eighth-century monk who had a vision that he was to take Andrew's remains to the west. The monk ended his journey in Scotland, where he founded St. Andrew's church. Soldiers from the area, fighting a battle against the English, reported that they saw and were guided by the cross of St. Andrew shining in the sky above the battlefield. Today, Andrew is the patron saint of Russia, Greece, and Scotland. The disciple who carried on his mission quietly and often in the shadows continues to represent Christ to the world.

Thomas

Thomas saith unto him, Lord, we know not whither thou goest; and how can we know the way? Jesus saith unto him, I am the way, the truth, and the life: no man cometh unto the Father, but by me.
John 14:5, 6

Thomas was a man of pessimism and doubt. It was he who continually questioned Jesus, he who was troubled by his inability to understand. In the Upper Room, Thomas resisted Jesus' prophecy of His fate; after the resurrection, Thomas withheld his belief until his eyes and hands confirmed what his ears had heard.

Doubt alone is not the story of Thomas. It is the answer Jesus provides, the resolution of Thomas's doubt, that is instructive. Jesus does not condemn Thomas for expressing doubts, which arise from a desire for more complete understanding, nor does He try to persuade. Jesus' answer is Himself. "I am the way," He tells Thomas in the Upper Room; and after the resurrection, He presents His body for Thomas's doubting hands to feel. Jesus' challenge to the doubter is to battle doubts with faith. Thomas exclaims to Jesus upon putting his fingers in the resurrected Lord's wounds: "My Lord and my God." Faith born in struggle emerges strong and pure.

One legend concerning Thomas, although its authenticity is questionable, nevertheless demonstrates the disciple's personality. After Christ's resurrection, Thomas was supposedly assigned the ministry of India by the group of disciples. Thomas refused to go, doubtful that he could carry Jesus' message to this foreign land. Jesus appeared to him in a vision, however, calmed his doubts, and convinced Thomas to go. The legend continued that, once in India, Thomas became a man of great and inspirational faith. True or not, the legend emphasizes the lesson of Thomas's life: doubt and pessimism in mankind are natural, but deep faith in Christ reveals that through God all things are possible.

Matthew

He went forth, and saw a publican, named Levi, sitting at the receipt of custom: and he said unto him, Follow me. And he left all, rose up, and followed him. And Levi made him a great feast in his own house: and there was a great company of publicans and of others that sat down with them. But their scribes and Pharisees murmured against his disciples, saying, Why do you eat and drink with publicans and sinners? And Jesus answering said unto them, They that are whole need not a physician: but they that are sick. I came not to call the righteous, but sinners to repentance.
Luke 5:27b–32

W̲e know the publican Levi as the disciple Matthew, a tax collector from Capernaum who left his work to follow Jesus. In Jesus' time, there were few men more despised than those who collected the Roman taxes, since payment to Rome was against the Jews' religion that taught that only God deserved such tribute.

In addition to the religious concern, there was a more earthly reason to hate the tax collectors. They had a reputation for immorality and injustice: more often than not, they collected more money than was required and kept the difference. We don't know whether Levi was such a scurrilous man, but as a tax collector, he was indeed an unlikely disciple.

Yet once chosen, Matthew proved truly faithful and desired to spread the good word immediately. Evidence of his faith exists in the use he made of one of the tools of his former trade: his pen. Blessed with the skill of writing, Matthew left a record of the life and teachings of Jesus.

Although scholars dispute how much of the Book of Matthew in the biblical canon was actually written by the disciple, it is certain that Matthew wrote about Jesus and thus was instrumental in bringing countless people to Christianity. Jesus called Matthew to repentance. Matthew answered, and his life was transformed.

Judas Iscariot

Then one of the twelve, called Judas Iscariot, went unto the chief priests, And said unto them, What will ye give me, and I will deliver him unto you? And they covenanted with him for thirty pieces of silver. And from that time he sought opportunity to betray him.
Matthew 26:14-16

Judas Iscariot was the only one of the twelve apostles not from Galilee. Scholars believe that his name means Judas from Kerioth and that he hailed from a city by that name in Judea. Judas is the disciple who betrayed Jesus to the Roman authorities who arrested and eventually crucified Him.

Christians have debated Judas' motives for hundreds of years. One argument is that Judas lost faith in Jesus as the true Messiah and was greedy; another has Judas troubled by Jesus' association with sinners and questioning His leadership. Judas has also been portrayed as a man frustrated by Jesus' unwillingness to use force to assert His rule—perhaps Judas was a member of a radical group who wanted to overthrow Roman rule by violence. Perhaps he believed so strongly that Jesus was the Messiah who would lead the Jews to earthly freedom that he lost track of Jesus the Son of God who taught peace and love and repentance. Perhaps Jesus chose Judas, knowing he would betray Him, specifically so that the Scriptures might be fulfilled. The answers to these questions can never be known.

Accounts of Judas' downfall after the betrayal differ in their details. In the Book of Matthew, Judas immediately hangs himself. In the Acts of the Apostles, Judas buys a burial field with the thirty pieces of silver, then collapses and dies there. Whatever the circumstances, Judas could not live with the consequences of his act.

Judas is an example of a person who could never fully accept Jesus as Lord. Like the rich, young ruler, Judas could not relinquish his worldly life and commit himself to his Lord. When the time came to choose, he betrayed his Lord and lost his life in the process.

Philip

Philip saith unto him, Lord, shew us the Father, and it sufficeth us. Jesus saith unto him, Have I been so long time with you, and yet hast thou not known me, Philip? he that hath seen me hath seen the Father.
John 14:8, 9a

Philip, from Bethsaida on the north coast of the Sea of Galilee, was the first disciple to hear the simple command, "Follow me" (John 1:43) from Jesus; he answered the call and became a devoted missionary. Philip appears in the first three Gospels only in lists of the apostles. He comes to life, however, in the book of John.

Philip's first act after hearing Jesus' call was to find Nathanael and tell him the news that the Messiah, long promised by the prophets and by Moses, had come. Nathanael was skeptical; rather than argue with him, Philip simply urged Nathanael to go and see Jesus for himself.

Later, when a group of Greeks approached Philip in Jerusalem, hoping to be taken to meet Jesus, the disciple sought out Andrew and together they took the Greeks to Jesus, certain that the Greeks too would be overcome by faith in the presence of the Master.

A legend of Philip proves that the faith born in his first encounter with Christ remained his guiding light. Philip had been preaching in Hierapolis, and his church was composed of a large group of Christians. When sentenced to die by the leaders of Hierapolis for his preaching, Philip did not just quietly accept his fate. At his execution, he called upon the ground to open up and swallow the thousands who looked upon him. At that, Jesus appeared to Philip and rebuked him. Calmed by the vision of the risen Christ, Philip accepted death and requested only that his body be wrapped in papyrus rather than linen, which was used to wrap the body of Christ.

In this final act, Philip recalled the faith born out of his first step as a disciple, when he heard the two words that would ever after guide his life: "Follow me."

imon, known both as Simon the Canaanite and Simon the Zealot, is mentioned only four times in the New Testament. In the Gospels of Matthew, Mark, and Luke, his name appears only as part of a list of apostles; in the passage at left, from Acts, we learn only that Simon remained with the disciples after Jesus' ascension.

What little we know about the man Simon comes from his designation as a Zealot. The Zealots were a radical Jewish party that emerged after the death of Herod the Great, when Judea fell under the rule of a Roman governor. Zealots were devoted to strict adherence to Jewish law, which included the belief that God alone was their ruler. Their resistance to Roman rule was absolute and violent; Zealots were prepared to sacrifice their own lives and the lives of any who cooperated with the Roman government. For a Zealot to become a disciple of Christ is then truly amazing. To follow Jesus, Simon had to lay down his weapons, quiet his anger, and pledge his belief in the sacrificial love of Jesus as the source of salvation.

Simon

And when they were come in, they went up into an upper room, where abode both Peter, and James, and John, and Andrew, Philip, and Thomas, Bartholomew, and Matthew, James the son of Alphaeus, and Simon Zelotes, and Judas the brother of James. These all continued with one accord in prayer and supplication, with the women, and Mary the mother of Jesus, and with his brethren.
Acts 1:13, 14

James

And going on from thence, he saw other two brethren, James the son of Zebedee, and John his brother, in a ship with Zebedee their father, mending their nets; and he called them. And they immediately left the ship and their father, and followed him.
Matthew 4:21, 22

ames of Zebedee answered the call of Jesus without doubt or hesitation; he left behind his fishing boat, his nets, and his father to become a disciple along with his brother John. Very little is known of James. Along with John and Peter, he was part of Jesus' inner circle of disciples; these three witnessed Jesus' transfiguration on the mountaintop, and Jesus selected them to accompany Him as He prayed in the Garden of Gethsemane.

Jesus' characterization of James and his brother as "sons of thunder" implied that James had a fiery spirit. We know that he was outspoken and ambitious from the Gospel of Mark. Mark relates the story of a request made of Jesus by James and John, who asked that they be given places by His side in His kingdom. Jesus answered, "Ye know not what ye ask. Can ye drink of the cup that I drink of? and be baptized with the baptism that I am baptized with?" (Mark 10:38). Without hesitation, James joined John in answering, "We can." James was bold enough to ask for a place by Jesus' side and confident enough to profess himself worthy.

In A.D. 44, James proved his faith as strong as his words. In that year he became the first of the apostles to die for his faith when Herod Agrippa ordered him beheaded. Facing death, James did not waver from his strong faith. Tradition tells that on the way to his execution, James converted his jailer, who professed his own belief in Jesus as Christ and was executed alongside the apostle.

Bartholomew

And it came to pass in those days, that he went out into a mountain to pray, and continued all night in prayer to God. And when it was day, he called unto him his disciples: and of them he chose twelve, whom also he named apostles; Simon (whom he also named Peter,) and Andrew his brother, James and John, Philip and Bartholomew, Matthew and Thomas, James the son of Alphaeus, and Simon called Zelotes, and Judas the brother of James, and Judas Iscariot.
Luke 6:12–16a

Little is known of Bartholomew; he appears by name alone in the Gospels of Matthew, Mark, and Luke. And in John, when the disciples are mentioned, the name Bartholomew seems to be replaced with that of Nathanael. Many scholars believe that Bartholomew and Nathanael are the same man. If this is the case, then the Gospel of John offers our only glimpse at the character of this silent disciple.

In John 1:45–51, Philip told Nathanael that Jesus of Nazareth was the Messiah of whom the prophets spoke. Nathanael doubted, yet followed Philip out of curiosity, perhaps, to see the man called Jesus.

In His presence, Nathanael's doubts dissolved to be replaced by faith in Jesus as the Messiah. No great miracle precipitated this belief, simply Jesus' words of recognition: He already knew Nathanael. He saw into Nathanael's heart, and Nathanael instantly acknowledged Him as Lord: "Rabbi, thou art the son of God: thou art the King of Israel." Nathanael (Bartholomew), a thoughtful man who waited to make up his own mind about Jesus of Nazareth, was moved to discipleship by the simple presence of the Son of God.

James, Son of Alphaeus

And he ordained twelve, that they should be with him, and that he might send them forth to preach, And to have power to heal sicknesses, and to cast out devils: And Simon he surnamed Peter; and James the son of Zebedee, and John the brother of James, . . . And Andrew, and Philip, and Bartholomew, and Matthew, and Thomas, and James the son of Alphaeus, and Thaddaeus, and Simon the Canaanite, And Judas Iscariot.

Mark 3:14–19a

L ess is known about James of Alphaeus than about any of Jesus' twelve apostles. James's name appears four times in lists of the apostles, and that is all. Even legends are few.

It is believed that James preached in Persia and was eventually crucified for his faith. Some scholars have argued that James was the brother of Matthew, who is also identified as a son of Alphaeus. Others believe that James was a Zealot like Simon, for his name always appears joined with that of Simon the Zealot. Given these two assumptions, James would have been in an interesting position: a brother of a tax collector—a Roman collaborator—and a member of a group that believed all such men as Jesus should be put to death for their "betrayal of God." Only in discipleship and with the peaceful message of Jesus could such an inner and personal conflict have been resolved.

There is additional conjecture that James son of Alphaeus is the same man as James the Less, whose mother—a woman called Mary—is present at Christ's death upon the cross (Mark 15). James of Alphaeus, at last, remains a true mystery: a man of faith and devotion whose life was given to Jesus.

Judas, Brother of James

Judas saith unto him, not Iscariot, Lord, how is it that thou wilt manifest thyself unto us, and not unto the world? Jesus answered and said unto him, If a man love me, he will keep my words: and my Father will love him, and we will come unto him, and make our abode with him.

John 14:22, 23

The apostle named Judas, not Iscariot, in the passage from John, is identified as Thaddeus in the Gospels of Matthew and Mark, and as Judas, the brother of James, in Luke and Acts. Scholars, for the most part, agree that the references in these five books refer to one man.

The passage at left is the only biblical evidence we have as to the character of this disciple. The question Judas put to Jesus indicates that Judas had some desire that Jesus make use of His great power to forcibly take command of the kingdom of the Jews. Jesus used the opportunity to remind Judas that His was a rule of love, not of violence, and it was not faith surrendered to force that would gain salvation for man, but only by following Christ.

One legend exists of Thaddeus. After Christ's resurrection, Thaddeus traveled to the city of Edessa to preach the gospel and to fulfill a promise made by Jesus to that city's king who, sight unseen, had accepted Jesus as the Son of God. Jesus had promised him that for his faith, the king would be healed. If Thaddeus and Judas are one, then his selection as the disciple to heal the King of Edessa is ironic. The disciple who urged Jesus to show His power to the world comes face to face with a man whose faith required no such display of worldly sign.

What Good Can Come from Nazareth?

hilip could hardly wait to tell somebody, and the first person he found was Nathanael. Ever since Moses they'd been saying the Messiah was just around the corner, and now he had finally turned up. Who would have guessed where? Who would have guessed who?

"Jesus of Nazareth," Philip said. "The son of Joseph." But he could hear his words fall flat.

"Can anything good come out of Nazareth?" Nathanael said.

Philip told him to come take a look for himself then, but Jesus got a look at Nathanael first as he came puffing down the road toward him, near-sighted and earnest, no doubt with his yarmulke on crooked, his dog-eared Torah under his arm.

"Behold, an Israelite indeed, in whom is no guile," Jesus said. Nathanael's jaw hung open. He said, "How do you know me?"

"Before Philip called you," Jesus said. "When you were under the fig tree, I saw you."

It was all it took apparently. "Rabbi!" Nathanael's jacket was too tight across the shoulders and you could hear a seam split somewhere as he made an impossible bow. "You are the Son of God," he said. "You are the king of Israel."

"Because I said I saw you under the fig tree, do you believe?" Jesus said. There was more to it than parlor tricks. He said, "You shall see greater things than these." But all Nathanael could see for the moment, not daring to look up, were his own two feet.

"You will see heaven opened," he heard Jesus say, "the angels of God ascending and descending upon the Son of Man." When Nathanael decided to risk a glance, the sun almost blinded him.

What Nathanael did see finally was this. It was months later, years— after the Crucifixion of Jesus. One evening he and Peter and a few of the others took the boat out fishing. They didn't get a nibble between them but stuck it out all night. It was something to do anyway. It passed the time. Just at dawn, in that queer half-light, somebody showed up on the beach and cupped his mouth with his hands. "Any luck?" The answer was no. "Then give it another try," the man said. "Reel in the nets and cast them off the port beam this time." There was nothing to lose they hadn't lost already, so they did it, and the catch had to be seen to be believed, had to be felt, the heft of it almost swamping them as they pulled it aboard.

Peter saw who the man was first and heaved himself overboard. The water was chest-high as he plowed through it, tripping over his feet in the shallows so he ended up scrambling ashore on all fours. Jesus was standing there waiting for him by a little charcoal fire he had going. Nathanael and the others came ashore, slowly, like men in a dream, not daring to speak for fear they'd wake up. Jesus got them to bring him some of their fish, and then they stood around at a little distance while he did the cooking. When it was done, he gave them the word. "Come and have breakfast," he said, and they sat down beside him in the sand.

Nathanael's name doesn't appear in any of the lists of the twelve apostles, but there are many who claim he was known as Bartholomew, and that name does appear there. It would be nice to think so. On the other hand, he probably considered it honor enough just to have been on hand that morning at the beach, especially considering the unfortunate remark he'd made long ago about Nazareth.

They sat there around the fire eating their fish with the sun coming up over the water behind them, and they were all so hushed and glad and peaceful that anybody passing by would never have guessed that, not long before, their host had been nailed up on a hill outside the city and left there to die without a friend to his name.

FREDERICK BUECHNER
FROM *PECULIAR TREASURES*

Nathanael saith unto him, Whence knowest thou me? Jesus answered and said unto him, Before that Philip called thee, when thou wast under the fig tree, I saw thee. Nathanael answered and saith unto him, Rabbi, thou art the Son of God; thou art the King of Israel.
John 1:48, 49

Artist Joseph Maniscalco has caught the wonder of two disciples as they struggle to pull an abundant catch into their boat. Jesus, standing on the shore, performed a small miracle by filling their nets.

Jesus Healed Them

I n a world where disease and death were constant companions, where illness and blindness were mysteries, where leprosy and insanity were God's punishment for transgression, many men claimed powers of healing; and sufferers traveled far and wide in search of a miraculous cure.

When word of Jesus' healing miracles began to spread throughout Judea, some dismissed the stories as the same exaggerated and false claims they had heard before. Those who witnessed Jesus' miracles, however, believed He was the great healer the prophets had foretold. He made the blind to see, the lame to walk, the leper to lose his disease with a mere touch of His hand or a simple command from His lips.

The healer Jesus simply asked those who sought healing to believe in Him and no more. Jesus was a healer who offered more than relief from illness and pain; He offered hope.

On the west coast of the Sea of Galilee lies the city of Tiberias. In Jesus' era, the population was almost entirely Gentile; many of the residents had been brought there by force by the city's founder, Herod Antipas, who fought to populate the city with Roman citizens. Only ten miles from Capernaum, the center of Jesus' Galilean ministry, Tiberias nonetheless is never mentioned in the gospel accounts of Jesus' travels. At right is part of the old city wall.

The Master's Touch

"He touched her hand,
   and the fever left her."
He touched her hand
   as He only can,
With the wondrous skill
   of the great Physician,
With the tender touch
   of the Son of Man,
And the fever pain
   in the throbbing temples
Died out with the flush
   on brow and cheek;
And the lips that had been
   so parched and burning
Trembled with thanks
   that she could not speak;
And the eyes, where the fever
   light had faded,
Looked up—by her grateful
   tears made dim;
And she rose and ministered
   to her household—
She rose and ministered unto Him.
"He touched her hand,
   and the fever left her."
O blessed touch of the Man Divine!

AUTHOR UNKNOWN

*They entered into the house of
Simon and Andrew. . . . But
Simon's wife's mother lay sick
of a fever, and anon they tell
him of her. And he came and
took her by the hand, and lifted
her up; and immediately the
fever left her, and she ministered unto them.*
Mark 1:29b–31

Peter's mother-in-law, pictured on page thirty-four in the painting CHRIST HEALING THE MOTHER OF SIMON PETER by J. Bridges, and all those who experienced physical contact with the Lord Jesus found the moment powerful, mysterious, and life changing.

Jesus Christ . . . began to cure sick people by only laying his hand upon them; for God had given him power to heal the sick, and to give sight to the blind, and to do many wonderful and solemn things . . . which are called *"the miracles"* of Christ. . . . For God had given Jesus Christ the power to do such wonders; and he did them, that people might know he was not a common man, and might believe what he taught them, and also believe that God had sent him. And many people, hearing this, and hearing that he cured the sick, did begin to believe in him; and great crowds followed him in the streets and on the roads, wherever he went. . . .

There came to him a man with a dreadful disease called the leprosy. It was common in those times, and those who were ill with it were called lepers. This Leper fell at the feet of Jesus Christ, and said "Lord! If thou wilt, thou canst make me well!" Jesus, always full of compassion, stretched out his hand, and said "I will! Be thou well!" And his disease went away, immediately, and he was cured.

Being followed, wherever he went, by great crowds of people, Jesus went, with his disciples, into a house to rest. While he was sitting inside, some men brought upon a bed a man who was very ill of what is called the Palsy, so that he trembled all over from head to foot, and could neither stand, nor move. But the crowd being all about the door and windows, and they not being able to get near Jesus Christ, these men climbed up to the roof of the house, which was a low one; and through the tiling at the top, let down the bed, with the sick man upon it, into the room where Jesus sat. When he saw him, Jesus, full of pity, said "Arise! Take up thy bed, and go to thine own home!" And the man rose up and went away quite well; blessing him, and thanking God.

There was a Centurion, too, or officer over the Soldiers, who came to him, and said "Lord! My servant lies at home in my house, very ill."

Jesus Christ made answer, "I will come and cure him." But the Centurion said "Lord! I am not worthy that thou shouldst come to my house. Say the word only, and I know he will be cured." Then Jesus Christ, glad that the Centurion believed in him so truly, said "Be it so!" And the servant became well, from that moment.

But of all the people who came to him, none were so full of grief and distress as one man who was Ruler or Magistrate over many people, and he wrung his hands, and cried, and said "Oh Lord, my daughter— my beautiful, good, innocent little girl, is dead. Oh come to her, come to her, and lay thy blessed hand upon here, and I know she will revive, and come to life again, and make me and her mother happy. Oh Lord we love her so, we love her so! And she is dead!"

Jesus Christ went out with him, and so did his disciples and went to his house, where the friends and neighbours were crying in the room where the poor dead little girl lay, and where there was soft music playing; as there used to be, in those days, when people died. Jesus Christ, looking on her, sorrowfully, said—to comfort her poor parents—"She is not dead. She is asleep." Then he commanded the room to be cleared of the people that were in it, and going to the dead child, took her by the hand, and she rose up, quite well, as if she had only been asleep. Oh what a sight it must have been to see her parents clasp her in their arms, and kiss her, and thank God, and Jesus Christ his son, for such great Mercy!

But he was always merciful and tender. And because Jesus did such Good, and taught people how to love God and how to hope to go to Heaven after death, he was called Our Savior.

CHARLES DICKENS
FROM *THE LIFE OF OUR LORD*

While he spake these things unto them, behold, there came a certain ruler, and worshipped him, saying, My daughter is even now dead: but come and lay thy hand upon her, and she shall live. And Jesus arose, and followed him, and so did his disciples. And when Jesus came into the ruler's house, and saw the minstrels and the people making a noise, He said unto them, Give place: for the maid is not dead, but sleepeth. And they laughed him to scorn. But when the people were put forth, he went in, and took her by the hand, and the maid arose. And the fame hereof went abroad into all that land.
Matthew 9:18, 19, 23–26

Capernaum was a community of fishermen, farmers, and merchants on the northwest shore of the Sea of Galilee. No such city exists today in Israel, but scholars believe the modern city of Tell Hum occupies the ground of ancient Capernaum. The synagogue ruins pictured here date from the second or third century A.D. Because it was customary to build new synagogues on the site of the old, it is believed that the Capernaum synagogue in which Jesus taught stood on this site.

Although others told him to
be silent, blind Bartimaeus
insisted in calling out to
Jesus, who recognized the
beggar's genuine faith and
immediately granted him
sight. Jesus' miraculous
power to heal is represented
at right in Carl Heinrich
Bloch's painting THE MAN
BORN BLIND.

Blind Bartimaeus

Blind Bartimaeus at the gates
Of Jericho in darkness waits;
He hears the crowd—he hears a breath
Say, "It is Christ of Nazareth!"
And calls in tones of agony,
"Jesus, have mercy now on me!"

The thronging multitudes increase;
Blind Bartimaeus, hold thy peace!
But still, above the noisy crowd,
The beggar's cry is shrill and loud;
Until they say, "He calleth thee!"
"Fear not, arise, He calleth thee!"

Then saith the Christ, as silent stands
The crowd, "What wilt thou at my hands?"
And he replies, "O give me light!
Rabbi, restore the blind man's sight."
And Jesus answers, "Go in peace,
Thy faith from blindness gives release!"

Ye that have eyes yet cannot see,
In darkness and in misery,
Recall those mighty Voices Three,
"Jesus, have mercy now on me!"
"Fear not, arise, and go in peace!
Thy faith from blindness gives release!"

HENRY WADSWORTH LONGFELLOW
1807–1882

And a certain woman, which had an issue of blood twelve years, And had suffered many things of many physicians, and had spent all that she had, and was nothing bettered, but rather grew worse, When she had heard of Jesus, came in the press behind, and touched his garment. For she said, If I may touch but his clothes, I shall be whole.

Mark 5:25–28

The Touch of Faith

nd his disciples said unto him, Thou seest the multitude thronging thee, and sayest thou, Who touched me?" (Mark 5:31). That is an electrifying question when you realize who asked it, and under what circumstances. You cannot escape the thrill of it—the tingle of excitement that grips you when you think of Christ stopping in response to the touch of a poor nameless woman. . . .

The incident takes place in a city street. It is a narrow twisted street packed with a crowd of gesticulating, excited people, surging past its bazaars and pavement stalls with all the noise and confusion of an eastern market place. . . . They are caught up in the infection of curiosity, and walking along in their very midst, wedged in the tightly packed procession is Someone. . . .

It is His face that will hold your gaze—and will haunt you long after the sun has gone down, and the purple night, cool and starlit, has stilled every noise in the city, while only the Syrian stars wink unsleeping.

One is aware of that face even in such a crowd. Having once seen it, one sees it everywhere, for it is a haunting face—an expression that will not fade . . . eyes whose fires never die out . . . a face that lingers in memory. Farmers were to see it as they followed the swaying plow, and fishermen were to watch it dancing on the sun-flecked water.

This One who walks like a king is named Jesus. They called Him the Nazarene or the Galilean. He called Himself the Son of man. The common people speak of Him softly, with deep affection, such as the shepherds know, who carry the little lambs in their bosoms.

The beggars whisper His name in the streets as they pass, and the children may be heard singing about Him. His name has been breathed in prayer and whispered at night under the stars. He is known to the diseased, the human flotsam and jetsam that shuffles in and out of the towns and drifts hopelessly along the dusty highways of human misery.

His name has trickled down to the streets of forgotten men, has seeped into the shadowed refuges of the unremembered women. It is Jesus of Nazareth . . . whom they are crowding to see. They want to look on His face to see the quality of His expression that seems to promise so much to the weary and the heaven-laden; that look that seems to offer healing of mind and soul and body; forgiveness of sin; another chance—a beginning again.

His look seemed to sing of tomorrow—a new tomorrow—in which there should be no more pain, no more suffering, nor persecution, nor cruelty, nor hunger, nor neglect, nor disillusionments, nor broken promises, nor death.

At the request of one Jairus, a ruler of the synagogue, He is on His way to restore to complete health a little girl. He is on a mission of restoration, and the crowd is following Him in order to see Him perform this miracle. . . .

There is in the crowd another face—the face of a woman. Strange that it should be so noticeable—yet not strange, for it is a face that portrays great depth of human emotion.

There is so much in it—pale, pinched, and wan. Great lines of suffering mar its beauty and sweetness, and even now her lips are drawn in a thin line of agony. The face is streaked with pain. Her body is racked with acute suffering.

Who is she? Well, some say her name is Martha and some say Veronica. Tradition gives her various names, but I cannot tell who she was. It does not matter. Is it not enough that she was a woman in pain? Call her Martha . . . or Mary . . . or Margaret . . . or mother . . . or sister . . . or wife. She is typical of countless cases of endless pain and suffering. For twelve years she had suffered and twelve years is a long time! Her malady seems to have been a pernicious hemorrhage or a form of bleeding cancer. She had gone to many physicians and was none better—but rather worse. She had spent all that she had, and every new day was another hopeless dawn. Every sunset was stained with the blood of her pain.

She is typical of human despair—not only physical despair but spiritual despair as well. For her the world could offer no healing—so she represents all the people who look everywhere for peace of mind and heart—for hope and comfort—and find none. She represents them all—whatever their wants, their fears, their hopes, their pains. . . .

Now this woman had heard of the Great Teacher, of His wonderful works. She had heard the lepers talk and them that had been blind from birth and now had thrown away their sticks, and looked around them with eyes that flashed or filled with tears as they spoke His name.

She had heard what He had done for others. Surely He had power to bring into the haven of health the lost explorers of the vast treasuries of pain! Surely, He had power to lift from the dust of disease the flowers whose stems had been crushed or withered in the mildews of human misery! As this thought burned itself into her mind her faith was curiously stirred as it wrestled in the birth-throes of a great resolve.

It was daring—fantastic, perhaps. Her heart thumped, but it was worth trying. It could only fail, and she was no stranger to failure. There came to the woman the assurance that if she could but touch Him— even only the hem of His garment—she would be healed of her awful malady. Cannot you imagine her nervous reasoning? "Touch Him . . . yes . . . just to touch Him—There would be no harm in that! . . .

"Besides, here is my great chance. He is coming this way; soon He will be gone. Why not touch Him as He passes? . . . It would be

And straightway the fountain of her blood was dried up; and she felt in her body that she was healed of that plague. And Jesus, immediately knowing in himself that virtue had gone out of him, turned him about in the press, and said, Who touched my clothes? And his disciples said unto him, Thou seest the multitude thronging thee, and sayest thou, Who touched me? And he looked round about to see her that had done this thing.
Mark 5:29–32

enough—just to touch the border of His robes. I must touch Him. I must get some of that power."

Thus reasoning, she pushes her way through the crowd and with the pertinacity of despair she struggles in that dense throng, nearer and nearer, pushing and crushing. People get in the way—not knowing her need. Now she is desperate. He must not pass so near and yet so far away. Was she to lose this opportunity? She must touch Him. Now just a little farther. He is drawing nearer. Now she can almost reach Him—another moment—at last just as He passes, she is able to reach out her hand, and with the tip of her finger touch His robe.

It was enough! She had actually touched the Great Doctor! With a trembling finger she had touched Him with the touch of a mighty faith! Like an electric shock there surged back into the shrunken veins, the panting lungs, the withered muscles, and the bloodless flesh, the rich glow of health and vitality. Once again a body had been redeemed and given life.

She had touched Him with secret and trembling haste and thrilled with the change that had come to her; she retreated back into the crowd unnoticed, she thought. No one had noticed her—no one—but Christ! Recognizing the one magnetic touch of faith amid the pressure of the crowd, He stopped and asked that terrific question: "Who touched me?"

The question seemed absurd to those who heard it. Impatiently, brusquely, almost with sarcasm, the disciples asked: "How should we know? There are hundreds of people here—pushing all about you. Look at the crowd—and yet you ask 'Who touched me?'"

But, looking around Him, Christ stood still—His kind, but searching, glance fell at last on the face of the woman who had done it.

His gaze held hers. Something passed between them, and she told Him her story while His eyes were fixed upon her; His eyes gave her confidence. They seemed to promise all that she had desired. Her fear disappeared.

Then He answered her . . . "Daughter, thy faith hath made thee whole. Go in peace . . . and be healed of thy plague."

That is the record. These are the facts. It is a matter of history. She had no money—only faith. She did not meet Him in a house of worship. She met Him on the street. She had no private audience with the Lord. She touched Him in a crowd. She touched Him in faith—in desperate believing faith and He stopped!

The touch of one anonymous woman in a crowd halted the Lord of glory. That is the glorious truth of this incident. She touched Him. So can we.

PETER MARSHALL
FROM *MR. JONES, MEET THE MASTER*

In the painting opposite, *HEALING OF THE WOMAN WITH AN ISSUE OF BLOOD*, the artist James J. Tissot has beautifully depicted the crush of the crowd and the desperation and weakness of the woman in the foreground who could only crawl to touch the hem of the Lord's garment.

The Woman Who Came Behind Him in the Crowd

Near him she stole, rank after rank;
She feared approach too loud;
She touched his garment's hem, and shrank
Back in the sheltering crowd.

A shame-faced gladness thrills her frame:
Her twelve years' fainting prayer
Is heard at last! She is the same
As other women there!

She hears his voice. He looks about,
Ah! is it kind or good
To drag her secret sorrow out
Before that multitude?

The eyes of the men she dares not meet—
On her they straight must fall!
Forward she sped, and at his feet
Fell down, and told him all.

To the one refuge she had flown,
The Godhead's burning flame!
Of all earth's women she alone
Hears there the tenderest name!

"Daughter," he said, "be of good cheer;
Thy faith hath made thee whole."
With plenteous love, not healing mere,
He comforteth her soul.

GEORGE MACDONALD
1824–1905

Christ's miraculous healings were popular subjects for artists throughout the ages. This painting, HEALING THE WOMAN WITH THE ISSUE OF BLOOD, by Venetian artist Paolo Veronese shows the renown of Christ and His disciples and the great courage that the woman must have had just to reach for His hem.

Medical Practices in Israel

And if there be in the bald head, or bald forehead, a white reddish sore; it is a leprosy sprung up in his bald head, or his bald forehead. Then the priest shall look upon it: and, behold, if the rising of the sore be white reddish in his bald head . . . He is a leprous man, he is unclean: the priest shall pronounce him utterly unclean. . . . his clothes shall be rent, and his head bare, and he shall put a covering upon his upper lip, and shall cry, Unclean, unclean.

Leviticus 13:42–45

Traditionally, the Jews viewed illness as punishment for disobedience of God's law; therefore, the sick turned to prayer and sacrifice for healing. The few physicians in practice were faced with deadly diseases, poor sanitation, and limited understanding of human physiology. They could offer balms, oils, healing waters, wines, and herbs, such as the wine mixed with myrrh, an ineffective painkiller, offered to Jesus on the cross. But to the seriously ill, they could offer little real hope.

The River Jordan flows from the foot of the 9,232-foot Mount Hermon southward into the Sea of Galilee and then on to its final destination, the Dead Sea. Between the Sea of Galilee and the Dead Sea are only sixty-five miles of territory, but the Jordan winds tortuously for two hundred miles to cover that ground. It is in most places a rough, quick-moving river, but gentle shallows do exist; it was in some of these shallows that John the Baptist conducted his ministry, baptizing, among others, Jesus of Nazareth. Pictured above is the Jordan River near Tel Beit Zaida in Israel.

Today, *leprosy* refers to a skin disease that is rare and controllable, if not curable. In the Bible, however, leprosy, which was diagnosed by the priests, comprised any skin disease or discoloration, and the worst cases were incurable lifelong maladies. The law of Moses concerning two colors of skin was the same as that which forbade plowing with two types of beasts or raising two different crops in the same field; and the law required that lepers be isolated as religiously unclean. Those lepers whom Jesus touched were offered not only physical relief, but spiritual healing as well.

Now there is at Jerusalem by the sheep market a pool, which is called in the Hebrew tongue Bethesda. . . . In these lay a great multitude of impotent folk, of blind, halt, withered, waiting for the moving of the water. For an angel went down at a certain season into the pool, and troubled the water: whosoever then first after the troubling of the water stepped in was made whole of whatever disease he had.

John 5:2–4

The healing pool of Bethesda lay in the northeastern part of Jerusalem. Tradition held that angels regularly came down and touched the pool's waters and that those who entered the water after the angels' descent would be cured of their disease. Countless men and women sought a miracle at Bethesda. The Book of John tells of one hopeful man who had been lame for thirty-eight years before traveling to Bethesda for a cure. Once at the pool, however, the man was too weak to crawl to the water and lay helpless only a short distance away. But this was the day Jesus came; and the lame man was healed, not by the waters of Bethesda, but by the Master's command.

The faithful pray at the only wall remaining of Herod's temple, the West or Wailing Wall. During Jesus' time, prayer for healing was the only hope available for the ill or lame.

In the time of Christ, stories abounded of "holy men" with miraculous powers who, through chanting, ritual, and prayers, healed the sick, lame, and insane. Jesus, however, used no chants or magic. By only a touch or a word, the lame, blind, and leprous were healed. Something else set Jesus apart from other healers: He did not want the healing to overshadow His message. Those He touched, believed; many of those who witnessed, believed; it was faith, not fame, that Jesus sought in healing.

At left are the ruins of the healing pool of Bethesda, situated in the northeastern part of Jerusalem. Archaeologists have uncovered two pools; the one shown is behind the Church of Saint Anna in the old city of Jerusalem. The man who was lame for thirty-eight years came to be healed by the waters at the pool, but instead he was healed by the word of Jesus.

The Ten Lepers

Not white and shining like an ardent flame,
Not like thy mother and the saints in bliss,
But white from head to foot I bear my blame,
White as the leper is.

Unclean! unclean! But thou canst make me clean:
Yet if thou clean'st me, Lord, see that I be
Like that one grateful leper of the ten
Who ran back praising thee.

But if I must forget, take back thy word;
Be I unclean again but not ingrate.
Before I shall forget thee, keep me, Lord,
A sick man at thy gate.

KATHARINE TYNAN HINKSON
1861–1931

*There met him ten men that
were lepers, which stood afar off:
And they lifted up their voices,
and said, Jesus, Master, have
mercy on us. And when he saw
them, he said unto them, Go
shew yourselves unto the priests.
And it came to pass, that, as
they went, they were cleansed.
And one of them, when he saw
that he was healed, turned back,
and with a loud voice glorified
God, And fell down on his face
at his feet, giving him thanks.*
Luke 17:12b–16a

Although Jesus healed ten lepers on His way to
Jerusalem, only one returned to thank Him and
received Jesus' praise for his faith. In this painting by
James J. Tissot entitled *HEALING OF THE TEN LEPERS*, Jesus
reaches out to the lepers, offering them relief of body
and soul.

Now when the sun was setting, all they that had any sick with divers diseases brought them unto him; and he laid his hands on every one of them, and healed them. And devils also came out of many, crying out, and saying, Thou art Christ the Son of God. And he rebuking them suffered them not to speak: for they knew that he was Christ. And when it was day, he departed and went into a desert place: and the people sought him, and came unto him, and stayed him, that he should not depart from them.
Luke 4:40-42

The photograph opposite is of a waterfall in the Banias area of the Golan in Israel. The word *Banias* comes from the Roman term meaning bath.

At Even, When the Sun Was Set

At even, when the sun was set,
The sick, O Lord, around Thee lay;
O in what divers pains they met!
O with what joy they went away!

Once more 'tis eventide, and we,
Oppressed with various ills, draw near;
What if Thy form we cannot see,
We know and feel that Thou art here.

O Savior Christ, our woes dispel;
For some are sick, and some are sad,
And some have never loved Thee well,
And some have lost the love they had;

And some are pressed with worldly care,
And some are tried with sinful doubt;
And some such grievous passions tear,
That only Thou canst cast them out;

And some have found the world is vain,
Yet from the world they break not free;
And some have friends who give them pain,
Yet have not sought a Friend in Thee;

And none, O Lord, have perfect rest,
For none are wholly free from sin;
And they who fain would serve Thee best
Are conscious most of wrong within.

O Savior Christ, Thou too art Man;
Thou hast been troubled, tempted, tried;
Thy kind but searching glance can scan
The very wounds that shame would hide;

Thy touch has still its ancient power;
No word from Thee can fruitless fall;
Hear, in this solemn evening hour,
And in Thy mercy heal us all.

HENRY TWELLS
1823–1900

The Leper

"Room for the leper! Room!" And, as he came,
The cry passed on—"Room for the leper! Room!"
And aside they stood—
Matron, and child, and pitiless manhood—all
Who met him on his way—and let him pass.
And onward through the open gate he came,
A leper, with the ashes on his brow,
Sackcloth about his loins, and on his lip
A covering, stepping painfully and slow,
And with a difficult utterance, like one
Whose heart is with an iron nerve put down,
Crying, "Unclean! Unclean!"
—Helon was a leper!

Day was breaking,
When at the altar of the temple stood
The holy priest of God. The incense lamp
Burn'd with a struggling light, and a low chant
Swell'd through the hollow arches of the roof
Like an articulate wail, and there, alone,
Wasted to ghastly thinness, Helon knelt.
The echoes of the melancholy strain
Died in the distant aisles, and he rose up,
Struggling with weakness, and bow'd down his head
Unto the sprinkled ashes, and put off
His costly raiment for the leper's garb:
And with the sackcloth round him, and his lip
Hid in a loathsome covering, stood still,
Waiting to hear his doom:—

Depart! Depart, O child
Of Israel, from the temple of thy God!
For He has smote thee with His chastening rod;
And to the desert-wild,
From all thou lov'st away, thy feet must flee,
That from thy plague His people may be free.

Depart! and come not near
The busy mart, the crowded city, more;
Nor set thy foot a human threshold o'er;
And stay thou not to hear
Voices that call thee in the way; and fly

From all who in the wilderness pass by.
Wet not thy burning lip
In streams that to a human dwelling glide;
Nor rest thee where the covert fountains hide;
Nor kneel thee down to dip
The water where the pilgrim bends to drink,
By desert well or river's grassy brink;

And pass thou not between
The weary traveller and the cooling breeze;
And lie not down to sleep beneath the trees
Where human tracks are seen;
Nor milk the goat that browseth on the plain,
Nor pluck the standing corn, or yellow grain.

And now, depart! and when
Thy heart is heavy, and thine eyes are dim,
Lift up thy prayer beseechingly to Him
Who, from the tribes of men,
Selected thee to feel His chastening rod,
Depart! O Leper, and forget not God!

And he went forth—alone! not one of all
The many whom he loved, nor she whose name
Was woven in the fibres of the heart
Breaking within him now, to come and speak
Comfort unto him. Yea—he went his way,
Sick, and heartbroken, and alone—to die!
For God had cursed the leper!

It was noon,
And Helon knelt beside a stagnant pool
In the lone wilderness, and bathed his brow,
Hot with the burning leprosy, and touched
The loathsome water to his fever'd lips,
Praying that he might be so blest—to die!

Footsteps approach'd, and with no strength to flee,
He drew the covering closer on his lip,
Crying, "Unclean! Unclean!" and in the folds
Of the coarse sackcloth shrouding up his face,
He fell upon the earth till they should pass.

*And it came to pass,
when he was in a cer-
tain city, behold a man
full of leprosy: who
seeing Jesus fell on his
face, and besought him,
saying, Lord, if thou
wilt, thou canst make
me clean. And he put
forth his hand, and
touched him, saying, I
will: be thou clean. And
immediately the leprosy
departed from him.*
Luke 5:12, 13

Nearer the Stranger came, and bending o'er
The leper's prostrate form, pronounced his name—
"Helon!" The voice was like the master-tone
Of a rich instrument—most strangely sweet;
And the dull pulses of disease awoke,
And for a moment beat beneath the hot
And leprous scales with a restoring thrill.
"Helon! arise!" and he forgot his curse,
And rose and stood before Him.
Love and awe
Mingled in the regard of Helon's eye
As he beheld the Stranger. He was not
In costly raiment clad, nor on His brow
The symbol of a princely lineage wore;
No followers at His back, nor in His hand
Buckler, or sword, or spear—yet in His mien
Command sat throned serene, and if He smiled,
A kingly condescension graced His lips,
The lion would have crouch'd to in his lair.

His garb was simple, and His sandals worn;
His stature modell'd with a perfect grace;
His countenance, the impress of a God,
Touch'd with the open innocence of a child;
His eye was blue and calm, as is the sky
In the serenest noon; His hair unshorn
Fell to His shoulders; and his curling beard
The fullness of perfected manhood bore.

He looked on Helon earnestly awhile,
As if His heart were moved, and stooping down,
He took a little water in His hand,
And laved the sufferer's brow, and said, "Be clean,"
And lo! the scales fell from him, and his blood
Coursed with delicious coolness through his veins,
And his dry palms grew moist, and his lips
The dewy softness of an infant's stole,
His leprosy was cleansed, and he fell down
Prostrate at Jesus' feet and worshipped Him.

NATHANIEL PARKER WILLIS
1806–1867

*And he charged him to
tell no man: but go, and
shew thyself to the
priest, and offer for thy
cleansing, according as
Moses commanded, for
a testimony unto them.
But so much the more
went there a fame
abroad of him: and
great multitudes came
together to hear, and to
be healed by him of
their infirmities. And he
withdrew himself into
the wilderness, and
prayed.*
Luke 5:14–16

HEALING THE LEPER AT CAPERNAUM
by James J. Tissot illustrates
the hope that compelled the
sick to seek out Christ as
well as the gentleness of
Jesus as He talks with a child.
Once while Jesus was at
Capernaum, the crowd was
so huge and so eager to
meet Christ that a paralytic
man was lowered down
through the roof on his cot
for Jesus to heal.

Religion and Doctrine

He stood before the Sanhedrim;
The scowling rabbis gazed at him;
He recked not of their praise or blame;
There was no fear, there was no shame
For one upon whose dazzled eyes
The whole world poured its vast surprise.
The opened heaven was far too near,
His first day's light too sweet and clear,
To let him waste his new-gained ken
On the hate-clouded face of men.

But still they questioned, Who art thou?
What hast thou been? What art thou now?
Thou art not he who yesterday
Sat here and begged beside the way,
For he was blind.

And I am he;
For I was blind, but now I see.

He told the story o'er and o'er;
It was his full heart's only lore;
A prophet on the Sabbath day
Had touched his sightless eyes with clay,
And made him see, who had been blind.
Their words passed by him on the wind

Which raves and howls, but cannot shock
The hundred-fathom-rooted rock.
Their threats and fury all went wide;
They could not touch his Hebrew pride;
Their sneers at Jesus and his band,
Nameless and homeless in the land,
Their boasts of Moses and his Lord,
All could not change him by one word.

I know not what this man may be,
Sinner or saint; but as for me,
One thing I know, that I am he
Who once was blind, and now I see.

They were all doctors of renown,
The great men of a famous town,
With deep brows, wrinkled, broad and wise,
Beneath their wide phylacteries;
The wisdom of the East was theirs,
And honor crowned their silver hairs;
The man they jeered and laughed to scorn
Was unlearned, poor, and humbly born;
But he knew better far than they
What came to him that Sabbath day;
And what the Christ had done for him,
He knew, and not the Sanhedrim.

JOHN HAY
1838–1905

In John 9:1–41, Jesus heals a blind man on the
Sabbath day, an act that violated the law and for
which the Pharisees called Him a heretic. But
Jesus was more concerned with relieving the
man's suffering than in the letter of the law. At
left is Martines Roerbye's painting CHRIST
HEALING THE BLIND.

The Great Physician

From Thee all skill and science flow,
All pity, care, and love,
All calm and courage, faith and hope;
Oh, pour them from above.

And part them, Lord, to each and all,
As each and all shall need,
To rise like incense, each to Thee,
In noble thought and deed.

And hasten, Lord, that perfect day
When pain and death shall cease,
And Thy just rule shall fill the earth
With health and light and peace.

CHARLES KINGSLEY
1819–1875

*When the even was come, they
brought unto him many that were
possessed with devils: and he cast out
the spirits with his word, and healed
all that were sick.*
Matthew 8:16

The painting JESUS HEALING THE LAME AND THE BLIND by
James J. Tissot magnificently illustrates the crowds that
must have come from all over the country once news of
the Lord's healing spread.

Jesus Taught Them

Jesus began His ministry in a society that believed the highest authority was the Law of Moses—the Ten Commandments and the rules of the first five books of the Old Testament. The most respected teachers were those rabbis who knew this law by heart, and who scrupulously applied it to every facet of their lives.

Jesus, however, was a teacher unlike any other. He rebuked the scholars whose obsession with the letter of the law made them slaves to ritual and blind to the spirit of the law. His principal method of teaching was the ancient, time-honored method of storytelling. These stories, or parables, conveyed deep theological truths in short, everyday speech. Even the simple and unlearned people understood what Jesus meant when He told of the prodigal son or the pearl of great price.

Jesus urged the faithful to follow God's law, not out of fear of reprisal or punishment, but out of a deep love of the Lord. He was a teacher from whom even the most studied scholars could learn, a teacher whose authority was not of this earth, but truly divine.

Pictured at right is a shallow shoreline of the Sea of Galilee, a modern name for this lake below sea level. On maps from Old Testament times it was called Lake of Chinnereth, and later, Lake Gennesaret (Luke 5:1) and then Sea of Tiberias (John 6:1).

And he opened his
mouth, and taught
them, saying,
Blessed are the poor in
spirit: for theirs is the
kingdom of heaven.
Blessed are they that
mourn: for they shall
be comforted.
Blessed are the meek:
for they shall inherit
the earth.
Blessed are they which
do hunger and thirst
after righteousness: for
they shall be filled.
Blessed are the merciful:
for they shall
obtain mercy.
Matthew 5:2–7

I n the Greek there is no verb in any of the Beatitudes, which means that the Beatitudes are not statements, but exclamations. They reproduce in Greek a form of expression which is very common in Hebrew, especially in the Psalms. Hebrew has an exclamatory word *ashere,* which means: "O the bliss of . . ." So the Psalmist says: "O the bliss of the man who walks not in the counsel of the ungodly . . . but whose delight is in the law of the Lord". . . . (Psalm 1:1) This is the form of expression which each of the Beatitudes represents; each of them is an exclamation beginning: "O the bliss of . . . !" That is to say that the Beatitudes are not promises of future happiness; they are congratulations on present bliss. They are not statements and prophecies of what is one day going to happen to the Christian in some other world; they are affirmations of the bliss into which the Christian can enter even here and now. That is not to say that this bliss will not reach its perfection and its completion, when some day the Christian enters into the nearer presence of his Lord; but it is to say that even here and now the foretaste and the experience of that bliss is meant to be part of the Christian life. . . .

The promised bliss is nothing less than the blessedness of God. Through Jesus Christ, the Christian comes to share in the very life of God. The bliss of the Beatitudes is another expression of what John calls Eternal Life. Eternal Life is *zoe aionios;* in Greek there is only one person in the universe to whom the word *aionios* may properly be applied, and that person is God. Eternal Life is nothing less than the life of God, and it is a share in that life that Jesus Christ offers to men.

If that is so, it means that the Christian bliss is independent of outward circumstances. . . . It is independent of all the chances and the changes of life. That, indeed, is why happiness is not a good name for it. Happiness has in it the root *hap,* which means *chance;* and happiness is something which is dependent on the chances and alterations of this life; but the Christian bliss is the bliss of the life of God, and is, therefore, the joy that no man can take from us.

If this Christian bliss is the bliss of the blessedness of God, we will not be surprised to find that it completely reverses the world's standards. O the bliss of the poor! O the bliss of the sorrowful! O the bliss of the hungry and thirsty! O the bliss of the persecuted! These are startling contradictions of the world's standards; these are sayings which no man could hear for the first time without a shock of amazement. . . . But when we look at the Beatitudes carefully, we see that they are very closely interwoven into a threefold bliss.

There is the bliss which comes when a man recognizes his deepest need, and discovers where that need can be supplied. There can be three periods in any life. There can be the period when a man lives placidly and in a kind of drab mediocrity, because he knows nothing better. There can be a period of restless dissatisfaction and even of mental agony, when something makes him realize that there is an unidentified something missing in his life. And there can be the period into which there enters a new joy and a new depth into life, because a man has found that wherein his newly discovered need can be supplied. So there is bliss for the man who discovers his own poverty, for the man who becomes sorrowfully aware of his own sin, and for the man who hungers and thirsts for a righteousness which he knows is not in him.

There is the bliss of living the Christian life. There is the bliss which comes in living in mercy, in meekness, in purity of heart, and in the making of peace. These were the qualities of Jesus Christ himself, and he who follows in the steps of Jesus Christ knows the joy of the Christian life.

There is the bliss of suffering for Jesus Christ. Long ago Plato said that the good man will always choose to suffer wrong rather than to do wrong. Herein is the bliss of loyalty, and there is the deepest of all satisfactions in loyalty, even when loyalty costs all that a man has to give.

On the face of it, it might look as if the Beatitudes looked for bliss all in the wrong places; but when we think again we can see that the way of the Beatitudes is the only way to bliss.

WILLIAM BARCLAY
FROM *THE PLAIN MAN LOOKS AT THE BEATITUDES*

Blessed are the pure in heart: for they shall see God.
Blessed are the peacemakers: for they shall be called the children of God.
Blessed are they which are persecuted for righteousness' sake: for theirs is the kingdom of heaven.
Blessed are ye, when men shall revile you, and persecute you, and shall say all manner of evil against you falsely, for my sake.
Rejoice, and be exceeding glad: for great is your reward in heaven: for so persecuted they the prophets which were before you.
Matthew 5:8–12

Richard Hook's painting *JESUS WASHING THE DISCIPLES' FEET* illustrates the passage in John 13:4, 5: "He riseth from supper, and laid aside his garments; and took a towel, and girded himself. After that he poureth water into a basin, and began to wash the disciples' feet, and to wipe them with the towel wherewith he was girded." In Jesus' day, it was generally a servant who washed his master's feet. Thus were the apostles astonished when, after the Last Supper, Jesus knelt to wash the feet of each of them. For Jesus, however, this was a symbolic gesture meant to emphasize what He had told them many times: "the Son of man came not to be ministered unto, but to minister" (Matthew 20:28).

The Sermon on the Mount

hink not that I am come to destroy the law, or the prophets: I am not come to destroy, but to fulfil. For verily I say unto you, Till heaven and earth pass, one jot or one tittle shall in no wise pass from the law, till all be fulfilled. Whosoever therefore shall break one of these least commandments, and shall teach men so, he shall be called the least in the kingdom of heaven: but whosoever shall do and teach them, the same shall be called great in the kingdom of heaven. For I say unto you, That except your righteousness shall exceed the righteousness of the scribes and Pharisees, ye shall in no case enter into the kingdom of heaven.

Ye have heard that it hath been said, An eye for an eye, and a tooth for a tooth: But I say unto you, That ye resist not evil: but whosoever shall smite thee on thy right cheek, turn to him the other also. And if any man will sue thee at the law, and take away thy coat, let him have thy cloak also. And whosoever shall compel thee to go a mile, go with him twain. Give to him that asketh thee, and from him that would borrow of thee turn not thou away.

Ye have heard that it hath been said, Thou shalt love thy neighbour, and hate thine enemy. But I say unto you, Love your enemies, bless them that curse you, do good to them that hate you, and pray for them which despitefully use you, and persecute you;

For if ye love them which love you, what reward have ye? do not even the publicans the same? And if ye salute your brethren only, what do ye more than others? do not even the publicans so? Be ye therefore perfect, even as your Father which is in heaven is perfect.

Take heed that ye do not your alms before men, to be seen of them: otherwise ye have no reward of your Father which is in heaven. Therefore when thou doest thine alms, do not sound a trumpet before thee, as the hypocrites do in the synagogues and in the streets, that they may have glory of men. Verily I say unto you, They have their reward.

But when thou doest alms, let not thy left hand know what thy right hand doeth: That thine alms may be in secret: and thy Father which seeth in secret himself shall reward thee openly.

And when thou prayest, thou shalt not be as the hypocrites are: for they love to pray standing in the synagogues and in the corners of the streets, that they may be seen of men. Verily I say unto you, They have their reward.

After this manner therefore pray ye: Our Father which art in heaven, Hallowed be thy name. Thy kingdom come. Thy will be done in earth, as it is in heaven. Give us this day our daily bread. And forgive us our debts, as we forgive our debtors. And lead us not into temptation, but

Jesus' audience for the Sermon on the Mount was His disciples, including the twelve apostles and others who had accepted Him as the Messiah. The sermon suggests, essentially, the new life His followers should lead and their relationship to each other and to God. Christ's words offer a model of life for His disciples and give a concise description of His doctrine of brotherly love, which replaced the laws of Moses.

deliver us from evil: For thine is the kingdom, and the power, and the glory, for ever. Amen.

Moreover when ye fast, be not, as the hypocrites, of a sad countenance: for they disfigure their faces, that they may appear unto men to fast. Verily I say unto you, They have their reward. But thou, when thou fastest, anoint thine head, and wash thy face; That thou appear not unto men to fast, but unto thy Father which is in secret: and thy Father, which seeth in secret, shall reward thee openly.

Lay not up for yourselves treasures upon earth, where moth and rust doth corrupt, and where thieves break through and steal: But lay up for yourselves treasures in heaven, where neither moth nor rust doth corrupt, and where thieves do not break through nor steal: For where your treasure is, there will your heart be also.

The light of the body is the eye: if therefore thine eye be single, thy whole body shall be full of light. But if thine eye be evil, thy whole body shall be full of darkness. If therefore the light that is in thee be darkness, how great is that darkness!

No man can serve two masters: for either he will hate the one, and love the other; or else he will hold to the one, and despise the other. Ye cannot serve God and mammon.

Therefore I say unto you, Take no thought for your life, what ye shall eat, or what ye shall drink; nor yet for your body, what ye shall put on. Is not the life more than meat, and the body than raiment? Behold the fowls of the air: for they sow not, neither do they reap, nor gather into barns; yet your heavenly Father feedeth them. Are ye not much better than they?

Which of you by taking thought can add one cubit unto his stature? And why take ye thought for raiment? Consider the lilies of the field, how they grow; they toil not, neither do they spin: And yet I say unto you, That even Solomon in all his glory was not arrayed like one of these. Wherefore, if God so clothe the grass of the field, which to day is, and to morrow is cast into the oven, shall he not much more clothe you, O ye of little faith?

Therefore take no thought, saying, What shall we eat? or, What shall we drink? or, Wherewithal shall we be clothed? . . . for your heavenly Father knoweth that ye have need of all these things. But seek ye first the kingdom of God, and his righteousness; and all these things shall be added unto you.

Judge not, that ye be not judged. For with what judgment ye judge, ye shall be judged: and with what measure ye mete, it shall be measured to you again.

And why beholdest thou the mote that is in thy brother's eye, but considerest not the beam that is in thine own eye? Or how wilt thou say to thy brother, Let me pull out the mote out of thine eye; and, behold, a beam is in thine own eye? Thou hypocrite, first cast out the beam out of thine own eye; and then shalt thou see clearly to cast out the mote out of thy brother's eye.

Give not that which is holy unto the dogs, neither cast ye your pearls before swine, lest they trample them under their feet, and turn again and rend you. Ask, and it shall be given you; seek, and ye shall find; knock, and it shall be opened unto you: For every one that asketh receiveth; and he that seeketh findeth; and to him that knocketh it shall be opened.

Or what man is there of you, whom if his son ask bread, will he give him a stone? Or if he ask a fish, will he give him a serpent? If ye then, being evil, know how to give good gifts unto your children, how much more shall your Father which is in heaven give good things to them that ask him?

Therefore all things whatsoever ye would that men should do to you, do ye even so to them: for this is the law and the prophets.

Enter ye in at the strait gate: for wide is the gate, and broad is the way, that leadeth to destruction, and many there be which go in thereat: Because strait is the gate, and narrow is the way, which leadeth unto life, and few there be that find it.

Beware of false prophets, which come to you in sheep's clothing, but inwardly they are ravening wolves. Ye shall know them by their fruits. Do men gather grapes of thorns, or figs of thistles? Even so every good tree bringeth forth good fruit; but a corrupt tree bringeth forth evil fruit.

A good tree cannot bring forth evil fruit, neither can a corrupt tree bring forth good fruit. Every tree that bringeth not forth good fruit is hewn down, and cast into the fire. Wherefore by their fruits ye shall know them.

Not every one that saith unto me, Lord, Lord, shall enter into the kingdom of heaven; but he that doeth the will of my Father which is in heaven. Many will say to me in that day, Lord, Lord, have we not prophesied in thy name? and in thy name have cast out devils? and in thy name done many wonderful works? And then will I profess unto them, I never knew you: depart from me, ye that work iniquity. Therefore whosoever heareth these sayings of mine, and doeth them, I will liken him unto a wise man, which built his house upon a rock: And the rain descended, and the floods came, and the winds blew, and beat upon that house; and it fell not: for it was founded upon a rock.

And every one that heareth these sayings of mine, and doeth them not, shall be likened unto a foolish man, which built his house upon the sand: And the rain descended, and the floods came, and the winds blew, and beat upon that house; and it fell: and great was the fall of it. And it came to pass, when Jesus had ended these sayings, the people were astonished at his doctrine: For he taught them as one having authority, and not as the scribes.

MATTHEW 5:17–20, 38–44; 46–48; 6:1–5, 9–13, 16–33; 7:1–29

A new commandment I give unto you, That ye love one another; as I have loved you, that ye also love one another. By this shall all men know that ye are my disciples, if ye have love one to another.
John 13:34, 35

Progress

The Master stood upon the Mount and taught.
He saw a fire in His disciples' eyes.
"The old Law," they said, "is wholly come to nought;
   Behold the new world rise!"

"Was it," the Lord then said, "with scorn ye saw
The old Law observed by Scribes and Pharisees?
I say unto you, see ye keep that Law
   More faithfully than these.

"Too hasty heads for ordering worlds, alas!
Think not that I to annul the Law have will'd.
No jot, no tittle, from the Law shall pass,
   Till all shall be fulfill'd."

So Christ said eighteen hundred years ago.
And what then shall be said to those today
Who cry aloud to lay the world low
   To clear the new world's way?

MATTHEW ARNOLD
1822–1888

Pictured at left is one of the many cone-shaped peaks of the Upper Golan. Ancient volcanoes, now extinct, dot the landscape; and centuries of eruptions left breathtaking views in the Upper Golan.

Sisters

Now it came to pass, as they went, that he entered into a certain village: and a certain woman named Martha received him into her house. And she had a sister called Mary, which also sat at Jesus' feet, and heard his word. But Martha was cumbered about much serving, and came to him, and said, Lord, dost thou not care that my sister hath left me to serve alone? bid her therefore that she help me.
Luke 10:38–40

ary's loveliness was twin sister to the dawn. She took the road to the village well, and as she walked, Life sang in her heart. Life—she saw it all about her—in the sun, whose strong hands pushed the mist aside and clutched the little white houses standing in huddled groups along the road, and in the very road itself stretching so comfortably before her.

Life—she felt it within her—surging up in her healthy young body, filling her with complete and unshadowed happiness. Life was so splendid a thing! Did it not hold Martha, and Lazarus, and Jesus, their Friend, who even now would be taking the road to Bethany that He might break bread with them at sundown?

As she pondered these things she lifted her face with a little gesture of expectancy, and, as though she had received a command, she stood perfectly still, poised, and attentive. Soon a smile of welcome illumined her face. They had come—the great unseen wings! She felt their gentle touch upon her cheeks. Always, when she thought of the Master and His Kingdom, they came. Sometimes they flew past, brushing against her lightly and quickly, leaving her filled with a great buoyancy, a great radiance of spirit, but at other times, when she was tired, when in the early evening she sat in the doorway and watched the stars, they folded and upheld her and filled her with a great peace.

She had never spoken about them to Martha. Dear, practical Martha would not understand. But the Master—*He* would understand. Very shyly she had told Him. "It is as the wings of a dove, covered with silver, and her pinions of yellow gold," He had answered her, quoting the words of the Sweet Singer of Israel. "God has gifted you with the sense of His presence."

This morning Mary felt their touch more vividly than ever, and her walk to the village well became a pilgrimage to the Source of Life. . . .

Noon came out of the dawn. Yet Mary lingered. . . . Time slipped by unheeded, *and Martha waited.*

When at last Mary lifted the latch of her door, the crisp fragrance of freshly baked loaves silently reproached her tardiness. She smiled ruefully. "I'm so sorry; I forgot it was our day to use the public oven." Mary put her arms around Martha. "But life's so big, dear, and, after all, tasks are so little—like ants, hundreds and hundreds of them, one after another, in a long line from morning until night. Oh, Martha, you ought to step over them once in a while—really you ought—and just forget them, the way I do. But you're tired, dear. Go and rest now, and don't worry about preparing the evening meal, just leave it all to me."

Martha smiled dubiously and patted her younger sister in much the same manner as one pets a charming but willful child.

With the first shadows of evening, Mary stood in the doorway, watching for Jesus. It was not long before she saw Him coming along the road. . . . Mary felt a sudden sense of awe. This Man, in whom Life was so vital, so unfettered and free, this great Man with the simple, courteous manners, this Poet of a Kingdom that lay hidden within the human heart, was Lazarus' Friend and Martha's Friend, and hers! . . .

Her task lay unheeded, her resolution forgotten; and Mary sat in the doorway, talking with the Master. . . .

"The wings of a dove—have you felt them today?"

"Yes; they seemed nearer than ever before. But how did You know?"

"The story of their coming is written in your eyes."

Mary and Jesus talked on and on. Busy Martha caught the hum of their voices. Now and then, passing the doorway as she went about her tasks, her eyes grew wistful. A whole radiant world lay open to them that somehow was locked and barred to her. She tried to enter in. Could it be that she was exiled because of some subtle difference between herself and Mary? The thought pressed upon her like a dull pain.

The ache in her heart became unbearable. "Master, Master," she said, and her voice was almost a sob, "don't you care that I do all the work alone? Tell Mary to come in and help me."

Mary was startled. Martha's words fell like stones into the quiet pool of her thinking, inopportunely recalling her promise. She was about to answer Martha, to make the usual excuses, when Jesus said, His voice full of compassion: "Martha, you are troubled with many things. Mary has chosen the better part, that shall not be taken from her."

Instantly the cloud that crossed Mary's eyes gave way to an expression of relief. "That's just what I keep telling Martha. Why, if I always remembered to do the things Martha says need to be done, I would be stirring up such a noisy business, clattering pots and swishing brooms, that the beautiful wings would fly by, ever so softly, far off, in some quiet place on a little pathway, or a hillside open to the sky.

Jesus laughed. "Yes, Mary, you have chosen the better part, but there is only one way to keep it."

"How?"

"I need not tell you, for you already know."

Mary scanned His face, that of a seer and a poet; then she looked at His hands, strong and brown from having worked . . . in the little carpenter shop in Nazareth; and she caught a glimpse of the working methods of Life, ever creating through dreams, and dreaming through deeds. "I believe I understand now," she said. "They are sisters, not strangers."

"Who?"

"Being and doing," she said, then rose and went in.

ELEANOR B. STOCK

And Jesus answered and said unto her, Martha, Martha, thou art careful and troubled about many things: But one thing is needful: and Mary hath chosen that good part, which shall not be taken away from her.
Luke 10:41, 42

Mary and Martha

Martha with joy received her blessed Lord;
Her Lord she welcomes, feasts, and entertains:
Mary sat silent; hears, but speaks no word;
Martha takes all, and Mary takes no pains:
Mary's to hear; to feast him Martha's care is;
Now which is greater, Martha's love, or Mary's?

Martha is full of trouble, to prepare;
Martha respects his good beyond her own:
Mary sits ill at ease, and takes no care;
Mary desires to please herself, alone:
The pleasure is Mary's; Martha's all the care is;
Now which is greater, Martha's love, or Mary's?

'Tis true, our blessed Lord was Martha's guest;
Mary was his, and in his feast delighted:
Now which hath greater reason to love best,
The bountiful inviter, or the invited?
Sure, both loved well; but Mary was the debtor,
And therefore should, in reason, love the better.

FRANCIS QUARLES
1592–1644

Not all of Jesus' lessons were taught in the synagogue, through parables, or with the drama of miracles. Jesus, the teacher, touched many lives in quiet ways. Such was the case with the sisters Martha and Mary, who learned by Jesus' gentle words that both the active Martha and the more contemplative Mary were true children of God. At left, the classic painting CHRIST IN THE HOUSE OF MARTHA AND MARY by Jan Vermeer offers a seventeenth-century Dutchman's artistic view.

The Prodigal Son

Young man—Young man—
Your arm's too short to box with God.

But Jesus spake in a parable, and he said:
A certain man had two sons.
Jesus didn't give this man a name,
But his name is God Almighty.
And Jesus didn't call these sons by name,
But ev'ry young man,
Ev'rywhere,
Is one of these two sons.

And the younger son said to his father,
He said: Father, divide up the property,
And give me my portion now.
And the father with tears in his eyes said: Son,
Don't leave your father's house.
But the boy was stubborn in his head,
And haughty in his heart,
And he took his share of his father's goods,
And went into a far-off country.

There comes a time, there comes a time
When ev'ry young man looks out from his father's house,
Longing for that far-off country.

And the young man journeyed on his way,
And he said to himself as he traveled along:
This sure is an easy road,
Nothing like the rough furrows behind my father's plow.

Young man—Young man—
Smooth and easy is the road
That leads to hell and destruction.
Downgrade all the way,
The further you travel, the faster you go.
No need to trudge and sweat and toil,
Just slip and slide and slip and slide
Till you bang up against hell's iron gate.

And the younger son kept traveling along,
Till at nighttime he came to a city.

And the city was bright in the nighttime like day,
The streets all crowded with people,
Brass bands and string bands a-playing,
And ev'rywhere the young man turned
There was singing and laughing and dancing.
And he stopped a passerby and he said:
Tell me what city is this?
And the passerby laughed and said: Don't you know?
This is Babylon, Babylon,
That great city of Babylon.
Come on, my friend, and go along with me.
And the young man joined the crowd.

Young man—Young man—
You're never lonesome in Babylon.
You can always join a crowd in Babylon.
Young man—Young man—
You can never be alone in Babylon,
Alone with your Jesus in Babylon.
You can never find a place, a lonesome place,
A lonesome place to go down on your knees,
And talk with your God, in Babylon.
You're always in a crowd in Babylon.

And the young man went with his newfound friend,
And bought himself some brand new clothes,
And he spent his days in the drinking dens,
Swallowing the fires of hell.
And he spent his nights in the gambling dens,
Throwing dice with the devil for his soul.
And he met up with the women of Babylon.
Oh, the women of Babylon!
Dressed in yellow and purple and scarlet,
Loaded with rings and earrings and bracelets,
Their lips like a honeycomb dripping with honey,
Perfumed and sweet-smelling like a jasmine flower;
And the jasmine smell of the Babylon women
Got in his nostrils and went to his head,
And he wasted his substance in riotous living,
In the evening, in the black and dark of night,
With the sweet-sinning women of Babylon.
And they stripped him of his money,
And they stripped him of his clothes,
And they left him broke and ragged
In the streets of Babylon.

And he would fain have filled his belly with the husks that the swine did eat: and no man gave unto him. And when he came to himself, he said, How many hired servants of my father's have bread enough and to spare, and I perish with hunger! I will arise and go to my father, and will say unto him, Father, I have sinned against heaven, and before thee, And am no more worthy to be called thy son: make me as one of thy hired servants. And he arose, and came to his father. But when he was yet a great way off, his father saw him, and had compassion, and ran, and fell on his neck, and kissed him.
Luke 15:16–20

And the son said unto him, Father, I have sinned against heaven, and in thy sight, and am no more worthy to be called thy son. But the father said to his servants, Bring forth the best robe, and put it on him; and put a ring on his hand, and shoes on his feet: And bring hither the fatted calf, and kill it; and let us eat, and be merry: For this my son was dead, and is alive again; he was lost, and is found.

Luke 15:21-24a

At right is the magnificent masterpiece RETURN OF THE PRODIGAL SON by Rembrandt Van Rijn, which depicts the tender scene of perhaps the most beloved of all Jesus' parables.

The young man joined another crowd—
The beggars and lepers of Babylon.
And he went to feeding swine,
And he was hungrier than the hogs;
He got down on his belly in the mire and mud
And ate the husks with the hogs;
And not a hog was too low to turn up his nose
At the man in the mire of Babylon.
Then the young man came to himself—
He came to himself and said:
In my father's house are many mansions,
Ev'ry servant in his house has bread to eat,
Ev'ry servant in his house has a place to sleep;
I will arise and go to my father.

And his father saw him afar off,
And he ran up the road to meet him.
He put clean clothes upon his back,
And a golden chain around his neck,
He made a feast and killed the fatted calf,
And invited the neighbors in.

Oh-o-oh, sinner,
When you're mingling with the crowd in Babylon—
Drinking the wine of Babylon—
Running with the women of Babylon—
You forget about God, and you laugh at Death.
Today you've got the strength of a bull in your neck
And the strength of a bear in your arms,
But some o' these days, some o' these days,
You'll have a hand-to-hand struggle with bony Death,
And Death is bound to win.

Young man, come away from Babylon,
That hell-border city of Babylon.
Leave the dancing and gambling of Babylon,
The wine and whiskey of Babylon,
The hot-mouthed women of Babylon;
Fall down on your knees,
And say in your heart:
I will arise and go to my Father.

JAMES WELDON JOHNSON
1871–1938

The Pearl

I know the ways of learning; both the head
And pipes that feed the press, and make it run;
What reason hath from nature borrowèd,
Or of itself, like a good housewife, spun
In laws and policy; what the stars conspire,
What willing nature speaks, what forced by fire;
Both the old discoveries and the newfound seas,
The stock and surplus, cause and history,—
All these stand open, or I have the keys:
    Yet I love Thee.

I know the ways of honour, what maintains
The quick returns of courtesy and wit;
In vies of favours whether party gains;
When glory swells the heart, and mouldeth it
To all expressions both of hand and eye;
Which on the world a true-love-knot may tie,
And bear the bundle, wheresoe'er it goes;
How many drams of spirit there must be
To sell my life unto my friends or foes:
    Yet I love Thee.

I know the ways of Pleasure, the sweet strains,
The lullings and the relishes of it;
The propositions of hot blood and brains;
What mirth and music mean; what love and wit
Have done these twenty hundred years and more.
I know the projects of unbridled store:
My stuff is flesh, not brass; my senses live,
And grumble oft that they have more in me
Than he that curbs them, being but one to five:
    Yet I love Thee.

I know all these, and have them in my hand:
Therefore not sealèd, but with open eyes
I fly to Thee, and fully understand
Both the main sale and the commodities;
And at what rate and price I have Thy love,
With all the circumstances that may move.
Yet through the labyrinths, not my grovelling wit
But Thy silk-twist let down from heaven to me,
Did both conduct and teach me how by it
    To climb to Thee.

GEORGE HERBERT
1593–1633

Again, the kingdom of heaven is like unto a merchant man, seeking goodly pearls: Who, when he had found one pearl of great price, went and sold all that he had, and bought it.
Matthew 13:45, 46

Jesus could have learned the use of parables as a boy studying in the synagogue in Nazareth. Parables are found in the writings of Plato and Aristotle, as well as in the Old Testament; and many Jewish scholars used them to provoke their students to deeper thought on the lessons of the scriptures. In the painting opposite, artist Joseph Maniscalco has depicted Jesus speaking from a boat.

Education in Jesus' Time

Jewish parents taught their children at home: girls learned about running the household and caring for the family; boys learned a trade with which they could support a family. Beginning about the first century B.C., however, boys began attending classes at synagogues at about six years of age. Here they learned to read and write, and, perhaps more importantly, they studied the ancient scriptures. This education continued until the age of ten when some boys went on to learn a trade while others continued as students of religious scholars. The Bible tells us that Jesus was a carpenter, a trade He probably learned from Joseph; but we also know that He was addressed as Rabbi, taught in the temple at age twelve, and was thoroughly grounded in the scriptures. We can assume then, that, as a boy, Jesus was a devoted student in the synagogue of Nazareth.

When Jesus began His own ministry, much of His teaching was conducted in synagogues, and He taught in the traditional method of sitting on the ground with His listeners gathered around Him and standing to read scriptures. Pictured here are the ruins of the synagogue at Capernaum.

King Solomon built the first Temple in Jerusalem for a sanctuary, a home for the Ark of the Covenant, and for animal sacrifices. Built on the eastern hill north of the city (where the Islamic Dome of the Rock now stands), it was completed in 950 B.C. The Temple was destroyed by fire by Babylonian King Nebuchadnezzar in 587 B.C.; thereafter, the Temple was destroyed and rebuilt, its fate reflecting that of the Jews themselves.

In 20 B.C., Herod the Great began remodeling the Temple and created a truly magnificent structure. His workmen used huge stones measuring about forty inches deep by three to ten feet high and thirteen feet long; the Temple's walls rose 158 feet above the valley floor.

In A.D. 70, the Roman Titus captured Jerusalem and burned Herod's Temple. According to Jewish tradition, the destruction took place on the anniversary of the day that Solomon's Temple had been burned by Nebuchadnezzar more than 650 years earlier. Today, only the west wall of Herod's Temple remains standing.

Jesus told stories that illustrated divine wisdom through everyday events and used illustrations that His audience would understand. He spoke to fisherman about fishing, to farmers about farming, to shepherds about sheep. In fact, scholars use the particulars of everyday life that Jesus used for His parables to verify the facts of His life. Yet His parables are not merely simple stories. They often rise to the poetic, as in stories of the prodigal son and the good Samaritan, which not only speak of theological truths, but are literary masterpieces.

Like other children of His day, Jesus probably received early religious instruction in His local synagogue, where classes would have been conducted by a man known as the *hazzan*, or the keeper of the scrolls. Students in the synagogue gathered around their instructor, who sat on the open floor of the synagogue giving instruction in scripture, reading, and writing. Pictured at left is a portion of one of the two scrolls of Isaiah found in the caves of Qumram, northwest of the Dead Sea. Jesus probably studied such a scroll as a student in the synagogue.

Below is a portion of the floor of the Beit Alfa Synagogue ruins in Israel.

And he taught in their synagogues . . . And he came to Nazareth, . . . and, as his custom was, he went into the synagogue on the sabbath day, and stood up for to read. And he closed the book, and he gave it again to the minister, and sat down. And the eyes of all them that were in the synagogue were fastened on him.
Luke 4:15, 16, 20

The exact origin of the Jewish synagogue is unknown, although most scholars believe that the first synagogues were built following the destruction of Solomon's Temple in 587 B.C., either during the Babylonian exile or upon the Jews' return to Judea. The synagogue grew into a community institution, a school, a meeting place, an inn, a home for the priests, and a judicial court.

During the years of Jesus' ministry, synagogues were widespread throughout the Holy Land. Because of these local synagogues, Jesus found people well-versed in the scriptures and strong in their beliefs—fertile ground for His teachings.

The parable of the good Samaritan was a reminder that Jesus' disciples should strive to uphold the spirit, not the letter of the law. The Samaritan does not think of himself, but only of the traveler in need; and it is he who lives up to Jesus' commandment: love thy neighbor. At right, artist John Walter has painted the THE GOOD SAMARITAN.

The Good Samaritan

A traveler fell among the
  thieves;
He was crushed like autumn
  leaves:
He was beaten like the sheaves
Upon the threshing-floor.

There, upon the public way,
In the shadowless heat of day,
Bleeding, stripped and bound
  he lay,
And seemed to breathe no more.

Void of hope was he, when lo!
On his way to Jericho,
Came a priest, serene and slow,
His journey just begun.

Many a silver bell and gem
Glittered on his harness' hem;
Behind him gleamed Jerusalem,
In the unclouded sun.

Broad were his phylacteries,
And his calm and holy eyes
Looked above earth's vanities,
And gazed upon the sky.

He the suffering one descried,
But, with saintly looks of pride,
Passed by on the other side,

And left him there to die.
Then approached with reverend
  pace
One of the elected race,
The chosen ministers of grace,
Who bore the ark of God.

He, a Levite, and a high
Exemplar of humanity,
Likewise passed the sufferer by,
Even as the dust he trod.

Then came a Samaritan,
A despised, rejected man,
Outlawed by the Jewish ban
As one in bonds to sin.
He beheld the poor man's need,
Bound his wounds, and with all
  speed
Set him on his own good steed,
And brought him to the inn.

When our Judge shall reappear,
Thinkest thou this man will hear,
"Wherefore didst thou interfere
With what concerned not thee?"

No! the words of Christ will run,
"Whatsoever thou hast done
To this poor and suffering one,
That hast thou done to me!"

AUTHOR UNKNOWN

The painting opposite is of Jesus and the woman at the well by Joseph Maniscalco. When Jesus spoke to the Samaritan woman at the well, ignoring the hatred between His own people and the Samaritans, He taught by example one of His most valuable lessons: the kingdom of God is open to all who will believe.

The Samaritan Woman

In order to return into Galilee, Jesus could have followed the Jordan as he did on his last return, as did almost all the Jews anxious to avoid Samaria, a region despised and accursed since the Assyrian colonists had brought their idols there. The Samaritans had done worse: they had harbored a renegade priest expelled from Jerusalem, and he had built an altar on Mount Gerizim.

If Jesus followed the road through the ripening fields of Samaria, it was to meet a soul, no less defiled nor better disposed than most. Yet for this soul, and not for another, he entered the enemy territory—the first soul he was to meet, the one he was to use in order to reach many others. Near the little town of Sychar he was overcome with weariness, and he sat down by the well which Jacob had dug. His disciples went away to buy bread; he awaited their return.

The first to come happened to be a woman. There were many reasons that Jesus might not have spoken to her. First, it was not fitting for a man to speak to a woman on the road. And then he was a Jew and she was a Samaritan. And then he who knew hearts—and bodies too—was not unaware of the identity of this graceful being. . . .

She might fully be what she was: a concubine, a woman who had dragged in the mire, passed from one to another, who had lain in the arms of six men, and he whose thing she now was, and who tasted pleasure with her, was not her husband. Jesus took what he found, gathered up no matter what, that his Kingdom might come. He looked at her and decided that on that very day this creature would seize Sychar in his name and would found in Samaria the kingdom of God. . . . Jesus looked at her closely; he had not that haughty air, that contraction of the virtuous before a woman who made a business of love. Neither did he look at her with indulgence, nor with connivance. She was a soul, the first to come, of which he was going to make use. A ray of sun lay across a potsherd in the dirt heap, the flame leaped up, and all the forest caught fire.

The sixth hour. It was hot. The woman heard someone call her. Was the Jew speaking to her? But yes; he said: "Give me to drink." At once coy and mocking, she replied to the perspiring stranger:

"How dost thou, being a Jew, ask to drink of me, who am a Samaritan?"

"If thou didst know the gift of God, and who he is who saith to thee, 'Give me to drink,' thou wouldst have asked of him, and he would have given thee living water."

Christ brooked no delay; his words were incomprehensible to the Samaritan woman, but like a thief he had already entered into

The woman saith unto him, Sir, thou hast nothing to draw with, and the well is deep: from whence then hast thou that living water? Art thou greater than our father Jacob, which gave us the well, and drank thereof himself, and his children, and his cattle? Jesus answered and said unto her, Whosoever drinketh of this water shall thirst again: But whosoever drinketh of the water that I shall give him shall never thirst; but the water that I shall give him shall be in him a well of water springing up into everlasting life.

John 4:11–14

that dark soul. She must have felt besieged on every side, and the stranger whose dripping face and dusty feet she saw before her entered into her soul, invaded her, and she was powerless before this living surge. Dumfounded, she ceased to mock, and . . . began to ask childish questions:

"Sir, thou hast no pail and the well is deep; whence then hast thou living water? Art thou greater than our father Jacob, who gave us this well, and drank thereof himself, and his sons and his cattle?"

Jesus had no time to lose; he was going to thrust her, with an impatient gesture, into the full glare of the truth. He said:

"Everyone that drinketh of this water shall thirst again; but whosoever drinketh of the water that I shall give him shall never thirst, but the water that I shall give him shall become in him a fountain of water springing up into everlasting life."

Every word of the Lord should be taken to the letter. That is why many have believed themselves drunk with this water and have been deceived; this was not the water of which Jesus spoke, since having drunk of it they thirsted still. Nevertheless, the woman replied:

"Sir, give me this water, that I may not thirst, nor come hither to draw."

"Go, call thy husband and come hither."

Always the same methods to persuade the simple: the same method he used with Nathanael when he said: "I saw thee under the fig tree." It revealed to them at once his knowledge of their lives, or rather his power to take up his abode within them, to enter into their most secret being; and that is why when the Samaritan woman said, "I have no husband," he replied:

"Thou hast said rightly, 'I have no husband': for thou hast had five husbands, and now he whom thou hast is not thy husband. This hast thou said truly."

The woman did not belong to the royal race of Nathanael and Simon, of those who immediately fell on their knees and struck their breasts. She was at first only a guilty woman caught in her sin, and, in order to divert the attention of this Rabbi who knew too much, she tried to put the discussion on a theological basis. After having stammered, "Sir, I perceive that thou art a prophet . . ." she added hastily:

"Our fathers worshipped on this mountain; yet ye say that the right place for worship is Jerusalem."

Jesus did not allow himself to be turned away; he laid aside the objection with several words. But he was pressed for time; the disciples were returning with provisions. He heard them talking and laughing. They must not come there until he had finished. The truth must be given this poor woman at once:

"The hour cometh and now is, when true worshippers shall worship the Father in spirit and truth. For indeed the Father seeketh such worshippers. God is a spirit; and those who worship him must worship in spirit and truth."

And the Samaritan woman: "I know that Messiah is coming; when he cometh, he shall declare unto us all things."

Already the disciples' steps could be heard on the road. To hear the secret he had never yet told anyone, Jesus chose this woman who had had five husbands and who then had a lover.

"I that speak with thee am he."

And at that very moment, the light of grace was given to the miserable woman; so strong was it that no doubt could ever assail her. Yes, this poor burdened Jew who had walked far in the sun and the dust and who so suffered from thirst that he must beg a little water from a woman of Samaria, was the Messiah, the Savior of the world.

She stood there petrified, until she heard the voices of those who accompanied this man, coming nearer. Then she started to run, like one whose garments were on fire. She entered Sychar to arouse the people. She cried:

"Come and see a man who hath told me all that I have done."

One would have said that Christ, still seated on the edge of the well, while his disciples gave him a morsel of bread, had trouble in returning to their narrow world. "Rabbi, eat!" they insisted. But incarnate love, unmasked by this woman, had not yet had time to become a man again, a man who hungered and thirsted.

"I have food to eat that ye know not."

This answer still came from another world. The poor people imagined that someone had brought him mysterious food to eat. He looked at their staring eyes, their gaping mouths, and beyond in the blinding light the harvest fields of Samaria, with their ripening ears of corn. Above the corn, heads were moving: a troop of people led on by the woman (her lover was perhaps among them!).

Finally, Jesus touched earth again. He spoke of the things of the soil which they knew, quoted a proverb, reassured them, led them to understand that they would reap what he had sown. He had already made them fishers of men, now they would be harvesters of human sheaves.

He tarried for two days in the midst of the outcast Samaritans, thus giving his followers an example which was to be transmitted in vain to the rest of the world. For if there is a part of the Christian message which men have refused and rejected with invincible obstinacy, it is faith in the equal value of all souls, of all races, before the Father who is in heaven.

FRANÇOIS MAURIAC
FROM *LIFE OF JESUS*

Jesus saith unto her, Woman, believe me, the hour cometh, when ye shall neither in this mountain, nor yet at Jerusalem, worship the Father. Ye worship ye know not what: we know what we worship: for salvation is of the Jews. But the hour cometh, and now is, when the true worshippers shall worship the Father in spirit and in truth: for the Father seeketh such to worship him. God is a Spirit: and they that worship him must worship him in spirit and in truth. The woman saith unto him, I know that Messias cometh, which is called Christ: when he is come, he will tell us all things. Jesus saith unto her, I that speak unto thee am he.
John 4:21–26

Jesus Amazed Them

During many periods throughout history, and especially in Jesus' time, people viewed natural events as signs of God's power over His creation. When floods, plagues, storms, and droughts ravaged the land, they were seen as expressions of God's wrath and displeasure at the transgressions of His people. Equally, good crops, favorable weather, and propitious rainstorms were taken as expressions of God's favor.

The people looked to nature for signs at all times; the Magi from the East found a sign in the heavens that led them to the newborn Jesus. Nature was, in effect, God's language of communication to His people. Those who witnessed Jesus walking on water, quieting the raging sea, and causing the fig tree to wither were amazed and believed He was the Son of God, for only God Incarnate could display such mastery over God's natural creation.

The photograph at right offers a serene view of the Sea of Galilee. The lake's approximately thirty-two miles of shoreline are skirted by steep hills; and cool winds often rush down the slopes, creating violent waves on the lake's warm surface. A storm such as this was easily calmed at Jesus' command.

Water into Wine

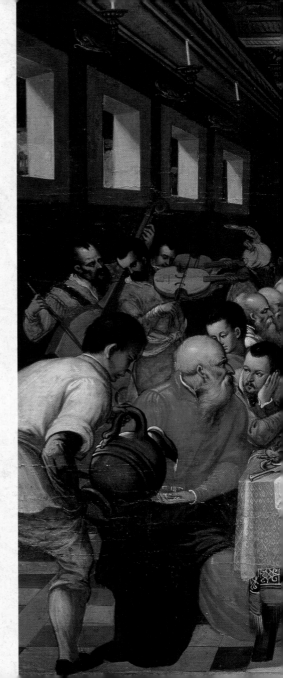

lizabeth rose and dressed carefully. . . . Some time during the morning would come the ceremonious entrance of the messengers from Philip [her betrothed] bearing her bridal dress and ornaments and the ointment and perfumes.

There was no breakfast to make, for she must fast until evening. But there were the prayers of Atonement with which her mind must be occupied most of the day. She knelt facing Jerusalem and recited softly the solemn, stately words of the confession. Later the messengers arrived. The bridal gown with all its expensive ornaments was spread upon the bed. She smiled tenderly at Philip's extravagance. He had sent perfumes enough for a lifetime.

In the early evening, while the neighbors swarmed about the rooms, trying to be helpful, Elizabeth stood before her mirror and let down her long black hair until it fell about her shoulders as a maiden bride's must hang. They helped her into her bridal dress, exclaiming at its beauty. With her own hands Elizabeth adjusted the "attire" about her waist and the crown of fresh myrtle leaves that she had preferred to the golden imitation. Then over all was thrown the long white veil of betrothal that would not be raised until Philip's own hands lifted it in the hush of the bridal chamber. Elizabeth was ready.

The early dusk had grown swiftly to darkness. The young girls who had been running in and out were gone hastily to their own homes to don their last bit of finery for the procession.

A shout came from the doorway. "Here they come! Look! Thou canst see the torches! And the flutes! Dost thou hear them? Oh, it will be a great procession. Call Elizabeth. Tell her they have started!"

The sounds came clearly through the night. Philip and his groomsmen were on their way to her. The neighbors were all thronging the streets. The maidens were waiting, ready to circle about

Jewish weddings in Jesus' day were often held at harvest time with music, dancing, and feasting. The betrothal, which generally happened a year before the wedding feast, was the official ceremony of marriage. There the parents, who had arranged the marriage, made the formal agreements that bound their children. The painting on the previous page is an elaborate depiction of Christ's first miracle, THE MARRIAGE FEAST AT CANA, from an unknown artist of the Venetian school of Italian painters.

her when she emerged from the house. All at once the shouting increased deafeningly. The torches again became a confused glare. They had reached her house. Elizabeth felt herself conducted through lines of laughing, bowing men and women on to the doorway, where Philip met her and drew her inside.

He led her proudly to the room reserved for the women and seated her on the soft-rug-covered dais prepared for her. The other women and maidens who were invited to the house crowded in and found seats on the floor and cushioned ledges. Through the door which led into the room where the feast was spread for the men, and where the singing and dancing would take place, Elizabeth could see the women who were to serve, carrying food to the table and chatting importantly to each other as they worked. She watched the form of Mary of Nazareth as she came and went. So gentle in her movements, so quiet of speech, so tender and smiling as she looked upon the group that clustered round the bridegroom.

Then Terenth came in with refreshments for the women. "There are many strangers," she commented, excitedly. "Four men are sitting with Nathanael, and he keeps calling one of them Rabbi. He is Mary's son from Nazareth, but I didn't know He was a rabbi. Philip's father is so excited. We can't bring things in fast enough to please him. He is mightily lavish with the wine. Philip will have to go clear to the new vineyards for more for tomorrow night. Thou shouldst see how the guests eat!"

She ran out, laughing, but it seemed only a moment until she was back with blanched face. "The wine is gone!" she gasped. "There isn't another drop and the feast but barely begun! We thought there were two more vats of it and they are empty! What can we do?"

At the first words Elizabeth had started in surprise. Now she sat tense with hands gripped together. No more wine! The feast begun in riotous plenty was to end in poverty and disgrace. . . . "Tell Mary of Nazareth!" she whispered. "She is always calm and wise. She will know how to tell the governor and the rest when it has to be known."

When Terenth had rushed away and the chatter of awed comment and criticism and speculation was in full flow about her, Elizabeth sat speechless and stunned behind her veil.

This was no small calamity that was about to fall upon them. It was a lifelong disgrace for Philip and his father. Never again could they hold up their heads in the village. No matter whose mistake it had been, the burden of reproach would rest upon them. And no one would ever let them forget it. This flagrant breach of hospitality, this unprecedented failure to make good the promise of their lavish invitations. No apology could be offered or accepted. There would be only the ugly fact to speak for itself. There would be a little while of forced merriment and then the guests would go. And Philip and his father would be left amid the ruins of the feast and the bitterness of their disgrace.

Suddenly she noticed that the women and maidens had stopped talking. A silence had fallen upon the feast-room, too. Elizabeth caught her breath. Some one must be telling Philip and his father now. For a long second the strange hush lasted. And then everything was as it had been before. The talking, the laughter, the women running to and fro with their platters and pitchers. And high above the other voices rose the strong tones of the governor of the feast.

"How is this, Philip?" he was demanding. "Every man when he maketh a feast doth first serve the good wine, and then when men have well drunk, he serveth that which is worse. But thou hast kept the good wine until now!"

The governor sounded well pleased. Then Philip replied, his voice still vibrant with pride and joy: "But, governor, is the best not worth waiting for always?"

Then overwhelmingly rose the shouts: "To the bridegroom! Fill your cups and drink again to the bridegroom! Joy to Philip and his bride!"

One of the maidens leaned cautiously toward the door of the feast-room. "They have wine! They are drinking it now. Terenth is silly and excitable. Alarming us for naught. Wait till she comes again! We shall teach her a lesson."

But Terenth was already there. "There has been a miracle. There is a man of God in this house!" Then, before the excited gasps of wonder had become coherent, Terenth went on: "There was no wine. Any of the women or the servants will tell you that. I did as Elizabeth bade me. I asked Mary of Nazareth to break the news to Philip and his father. I was just behind her as she entered the room. Instead of going to the end of the table she stopped beside her Son. I heard her whisper to Him: 'They have no wine'—only that. But she looked at Him beseechingly. Her Son looked grave for a moment and then He smiled a little and said in the gentlest voice: 'Woman, what have I to do with thee? Mine hour is not yet come.' But she smiled back at Him and touched His shoulder—they must love each other deeply, those two—and signed to a servant. 'Do whatever he telleth thee' she said.

"Then this Jesus told the servant to fill the six big water jars in the hallway, full of water. When it was done he said quietly: 'Draw out now and bear to the governor of the feast!'

"And as we drew, the water was changed to wine! They are drinking it now."

In the midst of it all, Elizabeth sat withdrawn, apart, trying to sense the awesome thing she had just heard. Under this roof, Philip's roof, which was now her home, water had been changed into wine! That quiet guest in the other room had wrought a miracle! God was dwelling in this place.

AGNES SLIGH TURNBULL
FROM *FAR ABOVE RUBIES*

Jesus saith unto them, Fill the waterpots with water. And they filled them up to the brim. And he saith unto them, Draw out now, and bear unto the governor of the feast. And they bare it. When the ruler of the feast had tasted the water that was made wine, and knew not whence it was: . . . the governor of the feast called the bridegroom, And saith unto him, Every man at the beginning doth set forth good wine; and when men have well drunk, then that which is worse; but thou hast kept the good wine until now. This beginning of miracles did Jesus in Cana of Galilee, and manifested forth his glory; and his disciples believed on him.
John 2:7–11

> Jesus . . . saw a great
> company come unto
> him, One of his disci-
> ples, . . . saith unto him,
> There is a lad here,
> which hath five barley
> loaves, and two small
> fishes: but what are they
> among so many? . . .
> And Jesus took the
> loaves; and when he had
> given thanks, he distrib-
> uted to the disciples,
> and the disciples to
> them . . . and likewise of
> the fishes as much as
> they would. When they
> were filled, he said unto
> his disciples, Gather up
> the fragments that
> remain . . . Therefore
> they gathered them
> together, and filled
> twelve baskets with the
> fragments of the five
> barley loaves, which
> remained over and
> above unto them that
> had eaten. Then those
> men, when they had
> seen the miracle that
> Jesus did, said, This is
> of a truth that prophet
> that should come into
> the world.
> John 6:5a, 8, 9, 11–14

The miracle of the loaves
and fishes is the only miracle
recounted in all four gospels.
Opposite, the Limbourg
Brothers, Flemish artists
from the fifteenth century,
depict BOOK OF HOURS: FEEDING
THE MULTITUDES.

The Boy with the Five Loaves

What time the Savior spread His feast
For thousands on the mountain's side,
One of the last and least
The abundant store supplied.

Haply, the wonders to behold,
A boy 'mid other boys he came,
A lamb of Jesus' fold,
Though now unknown by name.

Well may I guess how glow'd his cheek,
How he look'd down, half pride, half fear
Far off he saw one speak
Of him in Jesus' ear.

"There is a lad—five loaves hath he,
And fishes twain:—but where are they
Where hungry thousands be?"
Nay, Christ will find a way.

Oh, who can tell the trembling joy,
Who paint the grave endearing look,
When from that favored boy
The wondrous pledge He took?

Thou prayest without the veil as yet:
But kneel in faith: an arm benign
Such prayer will duly set
Within the holiest shrine.

And Prayer has might to spread and grow.
Thy childish darts, right-aim'd on high,
May catch Heaven's fire and glow
Far in the eternal sky:

Even as He made that stripling's store
Type of the Feast by Him decreed,
Where Angels might adore,
And souls for ever feed.

JOHN KEBLE
1792–1866

Natural Signs and Wonders

There are instances in the Old Testament when the truly miraculous took place in the natural world. The sun stood still to give Joshua and his army more time in battle. The Red Sea parted so that Moses could lead the Israelites out of captivity in Egypt, and then returned to drown Pharaoh's army. Joshua and Moses called upon God to work these natural miracles. Jesus, however, worked miracles by His own authority over the forces of nature.

Pictured here is a star of David on part of the ruins of old Jericho. Jericho is one of the oldest settlements in the world, with archaeological remains dating back ten thousand years. The city's rich history includes the story of the city's conquest in Joshua chapter 6. After faithfully following God's instructions, Joshua and his army watched the walls of Jericho tumble, tangible evidence of God's miraculous power.

The Gezer Calendar, the first known agricultural calendar, dates from the tenth to sixth century B.C. One of the oldest known Hebrew documents, the calendar once helped farmers determine when to sow their crops.

Then spake Joshua to the LORD . . .
and he said in the sight of Israel,
Sun, stand thou still upon Gibeon;
and thou, Moon, in the valley
of Ajalon. And the sun stood still,
and the moon stayed, until
the people had avenged themselves
upon their enemies. And
there was no day like that
before it or after it,
that the LORD hearkened
unto the voice of a man.
Joshua 10:12, 13a, 14a

The people Jesus taught were, for the most part, farmers, fishermen, or shepherds. They grew grain, grapes, olives, and figs and tended sheep, goats, and occasionally cattle. Much of Judea is desert; but even in the fertile Jordan River valley, people were dependent upon nature for their survival. They believed a merciful God sent rain; a fierce storm came from God's wrath. In an ever-changing natural world, they read the judgment of God upon their worthiness. For these people, Jesus, who demonstrated His mastery over the powerful forces of nature, was truly the Son of God.

Jesus displayed His lordship over the natural world by calming a storm, walking on water, turning water into wine, and feeding thousands from a handful of loaves and fishes. But nowhere in the Bible does nature bow so low as on the day of the Crucifixion. The sky turned dark for three hours until Jesus died, a great earthquake shook the city, stones were broken, the huge temple veil was torn in half, and graves were opened so the resurrected could walk among their kinsmen. Here was physical evidence that the world and all nature remained under His command. Here was real evidence of not only the power and the might of God, but of the love and compassion for His Son and all mankind.

And the LORD said unto Moses, Stretch out thine hand over the sea, that the waters may come again upon the Egyptians, upon their chariots, and upon their horsemen. And Moses stretched forth his hand over the sea.
Exodus 14:26–27a

Fishing methods and equipment have changed little in two thousand years; and it is easy to imagine Peter, James, Andrew, and John perhaps fishing the same waters in a boat similar to the one pictured, casting their nets into the Sea of Galilee.

Israel varies from fertile farmland to thick forests to river valleys to semi-arid desert. But everywhere, the people respected the power of nature, for their livelihoods were at its mercy. When Jesus displayed His lordship over the natural world, calming the storm and making the fig tree wither, the farmers and herdsmen of the Holy Land took notice. On the opposite page, a lone palm and a herd of goats share a stretch of the Judean wilderness.

Miracle

He was on His way from Bethany to Jerusalem,
Languishing under the sadness of premonitions.

The slope's prickly scrubwood had been scorched by the sun;
No smoke rose from a nearby hut.
The air was hot; the reeds did not stir
And the calm of the Dead Sea was unbroken.

And, knowing a bitterness that rivaled the bitterness of the sea,
Accompanied only by a small band of clouds,
He went on along the dusty road
Intent on reaching a certain religious school.
He was on His way to attend a gathering of disciples.
And so deeply was He plunged in His thoughts
That the countryside sent forth an odor of wormwood.
A stillness fell over all things. He stood alone
In the midst of it all. And all the region lay prostrate
As if in a swoon. All things became confused:
The sultriness and the desert,
And lizards, and wellsprings and streams.

A fig tree rose up a short distance ahead—
Utterly fruitless, putting forth only branches and leaves.
And He said unto it: "Of what use art thou?
What joy have I from thee, standing there petrified?
I am enhungered and athirst, yet thou art all barren
And coming upon thee is of less joy than stumbling on granite.
Oh, how thou dost offend, how void of any gift!
Remain, then, even as thou art until the end of time."

A shudder at the condemnation ran through the tree
Even as a spark of lightning runs down a rod.
The fig tree was instantly consumed to ashes.

If at that point but a moment of free choice had been granted
To the leaves, the branches, to the trunk and roots
The laws of nature might have contrived to intervene.

But a miracle is a miracle—and miracle is God.
When we are in confusion, then in the midst of our straggling
It overtakes us and, on the instant, confounds us.

BORIS PASTERNAK
1890–1960

Christ
Stilling the Tempest

Fear was within the tossing bark,
   When stormy winds grew loud;
And waves came rolling high and dark,
   And the tall mast was bowed:

And men stood breathless in their dread,
   And baffled in their skill—
But One was there, who rose and said
   To the wild sea, "Be still!"

And the wind ceased—it ceased!—that word
   Passed through the gloomy sky;
The troubled billows knew their Lord,
   And sank beneath his eye.

And slumber settled on the deep,
   And silence on the blast,
As when the righteous falls asleep,
   When death's fierce throes are past.

Thou that didst rule the angry hour,
   And tame the tempest's mood,
Oh! send thy spirit forth in power,
   O'er our dark souls to brood!

Thou that didst bow the billows' pride
   Thy mandates to fulfill,
Speak, speak, to passion's raging tide,
   Speak and say—"Peace, be still!"

FELICIA DOROTHEA HEMANS
1793–1835

And the same day, when the even was come, he saith unto them, Let us pass over unto the other side. And when they had sent away the multitude, they took him even as he was in the ship. And there arose a great storm of wind, and the waves beat into the ship, so that it was now full. And he was in the hinder part of the ship, asleep on a pillow: and they awake him, and say unto him, Master, carest thou not that we perish? And he arose, and rebuked the wind, and said unto the sea, Peace, be still. And the wind ceased, and there was a great calm. And he said unto them, Why are ye so fearful? how is it that ye have no faith? And they feared exceedingly, and said one to another, What manner of man is this, that even the wind and the sea obey him?
Mark 4:35–36a, 37–41

The magnificent painting opposite by Rembrandt Van Rijn, THE STORM ON THE SEA OF GALILEE, shows the overwhelming danger the apostles faced on the Sea of Galilee, making the calm that followed Jesus' words, "Peace, be still," even more remarkable.

Walking on the Sea

When the storm on the mountains
  of Galilee fell,
And lifted its water on high;
And the faithless disciples were bound
  in the spell
Of mysterious alarm—their terrors to quell,
Jesus whispered, "Fear not, it is I."

The storm could not bury that word in the wave,
For 'twas taught through the tempest to fly;
It shall reach his disciples in every clime,
And his voice shall be near
  in each troublous time,
Saying, "Be not afraid, it is I."

When the spirit is broken
  with sickness or sorrow,
And comfort is ready to die;
The darkness shall pass,
  and in gladness tomorrow,
The wounded complete consolation
  shall borrow
From his life-giving word, "It is I."

When the waters are passed,
  and the glories unknown
Burst forth on the wondering eye,
The compassionate "Lamb in the midst
  of the throne"
Shall welcome, encourage, and comfort his own,
And say, "Be not afraid, it is I."

NATHANIEL HAWTHORNE
1804–1864

Simon Peter saith unto them, I go a fishing. They say unto him, We also go with thee. They went forth, and entered into a ship immediately: and that night they caught nothing. But when the morning was now come, Jesus stood on the shore: but the disciples knew not that it was Jesus. Then Jesus saith unto them, Children, have ye any meat? They answered him, No. And he said unto them, Cast the net on the right side of the ship, and ye shall find. They cast therefore, and now they were not able to draw it for the multitude of fishes. Therefore that disciple whom Jesus loved saith unto Peter, It is the Lord.
John 21:3–7a

The painting on the previous page, entitled *CHRIST APPEARING TO THE APOSTLES ON THE LAKE OF TIBERIAS*, by Duccio of Siena, shows the complete absorption and faith of Peter, if only temporarily, as he focuses solely on his Master and indeed walks on the water. Christ's compassion and love are also seen as He extends His hand to His disciple.

The Boat

(Simon Peter's Testimony)

I owned a little boat a while ago,
And sailed the morning sea without a fear,
And whither any breeze might fairly blow
I steered my little craft afar or near.

Mine was the boat
And mine the air,
And mine the sea,
Nor mine a care.

My boat became my place of mighty toil,
I sailed at evening to the fishing ground,
At morn my boat was freighted with the spoil
Which my all-conquering work had found.

Mine was the boat
And mine the net,
And mine the skill
And power to get.

One day there came along that silent shore,
While I my net was casting in the sea,
A Man who spoke as never man before.
I followed Him; new life began in me.

Mine was the boat,
But His the voice,
And His the call,
Yet mine the choice.

Ah! 'twas a fearful night out on the lake,
And all my skill availed not, at the helm,
Till Him asleep I waked, crying, "Take
Thou the helm—lest water overwhelm!"

And His the boat,
And His the sea,
And His the peace
O'er all and me.

Once from the boat He taught the curious throng
Then bade me cast my net into the sea;
I murmured but obeyed, nor was it long
Before the catch amazed and humbled me.

His was the boat,
And His the skill.
And His the catch,
And His my will.

GEORGE MACDONALD
1824–1905

Now when Simon Peter heard that it was the Lord, he girt his fisher's coat unto him, . . . and did cast himself into the sea. And the other disciples came in a little ship; . . . dragging the net with fishes. As soon then as they were come to land, they saw a fire of coals there, and fish laid thereon, and bread. Jesus saith unto them, Bring of the fish which ye have now caught. Simon Peter went up, and drew the net to land full of great fishes, an hundred and fifty and three: and for all there were so many, yet was not the net broken. Jesus saith unto them, Come and dine. And none of the disciples durst ask him, Who art thou? knowing that it was the Lord.
John 21:7b–12

Jesus Saved Them

Throughout the Gospels of the New Testament, Jesus Christ met people who asked, in one form or another, the same question asked by Nicodemus, "What must I do to have eternal life?" And to each, the answer Jesus gave was the same: "Ye must be born again."

Like Nicodemus, the thief on the cross confessed belief in the Son of God and was given the assurance that on that day he would be with Christ in paradise. Likewise Zacchaeus, a corrupt tax collector, invited Jesus into his home and was reborn into a life of righteousness. All found new life through their faith in Jesus.

Some who met Jesus, however, chose to reject His love. The rich young ruler would not sell all he had and follow Jesus. Pilate and Caiaphas were so close to the truth yet were unable or unwilling to grasp Christ's message.

Christ's message to them was His message to us all: He had come to earth to offer redemption to mankind. All He asked was complete faith, through which anyone, sinner or saint, could be transformed and born again to eternal life.

Shepherds and sheep are mentioned more than three hundred times in the Bible, and the work of the shepherd was familiar to most people living in Israel at the time of Jesus. Thus, Jesus was drawing upon fertile imagery when He called Himself the "Good Shepherd" who would lay down His life for His flock. At right, a shepherd tends his flock in modern-day Israel.

And a certain ruler asked him, saying, Good Master, what shall I do to inherit eternal life? And Jesus said unto him, Why callest thou me good? none is good, save one, that is, God. Thou knowest the commandments, Do not commit adultery, Do not kill, Do not steal, Do not bear false witness, Honour thy father and thy mother. And he said, All these have I kept from my youth up. Now when Jesus heard these things, he said unto him, Yet lackest thou one thing: sell all that thou hast, and distribute unto the poor, and thou shalt have treasure in heaven: and come, follow me.

Luke 18:18–22

The Rich Young Man

hildren were not the only ones who caused his heart to beat. With the audacity of youth, a boy interrupted him, saying: "Master, what am I to do to inherit life everlasting?" Jesus, without at first taking thought of him to whom he spoke, replied: "Thou knowest the commandments." He named them.

And the young man: "Master, all these have I kept from my youth."

This was said no doubt in a tone of simplicity, of humility, which touched Christ. Then only he lifted his eyes to him who spoke. "Jesus looked on him and loved him." After having looked at him . . . a certain expression touched the Son of Man, the grace of a young person, the light in his eyes which came from the soul. He loved him therefore, and like a God to whom all are subject, without preparation, almost brutally, he said:

"One thing is lacking to thee: go, sell all thou hast and give to the poor—and thou shalt have treasure in heaven—and come, follow me."

If Jesus had not loved him . . . no doubt he would have granted this young man the strength to leave all, as others had done. He would have submitted him to all-powerful grace. But love does not wish to obtain anything from him who is loved, unless it be freely given. He loved this stranger too much to capture him by force. From him the Son of Man hoped for a spontaneous movement of the heart. "But his face fell at the saying, and he departed grieved, for he had great possessions."

He was swallowed up in a crowd and with his eyes Jesus followed him far beyond space, into the depths of time, from misery to misery. For those whom Christ calls and who turn away, fall, lift themselves up, drag themselves about with eyes full of heavenly light, but with their garments stained, their hands torn and bleeding.

The sorrow which Jesus felt betrayed itself in the vehemence of [words] against the rich, which fell almost immediately from his lips. "With what difficulty shall they that have riches enter the kingdom of God . . . easier for a camel to pass through the eye of a needle."

Who, then, can be saved? Torturing thought for the saints themselves. His friends' sadness touched Jesus. Because he was the Son of God, the Author of life, he was going to destroy with one word all that he had said (perhaps also he saw in spirit that final moment when the young being who was turning away would come back to him of his own accord). "With men it is impossible . . . all things are possible with God." Even to save as many rich men as he pleased to save, even to bring back those creatures who have fallen the lowest, to take them by force, to gather to himself a soul, still begrimed, from the lips of a dying man. All things are possible with God; this is as literally true as all the other words of the Lord. All! He had already said: "I will draw all men to myself!" O divine and hidden stratagem of that mercy which knows no control nor limit! All things are possible with God.

Jesus' severity frightened the Apostles, but his indulgence made them jealous. What now? Then all the world would be saved? And we?

Peter murmured: "Behold, we have left all things and have followed thee."

Jesus covered them with a glance that reached beyond them and saw, throughout the ages, the innumerable multitude of consecrated and crucified souls.

"Amen I say to you, no one hath left home, or brothers, or sisters, or mother, or father, or children, or lands, for my sake and for the sake of the gospel, but shall receive a hundred-fold now in this time, houses, and brother, and sisters, and mothers, and children, and lands— together with persecutions—and in the world to come life everlasting."

FRANÇOIS MAURIAC
FROM *LIFE OF JESUS*

The painting by artist Heinrich Hoffmann entitled *RICH MAN WHO WENT AWAY SORROWFUL* perfectly captures the haughty arrogance of the "certain ruler" of Luke 18 who asked Jesus what he must do to have eternal life. Unable to sacrifice his great wealth, the rich man chose worldly riches over following the Lord.

And, behold, there was a man named Zacchaeus, which was the chief among the publicans, and he was rich. And he sought to see Jesus who he was; and could not for the press, because he was little of stature. And he ran before, and climbed up into a sycamore tree to see him: for he was to pass that way. And when Jesus came to the place, he looked up, and saw him, and said unto him, Zacchaeus, make haste, and come down; for today I must abide at thy house. And he made haste, and came down, and received him joyfully.

Luke 19:2–6

A Parable for Public Officials

t a time when many public officials are under charges of betraying their country, and business leaders of creating monopolies with restraint of trade, and labor leaders of confiscating union dues for their personal profit, it may be worth recalling the history of a very famous public official who suddenly turned and became a worthy citizen. His name was Zacchaeus, and his particular official title was publican. A publican worked for the Income Tax Bureau of the Roman government in Judea. He was a despised citizen, not just because he was an income tax collector, but because he was also a traitor. Just as some Americans betray their country to help Russia enslave the world, so Zacchaeus deserted his own people to serve the conquerors of his native land.

Zacchaeus did not trouble much about getting mink coats for his wife, but he was tremendously concerned with "kickbacks." He would collect in our money, say, $500,000 from a given area, give $100,000 of that to the foreign conquerors, and pocket the rest himself. Reputation is what men say about us, character is what a man is. No one spoke kindly about this "crook," but at heart he seemed to have very good instincts. The story of his transformation is familiar. One day when the Divine Savior came to his native town of Jericho, Zacchaeus tried to see Him. Being a "shorty" he could not look over the heads of the crowd, so he climbed into a sycamore tree. One cannot imagine the Director of the Tax Bureau of any great city climbing a tree to see a parade, or to catch a glimpse of a visitor, but apparently Zacchaeus was more humble. When a man begins looking for God, he will soon discover that God is looking for him.

The Good Lord looked up and called him by name, and then said: "Make haste and come down; I am to lodge today at thy house." The artificial elevation where our pride has thrust us, or the false compensations we make by climbing trees of egotism must all be negated. Of all the people in that wicked city, the one home to which the Savior chose to invite Himself was that of a despised public official. When the crowd saw the majestic figure of Christ and the tiny tax collector walking side by side into Zacchaeus' home, so well furnished by raiding the treasuries, they said sneeringly: "He has gone in to lodge with one who is a sinner." It is not likely that the mob would ever say that today, because few admit they are sinners. What they would probably say is: "He has gone to the home of that racketeer who was mentioned by the columnists and is about to be convicted by the Grand Jury."

As they converse in secrecy, something happens to the soul of the tax official. Up to this point Zacchaeus was concerned only with whether what he did was "legal"—"legal" meaning anything is justifiable providing you do not get caught; if you are convicted it means that you violated the law, not that you did what was morally wrong. Zacchaeus shifted his mind from "legality" to "morality," from "being caught" to "doing wrong," from "convention" to "conscience." Where there is wrong there has to be restitution; injustice disturbs the equilibrium of the due order that ought to prevail in society. Giving back the stolen goods restores that balance. Zacchaeus is now ready to make reparation. "Here and now, Lord, I give half of what I have to the poor; and if I have wronged anyone in any way, I make restitution of it fourfold."

Shame is not enough; remorse is not enough; there must also be restitution. As Shakespeare said:

> May one be pardon'd and retain the offence?
>> In the corrupted currents of this world
> Offence's gilded hand may shove by justice,
>> and oft 't is seen the wicked prize itself
> Buys out the law; but 'tis not so above;
>> There is no shuffling, there the action lies
> In his true nature, and we ourselves compell'd
>> Even to the teeth and forehead of our faults
> To give in evidence.

Many other crimes are cancelled out by mere sorrow and repentance, but the guilt of robbery, even when dignified with the name of "kickbacks" or "legality," remains, so long as we retain the fruits of it in our own hands. Those who make such restitutions rightly call it "conscience money." A public official who serves ten years in prison for his dishonesty, but all the while keeps the spoils, has not made reparation for his crime either before his country or before his God.

The point of the parable is that honesty in business, honesty among labor unions, honesty in public officials must be based not on "legality" or what they can get away with, but on conscience, that is, giving to every man his due; not because I cannot live away from prison if I am dishonest, but because I cannot live with myself, and I cannot live with myself because I am not living right before my God.

FULTON J. SHEEN
FROM *THOUGHTS FOR DAILY NEEDS*

And Zacchaeus stood, and said unto the Lord; Behold, Lord, the half of my goods I give to the poor; and if I have taken any thing from any man by false accusation, I restore him fourfold. And Jesus said unto him, This day is salvation come to this house . . . For the Son of man is come to seek and to save that which was lost.
Luke 19:8–10

The Hill Road

 od had a song He wanted to sing, and when He had finished it He created a man to sing it. You see, it was a mighty song and needed a Godlike singer. And the man was Jesus, a carpenter of Nazareth. He went up to Jerusalem, and as He walked up and down its narrow, crowded streets, God's song swept across the hearts of people.

Some ran to meet it, it was so full of strength and beauty. But others ran from it, trembling with fear. And these were they who dreaded lest it rend the hate and uproot the falsehood in which their lives were so comfortably grounded.

When the rulers of Israel—priests, scribes, and Pharisees—heard it, they shuttered the windows of their souls and barred the gates of their minds against it; that is, all of them except Nicodemus and one or two others who, when they heard it, stopped to listen.

Nicodemus was no longer a young man, and at first he listened with the gentlemanly indifference of one who is tired of life. But a day came when the swift, clean words cut through the mist of indifference and with a lightning flash revealed Nicodemus to himself. . . .

That night he took the hill road to the Mount of Olives. He had heard that Jesus was in the habit of spending His nights there. . . . The road ended abruptly among a clump of olive trees. . . .

As he stood looking down upon Jerusalem, he felt the presence of long-forgotten memories, and the . . . dreams of his boyhood seemed to rise from the city . . . lying there so quiet and clean in the white radiance of the Eastern night. Unconsciously he lifted his face toward heaven and stretched out his hands, palms upward, in prayer. In the light of the moon and stars his thin, tired face was like an exquisite cameo of old ivory, carved against the onyx shadows of the olive trees.

Jesus saw him thus. The beauty and pathos of the old man tugged at His heart and quietly, lest He break in upon the prayer, Jesus came and stood beside him. He watched the labored rise and fall of the old man's breathing, the throbbing pulse in the thick veins of his forehead, and at once sensed the courage and endurance it had cost Nicodemus to come out alone and by night up the hill road.

Nicodemus looked up. "You are here. I am so glad." . . .

Now that he was face to face with the young Teacher, Nicodemus was at a loss for words. . . . How could he tell Jesus that for an old man to seek the comradeship of a younger, and for a ruler of Israel, a Hebrew of the Hebrews, a member of the Sanhedrin, to have any dealings whatsoever with a Sabbath-breaking Nazarene was not only flagrantly undignified, but dangerously unconventional. But Jesus came to his relief, sensing with instinctive kindliness the older man's difficulty.

"I understand perfectly. It is a bitter experience to be scorned by one's own, an experience from which we may well shrink unless we live so near to God that we are filled with His life."

No sooner had the word *life* been spoken, than Nicodemus found the words for lack of which he had been unable to make his need known. Now he spoke slowly, hesitatingly: "You are a teacher come from God. . . ."

"Are you sure, Nicodemus?" And there was both sadness and a smile in the Master's voice, which Nicodemus was quick to catch.

"You may well ask that. We priests and Pharisees have so often tried to bait you with those very words, but I speak them in all sincerity. Only You can tell me, and my need is too great to be denied—how I, an old man, may find life, *eternal life*. . . ."

Jesus put His hand on that of the old man. "By knowing the God within you, by catching a vision of His Kingdom."

"But it is so long since I have felt God within me—and the eyes of my soul have grown too dim to see so divine a thing as His Kingdom. Surely you realize that I cannot do these things. And if I could—how?"

"There is only one way; you must be born anew."

Nicodemus shook his head and answered with bitter irony: "How can a man be born when he is old? Can he enter his mother's womb over again, and be born?"

"Do not wonder, Nicodemus, at My telling you that you must be born again, spiritually. The wind blows wherever it chooses, and you hear the sound thereof, but you do not know where it comes from or where it goes. This is the way with everyone who owes his birth to the Spirit."

"But how can that be?" Nicodemus asked, bewildered.

"You are a teacher of Israel and yet ignorant of this? I speak of that which I know, and of that which I have seen. You remember how it is told that Moses in the desert lifted the serpent up in the air—even so the Son of Man must be lifted up, so that everyone who believes in Him may have life. Don't you see, Nicodemus? You said your soul seemed to you like a barren, hemmed-in plain. Break down its barriers, widen its horizons, let God's light flood it, and even as the spring sunshine makes the fields blossom, so His light will make your soul alive with new interest, new hope, new joy, new life, life in its fullest sense. Lift up the Son of man within you, and this new life will be life eternal. That's what it means to be born again, Nicodemus, not once, but every day and every hour."

As Jesus spoke these words, night gave place to dawn. The untrammeled song of a lark swept over the hillside and lost itself in the immensity of life waking everywhere.

"It is as though that song had come of my heart," Nicodemus began. He wanted to say more, to make some expression of gratitude, but he could not find the right words. "I came to you in the night," he hesitated, "a soul seemingly without life; now in the dawn I go back—reborn."

ELEANOR B. STOCK

Jesus answered, Verily, verily, I say unto thee, Except a man be born of water and of the Spirit, he cannot enter into the kingdom of God. That which is born of the flesh is flesh; and that which is born of the Spirit is spirit. Marvel not that I said unto thee, Ye must be born again.
John 3:5–7

The painting opposite, *Visit of Nicodemus to Christ* by John La Farge, portrays the conversation of Nicodemus the Pharisee and Jesus Christ.

Conversion from "Nicodemus"

Nicodemus. Tell me one thing; why do you follow Jesus?

John. It was because of John the Baptist first.

Nicodemus. But why because of him?

John. One day when we were standing by the Jordan, John and my cousin Andrew and myself, we saw a man pass by, tall as a spirit; he did not see us though he passed quite near; indeed we thought it strange; His eyes were open but he looked on nothing; and as he passed, John, pointing with his finger, cried—I can hear him cry it now—"Behold, the Lamb of God!"

Nicodemus. And He, what did He say? What did He do?

John. Nothing; we watched Him slowly climb the hill; His shadow fell before Him; it was evening. Sometimes He stopped to raise His head to the home-flying rooks or greet a countryman with plough on shoulder.

Nicodemus. John said, "Behold, the Lamb of God"?

John. He said so.

Nicodemus. And from that day you followed Him?

John. No, that was afterwards in Galilee.

Nicodemus. But tell me why; why did you follow Him?

John. I think it was our feet that followed Him; it was our feet; our hearts were too afraid. Perhaps indeed it was not in our choice; He tells us that we have not chosen Him, but He has chosen us. I only know that as we followed Him that day He called us, we were not walking on the earth at all; it was another world, where everything was new and strange and shining; we pitied men and women at their business, for they knew nothing of what we knew—

Nicodemus. Perhaps it was some miracle He did.

John. It was indeed; more miracles than one; I was not blind and yet He gave me sight; I was not deaf and yet He gave me hearing; Nor was I dead, yet me He raised to life.

Andrew Young
1885–1971

The painting on the opposite page by Ted Hoffman portrays Christ in the garden prior to His arrest and crucifixion on the cross. Simon of Cyrene who helped Jesus carry the cross was probably a Jew coming in from the country to observe Passover in Jerusalem. Tradition has identified Simon of Cyrene with Simeon called Niger of Acts 13:1 who was from Africa.

Simon the Cyrenian Speaks

He never spoke a word to me,
   And yet He called my name;
He never gave a sign to me,
   And yet I knew and came.

At first I said, "I will not bear
   His cross upon my back;
He only seeks to place it there
   Because my skin is black."

But He was dying for a dream,
   And He was very meek,
And in His eyes there shone a gleam
   Men journey far to seek.

It was Himself my pity bought;
   I did for Christ alone
What all of Rome could not have wrought
   With bruise of lash or stone.

COUNTEE CULLEN
1903–1946

Near the Cross

Near the Cross, her vigil keeping,
Stood the mother, worn with weeping,
   Where He hung, the dying Lord:
Through her soul, in anguish groaning,
Bowed in sorrow, sighing, moaning,
   Passed the sharp and piercing sword.

O the weight of her affliction!
Hers, who won God's benediction,
   Hers, who bore God's Holy One:
O that speechless, ceaseless yearning!
O those dim eyes never turning
   From her wondrous, suffering Son!

Who upon that mother gazing,
In her trouble so amazing,
   Born of woman, would not weep?
Who of Christ's dear mother thinking,
While her Son that cup is drinking,
   Would not share her sorrow deep?

For His people's sin chastisèd
She beheld her Son despisèd,
   Bound and bleeding 'neath the rod;
Saw the Lord's Anointed taken,
Dying desolate, forsaken,
   Heard Him yield His soul to God.

Near Thy Cross, O Christ, abiding,
Grief and love my heart dividing,
   I with her would take my place:
By Thy guardian Cross uphold me,
In Thy dying, Christ, enfold me
   With the deathless arms of grace.

FROM THE LATIN, 13TH CENTURY;
TR. COMPILED BY LOUIS F. BENSON, 1855–1930

Now there stood by the cross of Jesus his mother, and his mother's sister, Mary the wife of Cleophas, and Mary Magdalene. When Jesus therefore saw his mother, and the disciple standing by, whom he loved, he saith unto his mother, Woman, behold thy son! Then saith he to the disciple, Behold thy mother! And from that hour that disciple took her unto his own home.
John 19:25–27

Jesus was crucified on a hill called Golgotha (a Semitic word meaning skull or place of the skull) outside the gates of Jerusalem. The Romans reserved crucifixion for slaves, thieves, and political prisoners, and this particularly cruel death was imposed upon Roman citizens only for the crime of high treason. Two other men were crucified alongside Jesus; one mocked the dying Jesus, but the other recognized His divinity and asked to be remembered in God's kingdom. The painting opposite by Joseph Maniscalco depicts the agony of the women, especially Jesus' mother, in witnessing this horrible act.

In fulfillment of the Psalms, "They part my garments among them, and cast lots upon my vesture" (Psalm 22:18), the soldiers cast lots to see which among them would take Jesus' tunic. He suffered six hours on the cross before His life on earth ended. The painting on the opposite page by Peter Bianchi shows a Roman soldier at the moment of Christ's death, when the world turned dark and the earthquake struck.

Gambler

And sitting down, they watched Him there,
The soldiers did;
There, while they played with dice,
He made His sacrifice,
And died upon the Cross to rid
God's world of sin.

He was a gambler, too, my Christ,
He took His life and threw
It for a world redeemed.
And ere His agony was done,
Before the westering sun went down,
Crowning that day with crimson crown,
He knew that He had won.

G. A. STUDDERT-KENNEDY
1883–1929

Upon a Hill

Three men shared death upon a hill,
But only one man died;
The other two—
A thief and God himself—
Made rendezvous.

Three crosses still
Are borne up Calvary's Hill,
Where Sin lifts them high:
Upon the one sag broken men
Who, cursing, die;

Another holds the praying thief,
Or those who, penitent as he,
Still find the Christ
Beside them on the tree.

MIRIAM LEFEVRE CROUSE

Peter V. Bianchi

Now at that feast he released unto them one prisoner, whomsoever they desired. And there was one named Barabbas, which lay bound with them that had made insurrection with him, who had committed murder in the insurrection. And the multitude crying aloud began to desire him to do as he had ever done unto them. But Pilate answered them, saying, Will ye that I release unto you the King of the Jews? For he knew that the chief priests had delivered him for envy. But the chief priests moved the people, that he should rather release Barabbas unto them. And so Pilate, willing to content the people, released Barabbas unto them, and delivered Jesus, when he had scourged him, to be crucified.

Mark 15:6–11, 15

The cedar trees of Lebanon grow up to one-hundred-twenty-five feet tall, and some are believed to be more than one thousand years old. Knot-free and rot-resistant, these great cedars forested the mountain slopes north of Israel and from Old Testament days have come to represent the steadfastness of God.

Good Friday

Am I a stone, and not a sheep,
    That I can stand, O Christ, beneath Thy cross,
    To number drop by drop Thy Blood's slow loss,
And yet not weep?

Not so those women loved
    Who with exceeding grief lamented Thee;
    Not so fallen Peter weeping bitterly;
Not so the thief was moved;

Not so the Sun and Moon
    Which hid their faces in a starless sky.
    A horror of great darkness at broad noon—
I, only I.

Yet give not o'er
    But seek Thy sheep, true Shepherd of the flock;
    Greater than Moses, turn and look once more
And smite a rock.

CHRISTINA ROSSETTI
1830–1894

Barabbas Speaks

I heard a man explaining
(they said his name was Paul)
how Jesus, on that fateful day,
had died to save us all.

I found it hard to follow
His fine-spun theory,
but I am very, very sure
He died that day for me.

EDWIN MCNEILL POTEAT
1892–1955

Easter Eve

His murderers met. Their consciences were free:
The sun's eclipse was past, the tumult stilled
In Jewry, and their duty well fulfilled.

Quoth Caiaphas:—
It wrung my heart to see
His mother's grief, God knows. Yet blasphemy
Was proven, the uprising imminent,
And all the church-supporting element
Demanded action, sir, of you and me.

Quoth Pilate:—
When this Nazarene denied
Even Caesar's rule, reluctantly I knew
My duty to the state, sir. Still, I tried,
But found no way, to spare him yet stay true

In loyalty. . . . And still, the poor lad cried,
"Forgive them, for they know not what they do!"

JAMES BRANCH CABELL
1879–1958

*Pilate saith unto them,
What shall I do then
with Jesus which is
called Christ? They all
say unto him, Let him
be crucified. And the
governor said, Why,
what evil hath he done?
But they cried out the
more, saying, Let him
be crucified. When
Pilate saw that he could
prevail nothing, but
that rather a tumult
was made, he took
water, and washed his
hands before the multi-
tude, saying, I am
innocent of the blood of
this just person: see ye
to it. Then answered all
the people, and said,
His blood be on us, and
on our children.*
Matthew 27:22–25

Opposite is a lovely view of a
sunset over the Sea of Galilee.

Religious Leaders and Factions

In the second century B.C., Jews in Palestine divided into various religious and political parties, one of the most powerful being the Pharisees, whose name came from a word that means separate. The Pharisees were teachers in the synagogues who diligently studied the scriptures, particularly the strict laws of purity. They followed an intense daily set of rules and religious laws that covered everything from how they ate to how they prayed, and they held themselves apart from the rest of the Jewish community. Jesus disagreed with the Pharisees' emphasis on maintaining the appearance of holiness, and He unmasked their self-righteousness and hypocrisy.

The painting below is entitled THE PHARISEES CONSPIRE TOGETHER, by James J. Tissot. Declaring that Jesus "not only had broken the Sabbath, but said also that God was his father, making himself equal with God" (John 5:18), the Pharisees called for Jesus' arrest and trial as a blasphemer.

The Pharisees also with the Sadducees came, and tempting desired him that he would shew them a sign from heaven. He answered and said unto them, A wicked and adulterous generation seeketh after a sign; and there shall no sign be given unto it."
Matthew 16:1, 2a, 4a

The Sadducees were the Pharisees' chief rival for religious power. They traced their lineage to the high priests of Solomon's Temple; and their name may have come from Zadok, the high priest from the time of King David. Sadducees based their lives on the books of Moses, Genesis through Deuteronomy. Unlike the Pharisees, they did not believe in an afterlife nor were they interested in the strict rules of purity. The Sadducees enjoyed good relations with Rome, and they worried that Jesus would create a Jewish uprising and bring down the wrath of Rome's rulers. Although they argued with the Pharisees about most issues, the Sadducees agreed that Jesus must be silenced.

The Zealots began in A.D. 6 in response to a census which they believed was the first step toward increased taxation; they became a powerful political party and were uncompromising in their hatred of Rome. During the destruction of Jerusalem by Roman soldiers in A.D. 70, the Zealots became the last holdouts in the stronghold on top of the Masada, a thirteen-hundred-foot high butte overlooking the Dead Sea on which King Herod built a magnificent palace. Here is where more than one thousand men, women, and children chose suicide over surrender; only two women and five children survived. With the fall of Masada, the Romans would not allow the rebuilding of the temple, the Sanhedrin was abolished, the high priesthood came to an end, and the Sadducees ceased to exist.

This relief depicting soldiers parading through Rome with bounty looted from the Temple in Jerusalem is from the Arch of Titus in Rome, a monument built to commemorate the victory of Rome in the first Jewish revolt of A.D. 73. Roman soldiers under Titus, son of the Roman emperor Vespasian, burned and looted the city, crushing all resistance. Rome's victory fulfilled Jesus' prophecy of Matthew 24:2b: "Verily I say unto you, There shall not be left here one stone upon another, that shall not be thrown down."

Essenes interpreted the religious law in the strictest manner, even more so than the Pharisees; and they lived in isolated communities of self-discipline and self-denial. Essenes believed that a judgment day would come when the Sons of Light would prevail over the Sons of Darkness, destroy life on earth as it existed, and usher in a time of peace and contentment. Their communities clustered in the deserts on the north coast of the Dead Sea, the most celebrated of which was at Qumran, where in the 1940s the Dead Sea Scrolls, written by the Essenes, were discovered.

Pictured below are the ruins of Herod's palace and fortress atop the Masada on the western shore of the Dead Sea. The Masada was only one of many mountaintop fortresses built by Herod the Great; water was provided by a series of deep cisterns fed by an aqueduct that brought water from a dammed wadi. A trail called the Snake Path was the road to the top during the days of Herod; on the opposite side a huge ramp was built by the Roman commander Silva during the siege. In part because of the water supply, the Zealots, who had captured Masada in A.D. 66, were able to hold out for eight years.

Pilate Remembers

Do I remember such and such an one?
Nay, Marcus mine, how can I? Every day
The judgment hall was crowded. Every week
A motley throng of victims met their doom.
One Jesus? No. And yet,—and yet,—the name
Does sound familiar. Let me think again—
Jesus from Nazareth in Galilee?
Yes, I recall him now: a strange, still man
With eyes that searched one's very soul, a voice
Of marvelous sweetness, and a face so pure
It scarce seemed human. There again he stands!
All bruised and bleeding, he was dragged in chains
Before the judgment seat. . . .

. . . Innocent he was
As babe new born. I felt a certain awe
As there with folded hands he stood, and gazed
Right in my eyes, yet gave nor sign nor sound.
He seemed the judge, and I the criminal.
I would have freed him, by the Gods I would,
And strove to do so; but those cursed priests—
Nay, boy, enough, enough. Let memory rest.
Here pass the wine and let us drink to her,
The fair, young slave whom Publius brought from Spain,
Whose queenly grace, and rounded loveliness
Have turned all heads in Rome. Your questions, lad,
Have made me squeamish, turned to sourness
The milk of my content. Let be the past.
I thank the Gods, that two divinities
Have power to lay the peeping ghosts that slip
Through memory's doorway. Thank the Gods, I say,
For wine and women. Fill the cup again!

THOMAS DURLEY LANDELS
1862–?

Pilate denied responsibility for the decision to crucify Jesus.
In his mind, he had left the choice to the crowd, and they had
determined that Jesus would die on the cross. The painting
PILATE WASHING HIS HANDS by Rembrandt Van Rijn depicts Pilate
as he ceremoniously washes his hands of responsibility.

*And as he journeyed, he
came near Damascus:
and suddenly there
shined round about him
a light from heaven:
And he fell to the earth,
and heard a voice say-
ing unto him, Saul,
Saul, why persecutest
thou me? And he said,
Who art thou, Lord?
And the Lord said, I am
Jesus whom thou perse-
cutest: it is hard for
thee to kick against the
pricks. And he trem-
bling and astonished
said, Lord, what wilt
thou have me to do?
And the Lord said unto
him, Arise, and go into
the city, and it shall be
told thee what thou
must do. And the men
which journeyed with
him stood speechless,
hearing a voice, but see-
ing no man. And Saul
arose from the earth;
and when his eyes were
opened, he saw no man:
but they led him by the
hand, and brought him
into Damascus.*
Acts 9:3–8

The painting opposite is THE
CONVERSION OF ST. PAUL by
Caravaggio. Blinded and
humbled on the road to
Damascus, Saul was
transformed into Paul to
become what he called an
apostle of Christ Jesus by the
will of God.

The Conversion
of Saint Paul

The midday sun with fiercest glare,
Broods o'er the hazy, twinkling air;
  Along the level sand
The palm tree's shade unwavering lies,
Just as thy towers, Damascus, rise
  To greet yon wearied band.

One moment—and to earth he falls;
What voice his inmost heart appalls?
  Voice heard by him alone.
For to the rest both words and form
Seem lost in lightning and in storm,
  While Saul, in wakeful trance,
Sees deep within that dazzling field
His persecuted Lord revealed
  With keen yet pitying glance:
And hears the meek upbraiding call
As gently on his spirit fall
  As if th' Almighty Son
Were prisoner yet in this dark earth,
Nor had proclaimed His royal birth,
  Nor His great power begun.

"Ah, wherefore persecut'st thou me?"
He heard and saw, and sought to free
  His strained eye from the sight;
But heaven's high magic bound it there,
Still gazing, though untaught to bear
  Th' insufferable light.

"Who art Thou, Lord?" he falters forth:
So shall sin ask of heaven and earth
  At the last awful day.
"When did we see Thee suffering nigh,
And passed Thee with unheeding eye?
  Great God of judgment, say?"
Ah! little dream our listless eyes
What glorious presence they despise,
  While in our noon of life,
To power or fame we rudely press,

Christ is at hand, to scorn or bless,
  Christ suffers in our strife.

And though Heaven's gates long since have clos'd,
And our dear Lord in bliss repos'd
  High above mortal ken,
To every ear in every land
(Though meek ears only understand)
  He speaks as He did then.

"Ah! wherefore persecute ye me?
'Tis hard, ye so in love should be
  With your own endless woe.
Know, though at God's right hand I live,
I feel each wound ye reckless give
  To the least saint below.
I in your care My brethren left,
Not willing ye should be bereft
  Of waiting on your Lord.

The meanest offering ye can make—
A drop of water—for love's sake,
  In heaven, be sure, is stor'd."

As to Thy last Apostle's heart
Thy lightning glance did then impart
  Zeal's never-dying fire,
So teach us on Thy shrine to lay
Our hearts, and let them day by day
  Intenser blaze and higher.
And as each mild and winning note
(Like pulses that round harp string's float,
  When the full strain is o'er)
Left lingering on his inward ear
Music, that taught, as death drew near,
  Love's lesson more and more:
So, as we walk our earthly round,
Still may the echo of that sound,
  Be in our memory stor'd:
"Christians! behold your happy state:
Christ is in these, who round you wait;
  Make much of your dear Lord!"

JOHN KEBLE
1792–1866

And there was a certain disciple at Damascus, named Ananias; and to him said the Lord in a vision, Ananias. And he said, Behold, I am here, Lord. And the Lord said . . . enquire in the house of Judas for one called Saul of Tarsus: for, behold, he prayeth, And hath seen in a vision a man named Ananias coming in, and putting his hand on him, that he might receive his sight. Then Ananias answered, Lord, I have heard by many of this man, how much evil he hath done to thy saints at Jerusalem: But the Lord said unto him, Go thy way: for he is a chosen vessel unto me, to bear my name before the Gentiles, and kings, and the children of Israel: For I will shew him how great things he must suffer for my name's sake.
Acts 9:10-13, 15-16

On the opposite page are the ruins of Caesarea. Philip and Peter brought Jesus' message to this Mediterranean city, as did Paul, who embarked from the city on many of his westward travels.

Jesus Gave Them Life

For the most part, the Jews of Jesus' time held to the belief that the day would come when God would send the Messiah, the king of the Jews who would save His people. Prophets of old such as Isaiah and Daniel foretold of this day.

As the trials of Roman occupation weighed increasingly heavy on the Jewish people, they became especially alert for signs of the Messiah, whose coming would signal the beginning of God's Kingdom.

As word of Jesus' miracles of resurrection spread through the land, the faithful took notice. But it was not until Jesus was crucified and rose from the dead that the ancient prophecies were fulfilled and the promise of eternal life given to all men and women of true faith.

A master teacher, Jesus used familiar language and images to help His disciples more fully understand the kingdom of God. Calling them to follow Him, Jesus told the apostles—many of them fishermen who left behind their boats and nets to serve Him—that He would make them "fishers of men." Later, He compared the kingdom of God to "a net, that was cast into the sea, and gathered of every kind: Which, when it was full, they drew to shore, and sat down, and gathered the good into vessels, but cast the bad away" (Matthew 13:47, 48). For men who had lived their lives in a part of the world where fishing was a way of life, such imagery was clear and powerful. At right, a lone fishing boat on the Sea of Galilee.

The Daughter of Jairus

And, behold, there came
a man named Jairus,
and he was a ruler of
the synagogue: and he
fell down at Jesus' feet,
and besought him that
he would come into his
house: For he had one
only daughter, about
twelve years of age, and
she lay a dying. While
he yet spake, there
cometh one from the
ruler of the synagogue's
house, saying to him,
Thy daughter is dead;
trouble not the Master.
But when Jesus heard
it, he answered him,
saying, Fear not: believe
only, and she shall be
made whole.

Luke 8:41, 42a, 49, 50

The Gospels tell of three times when Jesus raised the dead. He resurrected the widow of Nain's son during a funeral procession (Luke 7:11–18); He brought Lazarus from his tomb back to life (John 11:1–44); and He raised the daughter of Jairus, as depicted opposite in the painting RAISING OF JAIRUS'S DAUGHTER by Johann Friedrich Overbeck. These three miracles recall three Old Testament miracles of resurrection—two by Elisha and one by Elijah—and they also foreshadow Jesus' own resurrection, which was unique in that, unlike those raised from the dead before Him, Jesus was raised not to continue in His earthly life, but to demonstrate life eternal.

Jesus was at home once more, but He was not permitted to rest. Crowds, larger than He had left, received Him. He was surrounded and overwhelmed. . . . In the heart of His busiest and weariest hour an urgent demand came. . . .

An officer of the Jewish church, an important person, Jairus by name, had a little daughter, dearly cherished. She was scarcely twelve years old, . . . her father's darling. She lay at the point of death, and in hot haste messengers had been sent for the Nazarene.

At the feet of Jesus, Jairus flung himself down like a slave, and such an agony went up in his face and attitude as a cold man could not easily have resisted. Jesus, melting with sympathy, tenderly reassured the father, and started at once in the direction of the ruler's house.

But what a throng! When He tried to pass through the people, they closed like a round wall about Him. Such a mass of humanity pressed upon Him that it was impossible to move. At that moment, stealing past the push and rush of the thoughtless throng, a timid hand touched the fringe of his garment, then, terrified, withdrew instantly.

"Who touched me?" Jesus asked quickly. No person in the crowd replied. "Strength goes out of me," insisted the Master. "Who was it?" And the crowd marveled that he even felt it, so great was the press of the multitude.

Jesus and Jairus walked together to the ruler's house. The father did not speak again. He was afraid of offending the rabbi. . . . When the servant came, weeping, and told him that it was too late, not to trouble the Master, for the little maid was gone—his heart had broken in one mad outcry. This great Healer, this mysterious man, so famous for His tenderness, so marvelous for His pity, must needs fail him, him, Jairus, out of all Palestine, and that in the hour of his terrible need! For . . . Jesus had stopped on the way to a dying patient to cure an old, chronic case. That woman could have been healed just as well tonight, tomorrow, or next week. But He had lingered. And the child was dead.

"Do not be afraid," said Jesus, tenderly; "only believe!" But His face was very grave. And by a single motion of His expressive hand He ordered all His disciples back but three—Peter, James, and John, His dearest. The group entered the ruler's house. . . . Jesus seemed surprised at the condition in which He found the family.

"The child is not dead," He said, decidedly. Some of the neighbors, who did not altogether believe in the famous Healer, began to laugh. It was a derisive laugh, a cold sound in that house of woe, and it did not please Him. A keen rebuke shot from His mild eyes at the unseemly scorn. "Nay," He repeated, "she is not dead. She is asleep."

He spoke in the tone of a man who was not to be gainsaid. . . . He went into the sick room and looked at the child. "This is sleep," he persisted. . . . The father's sobs had ceased. The mother lifted her face, discolored with tears, worn with watching, and piteously raised her hands. The three friends of the rabbi reverently wondering.

Jesus silently regarded the little maid. She lay unconscious and was quite rigid. Jesus looked at her with a strange expression. His eyes seemed to say: "It is between Me and thee, little maid. We understand." . . .

Now He looked at the little girl with the tenderness that is only to be expected of those in whom the love of children is profound and genuine. She seemed to quiver beneath His look, but her color and her attitude did not change. Then He took her by the hand.

Her little wasted fingers lay for a few moments in His . . . grasp; then He felt them tremble. . . . Who sees the instant when the lily blossoms? Who could have detected the moment of time in which the child began to stir? Was it His hand that moved, or hers that directed His slowly upward till it reached her pillow, and so came upon a level with her face?

It did not seem sudden or startling, but only the most natural thing in the world, when the little girl laid her cheek upon His palm.

Elizabeth Stuart Phelps
from *The Story of Jesus Christ*

And when he came into the house, he suffered no man to go in, save Peter, and James, and John, and the father and the mother of the maiden. And all wept, and bewailed her: but he said, Weep not; she is not dead, but sleepeth. And they laughed him to scorn, knowing that she was dead. And he put them all out, and took her by the hand, and called, saying, Maid, arise. And her spirit came again, and she arose straightway.
Luke 8:51–55a

Now a certain man was sick, named Lazarus, of Bethany, the town of Mary and her sister Martha. Therefore his sisters sent unto him, saying, Lord, behold, he whom thou lovest is sick. When Jesus heard that, he said, This sickness is not unto death, but for the glory of God, that the Son of God might be glorified thereby. Now Jesus loved Martha, and her sister, and Lazarus. When he had heard therefore that he was sick, he abode two days still in the same place where he was. And after that he saith unto them, Our friend Lazarus sleepeth; but I go, that I may awake him out of sleep. Then said his disciples, Lord, if he sleep, he shall do well. Howbeit Jesus spake of his death: but they thought that he had spoken of taking of rest in sleep. Then said Jesus unto them plainly, Lazarus is dead. And I am glad for your sakes that I was not there, to the intent ye may believe; nevertheless let us go unto him. Then said Thomas, which is called Didymus, unto his fellowdisciples, Let us also go, that we may die with him.

John 11:1, 3–6, 11b–16

Now as Christ
Drew near to Bethany, the Jews went forth
With Martha mourning Lazarus. But Mary
Sat in the house. She knew the hour was nigh
When He would go again, as He had said,
Unto his Father; and she felt that He,
Who loved her brother Lazarus in Life,
Had chose the hour to bring him home thro' Death
In no unkind forgetfulness. Alone—
She could lift up the bitter pray to heaven,
"Thy will be done, O God!" But once more
Came Martha, saying, "Lo, the Lord is here
And calleth for thee, Mary!" Then arose
The mourner from the ground, whereon she sat
Shrouded in sackcloth, and bound quickly up
The golden locks of her dishevel'd hair,
And o'er her ashy garments drew a veil
Hiding the eyes she could not trust. And still,
As she made ready to go forth, a calm
As in a dream fell on her.
    At a fount
Hard by the sepulchre, without the wall,
Jesus awaited Mary. Seated near
Were the wayworn disciples in the shade;
But, of himself forgetful, Jesus lean'd
Upon his staff, and watch'd where she should come,
To whose one sorrow—but a sparrow's falling—
The pity that redeem'd a world could bleed!
And as she came, with that uncertain step,—
Eager, yet weak, her hands upon her breast,—
And they who follow'd her all fallen back
To leave her with her sacred grief alone,—
The heart of Christ was troubled. She drew near;
Then, with a vain strife to control her tears,
She stagger'd to the midst, and at His feet
Fell prostrate, saying, "Lord! hadst thou been here,
My brother had not died!" The Savior groan'd
In spirit, and stoop'd tenderly, and raised
The mourner from the ground, and in a voice
Broke in its utterance like her own, He said,
"Where have ye laid him?" Then the Jews who came
Following Mary, answer'd through their tears

"Lord, come and see!" But lo! the mighty heart
That in Gethsemane sweat drops of blood,
Taking from us the cup that might not pass—
The heart whose breaking cord upon the cross
Made the earth tremble, and the sun afraid
To look upon His agony—the heart
Of a lost world's Redeemer—overflowed,
Touched by a mourner's sorrow! Jesus wept.
Calm'd by those pitying tears, and fondly brooding
Upon the thought that Christ so loved her brother,
Stood Mary there; but that lost burden now
Lay on His heart who pitied her; and Christ,
Following slow and groaning in Himself,
Came to the sepulcher. It was a cave,
And a stone lay upon it. Jesus said,
"Take ye away the stone!" Then lifted He
His moisten'd eyes to heaven, and while the Jews
And the disciples bent their heads in awe,
And, trembling, Mary sank upon her knees,
The Son of God pray'd audibly. He ceased,
And for a minute's space there was a hush,
As if th' angelic watchers of the world
Had stayed the pulse of all breathing things,
To listen to that prayer. The face of Christ
Shone as He stood, and over Him there came
Command as 'twere the living face of God,
And with a loud voice, He cried, "Lazarus!
Come forth!" And instantly, bound hand and foot,
And borne by unseen angels from the cave,
He that was dead stood with them. At the word
Of Jesus, the fear-stricken Jews unloosed
The bands from off the foldings of his shroud;
And Mary, with her dark veil thrown aside,
Ran to him swiftly, and cried, "Lazarus!
My brother Lazarus!" and tore away
The napkin she had bound about his head—
And touched the warm lips with her fearful hand—
And on his neck fell weeping.

NATHANIEL PARKER WILLIS
1806–1867

Then when Jesus came, he found that he had lain in the grave four days already. And many of the Jews came to Martha and Mary, to comfort them concerning their brother. Then Martha, as soon as she heard that Jesus was coming, went and met him: . . . Then said Martha unto Jesus, Lord, if thou hadst been here, my brother had not died. But I know, that even now, whatsoever thou wilt ask of God, God will give it thee. Jesus saith unto her, Thy brother shall rise again. Martha saith unto him, I know that he shall rise again in the resurrection at the last day. Jesus said unto her, I am the resurrection, and the life: he that believeth in me, though he were dead, yet shall he live.
John 11:17, 19–25

The Touch of the Master's Hand

'Twas battered and scarred, and the auctioneer
Thought it scarcely worth his while
To waste much time on the old violin,
But held it up with a smile.
"What am I bidden, good folks," he cried,
"Who'll start the bidding for me?"
"A dollar, a dollar;" then "Two! Only two?
Two dollars, who'll make it three?
Three dollars, once; three dollars, twice;
Going for three—" But no,
From the room, far back, a gray-haired man
Came forward and picked up the bow;
Then, wiping the dust from the old violin,
And tightening the loose strings,
He played a melody pure and sweet
As a caroling angel sings.

The music ceased, and the auctioneer,
With a voice that was quiet and low,
Said: "What am I bid for the old violin?"
And he held it up with the bow.
"A thousand dollars, and who'll make it two?
Two thousand! And who'll make it three?
Three thousand, once; three thousand, twice,
And going, and gone," said he.
The people cheered, but some of them cried,
"We do not quite understand
What changed its worth." Swift came the reply:
"The touch of a master's hand."

And many a man with life out of tune,
And battered and scarred with sin,
Is auctioned cheap to the thoughtless crowd,
Much like the old violin. . . .
He is "going" once, and "going" twice,
He's "going" and almost "gone."
But the Master comes, and the foolish crowd
Never can quite understand
The worth of a soul and the change that's wrought
By the touch of the Master's hand.

MYRA BROOKS WELCH
?–1959

When Jesus therefore saw her weeping, and the Jews also weeping which came with her, he groaned in the spirit, and was troubled, And said, Where have ye laid him? They said unto him, Lord, come and see. Jesus wept. Then said the Jews, Behold how he loved him! Jesus therefore again groaning in himself cometh to the grave. It was a cave, and a stone lay upon it. Jesus said, Take ye away the stone. Then they took away the stone from the place where the dead was laid. And Jesus . . . cried with a loud voice, Lazarus, come forth. And he that was dead came forth.
John 11:33–36, 38, 39a, 41, 43b, 44a

When Lazarus died, Jesus was in Perea, east of Jerusalem. When Martha and Mary sent for Jesus, He knew that danger awaited Him in Jerusalem, yet He went. Although Lazarus had been dead four days, Jesus brought him back to life. The miracle aroused the people of Jerusalem, and the furor over the raising of Lazarus helped force the confrontation between Jesus and the Sanhedrin to its final climax. The painting opposite is THE RESURRECTION OF LAZARUS by the artist Jean-Baptiste Corneille.

Mary Magdalene

But Mary stood without at the sepulchre weeping: and as she wept, she stooped down, and looked into the sepulchre, And seeth two angels in white sitting, the one at the head, and the other at the feet, where the body of Jesus had lain. And they say unto her, Woman, why weepest thou? She saith unto them, Because they have taken away my Lord, and I know not where they have laid him. And when she had thus said, she turned herself back, and saw Jesus standing, and knew not that it was Jesus.

John 20:11–14

I t was in the month of June when I saw Him for the first time. He was walking in the wheatfield when I passed by with my handmaidens, and He was alone.

The rhythm of His step was different from other men's, and the movement of His body was like naught I had seen before. Men do not pace the earth in that manner. And even now I do not know whether He walked fast or slow.

My handmaidens pointed their fingers at Him and spoke in shy whispers to one another. And I stayed my steps for a moment, and raised my hand to hail Him. But He did not turn His face, and He did not look at me. . . . I was swept back into myself, and I was as cold as if I had been in a snowdrift. And I shivered.

That night I beheld Him in my dreaming; and they told me afterward that I screamed in my sleep and was restless upon my bed.

It was in the month of August that I saw Him again, through my window. He was sitting in the shadow of the cypress tree across my garden, and He was still as if He had been carved out of stone, . . . And my slave, the Egyptian, came to me and said, "That man is here again. He is sitting there across your garden."

And I gazed at Him, and my soul quivered within me, for He was beautiful. . . . Then I clothed myself with raiment of Damascus, and I left my house and walked towards Him. . . . Was it hunger in my eyes that desired comeliness, or was it His beauty that sought the light of my eyes? Even now I do not know.

I walked to Him with my scented garments and my golden sandals . . . and when I reached him, I said, "Good-morrow to you."

And He said, "Good-morrow to you, Miriam."

And He looked at me, and His night-eyes saw me as no man had seen me. And suddenly I was as if naked, and I was shy. Yet He had said only, "Good-morrow to you."

And then I said to Him, "Will you not come to my house? . . . Will you not have wine and bread with me?"

And He said, "Yes, Miriam, but not now."

Not now, not now, He said. And the voice of the sea was in those two words and the voice of the wind and the trees. And when He said them unto me, life spoke to death.

For mind you, my friend, I was dead. I was a woman who had divorced her soul. I was living apart from this self which you now see. I belonged to all men, and to none. They called me harlot, and a woman possessed of seven devils. I was cursed, and I was envied.

But when His dawn-eyes looked into my eyes all the stars of my night faded away, and I became Miriam, only Miriam, a woman lost to the earth she had known, and finding herself in new places.

And now again I said to Him, "Come into my house and share bread and wine with me."

And He said, "Why do you bid me to be your guest?"

And I said, "I beg you to come into my house." And it was all that was sod in me, and all that was sky in me, calling unto Him.

Then He looked at me, and the noontide of His eyes was upon me, and He said, "You have many lovers, and yet I alone love you. Other men love themselves in your nearness. I love you in yourself. Other men see a beauty in you that shall fade away sooner than their own years. But I see in you a beauty that shall not fade away, and in the autumn of your days that beauty shall not be afraid to gaze at itself in the mirror, and it shall not be offended. I alone love the unseen in you."

Then He said in a low voice: "Go away now. If this cypress tree is yours and you would not have me sit in its shadow, I will walk my way."

And I cried to Him and I said: "Master, come to my house. I have incense to burn for you, and a silver basin for your feet. You are a stranger, and yet not a stranger. I entreat you, come to my house."

Then He stood up and looked at me even as the seasons might look down upon the field, and He smiled. And He said again: "All men love you for themselves. I love you for yourself."

And then He walked away. But no other man ever walked the way He walked. Was it a breath born in my garden that moved to the east? Or was it a storm that would shake all things to their foundations?

I knew not, but on that day the sunset of His eyes slew the dragon in me, and I became a woman, I became Miriam, Miriam of Migdel.

KAHLIL GIBRAN
FROM *JESUS THE SON OF MAN*

Jesus saith unto her, Woman, why weepest thou? whom seekest thou? She, supposing him to be the gardener, saith unto him, Sir, if thou have borne him hence, tell me where thou hast laid him, and I will take him away. Jesus saith unto her, Mary. She turned herself, and saith unto him, Rabboni; which is to say, Master. Jesus saith unto her, Touch me not; for I am not yet ascended to my Father: but go to my brethren, and say unto them, I ascend unto my Father, and your Father; and to my God, and your God. Mary Magdalene came and told the disciples that she had seen the Lord, and that he had spoken these things unto her.
John 20:15–18

A Guard
of the Sepulcher

I was a Roman soldier in my prime;
Now age is on me and the yoke of time.
I saw your Risen Christ, for I am he
Who reached the hyssop to Him on the tree;
And I am one of two who watched beside
The Sepulcher of Him we crucified.
All that last night I watched with sleepless eyes;
Great stars arose and crept across the skies.
The world was all too still for mortal rest,
For pitiless thoughts were busy in the breast.
The night was long, so long, it seemed at last
I had grown old and a long life had passed.
Far off, the hills of Moab, touched with light,
Were swimming in the hollow of the night.
I saw Jerusalem all wrapped in cloud
Stretched like a dead thing folded in a shroud.
Once in the pauses of our whispered talk
I heard a something on the garden walk.
Perhaps it was a crisp leaf lightly stirred—
Perhaps the dream-note of a waking bird.
Then suddenly an angel burning white
Came down with earthquake in the breaking light,
And rolled the great stone from the Sepulcher,
Mixing the morning with a scent of myrrh.
And, lo, the Dead had risen with the day:
The Man of Mystery had gone His way.

Years have I wandered, carrying my shame;
Now let the tooth of time eat out my name.
For we, who all the wonder might have told,
Kept silence, for our mouths were stopt with gold.

EDWIN MARKHAM
1852–1940

Now the next day, that
followed the day of the
preparation, the chief
priests and Pharisees
came together unto
Pilate, Saying, Sir, we
remember that that
deceiver said, while he
was yet alive, After
three days I will rise
again. Command there-
fore that the sepulchre
be made sure until the
third day, lest his disciples come by night, and
steal him away, and
say unto the people, He
is risen from the dead:
so the last error shall be
worse than the first.
Pilate said unto them,
Ye have a watch: go
your way, make it as
sure as ye can. So they
went, and made the
sepulchre sure, sealing
the stone, and setting a
watch.
Matthew 27:62–66

The Gospels tell us that, after
the crucifixion, Joseph of
Arimathaea took possession
of Jesus' body, prepared it for
burial, and brought it to a
tomb near Golgotha. The
traditional site of Jesus' tomb
is located within the modern
city of Jerusalem and marked
by the Church of the Holy
Sepulchre. The tomb in which
Christ's body was laid probably looked much like the one
opposite, located in a garden
in modern Jerusalem.

And . . . then came Jesus, the doors being shut, and stood in the midst, and said, Peace be unto you. Then saith he to Thomas, Reach hither thy finger, and behold my hands; and reach hither thy hand, and thrust it into my side: and be not faithless, but believing. And Thomas answered and said unto him, My Lord and my God. Jesus saith unto him, Thomas, because thou hast seen me, thou hast believed: blessed are they that have not seen, and yet have believed.

John 20:24–29

Thomas is often remembered as the doubter among Jesus' apostles, yet there is more to Thomas than doubt alone. When Jesus tells His disciples that He is going to Jerusalem to seek out Lazarus, despite the fact that danger awaits Him there, all but Thomas urge Him not to go. Thomas declares they should not prevent Jesus from going, but rather go with Him. This is not a man plagued by doubt, but a man guided by devotion to His Master. Opposite, in a painting by Leslie Benson, Thomas reaches to touch Jesus' wounds after His resurrection.

Unbelieving Thomas

There was a seal upon the stone,
A guard around the tomb:
The spurned and trembling band alone
Bewail their Master's doom.
They deemed the barriers of the grave
Had closed o'er Him who came to save;
And thoughts of grief and gloom
Were darkening, while depressed, dismayed,
Silent they wept, or weeping prayed. . . .

But soon the gates asunder flew,
The iron bands were riven;
Broken the seal; the guards dispersed,
Upon their sight in glory burst
The risen Lord of Heaven!
Yet one, the heaviest in despair,
In grief the wildest was not there.

Returning, on each altered brow
With mute surprise he gazed,
For each was lit with transport now,
Each eye to heaven upraised.
Burst forth from each th' ecstatic word—
"Hail, brother, we have seen the Lord!"
Bewildered and amazed
He stood; then bitter words and brief
Betrayed the heart of unbelief. . . .

"Reach, doubter! Reach thy hand," he said;
"Explore the wound the spear hath made,
The front by nails impressed:
No longer for the living grieve,
And be not faithless, but believe." . . .

How could he trace to human eyes
The rainbow of the heart;
When love, joy, fear, repentance, shame,
Hope, faith, in swift succession came,
Each claiming there a part;
Each mingling in the tears that flowed,
The words that breathed—"My Lord! My God!"

THOMAS DALE
1797–1870

On the Road to Emmaus

And, behold, two of them went that same day to a village called Emmaus, which was from Jerusalem about threescore furlongs. And they talked together of all these things which had happened. And it came to pass, that, while they communed together and reasoned, Jesus himself drew near, and went with them. But their eyes were holden that they should not know him. And he said unto them, What manner of communications are these that ye have one to another, as ye walk, and are sad? And the one of them, whose name was Cleopas, answering said unto him, Art thou only a stranger in Jerusalem, and hast not known the things which are come to pass there in these days?

Luke 24:13–18

It was one of those evenings when every tree seems to have been dipped in crystal, and the scarlet anemones on the hills glowed like molten rubies. . . .

Nathanael and Cleopas had set out from Jerusalem in the forenoon; now their shadows were lengthening. During the journey they exchanged few words between them, until they came close to Emmaus. Then, when it was growing darker, and their spirits were oppressed by the memories that crowded on them with the coming of night, they spoke more often, with long silences between.

"Is he alive or dead—that's the question!" Cleopas said sharply . . . "If he is alive, where is he? . . . Well, I saw the empty tomb! How do you explain it, Nathanael?"

"Did not the woman say she saw him?" Nathanael said after a pause.

"Yes, she did. She said there was a gardener standing in the garden, and wearing a hat to shade his face, and she knew he was Jesus. But when I asked her to describe him—whether there were wounds on his hands and feet, and whether there was blood on his forehead from the crown of thorns, and what clothes he was wearing, why, she answered nothing at all. . . . As for the story of the angel sitting on the tomb— why, that's an old wives' tale. It was a fool's journey, and we were fools to follow him! I shall have no sleep at night, thinking of the trick he has played upon us! You have your faith, but as for me, I won't believe he is alive until I see him with my own eyes."

"Then what will you do?"

"I will do what all men do when they see a friend who has returned. I shall run into his arms with such joy that the sound of my cry will be heard for a hundred miles! I loved him with all my heart, but loving a dead man is something else altogether. Didn't he say: 'Let the dead bury the dead'? Well, let the dead Christ bury the dead Christ!"

With these words Cleopas shook his head, fell into a long silence, and said nothing more until the walls of Emmaus came in sight. . . . The two men were halfway through the walnut grove when they heard footsteps behind them. Nathanael looked over his shoulder, but there was no one in sight. Probably the man, whoever he was, was hidden by the walnut trees, or it might be someone walking within the town. It had been a strange afternoon, with a lowering sky and the threat of a storm; they were glad to be close to the village, for the strangeness and emptiness of the evening frightened them. The wind was rising, and a thick white dust came through the trees.

The sound of footsteps grew louder, and soon they became aware that someone else was walking near them. There were three long bluish shadows on the dusty road between the walnut trees. They turned and saw a man of middle height, who wore the costume of a Passover pilgrim, and to judge by the blue tassels on the edge of his cloak, he was a rabbi or a scribe. His gown was covered with dust, and to keep the dust from his mouth and nostrils he wore a scarf over the lower part of his face, and he concealed his hands within the folds of his cloak. They saw only the deep smoldering eyes, and they could barely guess at the shape of his face.

The man must have heard the muttering of Cleopas, for he said: "Why are you so sad, brother?"

"We are all sad these days," Cleopas answered. "Who can be happy now that Jesus is dead?"

"Look upon me," said the stranger quietly. "Surely you know me?" he insisted.

"I see you are a rabbi and a learned man, but you have a rag across your mouth—"

"Surely you know my voice?"

"There are many who speak like you. Forgive me, I do not remember everyone I have seen."

"Look upon me," the stranger repeated, and his hand tore away the scarf covering his mouth.

He looked at the stranger, but it was too dark for him to see the man's features clearly. The hand was wet with blood, but it meant nothing to him, for the stranger might have scratched it on a thorn tree.

"Surely you know me!" the stranger said. "Have we journeyed together all these years in vain? I plucked you, Cleopas, from the fields one day when you were sick unto death, and you, Nathanael, I plucked you from under a fig tree. Do you not know me?"

"Yes, we know you," Cleopas answered, but he spoke like a man who did not know.

In silence they walked into Emmaus. . . . They walked through the shadowy streets like sleepwalkers, and when they came to an inn Nathanael said: "Abide with us, for it is late and the day is far spent, and let us feast as we feasted in days gone by."

And still Nathanael did not believe that Jesus was at his side. He would glance at the stranger, who was very pale and curiously withdrawn, speaking in an unrecognizable voice, his eyes glowing like coals which have been blown upon. It was perhaps some messenger of Jesus, or a brother, or even a distant relative. Nathanael felt no alarm at the stranger's presence. . . . What puzzled him more than anything else was the unnatural stillness which had descended upon the village. At this hour of the evening you expected to hear a great number of distinct sounds . . . But even the birds which usually sang in the evening sky were silent.

ROBERT PAYNE
FROM *THE LORD JESUS*

And they drew nigh unto the village, whither they went: and he made as though he would have gone further. But they constrained him, saying, Abide with us: for it is toward evening, and the day is far spent. And he went in to tarry with them. And it came to pass, as he sat at meat with them, he took bread, and blessed it, and brake, and gave to them. And their eyes were opened, and they knew him; and he vanished out of their sight. And they said one to another, Did not our heart burn within us, while he talked with us by the way, and while he opened to us the scriptures? And they rose up the same hour, and returned to Jerusalem, and found the eleven gathered together, and them that were with them, Saying, The Lord is risen indeed, and hath appeared to Simon.
Luke 24:28–34

The Walk to Emmaus

It happened, on a solemn eventide,
Soon after He that was our surety died,
Two bosom friends, each pensively inclined,
The scene of all those sorrows left behind,
Sought their own village, busied, as they went,
In musings worthy of the great event:
They spake of Him they loved, of Him whose life,
Though blameless, had incurred perpetual strife
Whose deeds had left, in spite of hostile arts,
A deep memorial graven on their hearts.
The recollection, like a vein of ore,
The farther traced, enriched them still the more;
They thought Him, and they justly thought Him, one
Sent to do more than He appeared t' have done;
To exalt a people, and to place them high
Above all else, and wondered He should die.
Ere yet they brought their journey to an end,
A Stranger joined them, courteous as a friend,
And asked them, with a kind engaging air,
What their affliction was, and begged a share.
Informed, He gathered up the broken thread,
And, truth and wisdom gracing all He said,
Explained, illustrated, and searched so well,
The tender theme, on which they chose to dwell,
That reaching home, "The night," they said, "is near,
We must not now be parted, sojourn here."
The new acquaintance soon became a guest,
And, made so welcome at their simple feast,
He blessed the bread, but vanished at the word,
And left them both exclaiming, "'Twas the Lord!
Did not our hearts feel all he deigned to say,
Did they not burn within us by the way?"

WILLIAM COWPER
1731–1800

The painting at left is *THE SUPPER AT EMMAUS* by Caravaggio. Some scholars believe the city Nicopolis, northwest of Jerusalem, is the modern location of the town of Emmaus. The word Emmaus comes from a root word meaning warm water, and within Nicopolis are two wells known for their lukewarm water.

The End of Life

The Hebrew word *Sheol* described the region below the earth to which all souls descended after death. To the Old Testament faithful, it represented neither punishment nor reward, but was simply a powerless, unconscious state of being. The prospect of passing into Sheol was frightful to most ancient Hebrews, since all knowledge and consciousness of their God would be gone once their earthly lives ended. Jesus provided a release from this fear of death, however, when He rose from the grave. Through His physical resurrection, He offered the hope of salvation and everlasting life to all those who believed in Him.

But is now made manifest by the appearing
of our Saviour Jesus Christ,
who hath abolished death,
and hath brought life and immortality
to light through the gospel.
II Timothy 1:10

Below, the exterior of Old Testament tombs stands as a reminder of ancient Israel.

Death was ever-present in biblical Judea, and the Jews had strict rules for handling the dead. Fifty percent of the people did not live to the age of eighteen. Anyone who touched a corpse was considered unclean for seven days, and required to undergo ritualistic washing on the third and seventh days. Priests were allowed near the corpses only of their own family members. Jesus taught a distinction between physical impurity, such as that which came from unwashed hands, and moral impurity, which was of greater concern.

Ancient Jews expressed grief not only with crying, but also in wailing and the tearing of clothes. If the deceased were especially important to the mourners, they wore sackcloth to symbolize grief. Other traditional rituals included rolling in dust and removing head coverings. The wealthy often hired mourning women to follow the funeral procession and wail in the traditional manner.

Whatsoever thy hand findeth to do,
do it with thy might;
for there is no work, nor device,
nor knowledge, nor wisdom,
in the grave, whither thou goest.
Ecclesiastes 9:10

For out of the heart proceed
evil thoughts, murders, adulteries,
fornications, thefts, false witness,
blasphemies: These are the things
which defile a man:
but to eat with unwashen hands
defileth not a man.
Matthew 15:19, 20

The Jews did not embalm their dead; but generally washed, wrapped, and buried or entombed the body within twenty-four hours. Proper burial displayed respect for the dead. Those without money to own a private tomb covered the bodies of their loved ones with stones or lay them in public grave sites. The wealthy had many-chambered family tombs built into the cliffs and caves outside the city limits. Here the body was covered with a shroud, placed on a bier, and carried to the tomb where it was laid on a stone ledge. Eventually, each body was removed to a deeper chamber within the tomb, where it could lie forever with its ancestors and descendants.

At left, the interior of the tomb of the kings of Israel in Jerusalem. The tombs date from about the seventh century B.C. During this period, it was forbidden to all but kings to be buried inside the city walls.

Feed My Lambs

But when the morning was now come, Jesus stood on the shore: but the disciples knew not that it was Jesus. Then Jesus saith unto them, Children, have ye any meat? They answered him, No.

And he said unto them, Cast the net on the right side of the ship, and ye shall find.

They cast therefore, and now they were not able to draw it for the multitude of fishes. Therefore that disciple whom Jesus loved saith unto Peter, It is the Lord.

Now when Simon Peter heard that it was the Lord, he girt his fisher's coat unto him, (for he was naked,) and did cast himself into the sea. And the other disciples came in a little ship; (for they were not far from land, but as it were two hundred cubits,) dragging the net with fishes. As soon then as they were come to land, they saw a fire of coals there, and fish laid thereon, and bread.

Jesus saith unto them, Bring of the fish which ye have now caught.

Simon Peter went up, and drew the net to land full of great fishes, an hundred and fifty and three: and for all there were so many, yet was not the net broken. Jesus saith unto them, Come and dine. And none of the disciples durst ask him, Who art thou? knowing that it was the Lord.

Jesus then cometh, and taketh bread, and giveth them, and fish likewise. This is now the third time that Jesus shewed himself to his disciples, after that he was risen from the dead.

So when they had dined, Jesus saith to Simon Peter, Simon, son of Jonas, lovest thou me more than these?

He saith unto him, Yea, Lord; thou knowest that I love thee.

He saith unto him, Feed my lambs.

He saith to him again the second time, Simon, son of Jonas, lovest thou me?

He saith unto him, Yea, Lord; thou knowest that I love thee.

He saith unto him, Feed my sheep.

He saith unto him the third time, Simon, son of Jonas, lovest thou me?

Peter was grieved because he said unto him the third time, Lovest thou me? And he said unto him, Lord, thou knowest all things; thou knowest that I love thee.

Jesus saith unto him, Feed my sheep.

JOHN 21:4–17

Then the eleven disciples went away into Galilee, into a mountain where Jesus had appointed them. And when they saw him, they worshipped him: but some doubted. And Jesus came and spake unto them, saying, All power is given unto me in heaven and in earth. Go ye therefore, and teach all nations, baptizing them in the name of the Father, and of the Son, and of the Holy Ghost: Teaching them to observe all things whatsoever I have commanded you: and, lo, I am with you alway, even unto the end of the world. Amen.
Matthew 28:16–20

The painting on the opposite page by an unknown artist portrays the compassion of the resurrected Christ as He seeks out His followers. In providing food that satisfied His disciples' physical hunger, Jesus not only demonstrated His love for them but also His command to "Feed my sheep" with the food of the spirit: the saving gospel of Christ Jesus.

How He Came

When the golden evening gathered
  on the shore of Galilee,
When the fishing boats lay quiet by the sea,
Long ago the people wondered,
  tho' no sign was in the sky,
For the glory of the Lord was passing by.

Not in robes of purple splendor,
  not in silken softness shod,
But in raiment worn with travel came their God,
And the people knew His presence
  by the heart that ceased to sigh
When the glory of the Lord was passing by.

For He healed their sick at even,
  and He cured the leper's sore,
And sinful men and women sinned no more,
And the world grew mirthful-hearted,
  and forgot its misery
When the glory of the Lord was passing by.

Not in robes of purple splendor,
  but in lives that do His will,
In patient acts of kindness He comes still;
And the people cry with wonder,
  tho' no sign is in the sky,
That the glory of the Lord is passing by.

W. J. DAWSON
1854–1928

A spectacular sunset over the Sea of Galilee.

Places Where Jesus Touched Lives

BETHANY. The home of Mary, Martha, and Lazarus, Bethany was a small settlement outside of Jerusalem on a hill leading to the Mount of Olives.

BETHESDA. The pools of Bethesda, where Jesus healed the lame man, were just outside the triumphal arch of Jerusalem.

BETHSAIDA. This community by the Sea of Galilee was the home of Philip, Andrew, and Peter.

CANA. About ten miles northeast of Nazareth, Cana was the site of Jesus' first miracle.

CAPERNAUM. The home of Matthew, Capernaum was the center of Jesus' ministry. Excavators have unearthed a house believed to be where Peter lived.

DAMASCUS. The capital of Syria, Damascus is an ancient oasis and important trade center. On the road to this city, Paul met the risen Christ.

EMMAUS. This settlement, which no longer exists, was located about ten miles west of Jerusalem. On the road to Emmaus, the risen Christ appeared to two of His disciples.

GADARA. East of the Jordan River and seven miles south of the Sea of Galilee, Gadara was home to both Jairus and the woman with the issue of blood. Gadara joined nine other cities to form the loose confederation called the Decapolis.

JERICHO. A fertile oasis in the desert and the lowest town on earth, this community has survived for thousands of years. Outside Jericho, Jesus met Zacchaeus, the rich tax collector in the tree, and Bartimaeus, the blind man.

JERUSALEM. Jesus healed ten lepers outside this city, which was the home of Nicodemus and the rich young ruler as well as Pilate, the high priest Caiaphas, the Sanhedrin, the Sadducees, and the Pharisees.

JORDAN RIVER. The location of Christ's baptism by John the Baptist.

MAGDALA. A village on the western edge of the Sea of Galilee, Magdala was the home of Mary Magdalene and is the present-day el-Mejdel.

MOUNT OF OLIVES. This ridge was where Jesus went to pray after the Passover supper and where He was arrested.

NAZARETH. The hometown of Jesus, Nazareth still lies about ninety miles north of Jerusalem.

SEA OF GALILEE. Jesus' ministry was primarily in the region surrounding this large lake in the northern part of Israel. Through the centuries, the Sea of Galilee has also been called the Sea of Chinnereth, the Sea of Tiberias, and the Sea of Gennesaret.

SYCHAR. A town in Samaria near Jacob's well where Jesus met the Samaritan woman.

Index

Photography Credits

Jacket: Superstock. **Page 4–5:** World Image/FPG International. **9:** Ideals Publications Inc. **11:** Ideals Publications Inc. **12:** Superstock. **13:** top photo, Superstock; middle photo, Erich Lessing/Art Resource, NY; bottom photo, Superstock. **17:** Ideals Publications Inc. **31:** Ideals Publications Inc. **32–33:** Superstock. **34–35:** Superstock. **37:** FPG International. **39:** Superstock. **43:** Superstock. **44–45:** Superstock. **46:** Superstock. **47:** top right photo, Richard Nowitz/FPG International; bottom left photo, Erich Lessing/Art Resource, NY. 48–49: Superstock. **51:** Louis Goldman/FPG International. **54:** Superstock. **56:** Superstock. **58–59:** Superstock. **60–61:** Dave Bartruff/FPG International. **63:** Ideals Publications Inc. **65:** Dave Bartruff/FPG International. **68:** S. Kanna/FPG International. **72:** Superstock. **77:** Superstock. **78:** Ideals Publications Inc. **80:** Christian Michaels/FPG International. **81:** top left photo, Erich Lessing/Art Resource, NY; bottom right photo, Superstock. **83:** Ideals Publications Inc. **85:** Ideals Publications Inc. **88–89:** FPG International. **90–91:** Superstock. **95:** Superstock. **96:** lower left photo, FPG International; upper right photo, Erich Lessing/Art Resource, NY. **97:** FPG International. **99:** FPG International. **100:** Superstock. **102–103:** Art Resource, NY. **106–107:** Superstock. **109:** Superstock. **115:** National Museum of American Art, Washington, D.C./Art Resource, NY. **117:** Ideals Publications Inc. **118:** Ideals Publications Inc. **121:** Ideals Publications Inc. **123:** Superstock. **124:** Richard Nowitz/FPG International. **126:** top left photo, Superstock. **127:** top right photo; bottom right photo: Ulf Sjostedt/FPG International. **128–129:** Superstock. **131:** Superstock. **132:** Superstock. **134–135:** Richard Nowitz/FPG International. **137:** Superstock. **140:** Superstock. **144:** Superstock. **147:** Ideals Publications Inc. **150–151:** Superstock. **152:** Roy King/Superstock. **153:** Superstock. **154:** Ideals Publications Inc. **156–157:** Christian Michaels/FPG International.